ADJUDICATION IN ACTION

AF736693

Directions in Ethnomethodology and Conversation Analysis

Series Editors:
Stephen Hester, Honorary Senior Research Fellow, Bangor University, UK
Dave Francis, Department of Sociology, Manchester Metropolitan University, UK

Ethnomethodology and Conversation Analysis are cognate approaches to the study of social action that together comprise a major perspective within the contemporary human sciences. Ethnomethodology focuses upon the production of situated and ordered social action of all kinds, whilst Conversation Analysis has a more specific focus on the production and organisation of talk-in-interaction. Of course, given that so much social action is conducted in and through talk, there are substantive as well theoretical continuities between the two approaches. Focusing on social activities as situated human productions, these approaches seek to analyse the intelligibility and accountability of social activities 'from within' those activities themselves, using methods that can be analysed and described. Such methods amount to aptitudes, skills, knowledge and competencies that members of society use, rely upon and take for granted in conducting their affairs across the whole range of social life.

As a result of the methodological rewards consequent upon their unique analytic approach and attention to the detailed orderliness of social life, Ethnomethodology and Conversation Analysis have ramified across a wide range of human science disciplines throughout the world, including anthropology, social psychology, linguistics, communication studies and social studies of science and technology.

This series is dedicated to publishing the latest work in these two fields, including research monographs, edited collections and theoretical treatises. As such, its volumes are essential reading for those concerned with the study of human conduct and aptitudes, the (re)production of social orderliness and the methods and aspirations of the social sciences.

Other titles in this series

Ethnomethodology at Work
Mark Rouncefield and Peter Tolmie
ISBN 978-0-7546-4771-3

Preference Organisation and Peer Disputes
How Young Children Resolve Conflict
Amelia Church
ISBN 978-0-7546-7441-2

Adjudication in Action
An Ethnomethodology of Law, Morality and Justice

BAUDOUIN DUPRET
CNRS, France

Translated by
PASCALE GHAZALEH

First published in French as Le Jugement en action. Ethnométhodologie du droit, de la morale et de la justice en Egypte, *by Librairie Droz, CH-1206 Geneva,*
© 2006 Librairie Droz SA. All rights reserved.

Routledge
Taylor & Francis Group
LONDON AND NEW YORK

First published 2011 by Ashgate Publishing

Published 2016 by Routledge
2 Park Square, Milton Park, Abingdon, Oxfordshire OX14 4RN
711 Third Avenue, New York, NY 10017, USA

First issued in paperback 2016

Routledge is an imprint of the Taylor & Francis Group, an informa business

Copyright © 2011 Baudouin Dupret

Baudouin Dupret has asserted his right under the Copyright, Designs and Patents Act, 1988, to be identified as the author of this work.

All rights reserved. No part of this book may be reprinted or reproduced or utilised in any form or by any electronic, mechanical, or other means, now known or hereafter invented, including photocopying and recording, or in any information storage or retrieval system, without permission in writing from the publishers.

Notice:
Product or corporate names may be trademarks or registered trademarks, and are used only for identification and explanation without intent to infringe.

British Library Cataloguing in Publication Data
Dupret, Baudouin.
Adjudication in action : an ethnomethodology of law, morality and justice. -- (Directions in ethnomethodology and conversation analysis)
1. Law--Methodology. 2. Law and ethics. 3. Ethnological jurisprudence. 4. Justice.
I. Title II. Series
340.1'12-dc22

Library of Congress Cataloging-in-Publication Data
Dupret, Baudouin.
Adjudication in action : an ethnomethodology of law, morality and justice / by Baudouin Dupret.
p. cm. -- (Directions in ethnomethodology and conversation analysis)
Includes bibliographical references and index.
ISBN 978-1-4094-3150-3 (hardback) 1. Law--Methodology. 2. Law and ethics. 3. Ethnological jurisprudence. 4. Justice. I. Title.

K212.D87 2011
340'.112--dc22

2011016479

ISBN 13: 978-1-138-25541-8 (pbk)
ISBN 13: 978-1-4094-3150-3 (hbk)

Contents

PART IV: PRAXEOLOGICAL STUDY OF JUDGMENTS ON MORALITY

List of Figures and Tables

Figures

Tables

Introduction
A Grammar of Law in Context and Action

This book aims to deal with law and judicial activity, in their moral dimension as well as when they are faced with questions of morality. The context of this study is a specific one: that of public prosecutors' offices and courts of justice in Egypt, as well as the cases brought before them in the past ten to fifteen years. The intention, however, is neither to present the Egyptian legal system nor to take that system as a case study of a larger entity – which some might call "Islamic law". It is even less to postulate any form of Arab or Muslim cultural specificity. On the contrary, this book's goal is to observe the contextualized deployment of various practices, and the activities of very diverse people who, in different capacities, found themselves involved in or faced with institutional judicial space. More specifically, the objective is to observe and describe, in an empirically documented and detailed manner, the moral dimension of judicial activity, and the judicial approach to questions of morality. In other words, the point is to detail the production and manifestation of judicial activity in its necessarily moral dimension, and to examine how that activity mediates and modulates the treatment of cases dealing with sexual morality, among others.

To state that this is a study of law in context and action clearly specifies the perspective within which the work is situated. Inspired by the later Wittgenstein and aligned with ethnomethodology and conversation analysis, this perspective may be described as praxeological. In the following chapters, there will be abundant reference to works of ethnomethodology and conversation analysis, in general, and to the analysis undertaken by some of these works of legal and judicial objects, in particular. This introduction will be restricted to a general presentation of the ethnomethodological way to proceed and a few of its fundamental axes: the respecification of sociological objects; the attention paid to the practical grammar of actions, notably acts of language; the rejection of sociological irony and overhanging stance vis-à-vis the people and the actions they undertake. Having posited these basics, it will be possible to sketch out the general lines followed in the book.

Ethnomethodology

The invention of the term "ethnomethodology" must be attributed to Harold Garfinkel, who explained the conditions under which the term emerged (Garfinkel,

1974b). It was necessary to designate the study of the ways (the "method" part of ethnomethodology) in which people (the members of a given "ethnic" group: the "ethno" in ethnomethodology) give meaning to their world of action, orient to this world, and practice it in a routine manner and on a daily basis. In other words, ethnomethodology is concerned with the "procedures" by which actors analyse the circumstances in which they find themselves, and conceive and implement modes of action (Heritage, 1984: 9).

It would be impossible, here, to go back to the Parsonian counterpoint or the phenomenological contribution that did so much to determine the genesis of ethnomethodology. Suffice it to say, as John Heritage did (1984: 33-34), that Garfinkel, although he was Parsons' student, opposed Parsons on every essential point in his sociology, and particularly on the idea that modelling courses of action could be a pertinent way of studying social activity empirically, or that it could serve as a standard by which to measure the more or less rational character of actions people undertake. He also opposed the idea that norms and rules constitute factors that constrain people's behaviour in a deterministic way. As for the contribution of phenomenology, it comes through in the constant concern for taking into account people's "natural attitude" – the expression used by Edmund Husserl to designate the "worldly" framework through which we apprehend, perceive, and interpret the world in which we live, and through which we intervene in it. Alfred Schütz's influence, and his sociological adaptation of Husserl's philosophy, must be emphasized in this regard (Cefaï, 1998). For that author, the social world is experienced, first and foremost, through interpretation by those who live in it, as something intelligible and meaningful, in the form of social categories and constructs (Schütz, 1990; Cefaï, 1994; Coulon, 1994a). But it is the idea of ordinary knowledge having an intersubjective character and, more specifically, of insertion in a game of reciprocal perspectives – and the resulting idealizations: the interchangeable nature of points of view and the congruence of systems of pertinence – that constitute the main elements in Schütz's sociology. These types and categories, once Garfinkel and Sacks, among others, revisited and transformed them, became one of the cornerstones of ethnomethodology (see among others Watson, 1994).

In ethnomethodology, social facts are seen as practical achievements. In that perspective, Durkheim's aphorism – that social facts are objective reality – was, for Garfinkel, a constant source of inspiration and disputation. In *Studies in Ethnomethodology*, he pointed this out:

> ... the objective reality of social facts *as* an ongoing accomplishment of the concerted activities of daily life, with the ordinary, artful ways of that accomplishment being by members known, used, and taken for granted, is, for members doing sociology, a fundamental phenomenon. (Garfinkel, 1967: vii)

His most recent book goes further, extending Durkheim's metaphor and using it as its cornerstone (Garfinkel, 2002). In this perspective, the objective reality of social facts becomes the group of themes that can be linked, in each concrete case, to an indigenous production of order, carried out locally, generated through collaboration, and describable through natural language:

> Produced in a concerted manner by population cohorts, these phenomena of order are intelligible, recognizable, and recognized. They correspond to practices of production, monstration, observation, and recognition. (Garfinkel, 2001: 440)

This sort of concern for the way in which people conduct their methodical activities, establishing pragmatically what may be considered adequate, precise, and appropriate, supposes that the analysis rejects the search for external criteria in the establishment of truth and intelligibility (sociology's methodological discourse) and focuses only on the ordinary modes of practical sociological reasoning. This is what Garfinkel's call for "ethnomethodological indifference" means:

> 'Scientific methodology' ['m]ethods' (whether avowedly scientific or not) do not provide a priori guarantees, and the initial requirement for an ethnomethodological investigator is to find ways to elucidate methods from within the relevant competence systems to which they are bound. (Lynch, 1993)

Among the terms one encounters frequently in ethnomethodological literature, four deserve particular attention: accountability, the documentary method of interpretation, indexicality, and reflexivity. The first suggests both the account and responsibility. Contrary to the theory of correspondence, for which language exercises the function of representing reality, ethnomethodology asks what people do in action and through the action of accounting for something. Rather than speaking in terms of incorporation, habitus, self-mystification, lies, or double-speak, ethnomethodology considers that people are generally able to know and describe their daily business in a competent and adequate manner. Far from being idiots or dopes (in cultural, "judgmental", or cognitive terms), people generally act and speak in and of their world in an informed way. In so doing, they describe it and orient intersubjectively towards this description, its relevance, and its intercomprehension. Accounts, in this perspective, are the manifestation of emergent relevancies to which consequences are attached, retrospectively and prospectively.

The prospective and retrospective meaning that people give to the events they account for is behind what Garfinkel (1967: 77-79) calls the documentary method of interpretation – the second important term in ethnomethodological literature. This is the method anyone uses to understand the events or objects of the world, as an underlying schema used prospectively to give meaning to future events, and, because judgments are always subject to revision, retrospectively as well, so that meanings of past events can change (Travers, 2001: 353). To say that someone is insane, for example, is at one and the same time a retrospective judgment on his past actions and the prospective basis on which to evaluate his future actions. The concept of a documentary method of interpretation, taken from Mannheim, thus refers to the use of a structure or an underlying model by its members simultaneously with its practical actualization. In this way, ethnomethodology is concerned with '… the way in which these models are apprehended by the members themselves at the moment of their particular situational manifestations.' (Watson, 2001: 21)

This leads us to observe that accounts made by the members of a given social group are irreducibly contextual, in the sense that they are loosely adapted to the events they describe, that they are subject to ad hoc adjustments, and they are understood by reference to a mass of postulates which are not made explicit (Heritage, 1984: 141).

This orientation of accounts to the context of their production, the fact that they point toward this context, is what Garfinkel calls their indexicality. Ethnomethodology is not the only method concerned with deictic terms, those which point towards their context. Still, Garfinkel, along with Harvey Sacks, placed the indexicality of accounts at the very heart of sociological work (Garfinkel and Sacks, 1986). The central question raised by indexical terms is due to the fact that they refer to different things according to the circumstances in which they are formulated. This problem is not at all limited to the correspondence between an indexical term and an indexed object, but rather extends to every descriptive action. The version of indexicality that Garfinkel proposes thus consists of showing [that] 'the intelligibility of what is said rests upon the hearer's ability to make out what is meant from what is said according to *methods* which are tacitly relied on by both speaker and hearer. These methods involve the continual invocation of commonsense knowledge and of context as resources with which to make definite sense of indefinite descriptive terms.' (Heritage, 1984: 144)

In a manner closely linked to indexicality, ethnomethodology is particularly concerned with analysing the reflexive character of social practices. According to Garfinkel, '[n]ot only does common sense knowledge portray a real society for members, but in the manner of a self fulfilling prophecy the features of the real society are produced by persons' motivated compliance with these background expectancies.' (1967: 53)

The notion of reflexivity thus refers to the fact that, as soon as they are formulated, our descriptions of social things become an integral part of what they seek to describe. Reflexivity therefore designates practices that describe and constitute a social framework: '… This is the property of activities that presuppose simultaneously their ability to reveal the same thing to observation.' (Coulon 1987: 37)

Conversation Analysis and the Ethnomethodological Study of Work

Ethnomethodology cannot be conceived of as a monolithic tradition. Among its ramifications are the phenomenological branch, incarnated mainly by the works of Melvin Pollner on "mundane reason" (1987); ethnographic ethnomethodology or the ethnomethodological study of work, essentially represented by the "second Garfinkel" (*Ethnomethodological Studies of Work*, 1986); and, finally, conversation analysis, incontestably initiated by Harvey Sacks (*Lectures on Conversations*, 1995). We will not dwell on the first of these trends for the time being, except to note that it was the subject of an interesting critique from within the ethnomethodological family

(Lynch, 1993: 35-8; Lynch and Bogen, 1996). For now, we will focus on conversation analysis and the ethnomethodological study of work.

Conversation analysis originated in Harvey Sacks's attempts to lay the foundations for a sociological method that would be able to grasp the primary data of the social world. In that sense, Sacks sought to deal with the details of natural events in a way comparable to that of the primitive natural sciences – in such a way that non-specialists could narrate them by going into the field, observing what took place there, and describing it in vernacular terms (Sacks, 1995, vol. 1: lecture 33). From this stemmed the idea that one way, or even the only way, allowing to obtain stable descriptions of courses of human action consisted of narrating the methods and procedures used to produce these courses of action (Schegloff, 1995). This becomes possible because commonsense actions are methodical, or in other words ordered, describable, recognizable, and reproducible (Lynch, 2001b: 265). They result from ordinary, usual, routine interactional skills, which are structurally organized and contextually oriented. Ordinary linguistic interaction can therefore be analysed in such a way that stable schemes organizing action, to which participants orient, begin to emerge (Heritage, 1984: 241). Conversation analysis thus brings out the fact that every act of communication is shaped by context, and simultaneously shapes this context. Further, conversation analysis underscores the ordered character of linguistic interaction: participants produce regularities and orient to them as normative grounds for action and inference (Heritage, 1984: 244).

Several major recurrences emerge in conversation analysis: first, the sequential organization of the conversation, by which Schegloff and Sacks (1973: 295-6) mean the fact that each utterance accomplishes a certain number of precise tasks in the course of a conversation, by sole virtue of its placement and its participation in a sequence of actions that are generally organized in adjacent pairs (question–answer, request–acceptance or refusal, invitation–acceptance or refusal, etc.). This sequential structure is normative: the first part of a pair (for example, a question) normally conditions its second part (for example, an answer). Any breach on this "conditional relevance" must thereby be justified. Conversely, the first part acquires significance only when the second part is uttered; in turn, the second can be sure that it is adapted to the first only when it is ratified by the first participant, pronouncing the third utterance. Conditional relevance is also subject to orders of preference (for instance, acceptance of an invitation is preferable to rejection). Finally, note must be made of the conversational context in its institutional dimension, and of all its consequences for the system of turns in conversation, the organization of participants' behaviour in interaction, its subjective perception, the organization of procedures, lexical choices, the routines of professional participants, and the asymmetry between professional and lay participants (Drew and Heritage, 1992).

The ethnomethodological study of work constitutes a third ramification of ethnomethodology, which it is important to discuss at this point, given that it occupies a central place in the method followed in the present work. This development of ethnomethodological research appeared as a critique of labour sociology and its tendency to ignore or to idealize the technical dimension of professional activities. Faced with a "missing-what", the ethnomethodology of work invited researchers to focus on the "just-this-ness" of activities in places of work, on their specifically practical dimension. This was, then, an invitation to observe and describe what practitioners do and how they understand what they do as they carry out an ordinary professional task (Travers, 2001: 360; see also Lynch, 1993: ch. 7). As Michael Lynch emphasizes (1993: 270), there is a vast gap between the methods used to study professional activity and the methods that make up the "what" (or, as Garfinkel termed it, the "quiddity") of the practices themselves. A good example of this is a certain type of legal sociology: the form that is more concerned with denouncing the injustice and inequality of law than with describing its practical deployment. In line with this project, Garfinkel called for the acquisition of dual skills, where mastery of a practical discipline would be combined with skill in ethnomethodology. The point was, in a sense, to encourage the hybridization of ethnomethodology with other disciplines. There is, however, a danger that consists of seeing each specialized discipline as a unique set of practices, defined by a singular essence to which access is determined by a strategy aiming to gain entrance into its epistemic circle. As Lynch points out, '[i]f we were to suppose that ethnomethodology could become an epistemic center from which inquiries into all other disciplines could be conducted, we might conclude that Garfinkel's ambition was to build a science capable of grasping the genetic essence of each praxeological species.' (1993: 276)

Garfinkel, who was aware of the risk inherent in such ambitions, abandoned the use of the term quiddity and instead used "just-this-ness". Although both terms can serve to designate "what makes an object what it is uniquely," "just-this-ness" emphasizes an indexical dimension in the construction of meaning that is free from any essentialism. Rather than producing accounts of accounts and documents abstract of the concrete, experienced operation that produces them; instead of dissociating documents from the activity that consists of producing documents, ethnomethodology of work attempts to grasp both parts of the pair (document and documentary activity) simultaneously, in the belief that they are indispensable to each other and indissociable from each other for a proper understanding of the phenomenon under consideration (Livingston, 1987; Lynch, 1993: 287-299).

Irony, Respecification, and Praxeological Grammar

Ethnomethodology thus posits itself as marking a clear break with sociological tradition. This position is expressed in its rejection of any position that would give sociologists a privileged vantage point on the world. Ethnomethodology has thus been led to respecify objects of sociological study. Finally, it has engaged in analytical study of the practical grammar of contextualized saying and doing.

Ethnomethodology and conversation analysis reject the form of irony that characterizes most sociology, placing the researcher "above" social and legal reality, and thereby claiming to grant a monopoly on understanding of what is "really" going on – and which actors could not see for themselves. The conventional approach thus tends to consider that, in a general framework where one recognizes the naturally perspectival character of social phenomena, it is appropriate to seek a perspective free from those adopted by social actors. In other words, sociology is required to find a position from which it can observe both impartially and holistically – observe, indeed, in a way that transcends worldly contingency; or, at least, when it is recognized that the transcendental point of view cannot be reached, it attempts to correct as much as possible the biases introduced by the perspectival nature of social phenomena. As for ethnomethodology, it approaches matters differently. Rather than adopting a corrective position, whereby it might attempt to attenuate the consequences of perspectivism, it focuses on this perspectivism in and of itself, as a dimension inherent to social and scientific activity. As Wes Sharrock and Rod Watson, adapting Heidegger, emphasize, sociologists are projected into the heart of the phenomena they seek to analyse. As a result, from the outset, any investigation is inevitably intertwined with the phenomenon it examines (1990: 229). Furthermore, sociologists cannot undertake their investigations outside their own common sense and background expectations as (competent) members of their society: to be able to propose anything regarding the events observed in social situation, sociologists must necessarily mobilize some degree of common sense understanding (*ibid.*).

It is therefore not sociology's task to overhang social reality, regarding it ironically, as if to say: I will reveal to you things that have been hidden since the world was created, thereby supposing that 'the meaning of social behaviour is inaccessible to the actors and reserved exclusively to those who can use certain tools of analysis.' (Livet, 2001: 422)

Sociological research cannot situate itself outside time or place. The analytical framework it proposes does not aim to compete with that of ordinary members of society. In that sense, there is no room for a "Goffmanization" of the world, in the words of Edward Rose (personal communication to Watson, 1998), which, by suggesting a dramatization of people's activities, waxes ironic on the ways in which they proceed, supposes that they are constantly setting the stage, and imputes to all the acts of anonymous, interchangeable actors supreme primary motives (Watson, 1998).

Ethnomethodology's refusal of an overhanging position is based on two corollary principles, among other things: a critique of the ambition to construct theories that propose global social models, and the principle, evoked early, of ethnomethodological indifference. The humanities and social sciences generally seem to emerge from a single epistemological and methodological matrix that incites theorizing, professional scepticism, and the application of mathematical reasoning to social phenomena (Button, 1991: 4). In contrast, ethnomethodology affirms that it is impossible to isolate a question from the circumstantial details that surrounded its emergence. Constructing grand explanatory models is classically tantamount to articulating empirical data and an abstract model in a system of correspondence. The problem arises precisely from this idea of correspondence between the model and events that are apprehended as instances of the model. As Douglas Benson and John Hughes (1991: 119) emphasize, however, even when researchers face no particular difficulty in classifying a phenomenon, they put this classification in action by using and paying attention, for the purpose in hand, to unexplained characteristics of the case, event, or person under observation. Once the purpose in hand changes, the relevant elements change as well, and other classifications are established. By referring to local situations as instances of a general model, researchers can ultimately hide the fact that a single word, for example, can mean very different things in very different contexts. One thus reaches authoritarian processes of categorization, where the relation between observation and observed object is presumed on the basis of postulates concerning both the model and its instances. The result is that one only knows what phenomena resemble through the prism of a format one has imposed upon them; but one knows very little with regard to the phenomenon's properties underlying this format (Benson and Hughes, 1991: 121). The very object that is supposed to be under study then becomes a mere function of the format imposed and of the implicit theory adopted by the researcher, rather than being a research object in and of itself. It is at this level that the idea of ethnomethodological indifference has a place. Rather than wondering whether sociologists can find identifications and characterizations of the phenomena they study that are adequate and acceptable in comparison to a given grand scheme, it is necessary to find out whether the members of a given social group identify and characterize something as an instance of something else (Lynch, 1991: 86 et seq.). Instead of searching for correspondences between the model and its instances, ethno-conversational analysis seeks to respecify its object in a manner leading it to observe, describe, and understand how people use categories in accomplishing their activities so as to make the world recognizable and subject to organization in a way that is relevant to them. Phenomena are no longer interpreted, then, according to a grid that we might impose upon them. Such a description cannot be carried out with abstract models that are external to the phenomena under study – herein lies the risk of irony and the overhanging attitude emphasized above. On the contrary, it is necessary to presume nothing theoretical with regard to phenomena, beyond their empirical description. In consequence, the social scientist's task is no longer to find the model of which such and such an event is the instance, but instead to try to find the social mechanisms that produced the event as it occurred.

Ethnomethodological respecification pledges the researcher to study the practical or praxeological grammar of contextualized doing and saying. In a perspective inspired by the later Wittgenstein (1961: §7-24 et seq.), it is necessary to study language games, in which linguistic usage and practical behaviour are seen as intertwined in a complex manner (Coulter, 1991: 27). Among Wittgenstein's favourite targets were "grand concepts", like the "mind", constructed as floating entities, totally decontextualized and retroactively projected onto the world as if they were its very nature – as if they were "something *beneath* the surface" (Wittgenstein, 1961: §92) independently of their actualization or the context in which they are used. In language games, '[g]rammars of concepts are rules which not only specify the linguistic frameworks within which words, phrases or types of words or phrases may be used, but also "what counts as an application of" such expressions. Grammars reveal the manifold connections between words and other words, phrases and expressions as these are used by "masters of natural language", and the manifold connections between kinds of expression and sorts of circumstance within which and about which they may be used.' (Coulter, 1989: 49)

For Wittgenstein, carrying out a grammatical investigation was a means of eliminating '[m]isunderstandings concerning the use of words, [misunderstandings] caused, among other things, by certain analogies between the forms of expression in different regions of language. Some of them can be removed by substituting one form of expression for another…' (Wittgenstein, 1961: §90)

A word's grammar, therefore, refers in a descriptive (and not an explanatory: *id.*: §496) manner to the modes of usage of that word. To investigate the grammar of concepts – legal concepts, in our case – therefore supposes inversing the tradition manner of doing research. Traditional philosophy easily incites one to give an essentialist significance to terms that have strong resonance, like "to know", "to represent", "to reason", and "true". It leads one to hypostasize concepts like "knowledge", "representation", "reason", and "truth". Researching the grammar of concepts, in contrast, allows us to problematize epistemology, by showing, in the daily use of "epistemological" expressions, variations, systematic ambiguities, and manifest sensibilities (Lynch, 1993: 199).

The description of situated activities that accomplish an epistemological task (for example, knowing, deducing, and finding causes) makes it possible to see the relevance the concept takes on in certain activity contexts. Respecifying sociological methods and analysing the practical grammar of epistemological concepts lead us to what Michael Lynch has called a study of "epistopics". This means that instead of participating in the construction of metatheoretical terms, on the basis of which the social sciences are elaborated, it is necessary to pay attention to these terms as "words" implicated in language games, and to examine the occasions on which such language games are practiced. In other words, it is necessary to examine the situated uses of epistemic themes, starting from the principle that nominal coherence alone (the use of the same word in different contexts) guarantees nothing with regard to the uses of that word. Quite the contrary: to return to the theme of quiddity advocated by Garfinkel, it is the irreducibly unique character of each occurrence that must be emphasized. In conclusion, Michael Lynch (1993: 265-308) thus suggests that investigations be carried out that begin with identifying epistopics, and then seek to follow their trail in various real cases of deployment, using ordinary words of observation, description, comparison, and reading.

The Morality of Law and the Law of Morality

This book seeks to respecify legal objects, in the moral dimension of their deployment and in their treatment of moral questions. To that end, we will start by attempting to lay the foundations of a praxeological approach to relations between law and morality. Next, we will examine judicial activity and the moral organization of its exercise. Thirdly, we will deal with the practical grammar of a few major questions of law. Finally, a fourth part will focus in detail on a legal case that bore on a question of morality.

It is difficult to perceive the entire value of the praxeological approach without bearing in mind the background and the counterpoint of the traditional way of dealing with relations between law and morality. Philosophy of law progressively established the positive status of norms by detaching them from their metaphysical anchors. From then on, moral norms were distinguished from legal norms. This is no doubt one of the fundamental principles on which modern law is based. Thus, for Herbert Hart, nothing makes it necessary to consider that legal rulings correspond to or reflect certain moral exigencies. Ronald Dworkin, for his part, impugned the positivist distinction, asserting that law, rather than a simple system of rules, is a combination of rules and principles. Dworkin thereby reintroduced morality as a major component of the legal phenomenon. This substantivist perspective, however, fails to resolve a major question: how are these principles constituted, mobilized, and characterized? In a way, Dworkin's substantivist approach, while claiming to reintroduce morality in law, sheds no light on the very phenomenon it is supposed to deal with: the modalities of law's moral dimension.

Grasping the moral dimension of the law in its practice implies envisaging, in a prejudicial way, what one could follow John Heritage in calling the morality of cognition. This expression suggests that the activities of competent members of a given social group are thoroughly imbued with a normative element, based on a certain number of background expectations that are realized, ratified, or contradicted. In turn, these expectations serve as a basis for other subsequent actions. This normative interaction, whether banal or extraordinary, is based on "mundane" ways of reasoning, understanding, interpreting, categorizing, and inferring, all of which orient to an intersubjectively constituted horizon of normalcy. Such normalcy, whether it is based on the nature of things or the things of nature, is a continuous achievement, with no time out, which permanently actualizes underlying shared schema of interpretation, projecting them in turn into the future, in the very thread of interaction, so that these relevancies are always already there and emerging.

The third chapter will deal with law in action. It will seek to synthesize works that have concerned legal objects in the ethnomethodological tradition. Law and justice, since the early works of Garfinkel and Sacks, have held a privileged place in ethnomethodology; the practices of various legal actors – lawyers, police officers, prisoners, jury members, judges, etc. – have provided the basis for the study of activities and language in context. In this perspective, the point was not so much to identify the defects of these practices in comparison with an ideal model or a formal rule to which they should have conformed, but rather to describe the modes of production and reproduction, the intelligibility and comprehension, the structuring and public manifestation of the structured nature of law and the different activities linked to it. Thus, rather than positing the existence of racial, sexual, psychological, or social factors, ethnomethodology and conversation analysis examined how activities are organized and how people orient to the structure of these activities, which can be and are read in a largely unproblematic way.

The second part of this book is concerned with legal and judicial activity in context. The first chapter will examine the judicial context. Action, understood as speech acts, cannot be understood in a vacuum, outside the locus of its production. Questions of identity and meaning, for example, depend strictly on the context in which they emerge and on the linguistic activities in which participants engage. In the course of interactions, people publicly manifest contextual relevancies to which they orient, as well as their understanding of these relevancies and their implications for subsequent actions. This contextual constraint is not a static given of interaction, but rather a reflexive and fluctuating framework, which members of the legal setting continuously reevaluate and according to which they carry out constant realignments. Linguistic expressions are conceived and formed for the purpose of intervening in particular sequential and social contexts, in a manner that is publicly recognizable and intelligible. This contextuality can also take on an institutional dimension, translated, in an empirical manner, through linguistic activity oriented to specific ends, modeled according to particular constraints, and inscribed within determined inferential frameworks and procedures.

Next, we will examine the effects of procedural constraints brought about by the inscription of action in a judicial context, since the judicial sequence follows a certain number of steps that – while they may well be formalized in the form of a sentence – nevertheless correspond to a series of empirically observable achievements, explicitly produced by the participants in the process. One of the major tasks facing a professional engaged in the routine exercise of his profession is to manifest publicly the correct performance of his work. The production of a procedurally impeccable sentence is one of the priorities to which legal professionals orient, and this is expressed to all public ends in the summary operated by the judge, the document of the judgment itself, and the effective accomplishment of all the legally necessary tasks. Most of the documents contained in a legal dossier translate this orientation of judges, prosecutors, and other professionals to this form of procedural correctness. This appears as directly linked to the general sequence of judgment, in which participants address people who are not necessarily physically present in the room, but who make up an audience that listens and, as it were, looks over the participants' shoulders – an audience that is virtually capable of invalidating procedure on a point of order. These procedural constraints, which the actors identify explicitly, do not correspond to a set of abstract rules drawn from an external legal system, with its own history and superior vantage point: rather, they correspond to the routine, bureaucratic dimension of people engaged in a variety of legal professions.

Procedural constraints aside, participants in legal interaction orient to what might be termed legal relevance. This indicates the qualifying operation that consists of bringing a factual instance into line with a formal legal definition. The qualifying operation may be endowed with a character of uncertainty, yet cannot be considered as totally problematic or arbitrary. The categories to which the judge refers have an objective nature, as far as the judge is concerned, even if it is qualification itself that makes them objective. Further, one may observe that the legal process of qualification depends narrowly on a sociological process of normalization, which designates all the operations through which the magistrate routinely selects some characteristics that belonged to a common, normal, or usual type in the case under consideration. Parties – the judges, prosecutors, lawyers, victim, accused, witnesses, etc. – therefore orient to these "normal" categories, which, even beyond their formal legal definition, belong to the realm of common sense. From this perspective, we must recognize that passing judgment operates as a justification, by identifying all the procedural and substantive rules that it satisfies, while dissimulating the practical character of its own constitution. It is possible, nevertheless, to measure these practical operations by reexamining the different stages through which they are formed, as well as the many documents that support the judge's work, and also by investigating the intertextual relation that brings them together.

The third part of the present work will put forth a sort of practical grammar for a number of legal epistemic themes. First, I will endeavour to reconstitute the doctrinal and jurisprudential background of Egyptian penal law. This will provide an opportunity to review textual legal formality, particularly with regard to questions of capacity, intentionality, and causality. I will highlight the vast distance between this type of textual documentation and the incarnate, lived conditions in which it is produced. To paraphrase Garfinkel, the normative enunciation of applied or implemented law finds itself in an asymmetrical relation to the detailed account of its practical, contextual elaboration, to the degree that the former dissimulates everything that contributed to its production, while the latter seeks precisely to reconstitute all the operations that led to the production of a formal, abstract document. While the different parties to a judicial process explicitly manifest their orientation to a certain number of rules of law, this does not mean that describing the mechanism of their orientation is strictly tantamount to simply enunciating the rule.

Having established this point, the following chapter will examine the grammar of the legal concept of personality and its corollary, capacity. The physical person constitutes the reference point for practical legal reasoning. Far from being an abstract, inaccessible category, it is made public through the methodical deployment, in social interaction, of shared linguistic resources. References to someone's person provide the opportunity for the selection and production of descriptions that depend strictly on the activity underway. In other words, what a person is officially for someone else depends on the course of action being taken. The realization of personality as a category is a public phenomenon through and through, and is articulated around a schema: that of the normative, normal person. Garfinkel's study of the case of Agnes shows how sexual identity is continually produced and managed in the course of social and institutional interactions. Persons and their identity function as a background that is constantly being mobilized, although that background remains largely unexplained and is loosely defined. The capacity to be defined as a person therefore depends mainly on people's ability to present a normal appearance and to expect treatment from others on that basis. Among other methods used to this end, we must note procedural incongruity, which contrasts expected behaviour with perceived behaviour, and draws from their convergence or divergence certain consequences with respect to the person under consideration.

In this attempt to constitute a practical grammar of some concepts of penal law, I will turn, next, to causality. It is impossible, when dealing with this question, to dispense with the reference work by Herbert Hart and Tony Honoré, *Causation in the Law*. The authors of this work laid the foundations for an exploration of causal reasoning in law, and, in particular, of its strong links to common sense, as well as its contextual sensitivity. Nevertheless, I will try to demonstrate that this type of approach, while it helps us identify the parameters of causality in legal practice, is not able to explain precisely the phenomenon with which it is dealing. This is due first and foremost to the fact that the authors studied material that had already been abstracted, formalized, and polished, leaving in shadow all the practical, contextual, and situated production of causal affirmations at the different stages of the judicial process. Legal reasoning and common sense are articulated, in practice and in context, around different notions, such as cause, reason, motive, intention, excuse, justification, or circumstance. All these are notions to which people orient throughout the judicial sequence. Here, too, it is necessary to note the importance of underlying schemes of normalcy and naturalness, and the inferences drawn from their invocation with respect to the qualification of an incriminated action.

A final chapter will deal with the practical grammar of intention. In penal law, intentionality is one of the central criteria in the work of judicial qualification. In this chapter, I will focus on showing how magistrates, and prosecutors in particular, organize their activities in practice around the establishment of this component of crime. After having painted a summary portrait of the literature that has dealt with this question in the field of legal theory, and after having pointed out the essentialist nature of previous approaches – which seek to grasp intention as a philosophical notion, independent of the institutional context of its mobilization – I will adopt an approach that is consistent with praxeology, and look at the question of intentionality as the result of interactions situated in the institutional legal context. This context forces professional actors to orient to the production of a legally relevant decision. We will thus observe how profane actors adjust their behaviour to the constraints of this institutional context, under the impact of induction carried out by professionals, and under the impact of their own anticipation, which causes them to act in such a way as to obtain (from the place and the people they are facing) the solution that will prove most favourable, least damaging, or at least most consistent with the routine achievement of their work.

In the fourth part of this work, I will undertake the praxeological study of a trial that rested on an operation allowing for the judicial definition of morality, among others. Whether the question is one of homosexuality, of prostitution, or of mental health, it is possible to observe and describe, in detail, the work of the various parties engaged before the courts in matters touching on morality. Here, morality is a constitutive part of a specific domain, to the degree that people orient to it as such. The so-called Queen Boat affair will provide a case study here. This part is organized in three chapters. First, I will specify the internal organization of the sentence as a specific text. In so doing, it will be possible to describe both the substance of the affair, in the formalization carried out by the judge, and the structure of the judgment, in its deployment on a specific occasion. Second, I will observe law and justice in action in moral questions of this type. This will lead us to examine in detail the conversational, sequential organization of judicial procedures in their entirety, without it being possible to affirm, pending further information, that their bearing on moral questions has the slightest influence on their outcome. Finally, I will undertake a category-based analysis of the interrogations enacted by the public prosecutor's office and the texts produced by various professional bodies. This will provide an opportunity to observe the modes whereby categories emerge and function, as well as their inferential properties.

While the first three parts deal with the moral nature of ordinary legal reasoning, the practical dimension of morality, and the ubiquity of morality in the course of judicial activity, the three chapters of the last part focus on morality as a specific domain on which certain human activities come to bear, such as religion, ethics, morality, philosophy, and, most importantly for us, law. Discourse on morality depends wholly on what we have called the morality of cognition. In the fourth part, we will try to show how this morality is exercised on the occasion of the judicial treatment of moral questions, and what modalities preside over the deployment of this treatment.

In conclusion, we will return once more to the articulation of the morality of judgement and judgements bearing on moral questions. On one hand, legal activity does not necessarily have to bear on moral questions in order to be morally constituted, organized, and practiced; nevertheless, on the other hand, it is important to note that this same legal activity can occasionally take as its object questions that evidently belong to the domain of morality. It is no doubt necessary to observe and describe the ways in which the morality of judgement and judgements on morality can mutually strengthen and shape each other. However, to remain consistent with the praxeological approach, we will not seek to propose a model that might enclose within its contours the abstract configurations that such relations might follow in the concrete course of events. Rather, we will seek to highlight two mechanisms: first, how the judge's activity aims not only at transforming moral questions into legal matters, but also, because this activity is moral through and through, how it cannot strip the law of its specifically moral dimensions; second, how the domain of morality not only constantly informs law and serves as a basis for the establishment of judgement as normalcy, but also, because it is associated, and yet not assimilated, with the law, how it can never entirely replace the law or people's orientation to the different practical ends they impute to it.

Justification of a Non-Culturalist Stance

Although this book is based on material taken from Egyptian legal activity, it must be clear by now that its aim is not to reveal the secrets of an "exotic" legal universe. On the contrary: it attempts to describe this activity without any prejudice with regard to what might distinguish Egyptian judicial space from other legal spaces. It does not even posit the existence of such differences. In other words, this book examines legal practice in an Egyptian environment, and not Egyptian culture observed through the prism of law. Actually, Egyptian culture is only one of the many components of the context in which the practices of Egyptian law are deployed – a context that is always unique, and never uniform. To suppose that this cultural component is primordial is to run the risk of not paying enough attention to other possible components, although, in practice, the members of the Egyptian judicial environment orient to many other things in the course of their actions. This also poses the threat of over-estimating the impact of culture; and yet, culturalism has untranslatability as its corollary. In this perspective, one could argue that a given concept, formulated in Arabic, cannot be perceived adequately in French or English, because its essence is accessible only in the language in which it was originally formulated. On the contrary, we consider that every phenomenon, whatever the language in which it is expressed, can always be translated into another language, and rendered accessible to observation and description. This implies, however, '[r]ather than pretending to read a culturally standardized finished text over the shoulder of an imagined native, we will be living in the line-by-line production of ongoing actual native talk.' (Moerman, 1988: 5)

What justifies the use of Egyptian legal data, then, the reader might ask, if it is not to substantiate the affirmation of cultural difference? The answer is, first, that there is no reason to consider that a given context is automatically more relevant, appropriate, or worthy of interest than any other. Second, we would add that, if this book manages to show the similarity of context rather that their irreducible difference, it will have been worth the effort, in a general atmosphere where the common humanity of humanity seems to have been denied in the name of cultural conflict or a clash between ineffably different civilizations. Of course, some specificities can ultimately be attributed to the Egyptian cultural context, but they may no longer be considered untranslatable. On the contrary: 'their meanings are knowable and, of course, known: they are governed by grammatical conventions which are determinable, and form part of the conceptual endowment of the human species, notwithstanding their differential empirical distributions of actual usage and the different kinds of language-games played with them in different cultures.' (Coulter, 1989: 101)

PART I
Law and Morality: Bases of a Praxeological Approach

Chapter 1
Law and Morality: Constructs and Models

This chapter seeks to offer a glimpse of the many approaches in legal theory and philosophy, which have sought to conceptualize the relations between law and morality. We hope to offer a brief, preliminary discussion of the models that a praxeological way of proceeding might in a certain sense respecify.

It is difficult to grasp the full value of the praxeological approach without keeping in mind as background and counterpart the traditional treatment of relations between law and morality. Legal philosophy gradually established the positive status of norms by disengaging them from their metaphysical anchors. From that point on, moral and legal norms were distinguished from each other. This is, no doubt, one of the fundamental principles on which modern law was built. The positivist distinction, however, was recused, and many attempts were made to reintroduce morality as a major component of the legal phenomenon. This substantialist perspective, however, does not answer the question of how law's moral dimension might be constituted, mobilized, and characterized. In a sense, the substantialist approach, which claimed to reintroduce morality in law, managed to leave in shadow the very phenomenon it sought to study: the modalities of law's moral dimension. By going over the main lines of the debate about law and morality, we will seek to establish a general framework in which to situate the praxeological respecification we suggest in the remainder of the book.

The Debate about Positivism

The distinction between law and morality may be considered one of the basic principles on which modern legal theory was built. For example, John Austin, the founder of legal positivism, argued that positive law is distinguished from other normative systems in that it is founded on a commandment issued by a factually legitimate authority that is endowed with the power to sanction (Austin, 1954 [1832]). The theory of commandment that Austin established, although it may appear paradoxical that this theory invokes the ruler's sovereignty in order to establish the state of law, sought to disengage law from the grip of the transcendental, and to make it, instead, susceptible to revision and prevision. The positivist way of proceeding is therefore completely in line with the dynamic separating "is" from "should be", the "true" from the "beautiful/good". This is precisely where attacks against positivist theory are lodged, aiming at its inability to explain the effective part taken up by meta- or extra-positive information in law.

The distinction between law and morality is taken up constantly in Durkheim's work, despite the considerable evolution that work underwent. Thus, in *La Division du travai social* (*The Division of Social Labor*; 1960 [1983]: 28), 'Law is nothing but the organization [of social life] in its most stable and precise form.' Law, however, does not include every type of regulation: 'It is necessary, in fact, to distinguish the rules emanating from law from those emanating from morality, or in other words rules with an "organized" sanction effect on one hand from those with a "diffused" sanction effect on the other.' (Chazel, 1991: 28)

Law and morality are therefore placed in the same category, the criterion being their punitive power, but they differ from each other due to the nature of the sanction they exercise. As for their articulation one to the other, it can occur at the level of the legal rule itself (morality of rules sanctioning crime, for example), or at the level of obligation engendered by the legal rule (morality of the obligation to obey the law). Later, in an article titled "*De la détermination du fait moral*" ("The Determination of the Moral Fact", 1924), Durkheim detached morality from the notion of sanction and caused it to evolve more towards the idea of duty and conscience, to which he added the dimension of desirability (which, nevertheless, was not independent from the feeling of obligation). In any case, constraint constitutes the central notion, making the junction between sanction and collective desire (Isambert, 1991). At the same time, it is important to emphasize the fact that law and morality, while they may be distinct, still evolve in an interdependent manner. In his first period (*Division*), Durkheim sees "primitive law" and its penal avatar as characterized by the close link they establish between legal and moral dimensions (repressive law, as against retribution). Historical evolution tends towards a process of desacralization and disjunction. In the second period (*Elementary Forms*), Durkheim sees historical evolution as testifying more to a process of displacement – the sacred moves more towards the individual – and duality pitting collective law (domestic or corporate) against individual law (contractual, etc.). Here, in a context of moral regression and faltering moral constraints, we witness the strengthening of the state's legal role (Génard, 1997). Durkheim's point of view was therefore certainly very liberating for a whole set of theoreticians of normativity, who saw in it 'the opportunity of freeing themselves from law in order to think about the social order.' This choice, nevertheless, adhered to 'a certain degree of legal positivism, since it admitted that the universe of regulations was vaster than that of the law, without striking at the integrity of the latter.' (Assier-Andrieu, 1996: 16)

Let us return to the demarcation established by legal positivism. We owe to John Austin an early formulation of the distinction between "laws, properly speaking", and other normative forms, i.e. metaphorical laws (for example, the laws of nature) and laws by analogy (laws that proceed from an opinion generally shared by a human group). Under "laws properly speaking", however, one can find "the laws established by God for His human creatures" as well as laws made by men for other men. In both cases, there is a conjunction of the two criteria for the definition of a law: the existence of a command and a sanction. What distinguishes the different categories of "laws, properly speaking", is the third criterion: effective authority, which can only be satisfied through the intervention of a human agent. In other words, intentionality coupled with the effective force of execution makes up positive law (Jackson, 1996).

To sum up: the idea of growing autonomy of the legal and ethical spheres is at the heart of all modern positivism. Kelsen, to cite an emblematic figure, called for a rigorous distinction between the two. Thus, he argued that law was defined subjectively, on one hand, by the Kantian criterion of exteriority and immanent legal punishment, organized and centralized by the state; and objectively, on the other, through its conformity with already existing legal norms and the establishment of conditions for competence allowing legal command (Kelsen, 1996). This perspective remained vulnerable to the classical critique of positivism, however, to wit:

> The impossibility, for the governed, of calling upon a metapositive legal norm in order to contest the legal significance of the positive order, and in order to free themselves from their obligation of obeying commandments that are no longer a law "worthy of the name". (Cayla, 1996)

Herbert Hart's perspective (1961) may be compared to that of Kelsen, but Hart sought to ward off a critique he took seriously, while reaffirming the need to distinguish law from ethics. Although he challenged Austin's theory of command, Hart sought to maintain a moderate positivist understanding of law. He therefore defined legal positivism as an expression of the thesis according to which it is not at all necessarily true that rules of law reflect or satisfy certain moral exigencies, although in reality they have often done so (Hart, 1961: 224).

What was at stake, therefore, was the need to demonstrate that no necessary relation existed between law and morality. Legal and moral obligations might indeed share certain characteristics: obligation is independent of the will of the individual who submits to it; obligation is recurrent, not occasional; obligation bears on the exigencies of collective life. But they remain different due to the importance of obligation (no moral rule can be considered unimportant), the inaccessibility of moral rules to deliberate changes, the necessarily intentional character of moral errors, and the form of moral pression that invites respect for the rules due to their importance and shared nature (Hart, 1961: 203-221). Hart's endeavour to distinguish law from morality can nevertheless be considered moderate ("soft positivism", according to Jackson, 1996), in the sense that it recognizes a "minimum content of natural law", which makes up a substratum shared by law and conventional morality in all societies that have progressed to the stage where law and morality are distinguished as different forms of social control (Hart, 1961: 232).

Still, for Hart this does not justify the confusion of the legal and moral levels. In order to be legally valid, a rule of law does not necessarily have to conform to moral standards. From this perspective, the rules of the law are 'all the rules valid according to the formal criteria of a system of primary rules (i.e. duty-imposing rules) and secondary rules (i.e. power-conferring rules), even though some of these rules violate the specific morals of a society or trespass what we can consider as an authentic morals.' (Hart, 1961: 250)

Egyptian Interlude

Egyptian legal doctrine asserts that there is a distinction between law and morality. For example, Hassan Gemei (aka Hasan Jami'i), a professor of civil law at Cairo University, aligns himself with Austin's theory of commandment with regard to the definition of law. Gemei sees law as a set of rules governing the behaviour of individuals in society, which people must obey, lest they expose themselves to sanctions imposed by a competent authority (Gemei, 1997: 6; see also Jami'i, 1996).

According to this author, legal rules are not the only ones on the path that aims to regulate and stabilize relations among members of any given societies. They act in concert with other rules, like those of courtesy, customs, traditions, and religious rules. As for moral rules, they are, according to Gemei, principles and teachings that the majority of the members of society consider as constraining behavioural rules that aim to realize elevated ideals (Gemei, 1997: 15).

Moral rules share a number of characteristics with legal rules: they change according to time and place; they tend toward organizing society; they have a constraining nature associated with sanctions. However, they differ from legal rules in three domains:

> First, with regard to their field of application: 'Whereas morality includes personal and social manners, law addresses the relationship between the person and the others from the perspective of the ostensible aspect of behavior without taking into consideration the intentions unassociated with physical action. (Gemei, 1997: 16)

They also differ with regard to the type of sanction imposed:

> Whereas the penalty of violating morality rules is a mere moral penalty ranging from remorse to denunciation and disdain, the penalty for violating legal rules is physical incarceration, imprisonment, hard labor, etc. (Gemei, 1997: 17)

They also differ in respect to their objectives: according to Gemei, while moral rules seek to attain perfection in man, legal rules seek to realize stability and order within society (Gemei, 1997: 17). Finally, they appear in different forms: legal rules, Gemei asserts, generally appear in a clear and specific form, while moral rules are not so clear, because they are linked to internal feelings, which may vary from one person to another (Gemei, 1997: 17).

The reader will note how Hassan Gemei deals with religious rules. He highlights their close relation to legal rules, but nevertheless insists on the fact that their field of action is far wider, and that violating them is punished in the afterlife (Gemei, 1997: 18). As for the distinction he establishes between moral and religious rules, it seems particularly tenuous, yet this does not lead him to accept a difference between religious and legal rules, for such a difference 'cannot be recognized from the perspective of Islamic *shari'ah*,' (Gemei, 1997: 18) in the sense that Islam is a total faith and encompasses law. This means that the field of application of *shari'a* is wider than that of law: Islamic *shari'ah*, he notes, is the source of legislation, from which legal rules must be derived in Islamic states (Gemei, 1997: 27):

> Islamic Shari'ah was ordained as a divine law to govern the conduct of the Islamic society, formulate the thought of the Moslems, and regulate the human relations. Revealed by Allah, Shari'ah guides the society to the highest ideals and seeks to achieve wisdom for which God has created man on earth. (Gemei, 1997: 28)

It is worth noting that, despite his refusal to distinguish law from *shari'ah*, Gemei's reasoning follows exactly the same lines that he had followed earlier, when examining moral and religious rules: although law differs from religious regulations because of its field of application, the nature of its sanctions, and its objectives, it must nevertheless proceed from these superior, ideal principles. In other words, Gemei, who is a good representative of Egyptian doctrine, seems to be making a dual statement, while demanding a particular status for *shari'ah*: Islamic rules are today very close to moral rules; law, with its specific technical means, serves objectives that do not generally contravene the principles of morality and religion.

The Critique of Positivism

There is no dearth of critiques targeting Hart's moderate positivist theory. They bear in part on the question of the disconnection between law and morality. This is explicit in the controversy pitting Hart against Fuller. It also emerges very clearly in the debate between him and Dworkin. In *The Morality of Law* (1964), Lon Fuller makes a distinction between the internal and external morality of law. Internal morality does not directly concern the content of legal rules, but affects the procedure followed in proclaiming them. Thus, a rule may be morally defective due to a lack of generality, insufficient publicity, a retroactive effect, its unintelligibility, its contradictory character, lack of feasibility, its instability, or the gap between its formulation and its implementation. Fuller argues that any total failure to fulfil one of these desiderata deprives the normative system its character as a system of law. This argument draws its inspiration from Locke's philosophy and Simmel's sociology, which are based on reciprocity between ruler and ruled, in a context where the social contract requires that the citizen obey and that the sovereign respect the citizen's natural rights. The model is an idealistic one, of course, and Fuller therefore introduces a distinction between total failure (the system as a whole fails to fulfil this requirement) and partial failure (only part of the system fails to fulfil it). The effect of a partial failure is to invalidate the flawed disposition and to offer the citizen the ability to choose between obeying and disobeying those parts of the system that are not directly flawed. Individuals thus find themselves confronted with a moral dilemma, especially since no precise criteria exist indicating the degree of failure. What is at stake is respect for a "morality of obligation", or in other words a form of morality that prescribes the minimum level of obligation necessary to life in society.

The conflict between Hart and Fuller is due to the fact that Hart does not consider procedural requirements as morality, but rather as simple mechanisms of social control that pose no obstacle to iniquity. In other words, law always remains separate from morality, because the only morality is external or substantial. In Fuller's view, on the contrary, procedural morality clearly exists, because there is a direct incidence of failure to fulfil procedural exigencies regarding the promulgation of rules on their substantial morality. As for the latter, it is based on a principle of communication: 'Open up, maintain, and preserve the integrity of the channels of communication by which men convey to one another what they perceive, feel, and desire.' (Fuller, 1964: 165 sqq.) This morality aspires to the complete realization of human faculties. Between the morality of duty of procedural exigencies, and the substantial morality of aspiration, there is a developmental progression that considers human beings as interactive, capable of increasing rationality and participation in the legal world (Freeman, 1979: 61, emphasizing the parallel with Piaget). The internal morality of law, as Fuller sees it, may therefore be considered as an ethic of legal communication understood as one of the means of opening, maintaining, and preserving channels that allow humans to perceive, feel, and desire. The debate between Fuller and Hart does not stop here. It also extends to the question of what an unjust law is. For Fuller, an unjust law is not a law, and this distinction has the advantage of not conferring on this norm the sanctity that surrounds the notion of law. For Hart, an unjust law is still a law; because it is unjust, there is no obligation to obey it, but preserving its quality as a law has the advantage of forcing us to ask whether or not it is just, and therefore of developing moral sensibility. One might note here that the internal morality of law according to Fuller is procedural above all, and void of substantive content. It affirms the role of reason alone in legal ordering. This procedural rationality, however, does not lack affinities with moral good or substantive justice, which are legal principles that contribute to humanity's realization of its moral goals and objectives (Fuller, 1969: 205). In that sense, Fuller explicitly aligns himself with schools of natural law (Tamanaha, 2001).

Ronald Dworkin is no doubt the author of the major critique of Hart's moderate positivism (Dworkin, 1977; 1986). According to Dworkin, the absence of any rule of knowledge among the rules Hart qualifies as secondary leads one to conclude that the law itself does not exist, in a manner allowing its existence or inexistence to be demonstrated. Dworkin seeks to show that this criterion is invalid in hard cases. In simple terms, what is at stake in the debate is the significance of a procedural conception of law – law is a system of rules that fulfil certain procedural conditions – and the significance of a conception of law that exceeds a system of rules alone – law is a set of rules and principles. The notion of principle, which opens the door to morality once again, is therefore central: it is in light of such principles that the judge, in hard cases, searches for the correct legal response. It is therefore part of the very nature of the judge's work to resort to these principles in finding a solution that already exists implicitly in the legal system – a solution he may deduce by adopting the forms of argument and reasoning that prevail there.

While Hart argued that laws only acquire legal existence if one can demonstrate their existence positively (otherwise, they belong to the order of morality), Dworkin argued that a law always exists implicitly and independently of any authority to edict it; a rational judgment entails only its legal recognition. What this means, in other words, is that moral norms are virtually legal. There are therefore "general and fundamental maxims of law", which may not enjoy the status of rules, and yet provide a legal basis for the judge's decision. In this way, law is made up of various normative components, with principles that are ultimately, according to Ricoeur (1995: 170), ethical-legal in nature. These principles are not univocal in and of themselves and, in consequence, must be interpreted. They have a weight and appropriateness that must be evaluated every time. In sum, Dworkin's theory emancipates law from the condition that it be issued by a legitimate authority, takes into consideration legal practice as it has unfolded historically, and situates law on a political horizon; in this way, it brings morality back home as an instance of the legal.

Realism

In this review of the theories that have sought to explain relations between law and morality, those that oppose the foundationalist perspective must be mentioned. Rather than attempting to analyse the substantive qualities of legal and moral norms, these theories would promote the adoption of a realistic approach that observes the way these norms were constituted as well as their practical relations. By emphasizing the pragmatic, procedural aspect of things and leaving aside determinism, idealism, and normativism, such theories focus on the practical moral dimension of legal activity.

Scandinavian legal realism tends to consider law in terms of a "feeling of obligation" produced by language. Contrary to the theory of command, which considers the law to be the product of an authority's resolve or determination, authors like Axel Hägerström, and especially Karl Olivecrona, pay closer attention to the effect an order has on its addressee. As a result, the emphasis is on perception of legal statements as orders, and on the linguistic formulation that translates this order. Such authors start from the observation that, if words have the ability to produce a "legal bind", that is because uttering a phrase produces "psychological states". In that sense, formulating a judgment is not the result of a simple syllogism, but of an act of will that emanates from psychological attitudes towards a norm. Thus, value judgments result from associating a feeling of pleasure with the idea of an action's reality (Olivecrona, 1953: XI). Value is thus produced by imputing an action with a quality under cover of objectivity, translated by the linguistic use of the indicative form. The Scandinavian realists therefore reject any idea of metaphysics in the legal system in favour of studying its emotional elements, and posit the principle that legal utterances are always based on valuation:

> Statements asserting the "existence" of rights, duties, and legal qualities [...] cannot be said to be either true or false. They are always based on valuation [...]

> Though ostensibly propositions concerning objective realities, they are only ascriptions of rights, duties and legal qualities in conformity with certain rules [...] Despite appearances, they are not statements about realities within the (legal) system; they form a part of the regularized use of language which makes the system work. (*id.*, 1971: 261 sqq.)

The essential character of a normative phenomenon resides in the emergence of a feeling of bindingness endowed with performative qualities. Here, the Scandinavian realists resort to the idea of "internalization" in order to explain that an obligation may be felt and evoked without direct, explicit external pressure having been exercised. Olivecrona thus makes a difference between the semantic content (*ideatum*) of legal rules and the act of communicating their authority (*imperantum*). The latter implies certain modes of enunciation (authoritative attitude and tone) and of reception (readiness to listen and obey). The enunciation and reception of rules operate through action models: rules are ideas of imaginary actions in imaginary situations, while their implementation by the judge is a process consisting of taking these imaginary actions as models (Olivecrona, 1939: 29, quoted by Freeman, 2001: 756).

An author like Alf Ross takes us a bit further in observing the constitution and implementation of these action models. Distinguishing judicial decisions from doctrine, he points out that norms created by judges consist of injunctions to do or not to do, buttressed by sanctions, while the legal concept is a linguistic shortcut that makes it possible to describe the law (Ross, 1958). Far from having a solely descriptive quality as their sole property, however, these terms gradually come to convey a moral connotation that contributes to their effectiveness (Jackson, 1996: 143). Ross bases the administration of justice, whether in "hard" or "easy" cases, on an act of volition. Such an act cannot be operated mechanically and, in that sense, legal decisions are the result of justification rather than interpretation. A judge, in fact, is 'a human being who will carefully attend to his social task by making decisions which he feels to be "right" in the spirit of the legal and cultural tradition.' (Ross, 1958: 116)

In this manner, law and morality intersect in the legal process: the façade of justification does not necessarily reflect the decision-making substratum. In this context, maxims of interpretation are:

> but implements of a technique which – within certain limits – enables the judge to reach the conclusion he finds desirable in the circumstances, and at the same time to uuphold the fiction that he is only adhering to the statute and objective principles of interpretation. (Ross, 1958: 152)

Legal reasoning, therefore, is not autonomous, but it is culturally and socially informed right through (see also Millard, 2002; Brunet, 2002; Serverin, 2002).

This orientation in Scandinavian realism is also found in American realism's scepticism with regard to facts (Jerome Frank) and to rules (Karl Llewellyn). These authors, seeking to demonstrate that judicial decisions are not principally deductive operations, tend to resituate action in a wider social and psychological context. The context of enunciation therefore becomes primordial, implying all the associated tendencies to erase distinguishing limits between law and morality. Then again, while still within a pragmatic perspective where the borders between law and ethics blur, Llewellyn sees the question of whether a decision is just and appropriate as dependent on a post facto evaluation of its adequacy. There may be certainty as to the justness (which coincides here with the justice) of a decision, but 'that certainty *after the event* which makes ordinary men and lawyers *recognize as soon as they see the result* that however hard it has been to reach, it is the right result. Then men feel that it has *therefore* really been close to inevitable.' (Llewellyn, 1960: 185 *sqq.*)

Evaluating a decision's justness is achieved through the perception of a situation, and this perception does not result from technical knowledge, but rather from common-sense understanding of the law, a legal culture that is acquired less through bookish learning that through the social and professional interactions of daily legal practice. This is why the law needs 'men – a bench – right-minded, learned, careful, wise, to find and voice from among the still fluid materials of the legal sun the answer which will satisfy, and which will render semisolid one more point, as a basis for a further growth.' (Llewellyn, 1960: 185) It is in natural law that Llewellyn seeks the source of inspiration, the natural law that jurists must transform into applicable legal rules. As Bernard Jackson emphasizes, 'natural law and realism are in common opposed to positivism, in that they claim that we cannot account for law in terms of rules laid down by institutional sources alone.' (1996: 166)

Natural Law and the Nature of Things

Whether because of the impact of the realist critique or of the repatriation of moral principles in the legal field, we are obliged to recognize that, where "Austin's axe" (Assier-Andrieu, 1996) radically severed the normative substance between law and morality, today we see 'a blurring of the criterion distinguishing law from ethics.' (Cayla, 1996) Several tendencies have called for a return to modern and renewed jusnaturalism, subordinating law to ethics.

In the work of the Brussels School, one thus finds references to the natural order of things. Chaïm Perelman and Paul Foriers both echo the idea of transcending legal positivism in order to find the criteria for the validity of the rule of law. In this case, we are speaking of natural law as it is induced from observing legal reality: 'the nature of things, which imposes itself by virtue of its sheer existences.' (Foriers, 1982: 809) The nature of things thus defined emerges from a consensus sought within a given group. It therefore contains a pragmatic dimension: that of the search for a consensus from which the natural order of things results. It also contains a contextual dimension as a corollary to this. Indeed, 'the nature of things refers to certain values that cover a consensus achieved at a given moment in a given society.' (Corten, 1998: 98)

It is not really certain, however, that these pragmatic and contextual dimensions were taken to their logical conclusions with the Brussels School. While that school does promote the idea of a sociological approach to law, it does so partly in order to emphasize that such an approach corresponds with a true natural order. Olivier Corten (1998: 100-101) makes a relevant point when he points out the weakness of the examples Foriers proposes: natural servitudes may be conventionally accepted as such, but there is no reason to think they are ontologically so; natural incapacities may just as conventionally be established, but they do not result from any immutable order. As for the notion of family, the work of Philippe Ariès offers sufficient proof that something that appears naturally evident one day is not necessarily so the next. Indeed, Perelman himself anticipated such reservations, and referred to Pareto, pointing out that 'universal consent as invoked is often nothing more than the illegitimate generalization of a particular intuition,' and that 'the history of "objective facts" or "evident truths" has been sufficiently varied for one to remain suspicious in this respect.' (Perelman and Olbrechts-Tyteca, 1992: 43) By cultivating certain ambiguities, however, these various authors have prevented themselves from bringing to fruition what their sociological, pragmatic, and contextual tendency had hinted at.[1]

The rejection of theories that grant the legal sphere autonomy from ethics was accompanied by a marked call for a return to natural law, or even to a science of jurisprudence that would have as its exclusive task the discovery of the nature of things. Faced with the problems posed by positivism, authors like Michel Villey suggested that positive law be anchored in the transcendent normative sphere of natural law. Villey (1976) thereby marked his preference for natural law that presented itself in the descriptive form of a discourse formulated by things themselves in relation to what is concretely just, and not in the prescriptive form of abstract principles commanding what should be. In other words, as Cayla emphasizes, legal science must now be observational, and constitute itself as a science of jurisprudence that aims to discover the nature of things (Cayla, 1996). This natural law method certainly transcends the logical dead-ends of state-centrism, but its critics still feel that it makes the concept of legality completely dependent on ethics, indeed causing legality to dissolve into ethics and making it impossible to account for the specificity of the law – which, in the natural law version, was to translate and actualize a human rights ethics through the state

1 We will see later in this work that the praxeological approach makes it possible to show how natural law exists only in invoked typicalities that are produced and reproduced by individuals. Natural law, then, is not what jurisprudence can discover, but rather what is situationally perceived as normal and expected by people engaged in an action. Rather than a limited series of very general, vague, and indeterminate maxims, which cannot serve as a basis for the least particular rule of common life, to which everyone could refer spontaneously, natural law refers to normality, or in other words to the prospective and retrospective reference point of the expectations formulated by those who are routinely engaged in situations of a similar type, and who orient towards these situations as such.

when such an ethical construct was ineffective on its own (*ibid.*). Those who called for positive law as a means of actualizing ethics thus insisted on the question of whether it was possible to identify natural law (a limited series of very general, vague, and indeterminate maxims, which cannot serve as a basis for any particular law of common life to which anyone might obey spontaneously), in order to advance a positivist principle (an obligation can result only from the exteriority of a will to command, expressed by a superior towards his subordinate) that restored state law to a specific place: the place that consists of making natural law present and effective in everyone's conscience.

Law and Ethics of Moral Disputation

Ethics in Jurgen Habermas's discussion is certainly part of this return to natural law, even while it claims to integrate essential points arrived at by the philosophy of language. Habermas's position appears as a critical extension of Max Weber's theory of rationalization of modern legal institutions[2] Weber states that the transition towards post-traditional forms of social organization is characterized by a continuous process of social differentiation and rationalization. The domains of public life that traditionally resulted from people's customary behaviour gradually became differentiated into autonomous spheres of activity, like art, science, and law, and each of these spheres developed its own distinct schemes of organization and rationality, thus gaining further autonomy from the others. The explanation of the tendency displayed by modern legal system to formalize substantive and procedural rules of law in a direction that grows increasingly specialized and technical – and, in that sense, increasingly detached from the traditional authority of practical moral life – is situated at this level. As a result, the legitimacy of legal rules does not emanate from principles of practical moral life, but from forms of rationality specific to the legal mode itself. The very idea of a confusion between law and morality is therefore a threat to the rationality of the law, and therefore to the very foundations of the legitimacy of legal dominance. With the emergence of the welfare state, however, we may observe precisely this type of inter-penetration of law and morality, since the legal system is constantly called upon to arbitrate among different sectors of society on the basis of notions like equity or social justice. Max Weber referred to "materialization of the law", by which he sought to target the formal destructuring of the legal system under the impact of pressures that required it to render substantive justice on questions that were external to it, because of its sensitivity to the impact of disputes bearing on practical moral questions. In other words, the return of a confusion between law and morality is said to threaten the autonomy of legal rationality, and therefore the viability of the legal system as a form of social control.

---

2 For a presentation of Habermas's thesis, see David Bogen (1999: 16-22).

Habermas based himself on this theory of legal rationalization to propose an alternative viewpoint on the socio-logical foundation of rational-legal authority. Contrary to Weber, who made the mistake of conceiving of legal rationality too narrowly, detaching it from the historical conditions that made this form of rationality specific to formal bourgeois law plausible and legitimate, Habermas emphasized that it was impossible to exclude every consideration of practical morality from legal rationality. There are different modes of formal rationality – procedural, intentional, scientific – which depend on relatively informal practical methods of moral reasoning. Practical reason, while it is concerned by collective moral life, is tightly encircled by formal procedures of deliberation and adjudication; and all these procedures are logical, rational methods, which are therefore open to formalization. In a word, Habermas argued that Weber, by relegating morality to the sphere of subjective orientations bearing on values, 'did not take ethical formalism seriously.' (Habermas, 1998: 227) In this perspective, legal rationalization must be related to processes of disputation that initially appeared outside the legal discourse. While Weber saw the autonomy of positive law being threatened by interventions from public discourse, therefore, Habermas treats such intrusions as the growing manifestation of practical moral forms of reasoning and argument, which are at the basis of the exercise of legal authority. The legitimacy of legal norms, in this perspective, depends on the cultural conditions of their construction, and the specific constraints of a logic of disputation: 'The legitimacy of legality is due to the interlocking of two types of procedures, namely, of legal processes with processes of moral argumentation that obey a procedural rationality of their own.' (*id.*: 230)

On this basis, Habermas makes his critical theory bear the task of restoring the rational basis – the procedural rationality – that underlies the legitimate processes of practical reasoning and argumentation. It must be possible to find the equivalent of a "natural law of communication" allowing for the definition of ethical norms that subjects must obey in order to constitute themselves as such and to preserve their own humanity. This law plays only the procedural role of a rational police of deliberation, allowing for the intersubjective elaboration of constraining legal norms. It is therefore a consensual type of law, called upon to replace state law.

Habermas's theory of communicational rationality is the outcome of an evolution towards the proceduralization of relations between law and morality. In that sense, it empties law of all moral normativity. It nevertheless operates through substitution: in the framework of pluralistic societies, where there can be no agreement on a substantive moral good, it is at least necessary to put in place a procedure through which the confrontation of opposite opinions may result in a decision. Like Fuller, Habermas seems to have argued that decisions taken in accordance with an ethics of rational communication would produce morally good results. The affinities of such an idea with good as defined in theories of natural law therefore appear explicitly.

Praxeological Critique

As we reach the end of this review of various approaches that have sought to grasp the relations between law and morality, it is necessary to offer a critique that will provide a basis for the praxeological method followed in the remainder of this work.

Questions about law and morality followed the same course as the general evolution of the social sciences and, in particular, of research into norms. While the fundamental question was initially about the connection between positive law and substantive morality, this was progressively transformed into an investigation into relations between positive law and procedural rationality:

> Until this shift [from substantive morality to procedural rationality], the connection between positive law and morality was always seen in substantive terms, in the sense that the key was law's consistency with the *content* of moral norms. [...] In a gradual process [...] law became separated from substantive morality [...] Just as reason came to be seen in substantively empty instrumental terms, so too with positive law. The culmination of this shift from substantive morality to procedural rationality in relation to law is tha positive law came to point to its own nature – to legality – for legitimation. (Tamanaha, 2001: 98)

It is possible to consider that this evolution had radical consequences. We will suggest, however, that it is also possible to think that these are simply two sides of a single coin, which present themselves as alternatives, but are based on the same fundamental ontology. Indeed, whether in substantive or procedural terms, law and morality are integrated within a general framework that establishes their conceptual connection or dissociation. As for praxeological respecification, it suggests that the line of questioning be shifted to focus only on the situated manifestations of an empirical connection – a connection, in other words, that is perceived, expressed, understood, interpreted, refuted, and argued – between law and morality.

It is worth emphasizing the need to distinguish morality as a normative modality operated by people on the different cognitive operations they are called upon to carry out contextually in the course of their actions, on one hand, from morality as an object on which these same cognitive operations come to bear, and to which people's attention and actions orient during a course of action, on the other. The praxeological respecification proposed here takes place at both these levels.

Law and Morality as Practical Objectivations

A critique of existing theories of legal pluralism will make it possible to show what should be understood by praxeological respecification of law and morality as objects on which cognitive operations come to bear, and to which people orient their attention and action in a given course of action.

Legal pluralism has become a major theme in the sociological and anthropological study of law. This general denomination, which includes very different perspectives, covers all the theories for which law is more than just positive and state law. In brief, three major critiques may be made against these theories, revolving around a definition problem, their functionalist understanding of law, and the culturalist, holistic, and essentialist perspective that underlies them.

According to John Griffiths, although the state presents itself as the sole lawmaker, legal pluralism points to the existence of many autonomous, self-regulating fields, which also produce legal rules. Brian Tamanaha sheds light on several weaknesses in the reasoning followed by Griffiths and his disciples, first among them the conclusion that all forms of social control are law (Tamanaha, 1993: 193). When proponents of the legal pluralism perspective make law synonymous with social norms, they generate an ambiguity, in the sense that they use a word with a common-sense meaning to achieve an analytical task that goes against that meaning. In other words, we may question the analytical usefulness of the word "law" to describe something that common sense would never associate with the law (like good manners, for example), especially if this supposed concept does not connote anything in particular to distinguish it from other, less loaded terms (like "norm"), or, on the contrary, to "secretly" bear the specific traits of that which it opposes. Tamanaha goes further, affirming:

> Lived norms are qualitatively different from norms recognized and applied by legal institutions because the latter involves "positivizing" the norms, that is, the norms become 'legal' norms when they are recognized as such by legal actors. (Tamanaha, 1993: 208)

This critique is perfectly well founded, although the dividing line runs not so much between lived and positivized norms as between law, as people (whoever they may be) recognize it and refer to it, and other moral and normative orders, as people (whoever they may be) recognize them and refer to them. In other words, law is not an analytical concept, but only what people say is law. This in no way prevents anyone from studying normativity in general, on the contrary; but it seriously challenges the possibility of doing so under the aegis of an ideology ("pluralism") that is not descriptive ("legal").[3] This ideology is not descriptive, in that its adherents use legal vocabulary to describe general normativity and its uses, the effect being to dilute law (as people refer to it in general) completely. It is an ideology, in that legal pluralism, while militating for recognition of all diffuse types of normativity, ignores the fact that it is impossible to recognize any normativity as law without an authority that has the right to say what is law and the capacity to interpret it as being law, the consequence being that every kind of militancy against state law would necessarily be promote militancy in favour of another authority of the same sort.

This definition-related problem of legal pluralism is linked to the fundamental postulate that lies beneath its construction. Law is considered as the concept that expresses the social function of ordering accomplished by social institutions.

---

3 This is why I had suggested replacing the notion of legal pluralism by that of "normative plurality" (Dupret, 1999).

Malinowski, Parsons, and Luhman are, according to Tamanaha (1997: 106), the main representatives of the functionalist approach to law. These authors fundamentally share the idea that: 1) law has a role and a nature; 2) this role and this nature are determined a priori by their social function; 3) this function is to maintain social order. And yet John Searle (1995), among others, has shown that functionalism implies an intentionalist conception of things. Thus, if I say that the heart's function is to pump blood, I necessarily indicate that an intentional force created the human body with a heart intended to pump its blood. Following the logic of this argument, a social function can be attributed to law if law is understood as an institution created to regulate human relations, but not when it is understood as an emanation of the social. In other words, a functional analysis can only operate if law is considered to be the product of an intentional agency, not as a spontaneous form of self-regulation. And even in the case of law as a product of social intentions, although it is clear that certain parts of the law were developed in order to fulfil functions (although they were never able to be completely effective in that task), it is equally clear that other sections of the law were not created in this way. Just as it is unlikely that the consumption of pork was prohibited for reasons of hygiene, it is unlikely that adultery was prohibited solely in order to preserve family harmony.

Legal pluralism has also shown itself to be heavily essentialist and culturalist. We will not dwell on nativistic interpretations, which offer a very naïve portrayal of law, one that is far from being supported by a substantial empirical base. Clifford Geertz's interpretive theory is altogether more interesting. Geertz understands law as a cultural code of significations that allow people to interpret the world: law, according to him, is just 'a distinct manner of imagining the real.' (Geertz, 1983: 184) In this hermeneutical project, 'words are keys to understanding the social institutions and cultural formulations that surround them and give them meaning.' (Merry, 1988: 886) This form of culturalism conceives of law in fundamentally holistic terms, meaning as one of many echoes of a larger explanatory principle: culture. Cultural unity, however, is not deduced from empirical observation, but rather postulated from the get-go. This type of approach has a powerful after-taste of genetic essentialism, whereby societies and the laws that characterize them are endowed, throughout their history, with identical, permanent, characteristic elements that historical incidents only scratch superficially. Interpretive culturalists also seem far more interested in the "why" than in the "how", even when paying attention to the latter question would allow them to remark that law is not necessarily or integrally part of culture, and that culture is not a set of permanent, pre-existing postulates. Rather, it is something that is continually being produced, reproduced, negotiated; it is something to which the members of any social group orient on specific occasions and in context (cf. also Sharrock and Anderson, 1982).

The praxeological respecification of the question of law, morality, and the relations between them consists first and foremost of emphasizing that the social sciences do not have the means of defining law and morality outside of what people say and do when they orient towards something that they identify as law or morality. Brian Tamanaha is also an advocate of this position. According to him, the project that consisted of portraying a concept of law of scientific nature was founded on the erroneous conviction that law constitutes a fundamental category, when in fact law *is* everything we attach to the label "*law*" (1997: 128).[4] In other words, people's common uses determine what law is, in the social field. It is not determined in advanced by theoreticians or social scientists (Tamanaha, 2000: 314). The merit of this approach – which makes it non-essentialist – resides in the fact that it is totally devoid of presuppositions about law (beyond the negative presupposition that law has no essence) (*id.*: 318).

It is possible to argue, nevertheless, that, even though Tamanaha's approach vastly improves the possibility of a sociological and anthropological study of law, it suffers from defects that could be attenuated by taking its intuitions further and adopting a praxeological perspective. The main problem with Tamanaha's conception of law results from his attempt to root it in a mixture of behaviorism and interpretivism. One of the difficulties in interpretivism is its culturalist and essentialist perspective. By preserving one of the dualities that mar contemporary theoretical enterprise in sociology, to wit the duality pitting meaning against action, Tamanaha perpetuates the problem rather than resolving it. In fact, what must be challenged is the very propensity to theorize. In other words, investigation 'into the *comprehensibility of society*, into the ways in which social life can be understood and described when seen from within by members' should substitute to the theoretical elaboration of 'a specific mode of comprehending society, a theoretical framework *within* which a substantive conception of society is to be construed.' (Sharrock and Watson, 1988: 59) Geertz's interpretivist culturalism is certainly not the paradigm that could enable such an investigation, as long as it postulates the constraint of a preexisting cultural order to which people conform, which would leave social scientists only the task of discovering the key word that can "epitomize" this cultural order, rather than observing practices and inferring the ways people orient to the multiple constraints of the necessarily local contexts in which they (inter)act. To the contrary, a praxeological approach requires the use of the criteria the participants have to determine the characteristics of interactional episodes (Maynard, 1984: 19), which does not provide an interpretation of people's behaviour: 'Rather, analysis is based on, and made valid by, the participants' own orientations, characterizations, and exhibited understandings.' (*ibid.*) In other words, while the opposition between meaning and behavior 'requires its solution by means [...] which are external to the orderliness observable in the sites of everyday activity' – for instance, social structures, local cultures, schemes of behavior – the praxeological respecification we suggest, in an ethnomethodological way, to consider '"the problem of social order" as completely *internal* to *those sites*'. (Sharrock and Button, 1991: 141) This also means that legal sociology must pay attention not to the question of "why" but rather to the questions of "what" and "how".

4 This is reminiscent of Nadel's remark (1954), according to which religion is what people say is religion.

Another major problem results from the fact that, while Tamanaha rightly criticizes legal pluralism for its "over-inclusiveness", or in other words its willingness to include phenomena that most people would not consider to be part of law, and its "under-inclusiveness", or in other words its exclusion of phenomena that many people would consider as a part of law (Tamanaha, 2000: 315), he ruins his argument by under-estimating the practical, contextual understanding people have of the word "law" and its equivalents. People do not use a single word indifferently to refer to different phenomena; those who use this word participate in producing it and making it intelligible, just as they orient to its production and intelligibility. The same word can be used to refer to another phenomenon in another context or another sequence, but that is a question of language game, in the sense Wittgenstein gave that expression, and it is necessary to respond to it empirically, by closely examining the grammar of this word in every interactional instance that occurs in each specific context (Wittgenstein, 1961; Coulter, 1989).

Morality as a Modality of (Legal) Action

Praxeological respecification also involves morality as the normative modalization people carry out on the different cognitive operations they carry out contextually in the course of their actions. Semiotics, as developed by Bernard Jackson (1985, 1988, 1995, 1996) constitutes an interesting endeavour in this perspective. We will seek to present it here, along with the critiques that may be formulated against it from an ethnomethodological point of view.

Legal semiotics clearly manifests its repudiation of the analysis of relations between law and morality in substantivist and conceptual terms. It takes several intuitions from American realism to the next step, in particular its questions about the Gestalt psychology of legal actors (Frank, 1949). It also takes inspiration from the models of narrativity, socio-linguistics, and social psychology, as developed – in the case of law – by authors like Lance Bennett and Martha Feldman (1981), Brenda Danet (1980), or John Conley and William O'Barr (1990). It also bases itself on Neil MacCormick's theory of narrative coherence (1984). It is the semiotics of Greimas, however, that inspires it in its elaboration of a grammar allowing for the construction of organized meaning in a general, abstract model centered on the notion of narrative unity (cf. Greimas and Courtès, 1979; Landowski, 1989). In this perspective, the construction of meaning implies the interaction of a certain number of different levels: a) the level of manifestation (surface), which is that of data and the meaning it is given; b) the thematic level, which contains the implicit stock of social knowledge that allows meaning to be given to the surface level data; c) the deep level, with the basic structures of meaning that are not linked to the environment but tend toward universality, not only in the framework of the different types of discourse in a given society, but also "interculturally" (Jackson, 1995). In this analytical context, every human action is seen as beginning with the establishment of a goal, instituting someone as the subject of this action, which it is necessary to realize or "perform". In that sense, the subject is helped or impeded by other actions carried out by other social actors, which affect the subject's ability to achieve the action. The action is complete when its realization (or non-realization) is recognized (or sanctioned). Human action thus results from a contract (institution of the subject through the establishment of goals and abilities), a performance (realization or failure to realize these aims), and recognition (sanction of (non-) performance). Every narrative structure implies a complex set of interactions. At the deep level, they pit actants against each other: emitter-receiver, subject-object, presence-absence of the ability required to carry out the action (know-how and can-do). The emitter-receiver pair seems primordial, however, since communication enters into the implementation of the three parts of the narrative syntagm (contract, performance, recognition). At the level of manifestation, one observes that the actants may appear in the form of one or several actors and that, conversely, a single actor can carry out different actant roles at different times (emitter and receiver can even be one and the same person). Finally, in a general way, one observes that the meaning of a term depends on its relation to the other relevant terms, and that substitutions result from choices, constrained by the need to preserve unaltered the meaning of the other elements.

On the basis of Greimas's semiotics, Bernard Jackson developed a narrative model to be applied to law. In the analysis of the thematic level, he starts from the notion of collective image, sketched out by Fletcher (1978), where factual situations are approximated with a collective image like that of "acting like a thief", for example. Jackson refined the concept and referred to narrative typification, meaning the paradigm that new situations approach to a greater or lesser extent when they occur and are evaluated. A collective image is thus at one and the same time the description of a typical action and the social evaluation of its performance. Jackson qualified this paradigm as "narrative typification of action", and distinguished three of its properties: a) it does not generate demonstrable judgments with regard to what is part of the collective image or not (it is not a definition setting out necessary and sufficient conditions), but it produces judgments of relative similarity; b) such a typification is not a neutral description, but is charged with a form of evaluation; c) some typifications are characteristic of certain semiotic groups that specific systems of meaning distinguish from each other (although they may overlap partially). All this social knowledge is internalized by the members of the relevant group and mobilized in a more or less conscious way, which means that some narrative typifications are internalized within a particular group. The content of the stereotype depends on what we have internalized as being typical based on our experience and culture. Judgments are therefore carried out by, among other means, comparing the manifestation level with the stereotype. Narrative typifications appear charged with tacit social evaluations, a fact contingent on the social knowledge specific to the members of a particular semiotic group. Furthermore, narrative typifications do not function mechanically. On the contrary, the model suggested here is negotiated and interactive. As Sbisà and Fabbri point out (1981), new narrative units do not emerge *ex nihilo*. It is necessary for someone to have enunciated them, and to have done so in a persuasive fashion. While a new narrative unit does not have a prefabricated substantive narrative typification, nevertheless it does take its place in the typifications of the pragmatics of new narrative-units creation (our social knowledge contains frameworks for the understanding of persons, behaviours, and discourses that persuade us that something new has been created). This process, of course, is not mechanical, but rather negotiated in interaction. In that sense, semiotics aims to explain *ex post facto* the construction of meaning as it occurred.

According to Jackson, law, whether it is defined as rules, decisions, requisitions, or pleas, can be envisaged as the sum of socially constructive narrative models of human experience that are implemented in a specific institutional framework (Jackson, 1988). Judiciary decisions, to take only one example, then become a procedure that evaluates rather than observing, and compares contending narrative units: that or those of facts and that or those of the rule. In general, the professional practice of law is a form (or, more precisely, a set of forms) of human behaviour that produces meaning. This definition is not restricted to legal practice, but is given to that practice by those who participate in it. It is, in a way, the common sense of those who are engaged in a given practice. We may already note here that the term "meaning" should be taken in a pragmatic, rather than a semantic, sense:

> In semiotic terms, the sense of professional practice is as much a matter of the meanings attributed to its pragmatics (*how* people use systems of signification) as those attributed to its semantics (*what* they say through the use of such systems). (Jackson 1994: 55)

The insertion of meaning in the social framework of its construction – meaning depends on the semiotic group that uses it; it is a use rather than an essence, and a resource rather than a source – implies that it is subjected to processes of accumulation: biographically, individuals stock frameworks for understanding, in which they tend to inscribe new experiences. Among these frameworks, we may include the different variants of legal activity.

Both because of his typification approach and because it takes the praxeological dimension into account, Jackson's legal semiotics constitutes a major turning point in the study of relations between law and morality. The narrative model makes it possible to resituate legal judiciary activity in the wider context where the determination of facts, their qualification, and the choice of the applicable rule are the object of tacit moral evaluations that respond very loosely to the actors' social and psychological information, and therefore to a common sense that they share with the lay people. Further, the typification of judicial pragmatics restores the fundamental dimension of action and interaction in the creation and transformation of norms, which incites us to see moral references not as an intangible essence, but rather, among other things, as a modality borne by the actors as they carry out their performance.

We may direct a number of major critiques against Jackson's semiotic perspective, however. These relate to his taste for the construction of a theory of meaning, his elaboration of such a theory on the basis of textual sources alone, the extremely reflexive nature of his conception of cognition (which is indeed utterly mentalist).

On his taste for the construction of models and theories of meaning – a critique that can also be made, of course, of Habermas's theory of communicational action – we would point out that it is impossible to account for the infinite variety of social phenomena using models, unless we accept to make these models unintelligible. We should also note, at the same time, that endogenous methods of reasoning and action are self-sufficient with regard to the organization and understanding of everyday events. In other words, we should not be endeavouring to formulate an alternative to ordinary reasoning, so much as describing the organized methods of practical action and rationality in practice (Bogen, 1999: 23). The modelling endeavour bears the risk of understanding practice and pragmatism in a sense restricted to the terms of formal linguistic analysis, which forces it to adopt an approach to meaning that is at one and the same time too general – because it relates the question of meaning to holistic, uniform entities like "culture", making these entities totally impermeable to each other – and too narrow, because it does not account for the diversity and contextual dimension of social practices (Sharrock and Anderson, 1982).

A second critique relates to the material that Jackson's semiotic theory is based on. Because semiotics takes its origin from literary criticism, it is not astonishing that it has developed an essentially textual conception of meaning and action: 'Semioticians see science as a form of fiction or discourse like any other, among which effects there is a "truth effect", which (like other literary effects) results from textual characteristics like the grammatical tense used, the structure of enunciation, modalities, etc.' (Latour and Woolgar, 1986: 184) This leads them to pose the question of indexicality, for instance, in terms of a problem of communicational intelligibility and uncertainty. For Michael Lynch, in contrast:

> Indexicality does not necessarily imply that the meaning or intelligibility of particular utterances is "problematic". Instead, it implies that words or isolated statements do not "contain" unequivocal meanings and that understanding and determinate reference are achieved through situated uses of indexical expressions. (1993: 101)

To explain practice, semiotics and its approach to language bears a whole apparatus of concepts that are independent of the discourses and abilities that make up this practice, in such a way that sociology finds itself overhanging the social context it is supposed to describe. The respecification we are suggesting here, on the contrary, consists of examining language games in law and morality in a way that is not external to the contexts we are studying. This requires that we use material that might be textual in part, but that is not simply a series of accounts of accounts, or in other words formalized texts that tell a stripped-down, retrospective version of practices that are already past – to use Garfinkel's terms, texts that are in a relation of asymmetrical alternation (the account of practices makes it possible to retrace the steps that led to the constitution of the text, whereas the textual account does not make it possible to find these practices again) (see Chapter 7). For example, although the text of a ruling makes it possible to accumulate data from which a sociologist can construct coherent analyses, it also produced a "gap in the literature" or a "missing-what", which is produced by the sheer fact and the sole existence of that "literature". (Lynch, 1993: 290)

The third and final critique of Jackson's semiotics relates to its excessively reflexive understanding of judgment and categorization, which makes these operations predicative in all cases. In a perspective close to cognitive psychology, and like classical conceptual theories (Quéré, 1994: 18), this approach grants logical priority to substantive categorization; it makes a relation that subsumes one content to another into a constitutive relation; it attributes a classificatory character to the act of identifying objects and phenomena (an object's identity is determined through the class to which it said to belong); it reduces awareness of a category to awareness of a representation (reasoning then becomes merely the aptitude of reproducing representative contents); it understands the construction of concepts as a process of abstraction and comparison; and finally, it considers words in language as reproductions of predetermined essences relating to the nature and world of representations. It is necessary to remark, however, that the very possibility of taking apart in its characteristics an object represented, and of relating it to others, already supposes that one has its concept, and that the emphasis placed on function as an extension of the concept detracts from the understanding it allows (the concept makes it possible to impose a form on impressions to make them into representations). It would no doubt be appropriate to adopt a more praxeological perspective: just as a concept sets off regulated procedures for the analysis, composition, and combination of concepts (the concept is the rule or method of these procedures), categorization is a moment in a process of descending into singularity, which functions according to a principle of selection that aims to detach a characteristic moment and make it the point to which attention is drawn (Quéré, 1994: 20).

Conclusion

Our investigation into the relationship between law and morality has followed the course of social science research into norms, moving from an examination of the link between positive law and substantive morality to questions about the relations between positive law and procedural rationality. This evolution certainly has consequences, but we suggested, in this chapter, that these are simply variations on a single fundamental ontology that integrates law and morality in the framework of conceptual connection or disconnection. The praxeological approach, on the other hand, suggests a respecification that examines only the situated manifestations of the empirical links between law and morality. At that level, we pointed out that it is necessary to distinguish morality as an object on which different cognitive operations comes to bear as people carry them out contextually in the course of their actions, from morality as people's normative modalization of these same operations. The next chapter will examine normative modalization in detail.

Chapter 2
The Morality of Cognition: The Normativity of Ordinary Reasoning

Taking an interest in the morality of judgment does not imply that it is necessary to await the act of judging, especially in law, before speaking of morality and normativity. Action is entirely normative and moral, and the following section will be devoted to elucidating this normativity.

First, we will synthesize the conclusions reached by ethnomethodological works on the morality of cognition. Next, we will focus on rules and on the debate that, since Wittgenstein, has examined the question of what it means "to follow a rule". We will also broach the question of ordinary reasoning, the categorizations it carries out, and their normative nature. For example, the question of causal imputation will be dwelt on in some depth. Finally, we will present a few remarks on reasoning about normality – in other words, the operations whereby a normative schema conforming to the average and to dominant morality is produced prospectively and used retrospectively at the same time.

The Moral Nature of Action

John Heritage (1984: 76), who inspired the title of this chapter, shows how Garfinkel sought to achieve the integration of morality and cognition when he took up Parsons's questions about the constraints that norms impose on actors and their actions, and Schütz's questions about commonsense judgment. While the former serves as a counterpoint to Garfinkel's procedure, however, the latter provides its backdrop.

Schütz's world is intersubjective: it is made up of routines and is largely unproblematic. This intersubjectivity is made possible by the principle of reciprocal perspectives, based on two fundamental idealizations that actors use: the interchangeability of the standpoints[1] and the congruency of the system of relevances.[2]

---

1 'I take it for granted – and assume my fellow-man does the same – that if I change places with him so that his "here" becomes mine, I shall be at the same distance from things and see them with the same typicality as he actually does' (Schütz, 1962, I: 12).

2 'Until counter evidence I take it for granted – and assume my fellow-man does the same – that the differences in perspectives originating in our unique biographical situations are irrelevant for the purpose at hand of either of us and that he and I, that "We" assume that both of us have selected and interpreted the actually or potentially common objects and

To the intersubjectivity of our knowledge we must add its being embedded in a "horizon of familiarity", which is the outcome of the work of rebuilding passed experiences and their accumulation in a stock of knowledge. Made of our habits, this stock, which ongoingly renews itself, represents the means at the disposal of every individual at any moment. It is organized around typified objects, and this is this typifying process that 'necessarily binds us to the past on one hand and implicates the anticipation of similar expression on the other.' (Coulon, 1994a: 456)

> All our knowledge of the world, in common-sense as well as in scientific thinking, involves constructs, i.e., a set of abstractions, generalizations, formalizations, idealizations specific to the respective level of thought organization. Strictly speaking, there are no such things as facts, pure and simple. All facts are from the outset facts selected from a universal context by the activities of our mind. They are, therefore, always interpreted facts, either facts looked at as detached from their context by an artificial abstraction or facts considered in their particular setting. In either case, they carry along their interpretational inner and outer horizon. This does not mean that, in daily life or in science, we are unable to grasp the reality of the world. It just means that we grasp merely certain aspects of it, namely those which are relevant to us either for carrying our business of living or from the point of view of a body of accepted rules of procedure of thinking called the method of science. (Schütz, 1962b: 5)

We observe, thus, that, according to Schütz (1962b: 5), 'relevance is not inherent in nature as such', but rather constitutes 'the result of the selective and interpretative activity of man within nature or observing nature.' In the perspective of Husserl's phenomenology, the operation of categorization must be apprehended below the level of predicative judgment – it does not constitute simply an object's being subsumed within a class. Husserl refers to 'typical precognition of every singular object of experience'. Schütz takes up this idea in sociological terms, by which it comes to mean that we grasp objects, events, and people a priori as being of a certain type; we apprehend their typical properties, according to general determinations, linked to their type, and not to their individual particularities. According to Daniel Cefaï (1994), Schütz's approach is neither cognitive (it posits already-there typicality) nor ontological (it focuses on operations of classification carried out by a subject). Reflection functions by referring to already available types, organized in schemes of experience, which were articulated in the course of past experience and have been stored in the actor's stock of experience (Husserl, 1970; Schütz, 1962b; Isambert, 1989).

In Schütz's sociology, actors behave as if events followed normal schemes and proceeded from normal causes. In other words, the social world is largely unproblematic. This shared world is valid until proven otherwise. The stable order

---

their features in an identical manner or at least an "empirically identical" manner, i.e., one sufficient for all practical purposes' (Schütz, 1962b, p. 12).

of things is assumed as a starting point. What remains – and this is Garfinkel's ambition – is to show how this stable order is produced, recognized, understood, and shared. This is the origin of the famous "breaching experiments", in which Garfinkel asked his students to produce situations that disrupted idealizations of the thesis of reciprocal perspectives. As a general rule, actors seem to find what their interlocutors seem to take for granted, without having to verify it; the meaning of the conversation is seen as clear and established, even when it has not been mentioned explicitly. Actors view this presumed clarity and intelligibility as something acquired, to which they have a moral right. In that light, any attack on such presumptions becomes illegitimate, and must therefore be the object of sanctions or repairs. As Heritage puts it, 'maintaining the "reciprocity of perspectives" (as one of the presuppositions of daily life) is not merely a cognitive task, but one which each actor "trusts" that the other will accomplish as a matter of moral necessity.' (1984: 82)

This moral necessity results from the fact that a breach has been inflicted to what is perceived as normal, and the normal order of events has been threatened (Garfinkel, 1963: 198). Using the documentary method of interpretation (see the introduction), Garfinkel also sought to show how, in an exchange, expressions are not necessarily taken literally, but in relation to an underlying scheme of presuppositions, which people expect will be confirmed and the invalidation of which, conversely, creates a problem. Heritage concludes that 'the "force" of the rules appears not to derive from a "moral consensus" on the "sacredness" of the rules, but rather from the fact that, if conduct cannot be interpreted in accordance with the rules, the social organization of a set of "real circumstances" simply disintegrates.' (1984: 83) In a word, the very order of action and interaction is normative.

The question then arises of how actors come to conform to the rules and procedures. Various theories have been put forth on this point. The sociological hypothesis of internalized norms, which provoke automatic, spontaneous behaviours, does not explain how actors perceive and interpret the world, recognize that which is familiar and construct that which is acceptable. Nor does it explain how rules concretely govern interactions (Coulon, 1994b: 648). On the contrary, ethnomethodology focuses on the mechanisms of normativity as they are deployed in concrete, public circumstances. From this perspective, Garfinkel adopts a procedural approach to the question of norms and meanings, which he presents as achievements that are anchored only in action and interaction. Without the slightest interruption being possible (with no time-out), people explain their conformity to a norm that is constantly being produced and reproduced, provide motives for their departures from this norm, and allow motives and significance to be attributed to departures from this normality. In that sense, behaviour appears susceptible to understanding, description, and evaluation. Ethnomethodology must therefore broach a whole series of questions bearing on norms and values, and describe in detail and in real contexts the diverse mechanisms in play.

> [These objects of inquiry might be:] the normative construction of features of those settings; the normative construction of facticity; the practical intelligibility

> of moral standards; the interactional logic of moral ascriptions etc. More specifically, some of the phenomena for analytic investigation might be: the ways agreements and disagreements are organised, generated, displayed and managed, and the activities they are constituents of; what counts as a reasonable warrant for certain sorts of action ascription; how particular action ascriptions are tied into responsibility ascriptions, and to the activities of blaming or praising; how factual disagreements are productive of different moral accountings (different verdicts, outcomes, interactional upshots); how different descriptions of an action can provide for different interactional tasks; how moral standards themselves can be interactionally assessed in consequential ways etc. (Jayyusi, 1991: 235)

Rather than dealing with morality in the framework of the ethical "big questions", and in line with the tradition of moral philosophy, we are therefore invited to undertake a "socio-logical" investigation of an empirical moral order, in a given situation and in action.

Following a Rule

Some sociologists argue that actors encounter action situations where sets of learned or incorporated rules apply, and that this leads to analyse their actions as guided or caused by such rules. In contrast, what is necessary is to examine the nature of rules and of the act of following them. This brings us inevitably back to Wittgenstein's analyses in *Philosophical Investigations* (1953).

Wittgenstein's interpretations on the question of rules are numerous and contradictory. Some readers have him say that ordered actions are not determined by rules, but by social conventions and learned dispositions that prevent the possibility of interpretive regression. Thus, the sociology of scientific knowledge adopted a conventionalist, sceptical posture, following the interpretation of Saul Kripke (1982). In this perspective, the relation between rules and behaviours is indeterminate. Others think Wittgenstein argued that rules cannot be separated from practical behaviour. They maintain that only a biased reading could lead one to read him in a conventionalist perspective (Lynch, 1993: 162-3). Thus, although ethnomethodological studies of work proceed from the investigation of the same epistemological objects and a reading of the later Wittgenstein, these studies also consider that rules and behaviour cannot be separated from each other, and that the relation between them is not the result of external sociological factors (a community's convention).

In his book, Kripke seeks to demonstrate that Wittgenstein adopted a skeptical position by giving a social-constructivist response to the problem of rule indeterminacy. To this end, he started with paragraphs 143-242 of the *Philosophical Investigations*, e.g. §185, where Wittgenstein suggested that the reader imagine an exercise where a teacher asks his student, who masters the cardinal numbers and has already carried out the exercise consisting of "n+2", to extend the series beyond 1,000.

> Now we get the pupil to continue a series (say +2) beyond 1000 – and he writes 1000, 1004, 1008, 1012. We say to him: "Look what you've done!" – He doesn't understand. We say: "You were meant to add *two*: look how you began the series!" He answers: "Yes, isn't it right? I thought that was how I was *meant* to do it."

According to Kripke, the pupil's error shows that the rule is indeterminate, in the sense that his actions are coherent with another, imaginable series such as: 'Add 2 up to 1,000, 4 up to 2,000, 6 up to 3,000…' Because he only practiced up to 1,000, his understanding of the rule does not contradict his previous experience. At the same time, it reveals the uncertainty inherent in this rule in the absence of any prior instruction. Thus we arrive at a radically relativistic position. Wittgenstein underlines this paradox:

> This was our paradox: no course of action could be determined by a rule, because any course of action can be made out to accord with the rule. The answer was: if everything can be made out to accord with the rule, then it can also be made out to conflict with it. And so there would be neither accord nor conflict here." (Wittgenstein, 1953: §201)

Kripke recognized that Wittgenstein did not stop at this relativistic paradox, which is founded on the postulate that our understanding of the rule is based on an interpretation, i.e. a private judgment regarding the rule's significance, formed independently of the regular practices of a given community. According to Wittgenstein, such an interpretation is impossible because the regularities of our common behaviour provide a context in which the rule is formulated and understood. This practice reveals few variations. Of course, it is possible to have the occasional doubt, and one can hesitate. This does not signify the existence of epistemological doubt, however; rather, it is doubt of a practical nature. In general, one follows the rule 'as a *matter of course*.' (Wittgenstein, 1953: §238) The question is then how it is possible to follow a rule "as a matter of course" beyond the cases where it has already been applied, and how the repetitive character of the action is obtained. Wittgenstein's reply seems to be: through example, guidance, the expression of agreement, encouragement, constraint, intimidation, etc.: 'When someone whom I am afraid of orders me to continue the series, I act quickly, with perfect certainty, and the lack of reasons does not trouble me.' (*id.*: §212)

According to Kripke's argument, therefore, we do not act in accordance with the rules of calculation, but for reasons extrinsic to the operation and linked to the language that people use, to their "form of life" (*id.*: §241) – in other words, with the social practices of a linguistic community that are so deeply rooted that the speakers do not think of them (Schulte, 1992: 125). Social conventions, then, are responsible for making us follow the rules in a certain way, and, in that case, Wittgenstein put forth a strong argument in favour of the conventionalist explanation. Agreement on a theory would then result from a social consensus and institutions shared by a community, rather than from the facts themselves. In that sense, social consensus would approve of and recognize the theory, rather than the other way around.

Kripke's skepticist theory has been widely debated and contested. According to Stuart Shanker (1987: 14), for example, 'far from operating as a skeptic, one of Wittgenstein's earliest and most enduring objectives was … to undermine the skeptic's position by demonstrating its unintelligibility.' The point on which Kripke articulates his argument, in his reading of Wittgenstein, corresponds to 'the culmination of a sustained *reductio ad absurdum.*' According to Shanker, Wittgenstein's reasoning aimed to demonstrate the absurdity of a "quasi-causal" representation of rule-following, which treats rules as abstractions engaging mental mechanisms. This deterministic vision should be replaced by a perspective that emphasizes the practical basis of rule-following: the impression of being guided by the rule reflects the fact that we apply it inexorably (Shanker, 1987: 17-8; Lynch, 2001a: 171).

Thus, if sceptics and non-sceptics agree in refusing the quasi-causal nature of rule-following, they diverge radically on the extent to which the rule can explain the action.

> The critical move in the skepticist strategy is to isolate the formulation of the rule from the practice it formulates (its extension). Once the rule statement is isolated from the practices that extend it to new cases, the relation between the two becomes problematic: No single rule is determined by the previous practices held to be in accord with it, and no amount of elaboration of the rule can foreclose misinterpretations consistent with the literal form of its statement. Such indeterminacy is then remedied by a skepticist solution, which is to invoke extrinsic sources of influence on the relation between rules and their interpretations. These extrinsic sources include social conventions, community consensus, psychological dispositions, and socialization – a coordination of habits of thinking and action that limits the alternative interpretational possibilities. (Lynch, 1993: 171)

Against the scepticist attitude, it is necessary to agree with Shanker that Wittgenstein's aim was not to resolve the question of rule indeterminacy. Rather than the sociological, conventionalist turn Kripke thought he could see, Wittgenstein shows a praxeological turn as he examines the grammar of something like "rule-following". Wittgenstein sought to show how mathematical knowledge could be considered "objective", which is not the same thing as giving it an objective or transcendental basis. Rather, he was attempting to show how the internal relation between the rule and the actions undertaken in accord with the rule was sufficient to engender the rule's extension to new cases, without it being necessary to look for a biological, psychological, or sociological basis for this extension. It must be emphasized that what is sufficient is the internal relation between the rule and its extensions, and not the rule alone. The rule is intelligible only because it is adhered to in practice; it finds meaning only in the order of concerted activities that are already in place when the rule is enunciated, violated, ignored, or followed. The enunciation of the rule is understood in and through these practices, and can in no way be abstracted from them (Lynch, 1993: 171-4; 2001a: 132-3).

Following a rule, then, is not just a matter of interpreting it, as if its significance were already wholly contained in its abstract formulation, but rather of acting and manifesting our understanding by acting in accordance with this rule. According to Wittgenstein (1953: §202), 'And hence also "obeying a rule" is a practice. And to think one is obeying a rule is not to obey a rule.' This does not preclude faulty interpretation of the rule or doubt as to its meaning or the steps to be taken in order to obey it; but these are exceptions and do not justify the adoption of a skepticist, interpretivist position. Understanding and interpreting are not the same thing. Interpretation is a reflexive activity, while understanding is neither a mental activity nor an experience that accompanies the act of hearing, seeing, or reading; nor is it a behaviour. Understanding manifests itself in behaviour.

> What distinguishes my actually understanding, i.e. having knowledge, from merely supposing or thinking that I do, from merely believing so, is nothing interior to my mind or brain (which I might find difficult to describe), but is my correct, ratifiable performance, my proper application, my exhibited capacity to do, say or in some other contextually appropriate manner to *satisfy the relevant criteria* for my having, indeed, actually understood whatever it was I *claimed* to have understood. (Coulter, 1989: 63)

To say that one has understood is to produce a gesture that signifies, in a manner that may be revised, that one possesses an ability.

The reference to internal relations between rules and practices signifies a grammatical relation between the expression of a rule and the techniques of a normative system, which has nothing to do with the idea of a private concept. An action may occasionally be qualified as a flawed interpretation of the rule, but this expression has meaning only to the extent that it is made from a place situated inside the recognized institution of a normative system. Rules are acquired and embedded in explanations, instructions, examples, errors, training, verification, etc. In other words, they are embedded in practices (Coulter, 1989: 67). There is no externality here, nor relativism that would make it possible to dismiss all theories, back to back, as equivalent alternatives based on nothing. Lack of understanding manifests the failure of understanding, not the relative nature of the rule's meaning and application. The established practices and techniques of a normative system may not be separated from the very terms in which a precise action is described as understanding, alternative understanding, or misunderstanding. A rule can only have meaning, can only be applied and followed, against a general backdrop of institutions, practices, and behavioural techniques that are socially shared and that provide criteria allowing one to distinguish a situation in which a rule is really being followed from another kind (Coulter, 1989: 66). Rules and the practice of rules are the expression of a form of life exhibited in the very coherence of our activities. And, due to this coherence, one notices errors, disturbances, and misunderstandings, and their authors are held accountable (Lynch, 1993: 176-80).

The Normativity of Ordinary Reasoning

In the ethnomethodological perspective, the social order is a cognitive and moral phenomenon produced by and in the methods of practical reasoning of the members of a given social group. This is what Garfinkel (1967: 74) calls their practical ethics. This practical ethics is expressed in ordinary, "mundane" reasoning (Pollner, 1987) and its various hypotheses regarding the objectivity and the intersubjectivity of the social reality we experience every day. In *Mundane Reason* (1987), Melvin Pollner examines precisely these ordinary hypotheses: how they are produced and maintained, as well as the solutions that ordinary reasoning provides when it is faced with conflicting versions or experiences of reality. Pollner's approach, which belongs in the same category as the phenomenology practiced by Schütz, starts from the observation that, in ordinary reasoning, the world is dealt with as an object. This objectivity is never examined. In other words, mundane reasoning is an underlying interpretive scheme that makes it possible for ordinary inferences and interpretations to be understood, described, and justified. The term scheme as used here indicates that mundane reasoning does not bear on the substantive nature of reality but rather on its formal properties.

Among the hypotheses and practices that make up mundane reasoning, Pollner identifies a number of idealizations that bear upon the coherent, determined, and non-contradictory character of reality. These idealizations 'function as constraints which the corpus of mundane determinations – reports, claims and experiences – of reality must satisfy insofar as it is to be counted as intelligible and rational.' (Pollner, 1987: 27) All these presuppositions regarding the determined, non-contradictory, internally consistent, and coherent nature of the world are beyond the possibility of invalidation. If contradictory observations on reality present themselves, they will not pose a challenge to these presuppositions; rather, it is the nature of the observations and the competence of those making them that will be in question. Thus, one will say that what observers saw was correct, but corresponded to two different moments in reality; or one will say that one of the observers could not have seen what he said he saw, because the conditions for correct observation were not present. Mundane reasoning, therefore, does not perceive multiple realities, but rather a single reality, of which the description may be faulty and patchy, which leaves it the task of filling in the gaps and empty spaces. Mundane reasoning anticipates a number of things with regard to the continuity, complementarity, and conformity of the various aspects of an object under observation. The fact that one expects accounts of an event to be harmonious, complementary, and coherent is behind the remarkable and remarked-upon character of the gaps that are noticed.

The task of ordinary reasoning then becomes that of reconciling contradictory accounts by affirming or discrediting various versions of reality. By that very token, suppositions that relate *a priori* to reality are invariably confirmed (Pollner, 1987: 46). The capacity of mundane reason to preserve itself is largely due to its intersubjective character and its insertion in a system of mutual perspectives that are translated in two other idealizations: the interchangeable nature of points of view and the congruence of systems of relevance (Schütz, 1987; 1990). To illustrate this point, Pollner cites Evans-Pritchard's description of the Azande oracle (1937). Just as the incongruous revelations of the oracle are repaired in such a way as to preserve the basic beliefs – so-called contradictions are thus explained in terms of interference with the normal functioning of the oracle – suppositions with regard to the objective nature of the world and the intersubjectivity of knowledge are incorrigible theses on which mundane reasoning bases itself as it searches for explanations to abnormal situations (Pollner, 1974; 1987). We may note that this incorrigibility, which is presupposed, is at one and the same time produced, reproduced, and realized each time people refer and orient to it. As for abnormal situations and disjunctions that arise from narrative accounts, they are explained, described, and justified by emphasizing the abnormal quality of the situation in which one or several observers could be found at the time of the event in question. The hypothesis is that, all else being equal, a single event can only produce identical descriptions. Mundane reasoning can only explain the incongruity of these descriptions by emphasizing the condition of normal observation that remained unfulfilled.

> Each explanation preserves the world as an objective and shared order of events by showing how unanimity would have been forthcoming had it not been for the absence, failure or violation of one of the presupposed but previously unformulated conditions necessary for unanimity. (Pollner, 1987: 65)

The existence of these idealizations, hypotheses, and background expectations, which make up what Cicourel (1968) called the prospective-retrospective horizon of reasoning, provides common sense with the methods that allow it to reconcile contradictory accounts of reality. Ethnomethodological analysis has focused on these methods and sought to show how they work. Garfinkel (1967) identified several of them: resorting to documentary methods of interpretation and indexical expressions; the reflexive constitution of language; the use of "ad hoc" methods and clauses like "etcetera", "ceteris paribus", "unless", etc. The clause "ceteris paribus", for example, refers to the method whereby people, in a situation of disjunction, seek out solutions that highlight the single condition, among an infinite variety of conditions dealt with from the outset as equivalent, which has not been fulfilled. In mundane or ordinary reasoning, modes of description applying to events, people, and actions are fundamental: firstly, because they select some of the many characteristics of the object being described – this selection is never neutral, but is always linked to the intention behind the description; secondly, because they necessarily reveal a background of understanding if the descriptions are to be intelligible. In sum, as Heritage points out (1984: 152), 'a wider context of interpretation is brought to bear on a description which is simultaneously being brought into rough correspondence with a referent state of affairs.' In descriptive action, people base their reasoning on well-established ways of evaluating the credibility of accounts and their correspondence to what occurred. All these methods are broadly articulated around procedures of categorization and category ascription.

The investigation of categories (cf. Fradin et al., 1994) and, in particular, of classes of membership, is one of the fundamental elements of ethnomethodological analysis. The analysis of membership categorizations, which rejects a semantic approach to categories, undertook the study of live categories, in a perspective that pays attention to context. According to the founder of this type of analysis, Harvey Sacks (1995), the problem – given the infinitely extensible variety of potentially correct categories in a given situation of categorization – is deciding how the criteria of correctness or exactitude of formal logic can shed light on the logic of real categorizations. At the very least, it is necessary to distinguish between "potentially correct" and "circumstantially correct", which implies that the activity of categorizing must be sensitive to the interlocutors' presumed time- and space-related knowledge. Sacks defines membership categories as classifications or social types that can be used to describe persons, groups, or objects. When these categories are associated in collections, they make up what he calls membership categorization devices, which he defines as follows:

> … any collection of membership categories, containing at least a category, which may be applied to some population containing at least a member, so as to provide, by the use of some rules of application, for the pairing of at least a population member and a categorization device member. A device is then a collection plus rules of application. (Sacks, 1974: 218)

For example, the categories "father", "mother", "brother", "sister", "uncle", and "cousin" belong to the membership categorization device "family". A single category, furthermore, can belong to several devices ("Catholic" can belong to "religion" or "church", for example). Sacks identifies two rules of application. On one hand, the economy rule: a single membership category suffices to describe a member of a given population. On the other, the consistency rule: the category of a device that has been used to categorize the first member of a given population may be used to categorize other members of that population (Sacks, 1974: 219). One of the major properties of membership categorization devices is the fact that classes of predicates may be ascribed to them conventionally, which includes category-bound activities, rights, expectations, obligations, knowledge forms, attributes, and skills. A sub-group of membership categorization devices is made up of what Sacks calls "standardized relational pairs". These are systems in which the collection of categories is limited to two. The simple fact of grasping the existence of such a dual relation, in different practical situations, may be "inferentially adequate" in terms of the attribution of moral rights and duties, or any other quality that may be imputed. Furthermore, these pairs are endowed with "programmatic relevance", by which Sacks means that each part of the pair implies the other. If the other is absent, this absence must be justifiable. Among these pairs, one may note a variation that Lena Jayyusi (1984: 124-7) calls "asymmetrical relational pairs". These display an asymmetrical distribution of knowledge, rights, and obligations between the two parties. Finally, Sacks points out that activities are very often linked in normative fashion to categorial systems. This often functions in a transitive way: a member of a category, although that category does not constitute a group in the sense of an organized community, is considered as the representative of that category, is endowed with its qualities, and, as such, is inexorably linked to whatever may involve it. In a symmetrical manner, one can also observe the procedure that consists of attributing a particular form of knowledge to a given category or a limited series of categories, which makes it possible to consider that such knowledge, in a commonsense way, is "held" by the members of those categories, entailing a certain set of rights and responsibilities (Watson, 1995: 2002). In sum, as Coulter says (1991: 47), membership categories and their use logic are immensely powerful resources. They can organize our perceptions, knowledge, beliefs, discourses, and other forms of practical behaviour, in a totally routine, predictable, and conventional – in a word, ordered – way (see also Hester and Eglin, 1997a; 1997b; 1997c).

Credit goes to Lena Jayyusi for having carried out an in-depth study of the intrinsically normative and moral nature of categorization. In her work on categorization and the moral order (1984; 1991a), she seeks to show how intersubjectivity rests on irremediably normative foundations. Pursuing the demonstration begun by Garfinkel on "breaching experiments", Jayyusi (1991a: 236) endeavours to describe the functioning of the moral bases from which the social order is praxeologically generated. These bases, in turn, are reestablished as the foundation of justifiable, rational, and intelligible actions, and of inferences and judgments in discourse. Communication practice presupposes, and is based on, ordinary ethics – "natural" ethics, in the sense that it is part of the natural attitude of everyday life, even while it is reflexively constituted by that attitude. In the course of all descriptive categorization work, the use and intelligibility of categories are deeply embedded in procedures that evaluate relevance, priorities, tasks to be accomplished, recipient, etc. Furthermore, in categorizations and in the normative imputations that we carry out while categorizing, we resort to inferential moral logic, even as we produce that logic. Ordinary, practical reason, in that sense, is morally organized.

> Very clearly, the use of even mundanely descriptive categories, such as "mother", "doctor", "policeman", for example, makes available a variety of possible inferential trajectories *in situ*, that are grounded in the various "features" bound up with or constitutive of, these categories as organisations of practical mundane social knowledge. These features might be "moral" features in the first place (such as the kinds of "rights" and "obligations" that are bound up with one's

> being a "mother", or a "doctor" or "policeman"), or they might be otherwise – such as the "knowledge" that is for example, taken to be bound up with a category such as "doctor", or the kind of "work" that is taken to be constitutive of, or tied to, a category such as policeman. But even in the later case, it turns out that as evidenced in our actual practices, for example, "knowledge" has its responsibilities – even *these* features provide grounds for the attribution of all kinds of moral properties, for finding that certain kinds of events or actions may or may not have taken place, for determining culpability, even for defeating the applicability of the category or description in the first place. (…) Intelligibility is constituted in practico-moral terms. (Jayyusi, 1991a: 241)

Such a varied group of questions, bearing on the constitution of actions and events, on what is factual or objective, on predictability, consequentiality, personhood, intentionality, causality, etc., appears thoroughly moral. Praxeological respecification, undertaken by ethnomethodological analysis, leads us to formulate a certain number of important considerations regarding the question of morality in ordinary reasoning, and the categories and categorizations on which that morality is based (Jayyusi, 1991: 243-7). First, moral values are publicly available, in the sense that they do not reside in some secret place of the mind or subjective perception; rather, they are given, made visible, laid out, and imputed on the basis of an actor's discourses and actions. Second, morality has a modal logic, meaning that, even if one had general principles, conventions, and rules, these would not provide their own applications in advance for different action contexts. Even if they are given conventionally, they must be explained situationally. Third, moral values and conventions have an open texture: their uses and applications are determined by multiple criteria (which is not evidence of disorder, but rather the indication of a practical order made up of multiple options, which are constantly being realized, contradicted, made relevant, or transformed). Fourth, objectivity is a practical achievement carried out by members of society. This does not mean that it is relative, but rather that it emerges from a shared world, in which the dimension everyone shares is at one and the same time presumed and discovered. Finally, fifth, it is important to note that the moral order is not one of Boltanski and Thévenot's "sites/cities" (1991): it is an omnipresent, constitutive characteristic of social practice; it is always available both as a resource and a topic of investigation, as a foundation and a project; it is not a locus of investigation restricted to moral philosophers alone. As Heritage emphasizes (1984: 100), 'the normative accountability of action is thus a seamless web, an endless metric in terms of which conduct is unavoidably intelligible, describable and assessable.'

Example: Causation

To illustrate the praxeological dimension of the moral order, we will explore a particular predicative operation that consists of ascribing a cause to an action.

Only causation in ordinary reasoning will be studied here; the practical grammar of causation in law being the specific topic of Chapter 9. Herbert Hart and Tony Honoré have dealt with the question of causation in common sense (1985), using it as a point of comparison in their examination of legal causation. The two authors start by underlining the fact that ordinary people master causal concepts as they are used daily. They also insist on the contextual sensitivity of many causal notions. Finally, they clearly assert that it is difficult to produce a complete survey of causation in general. Rather than attempting such a feat, they select "standard examples" of the way that people constantly use causal expressions in ordinary life. These examples, according to the authors, make up the core of relatively well-established common usage (Hart and Honoré, 1985: 27). In that regard, there is no single concept, but rather a variety of concepts that resemble each other. Consequences are perceived, for example, as the result of a complex, consciously formulated process; effects are perceived as desired secondary outcomes; and causes are perceived as the action whereby we bring about an initial change in the things we manipulate, or as the initial changes themselves (*id.*: 29). This, of course, is very far from causal theory as formulated by John Stuart Mill (1886). According to Hart and Honoré, the commonsense conception of causation turns around a certain idea of the normal or natural state of things and, therefore, of their abnormality (see herein). It is not necessary that an action be considered deliberate for it to be identified as the cause of an occurrence; however, deliberate actions hold a particular place in the commonsense search for causation, which seems to give human agency a particular status that leads the causal explanation to a halt These causal notions always remain vague, and their identification has more to do with a degree of plausibility than with absolute criteria. This is where Hart and Honoré find the context and the reason for the existence of causal ascription relevant.

While Hart and Honoré's research is extremely interesting, we may level two major critiques against it. The first concerns the material on which they base their work, while the second concerns the epistemology that underlies their analysis of this material. We will not dwell on these questions. Suffice it to emphasize that Hart and Honoré's approach, while it affirms that context has a determining role, and it is impossible to conceive a general theory of common-sense causation, is based on an understanding of language and speech acts that may be seen to echo, or more accurately to prefigure, the formal semantics and principle of expressibility formulated by John Searle.[3] The problem arises because the examples Hart and Honoré give are always imagined in an abstract way. This suggests that they are

3 According to Searle (1969: 20-1), this principle 'enables us to equate rules for performing speech acts with rules for uttering certain linguistic elements, since for any possible speech act there is a possible linguistic element the meaning of which (given the context of the utterance) is sufficient to determine that its literal utterance is a performance of precisely that speech act. To study the speech acts of promising/apologizing we need only study sentences whose literal and correct utterance would constitute making a promise or issuing an apology.'

of the same nature as the literal, exact expressions that Searle believes he can substitute indifferently for contextual utterances in order to repair their lack of precision and their indexicality. The canonical model of literal expression, however, can never serve as a gauge by which to measure the precision of an expression. Further, an expression cannot be formulated precisely outside the context of its utterance, and, in particular, of the set of illocutionary aims that adhere to it contextually (Bogen, 1999: 65). No utterance can be formulated outside a context: every utterance is formulated contextually, sequentially, and in a manner oriented to the realization of certain situated goals. As Sacks asserts (1995, vol. I: 742), the relevance of an expression depends on its location in a local interaction context, and on what immediately preceded it. Linguistic idealization is incapable of rendering the constitutive characteristics of the use of ordinary language. In sum, the type of material on which Hart and Honoré base their work must ignore the praxeological, contextual, and illocutionary dimensions of causal utterances. This does not invalidate their work in the sense that, contrary to Searle, they do not seek to base a general theory on imaginary examples; but it seriously restricts the field of application of their work.

To respecify the question of causation implies that the analysis must be brought to bear on causal reasoning as a practice in its own right. Following Pollner (1987: see above), we will begin by emphasizing that ordinary reasoning supposes the objectivity (the independent existence) and the intersubjectivity (shared postulates) of social realities. On the basis of this background understanding of the world, people describe, explain, and impute consequences to events, always supposing that reality is coherent, determined, and non-contradictory. If conflicting observations of reality arise, incongruity is explained and justified by designating the exceptional circumstances that prevailed at the time of the events. Circumstances explain the existence of contradictory causal accounts, and the reasons for their accurate or erroneous character.

Causation, description, and categorization are closely linked. The description and categorization effected by narratives contribute directly to the production of causal explanations, whether they are oriented to an object (material causes, objective reasons, etc.) or to a subject (agency, motives, intentions, subjective reasons, etc.). The individualization of action provides a good example in this respect. Following Jayyusi (1993), let us take the example of a person who pulls the trigger, fires a gun, wounds a man with the gunshot, and kills him. The philosophical response will be to consider either that four different actions have taken place (Goldman, 1971), or that four different descriptions of the same action have been provided (Austin, 1973). One may agree with Austin at first sight, but it is certainly necessary to go further and remark that these are four different types of description of a single action (Jayyusi, 1993: 436-7). Although these four descriptions are formally accurate, they do not take on interchangeable meanings and relevance. Each type of description refers to a particular type of context that justifies, describes, and attributes action; each type of description is used to accomplish specific practical tasks. These descriptions do not simply paraphrase each other; they are a paraphrase *and also* other things at the same time. They correspond to different wordplays, are inscribed in different courses of action, and orient to different objectives (Sacks, 1995, vol. I: 739-40). These descriptions are not equivalent from a praxeological point of view, because each points to different characteristics of the action context. In that sense, each description accomplishes a different causation effect. Whether the result was intended or a product of chance, negligence, or evil intent, whether or not knowledge of normal consequences was available, whether a person is considered as a direct agent or an indirect contributor – all this is organized in a routine and contextual manner by descriptive activity, which highlights, avoids, presumes, or raises specific consequential characteristics of the action described, in a way that may be accounted for. Thus, the attributes of knowledge, intention, agency, and causality, which are deeply embedded in practical contexts, are echoed in the descriptions, narrations, and attributions of responsibility that the members undertake.

In ordinary reasoning, motives are dealt with as causes of action. It may be true that motives are not, in the strict sense, causes of action, once action and motives for action are linked synchronically, once there is a wide margin of indeterminacy with regard to imputing motivation, and because there can always be multiple motives in accomplishing an action (Watson, 1983: 42), the fact remains that causation, dealt with as a social practice, does not correspond to nomological causality as presented by Mill (roughly, the causality of the laws of nature), but rather to causality as people refer to it in the course of their daily activities. The sociological question is no longer to know whether the causal reasons and explanations put forth are valid or real, but to observe, contextually, what it is that receives the status of valid or effective cause (cf. Goffman, 1959: 66). From that perspective, one observes that people often deal with motives as if they were the cause of action. Causal reasoning must therefore be understood as an action that aims to give reasons in context, which is closely linked to the processes of description and categorization whereby status, identity, and responsibility are attributed. In that sense, causation is a thoroughly moral practice. The complex selection and organization of categories operate in a "persuasive" manner (Watson, 1983: 39) with regard to actions for the causal imputation of which there are different possible candidates. Indeed, they can impute responsibility for committing the action, excuse it, justify it, or modify its tenor upward or downward (aggravating or extenuating circumstances). Furthermore, these causal categorizations are not imposed in a static way – far from it. Rather, they are constantly the object of selections, definitions, negotiations, formulations, reformulations, acceptance, denial, substitution, elision, and other transformations.

Normalcy and Incongruity Reasoning

In the contextual deployment of practical causal reasoning, one must observe the central role played by a certain ideal of the normal or natural state of things and, therefore, of what constitutes abnormality. According to Hart and Honoré (1985: 32-41), common sense considers that things have a "nature", and that they remain in their "natural" state as long as they have not been subjected to an intervention that interferes with their "normal" course. The cause of something is then an element that breaks the natural course of events; as for abnormality, it is defined as that which differentiates an accident from things following their customary course. By extension, abnormality may also arise from the failure to do something that should or could normally have been done. Causal explanation therefore does not seek the cause of a normal consequence in a normal course, but rather "why did this happen when it shouldn't have?" – in other words, a break in normalcy, which requires an explanation.

Furthermore, the Kantian idea that generally prevails is that each individual has an irreducible moral sense, which resides inside him or her, in a place that cannot be compressed. This moral sense, because it is common to everyone individually, becomes a universal attribute. At the same time, and paradoxically, this universal individual property is allegedly founded on certain unchanging ethical elements that allow, for example, for a conception of a general theory of justice. Individual moral sense is therefore characterized principally by its irreducible, identical nature. On the contrary, we seek to show here, through a praxeological approach, that moral sense and moral conscience are public phenomena, which only acquire significance when they are made explicit in public. This occurs through contextual operations, like description and categorization, and through the construction of categories, first and foremost the category of "normal" and "natural". Ethnomethodology thus seeks to observe the means and methods implemented by the members of a social group in order to affect the meaning of a given situation, so that it acquires a typical, uniform, unchanging dimension (Watson, 1998: 215).

As Sacks points out,

> In public spaces persons are required to use the appearances others present as grounds for treating them. Persons using public places are concurrently expected by others to present appearances which can be readily so used, and expect others to treat their own appearances at face value. (1972: 281)

Moral norms are thus perpetually produced, reproduced, manifested, and evaluated. Deviance, or a departure from the norm, is then evaluated by different means, among them the incongruity procedure, which compares expected and perceived behaviours (*ibid.*), or, in other words, a challenge to normality as perceived, produced, reproduced, and identified. In his analysis of the case of Agnes, a transsexual, Garfinkel (1967) deconstructs the practical conditions that make up the category "woman", and that allow Agnes to manifest the quality of "natural, normal woman", to which she aspires and which she claims. This leads him to argue that normally gendered people are cultural events in society. Gregory Matoesian (1997: 173; 2001; cf. ch. 2), analysing a rape sentence passed in the United States, shows how the fact of invoking a category ("rapist") somehow naturalizes the normative challenges linked to that category ("it is normal to be frightened of a rapist"), in such a way that any departure from these normative expectations violates "normalcy" and indeed leads to undermining the category that has been invoked ("he is not a rapist since you were not afraid when you met him"). In great detail, Matoesian shows how the use of a multitude of linguistic and sequential resources allows for a disjunction to be created between the activities and attitudes one might expect from the member of a category, on one hand, and that very category, on the other.[4] In other words, a lawyer's argument revolves around the idea that 'it is impossible that the witness would do "normal" things with someone who is supposed to be "abnormal".' (*id.*: 174) In general, we therefore observe that the evaluation of facts, objects, and persons is carried out on the basis of the typicality of routinized situations (Sacks, 1972), and normality is constructed on the basis of typical characteristics attributed to and expected of these situations (Sudnow, 1987). Normalcy covers situations that appear familiar, and are expected to reproduce typical characteristics. In sum, the idea of normalcy is the reference point of practical reason. It is because moral norms are constructed in such a way as to refer to what is supposedly known and expected by actors in a given context (normalcy) that they benefit from the status of unquestionable norms. They are somehow "naturalized", and therefore immune to challenge (Moore, 1993: 1); they also "naturalize", by giving the object on which they are brought to bear its normative dimension. Moral categories thus impose themselves by virtue of intersubjective constitution of their validity and of their desirable and compelling character (and not because they are anchored in society, defined as a "system of active forces", or in language). This constitution takes place through the reciprocal formation and attribution of mutual expectations, and through the naturalization and moralization of schemes and beliefs incorporated by these categories (Quéré, 1994: 35).

Normative constraints proceed essentially from the praxeological nature of operations of categorization. This means that ascribing categories is a circumstantial operation, aimed at orienting a debate by attributing to the categorized object a set of rights and obligations that are related not to the essence of the category but to the configuration of relations that it sets up. In other words, to describe a woman, for example, as modest, because she wears a certain type of clothing, is not related to the fact that her clothing conforms to religious, legal, natural, or social norms that have been dictated from time immemorial by God, Nature, or Society. On the contrary, this description entails inserting her clothing in a precise categorization device: that of female morality, which implies that all the activities carried out by a woman are evaluated according to the standard of rights and obligations that have been circumstantially attached to the members of the category. Inserting something in a category device, and the conventional imputations that result from such an operation, are based on a set of beliefs that are commonly accepted in a given social context. Reflexively, of course, the mobilization of a category device with the aim

4 Thus, lawyers tend to emphasize the abnormal nature of rapists, the normalcy of clients, and the interpretive choice that presents itself: either the witness who met the accused is irrational, since she knew he was a rapist, or she is not, since she knew that he was not.

of describing a person or a thing reinforces conventional acceptance of that device. It is perhaps this reflexive interplay that explains why a norm appears permanent: normalcy provides a basis for the mobilization of a norm, and the mobilization of a norm contributes to the construction of normalcy. In this way, normalcy proceeds from normalcy, through a continuous or fragmented series of rearrangements, and it would be pointless to search for the origins of this dynamic (Ferrié, 1998; 2008a). Also in this way, we observe that the morality of cognition and judgment dovetails with the question of judgments on morality. This is no doubt because the thoroughly moral dimension of cognition manifests all the more clearly when cognition comes to bear on questions located in the moral sphere. This is also because discourse on morality – or ethics, if one wants to be noble about it – cannot break free from the fundamental characteristics of ordinary reasoning, chief among them its moral nature.

Normalcy and Morality: An Egyptian Example

We would like to end this chapter with an example that allows us to show how, in a praxeological perspective, the idea of normalcy occupies a central position in articulating norms and morality.

In late October 1998, the Mufti of the Republic published a communiqué (*bayan*), which the press erroneously described as a fatwa, on rape and the rights of women who had been raped. The communiqué was followed by an interview in which he stipulated the conditions that, in his opinion, legitimized the reconstruction of a woman's hymen. A few days later, he gave an interview to the weekly magazine *Rose al-Yusuf* (26 October 1998), in which he confirmed the position he had taken. According to the Mufti, a virgin who has been raped and becomes pregnant as a result is allowed to have an abortion before the fourth month of pregnancy. Furthermore, she is entitled to ask a physician to restore her virginity. Finally, the Mufti also recognized such a woman's right to hide the fact that she had been raped from her future husband.

In his interview with Rose al-Yusuf, the Mufti justified his position by blaming society for failing to protect women sufficiently. He thus exonerated rape victims from the responsibility they would have borne, according to him, if their environment were not to blame. The text of the interview with the Mufti follows:

Press excerpt 1 (Rose al-Yusuf, 26 October 1998)

Question: Could you explain the legal authorization (*ibaha shar'iyya*) that you granted? Is a woman obliged to explain what happened to the man she is going to marry?

Answer: A girl who was kidnapped and lost her virginity when she was raped is the victim of considerable psychological and moral prejudice. She has been harmed psychologically, which constitutes a type of illness. If that can help cure her, then her virtue and honor must be restored to her. This obligation weighs heavily on society, which neglected her rights, failed to trust her, and is preventing her from retrieving what she lost through the fault of that same society. Whoever damages something must fix it. Surgery to restore the hymen repairs the damage here. As for the person

> who kidnapped and raped the girl, he committed an act of violence that is punished by death, as stipulated in article 290 of the Penal Procedure Code. He cannot be pardoned. Restoring her virginity and carrying out the operation does not amount to trickery. No objection. However, there are necessarily conditions and limitations. This can only be done if she has been kidnapped and raped, in the sense that real force has been applied to this end. If she agreed, then we enter the domain of fraud and trickery. This is why such an operation can only be carried out with the approval of the forensic doctor. He is the official and the specialist who can establish whether or not the girl was really raped, and that must be recorded officially. There must be specific conditions and explicit declarations that outline who is entitled to such an operation and who is not.
>
> I consider that society, which failed to defend this girl's rights, leading to her being raped, is responsible for rendering to her what she has lost … We need legislation that forbids doctors from carrying out such operations, and people from requesting them, in cases other than rape. To open the door to such practices would lead to trickery and fraud, which would lead people to perpetrate this kind of offence and undertake this procedure without anyone knowing about it.
>
> However, rape is public already, and that is why I demand that legal conditions and modalities be established that organize matters and determine who is in charge, so that trickery can be prevented. But Islamic law (*shar'*) does not forbid the surgical reconstitution of a raped woman's hymen, as long as she was really raped and did not consent in any way.
>
> Question: If a girl was raped and underwent an operation to reconstitute her hymen, should she tell her future husband or not say anything? What does Islamic law say about the matter of a girl who lies and denies that anything happened?
>
> Answer: If the husband doesn't know anything and hasn't asked anything, there is no reason to bring it up, and there's no reason for her to tell him. On the other hand, if the question is clear, in that a penal procedure is underway, and if the husband learns of this in one way or another, and if he asks her to tell him the truth, then she is not allowed to lie, because she has a legal justification. On the contrary, in such a situation, she will find more people willing to pardon her and evidence will be available to support the truth of her story. However, before her marriage, when her husband's consent is at stake, she is not obligated to tell him, and there is no shame in not telling him, even if he asks.
>
> Question: Wouldn't this open the door to such operations being performed even in cases other than real rape?
>
> Answer: This is a very important question, since rape is punishable by death. Establishing that rape with coercion has taken place is the task of the forensic doctor – the only person qualified to authorize [hymen reconstitution] surgery.

The communiqué and the interview both gave rise to many conflicting reactions. In many of these, however, we may observe the very deeply rooted idea that women generally consent to rape. Thus, one could read in the press reactions of the following sort:

Press excerpt 2 (source unknown)
A girl who gets raped is generally a girl who was going home late, wearing provocative clothes, or behaving improperly with her boyfriend, her fiancé, or anyone else, in isolated places at night. Thus, she provokes men.

Press excerpt 3 (source unknown)
Raping and penetrating a girl takes time. Why doesn't she scream? Because she wanted it.

In another interview with the daily newspaper *al-Ahram*, the Mufti of the Republic justified his position in the following terms:

Press excerpt 4 (al-Ahram, 17 April 1999)
I am in favor of anything that can protect a woman who has been raped. She is free to consult a specialized doctor and ask him to carry out an operation that will restore her virginity. This is a very common situation, and often even a necessary one, and there is nothing to say about it from the perspective of the *shari'a*, since she has been raped ... There is a very big difference between a girl who goes to the doctor because she has been raped and wants to protect her virtue, on one hand, and a girl who takes her clothes off in front of anybody who asks her to, and then wants her virginity back, on the other. There is nothing to object to, concerning the first, since she was raped. According to the *shari'a*, everything that results from rape is null and void, and cannot be taken into account. It's very good for her to go to a doctor; she has to be able to protect herself. To say that this is a way of fooling people is null and void ... Can you imagine a man who wants to get married and asks his fiancée: have you been raped? No one asks that sort of question. When a young man goes to visit a girl's family to ask for her hand in marriage, the man is completely convinced of her purity and her virtue. But as for a girl who takes her clothes off for anyone, who is in the habit of doing this, if she comes to ask me whether it is possible for her to undergo this operation in such circumstances, I will tell her: no, because she acted voluntarily. It's only logical. I am with the one who was raped and goes to the doctor afterwards. She has the right to erase from her body all the marks from this act, and to do everything she can to get her virginity back, especially if she was raped.

The press debate shows clearly that the question, if indeed there is one, is articulated around the definition of female normalcy. Virginity and legitimacy of sexual relations emerge as the primary components of the state of normalcy.[5] Sexual normalcy is manifestly based, in a prototypical way, on relations established

5 Taking this into account, it is possible to put the two following examples in perspective: on one hand, the reaction of a doctor, who felt that the mufti's communiqué aimed to 'remedy the girl's morality, and give her a normal life;' on the other, the comment of another doctor, who warned: 'If we give a woman the right to restore her virginity, how will we know if the membrane is artificial or not?'

legally through marriage, in an asymmetrical relationship between men and women. The gap between that state of normalcy and situations of adultery or rape underlines, in both cases, the abnormal behaviour of women, whose responsibility is presumed irrefragably. In other words, the Mufti's communiqué opens the door to an operation of normalization – an operation that can restore appearances and allow women to conform to the dominant moral order. Normality clearly depends on the idea of virginity, and the loss of virginity is only acceptable in the context of marriage.

The dividing line appears clearly in the question about hymen reconstitution for women who have been the victims of rape. Thus, we have the example of a jurist militating to have a new article included in the Code of Penal Procedure, which would allow rape victims to request hymenoraphy and to obtain an abortion if they become pregnant as a result of rape:

> **Press excerpt 5 (Sabah al-Khayr, April 1999)**
> The victim must have the feeling that society wants to protect her. She must be able to restore her honor, so that she can live a respectable life. She must be able to hold her head high, like other individuals of her sex. She must be freed from all pressure or constraint resulting from the conditions of her kidnapping and rape.

Many people consider that hymenoraphy for a rape victim cannot be equated with the same operation for a "slut". For the first, the operation is a right, since her abnormality is not the result of her will (she is not considered responsible). In contrast, for the second, it is not a right, and she must bear responsibility for her "immorality". The Egyptian religious authorities, for example, argue that *shari'a* does not oppose hymenoraphy for a girl who has been raped by force; the operation, according to them, will allow her to "start her life from scratch".

The debate over rape and hymenoraphy was always articulated around the moral category of "pure, virtuous, modest, normal womanhood". One might call this the typification of social events. In Egypt, if we stop to examine the way the press deals with rape cases, for example, we will see paradigmatic images of sexuality, sexual control, and female modesty. Most of the articles endeavour to reinforce these paradigms and undertake the necessary repression of transgression. Action always appears as linked to an archetype of morality or immorality. Thus, we find marriage as the only paradigm of "licit sexual relations", and, at the other end of the spectrum, rape and extramarital sexual relations (the two are usually associated) as its negative image. This archetype is the criteria according to which every sexual act is measured.

By examining the terms of the debate around hymenoraphy closely, we observed the deployment of a set of imputations and anticipations through which different actors construct and negotiate a form of knowledge, which they assume is shared, and which they present as such, thereby making it both normal and normative.

Conclusion

This chapter examined the morality or normativity of cognition. This does not mean that behaviour is tantamount to mechanical conformity to the rules; nor does it imply the conventional social construct of obedience to these rules. Following a rule results from practical obedience to it. Cognition of the rule and, more generally, of social reality is based on "mundane" methods of reasoning, understanding, interpreting, categorizing, and inferring. All these are oriented to a horizon of normalcy. Based on the nature of things or the things of nature, this horizon of normalcy is in a continual process of realization, which is continually actualizing underlying, shared schemes of interpretation and projecting them into the future. Law and morality are linked, not only because law may be brought to bear on moral questions, but also, and especially, because the practice of law is thoroughly impregnated with a form of morality – the morality of ordinary activity.

Chapter 3

Law in Action: A Praxeological Approach to Law and Justice

Sociology has traditionally sought to explain law in terms of power relations and domination, of modernity and rationalization, or as the symbolic translation of internalized culture. All these perspectives look at law, its manifestations, associated phenomena, and practices, from the outside. To paraphrase Dworkin, in a totally different sense, this external gaze does not take law seriously in its praxeological dimension. In contrast, ethnomethodological analysis focuses on law as a practical activity. In this chapter, we will critique the most glaring defects of culturalist research. Next, we will emphasize the "missing what" in sociological research and, on that basis, we will seek to shed light on the precise object of praxeological respecification, promoted by the ethnomethodological approach. Finally, we will undertake a synthesis of the literature inspired by ethnomethodology in the field of law and justice.

Substantivism in Legal Research: The Example of Islamic Law

It is often posited that in Egypt, as in many other Arab countries, family law or personal status law is the last bastion of Islamic law. Whereas in other domains law is supposed to have been "secularized", or largely "imported" from "the West", family law is said to have remained authentic and faithful to the *shari'a*, to such an extent that one should speak of "Islamic personal status law" as applied in Egypt, and not of Egyptian personal status law. In our opinion, this propensity to determine the extent to which such and such a part of the law is, in an orthodox or heterodox manner, Islamic, and to what extent such and such a part of the law may or may not be explained by some historical development in Islamic law, tends to impose an external structure upon legal phenomena and activities, instead of seeking to understand how they operate. This is due to the fact that many scholars start on the basis of strong assumptions regarding the general model of which a given legal system is supposed to be an instance. In this way, research misses phenomena it is supposed to document – in particular, the ways in which people understand and show their understanding of any given situation, orienting themselves to a context and its constraints, and behaving in a more or less orderly way within this spatially and temporally situated context. This is not something that may be observed from an overhanging position. In other words, the prior categorization of personal status law in Egypt as "Islamic law" does not give us access to what people do in the Egyptian judicial context when they deal with questions that pertain to personal status. All these are things that can only be carried out by describing people's practices, outside a preconceived interpretive framework.

This critique may be applied to most literature dealing with Islamic law in modern societies. As an example, suffice it to mention the article on *tashri'* by Aaron Layish and Ron Shaham in the new edition of the Encyclopedia of Islam (EI2, vol. X: 378-80). The authors start from the etymology of the word *tashri'*, which is the same as that of *shari'a* (religious law); but they totally disregard the fact that today, the term is used to designate legislation in the most general sense. Using their predefined knowledge of the word's etymological trajectory, they impose on legislation a nature that cannot be documented at all. And yet the endeavour does not end there. In an effort to evaluation the transformations undergone by *tashri'* in the contemporary world, Layish and Shaham establish a distinction between orthodox and deviant *shari'a*. They thereby affirm that certain countries, like Egypt and Sudan, while seeking to implement Islamic law, have deviated from *shari'a* to such an extent that they have caused it to become distorted. Such an assertion poses a major sociological and epistemological problem, however, since it implies that scholars can judge whether current practice is normal or deviant by comparing it to paradigmatic orthodox rules – rules it is up to them to identify. It also implies that scholars are entitled to adopt an ironic, overhanging stance with regard to the multiple ways people allegedly have of fooling themselves and being fooled by their governments when they adhere to a given conception of Islamic law. In a word, scholars supposedly hold a position that allows them to know what people engaged in daily practices are doing – better, indeed, than people themselves know. In this perspective, if people adopt deviant legislation, they do so despite themselves, unconsciously. Finally, this assertion also implies that categories are receptacles for meanings that travel through time and necessarily remain relevant in the context of their present usage. One could nevertheless remark that this assertion, at best, shows only that legal interpretations and practices do not remain constant throughout history. The benefit of the argument is weak – not to say non-existent – and its cost is high. Social sciences and philosophy have long known that texts do not float in a vacuum, that they have no meaning in and of themselves, and that they do not exist outside the acts of writing and reading them. In sum, they have no pure literal meaning. In other words, evaluating contemporary practices in terms of orthodoxy or deviance situates the debate on normative ground while avoiding the central question, which is what people do and how they do it when they refer to *shari'a* today.

In general, to describe law as "Islamic" refers simultaneously to two different things: Islamic law as a simple reference to Islam in a legal environment; and Islamic law as a legal system that may be assimilated to the corpus of classical *fiqh*. In the latter case, one must have available a substantive definition of Islamic law; furthermore, its criteria would have to be fulfilled by the specific type of law in which one is interested, which might then be seen as a specific example of the general model. This raises several questions: What are the constitutive criteria? Is there a paradigmatic Islamic legal system capable of serving as a standard by which to measure other examples of the model? Of what is this ideal legal system the model? Who has the authority to make this model the authoritative one? The literature dealing with this question goes through different stances. Occasionally, it advises that one adhere to the terms used by people; at other times, it suggests that people are lying to themselves and not saying what they mean – or that their beliefs are simply mistaken. Let us consider first the possibility of sticking to what people say. For example, people say that condemning apostasy is an Islamic legal principle. This must be considered as Islamic law since people refer to it as Islamic law. Determining whether the condemnation of apostasy to which they refer is the same as the condemnation of apostasy as provided for in *fiqh* manuals, however, is another question entirely. Here, once again, is the old problem of nominalism: the fact that the same word is used at different times does not necessarily mean that the word refers to the same meaning and technical definition. It is possible to establish connections, biographies of concepts, etc., but that should not lead us to presume that two or three uses of the same word are identical in character just because the linguistic form has stayed the same. Secondly, let us consider the idea that people lie to themselves. For example, some scholars have asserted that, although Egyptian judges no longer use the word "*dhimma*", the *dhimma* system[1] is still valid in Egyptian law (Berger, 2001). This is a perfectly ironic point of view, which implies that scholars are better informed with regard to a professional practice than are the people engaged in that practice, and that scholars occupy an overhanging position allowing them to say what reality is, and whether it is different from what people think it is. Furthermore, this is a metaphysical and deterministic understanding of things. It is metaphysical because it affirms that structures are permanent, even if people no longer understand them at all. Structures float in history, according to this perspective, and people are genetically enclosed in these structures and constrained by them. It is deterministic in the sense that people are determined by external constraints and do not produce or transform anything – they can only reproduce the past. One therefore presumes, when one claims that people do not say what they think, or that what they say is wrong, that scholars can occupy that overhanging position that allows them to tell people what is right and wrong, regardless of what they think, say, and do. Although the two positions are contradictory, in combination they make the argument impossible to falsify, since it always remains possible to pass from one to the other depending on the objection formulated or the problem one faces.

It is therefore necessary to reformulate the question. There is no reason to presume that what people refer to as being Islamic law is identical to the set of technical stipulations that make up the idealized model of Islamic law. Nor is there any reason to assume the contrary, however. Let us take the following example: in 1998, the question was raised in Egypt whether it was necessary to amend article 291 of the Penal Code, which stipulated that someone who had kidnapped a woman could go free if he married her. By extension, this meant that a rapist could escape punishment by marrying his victim. Historically, this article was inspired

1 The system providing for the submission and protection of minorities in classical Islamic law.

by French law, and was added to the Egyptian code in 1904, ostensibly to protect a man having kidnapped a woman in order to marry her without her family's consent from major penal sanction. With regard to this provision, one wonders how people would react if someone were to say: "That's French law!" At first sight, the reply would be: "It's a provision inspired by another provision that existed in the French penal code in the 19th century". That does not make article 291 of the Egyptian penal code French law, however. And yet, that is the kind of conclusion one arrives at when one asserts, for example, that repudiation (*talaq*) as provided for in laws 25/1929, 100/1985, and 1/2000 is Islamic law. Here we observe a double standard being applied, which leads observers to consider that *talaq*, as provided for in these laws, constitutes Islamic law, whereas article 291 of the penal code, in contrast, does not constitute French law. This is probably due to a bias in the analysis, which would tend to consider that the legacy of French law is less "natural" than that of Islamic law. The implicit dimension of this naturalistic argument is that societies are somehow endowed with cultural genes, which remain the same despite changes in time and place, and which continue to determine the essence of their destiny, beyond superficial appearances. In sum, to return to the thread of the argument, the question of whether or not what people refer to as Islamic law corresponds to the idealized model of Islamic law is simply irrelevant. It is impossible to answer it, because the question is totally dissociated from real practices. Furthermore, this question does not deal with the question it raises, which is the practice that consists of referring to Islamic law. Instead of "what is Islamic law?", we should be asking "what do people do when they refer to Islamic law?"

Ethnomethodological analysis underlines the fact that it is impossible to isolate a question from the circumstantial details of its deployment. In other words, studying law necessarily means studying "law in action" (Travers and Manzo, 1997). In that perspective, it becomes fairly meaningless to make a specific form of law – for example, Egyptian personal status law, into the example of a given model – for example, Islamic law. In the introduction, we highlighted the difficulties inherent in modelling. Suffice it to remind the reader here that the operation that consists of bringing an example back to a model implies a choice of characteristics that are assumed to be primordial in relation to others, characteristics that satisfy the requirements of identity and equivalence between the concrete case under observation and the formal abstraction to which it allegedly belongs. This choice consists, for example, of identifying those characteristics of Egyptian family law that make it possible to demonstrate that it belongs to Islamic family law, just like Algerian family law but in contrast to Danish family law. The cost of this operation is the massive dissimulation of everything, in those same legal systems, that does not correspond to the characteristics shared by all occurrences of the model, under cover of a purely nominal relation between the model and its occurrences. The result is that one learns nothing about the phenomena underlying this classification game, since the scholar has imposed a predetermined format on the research topic before even starting. Instead of this concern for finding something one can describe as "Islamic", we would suggest, rather, that attention be focused on the question of how people in various contexts orient to something they call

"Islamic law". This attitude turns its back on foundationalist approaches, which seek external criteria of measurement and intelligibility. Instead, it encourages researchers to examine the methods used by people engaged in an activity they describe as legal in order locally to produce the truth and intelligibility that allow them to cooperate and interact in a largely ordered way. One consequence of reformulating the question in this way is that we cease to define the object of study any differently from what people identify as such. In our example, Islamic law, then, we must be content to say that "Islamic law is what people call Islamic law" and focus exclusively on observing and describing how people engaged in legal practice conduct their activities and establish practically what counts for them as Islamic or legally Islamic. An occurrence is never anything but an occurrence of itself. The consequence is that there is no longer any need to look for the model of which the object of study is allegedly an example. Rather, what is needed is to shed light on the social mechanisms that caused this object to be produced as it was.

Three Problems in Legal Sociology and Their Ethnomethodological Respecification

One of the major characteristics of socio-legal research is thus that little attention is paid to the practical dimension of legal and judicial activity. This is particularly true of legal sociology in the Arab and/or Muslim context. In this regard, Ziba Mir-Hosseini's book, a comparative study of family law in Iran and Morocco (1993), is an exception. The author bases her research on abundant statistical and ethnographic sources. She also resorts to many hypotheses and problematic orientations, which will provide a basis on which we may advance in our efforts to carry out the praxeological respecification of our study of legal work.

Law on the Books and in Action

In the introduction to her work, Mir-Hosseini (1993: 3-10) asserts: 'From its inception, Islam has been both a political and a social order.' Islamic law is 'the divine law' that 'became the backbone of Muslim society; it has continued to define and guide it ever since.' Even in modern times, she describes the *shari'a* as forming the basis for family law, even though she specifies that it has been reformed, codified, and applied by a modern legal apparatus. Pitting Islamic legal theory against practice, she adds: 'What characterizes the Shari'a perhaps more than anything else is the distance between the ideal and the reality, between the law in theory and the law in practice.' *Shari'a* is supposed to be clear and intangible, since it is 'regarded as the divine blueprint for human action', but it is also understood in functional terms, so that it can remain viable and valid through the ages. According to Mir-Hosseini, this translates into the appearance of a dichotomy between legal validity and moral evaluation. She also asserts that the gap between theory and practice has a function: to 'ensure a voice for those who are in a position to define the terms of the divine law' and to check 'the power of those who can enforce it.' She concludes: 'It is precisely because this Divine Will needs to be discerned by human intellectual activity, and, more importantly, because it is enforced by human courts, that it is bound to bear the influence of the time and environment in which it operates.'

In seeking the nature of law – which she considers to be at the root of the functional gap between theory and practice – Mir-Hosseini misses the phenomenon of practice itself. Throughout the rest of her work, what she calls theory takes the form of a synthesis of applicable measures, whereas practice is represented by around 20 summarized cases and statistical data that are supposed to give us the necessary basis for understanding the patriarchal model that underlies the model of *shari'a*. Still, even if the *shari'a* is endowed with meaning, content, and an ideological orientation, people do not seem to orient to it in the cases summarized by Mir-Hosseini. In other words, we are in a double bind: on one hand, social actors remain external to the fundamental meaning of the law they practice; on the other, scholars, who claim to have access to the meaning of the law, have little grasp of its practical implementation. This is partially the result of an academic construct: the dichotomy between theory and practice. Law, as a social phenomenon, cannot be reduced to the stipulations of a legal code (law on the books). It would be equally misleading, however, to claim that law on the books is not an integral part of legal practice. The Platonic assertion that legal theory is nothing more than an appearance, and that the task of academics is to discover the object that lies behind the appearance, leads the analysis astray, because it does not do justice to people's natural attitude. People do not experience reality as something purely subjective, and they do not think of law on the books as something purely formal.[2] By opposing theory to practice and legal stipulations to "living law",

2 The best illustration of this is in the argument constructed by Pollner against symbolic interactionism and labeling theory, particularly on the question of deviance. Pollner emphasizes (1974: 27) that symbolic interactionism and ethnomethodologists converge in their critique of "deviance" as an essential property that somehow inheres in acts designated as deviant. They differ, however, on the question of what meaning to give deviance as a social construct. For Pollner, the problem comes from the fact that labelling theory, as presented by Howard Becker in *Outsiders* (1963), simultaneously and interchangeably uses two different models of the relation between social actors and deviance – the common-sense model and the sociological model. This leads to a sort of rejection of the common-sense model as relevant, whereas ethnomethodological research would deal with it as an integral part of the creation of deviance (*ibid.*). The common-sense model treats deviance as an action that exists independently of the community's response, while the sociological model treats it as a characterization that the community bestows upon an action (*id.*: 29). The sociological model, however, does not take into account the fact that 'even though deviance is created by … the response of the community, an integral feature of that response is the autobiographical conception of itself as confronting an order of events whose character as deviant is presupposed as independent of the immediate response of the community' (*id.*: 37). In other words, sociology may consider deviance as an artifact, but social actors consider it as a meaningful, objective category. To quote Pollner, 'thus, for example, while the community creates the possibility of traffic violations in the sense of making the rules

Mir-Hosseini misses an important part of the phenomenon she seeks to study. This might have been avoided, had she described in detail the legal categories to which people (professionals or laypeople) orient and the way they reify these categories in the course of their encounters with the legal fact, within the constraints of institutional frameworks and with the goal of achieving practical tasks.

The "Missing Whatness" of Research in Legal Sociology

Commenting on her own experience as a researcher in Iranian courts, Mir-Hosseini writes:

> One judge … assigned me the task of drafting court notes, the usual duty of the court clerk. This helped me a great deal to see the case from the court's viewpoint (or, more accurately, his), and I learned how to construct 'legal facts', how to translate the petitioners' grievances into court language, and how to discern the principles upon which the court operates. (1993:18)

In an ethnomethodological perspective, this excerpt is promising. The ethnomethodological study of legal work calls for more attention to be paid to the means of constructing legal facts, people's orientation to the judiciary context, the manifestation of their understanding of that context, its constraints, structures, etc. Mir-Hosseini, however, continues: 'later this duty became cumbersome as it prevented me from paying full attention while following the disputes during that session.' (*ibid.*) Mir-Hosseini suggests that one's attention is better used when it is turned toward two specific sources: legal statistic and case summaries. In the perspective that we are adopting, these two techniques are incapable of grasping law as a practical activity, because they cannot examine specific work-related skills through which jurists produce and coordinate legal actions. This is the problem that Garfinkel identifies as the "missing what" of the sociology of work. In the case of the legal professions, this refers to the fact that

> sociologists tend to describe various 'social' influences on the growth and development of legal institutions while taking for granted that lawyers write briefs, present cases, interrogate witnesses, and engage in legal reasoning (Lynch, 1993: 114)

The problem with statistics is that they erase the "here and now" dimension of each case, meaning that they hide the necessarily situated character of any activity. The use of statistics aims to establish a link between the general and the particular. It is necessary for the basic mathematic requirements in any computing operation –

---

which can be violated and developing the agencies for their detection, from within the court the rules may be treated as definitive of "real" deviance, as establishing that class of acts that are deviant whether or not they are concretely noticed or responded to as such' (*id.*: 39).

the requirements of identity and equivalence – to be fulfilled. Next, comparing the relative totals of each sub-group, which are generally expressed as percentages, allows the analysis of variables, for properties counted in similar fashion, to detect schemes of association between attributes. In the following stage, this makes it possible to transform statistical results into sociological discoveries (Benson and Hughes, 1991: 118). All this therefore depends on strict correspondence between the code and the encoded thing, between statistical entries and the reality they encode in order to render it statistically relevant. This correspondence, however, is not at all obvious: links are made on the basis of implicit assumptions and knowledge of common sense, while social reality is induced on the basis of statistical categories. In consequence, we remain incapable of understanding the underlying phenomenon, i.e. the practices of encoding.

> The 'visibility' of the phenomena is a function of the format and the natural theorising of researchers, rather than of the phenomena. Unfortunately … (it) says little about how persons themselves in constructing social activities use categories in the accomplishment of their activities. (Benson and Hughes, 1991: 123-4)

This is particularly true of law and the two fundamental operations it accomplishes: the formulation of legal categories and the legal characterization of facts. To paraphrase Michael Moerman (1974: 68), legal sociologists should describe and analyse the ways in which legal categories are used, rather than simply taking them as self-evident explanations.

The problem is different when it comes to case summaries. Legal work, in general, is a practical daily activity, inserted in a local environment. It operates as a constraint on what may be achieved in a given situation, and as a resource testifying to the fact that good work has been done. In a way, the aim of the ethnomethodological study of legal work is to have a grasp of the ways in which these constraints and resources affect jurists' work in a particular professional context (Travers, 1997: 7). The ethnomethodological perspective is not the only one that has sought to grasp certain aspects of the courts' work through ethnographic observation. Mir-Hosseini's study is also the result of a similar type of investigation. But few analyses look in depth at what is really done in the institutional context. This is particularly true of studies that resort to participant observation and interviews. Here, one observes a real descriptive short circuit, where the researcher's point of view is presented as the alternative to the actors' point of view, or where the researcher remains impervious to legal work as those who practice it every day understand it. Travers (1997: 5-16) speaks of a descriptive gap, which reduces legal work to the possession of a particular set of practical social skills;[3] considers law as the means used to reproduce the domination of dominant groups with the consent of subordinate groups;[4] or contrasts the clients' desire to express their feelings of injustice with the pragmatism of lawyers who seek

3 As is the case in the work of Mungham and Thomas (1979: 173).

4 See for example McBarnet, 1981.

only to negotiate a deal.[5] To fill the descriptive gap or replace the "missing what" implies that one must reorient to the content of legal work and to its character, which is practical first and foremost. This implies that one must turn to the technical aspects of legal work, its situated character, and the mixture of common sense and substantive knowledge that it bears. This cannot be achieved by staying at the back of the room, summarizing cases or resorting to interviews with the different parties to a case. On the contrary, the ethnomethodological study of legal work proposes a respecification

> ... involves understanding institutions like law or science in terms of the practical actions and understandings of scientists working in a particular laboratory, or lawyers in a particular legal office, rather than as a vehicle for advancing a political platform, or epistemological project, which is competitive whith the common-sense understandings of ordinary members of society. (Travers, 1997: 34)

Hyper-Explanation vs. Description of Situated Activities

This consideration leads us directly to a critique of dichotomous and "macro" explanations – what we call hyper-explanations. In her work, Mir-Hosseini presents a historical panorama of Islamic law, which allows her to examine those characteristics of *shari'a* that she finds relevant to her study. She asserts that a historical perspective is essential to an appreciation of the current place held by law in Muslim societies, and, in particular, to an exploration of the dynamic of changing relations between law and society (Mir-Hosseini, 1993: 3). Although she claims that 'those who ardently argue for the rule of the Shari'a ... tend to hold an idealized and totally ahistorical version of the development of the Islamic faith and its institutions', she simultaneously asserts that "Islamic law" has a "nature" that is linked to the "nature" of "Islamic civilization". One of the paradoxes inherent in Mir-Hosseini's position results from the fact that she considers the *shari'a* as having an intrinsic nature that reflects the influence of history. This position requires that one turn to historical developments to understand the current configuration of the *shari'a*, even though these historical contingencies are said to result from its essential nature. In other words, Mir-Hosseini seems to be claiming that, despite historical contingency, *shari'a* is endowed with an immanent nature; and yet combined past contingencies explain its current form. This paradox is strengthened when Mir-Hosseini asserts that modernization was achieved through 'the creation of a hybrid family law, which is neither the Shari'a nor Western.' (1993: 11) However, she goes on to argue: 'An indirect repercussion of the political changes that resulted in state intervention in the Shari'a has been the transformation of family law into its last bastion.' (*id.*: 12) In her introduction, she maintains:

> ... it is an error to equate family law, as applied in today's Muslim societies, with the classical Shari'a [, ...that] the very premise of the debate is flawed, [... and

5 See the work of Sarat and Felstiner, 1986.

> that] we know little of the ways in which Shari'a-based family law, this last bastion of the Islamic ideal of social relations, operates in today's Muslim world. (*id.*: 13)

In the conclusion, in contrast, she argues that: 1) there is something called "the model of Shari'a"; 2) effective marital schemes and family structures may be evaluated on the basis of this model; 3) these effective schemes ("patrifocal, matrifocal, bifocal") correspond more or less, or not at all, to the model of *shari'a* (the first corresponds to the *shari'a*, the second represents its negation, and the third its transformation); 4) this model is based on patriarchal ideology; 5) like all ideologies, it is open to manipulation (*id.*: 191 *sqq.*). One is entitled to ask precisely what these models, marital schemes, or ideologies are outside the practices in which they are incarnated. Of particular relevance to the present argument is the question of what explanatory purpose is served by a notion like patriarchy.

Gregory Matoesian's work (1993) on rape trials provides us with the means of critiquing the patriarchy argument. Matoesian's book contains a virtuoso conversational analysis of language in the context of the courts. At the end of the first chapter, he remarks:

> … the structures of talk-in-interaction generate the moral-inferential parameters which govern our interpretation of the rape incident, in particular our interpretation of the relationship and interaction between the victim and defendant, and propel (…) the assessment of blame and ascription of responsibility for that incident. (Matoesian, 1993: 22)

The ellipses in the above quote correspond to Mateosian's assertion that the structures of language in interaction function 'in conjunction with patriarchal ideologies.' (*ibid.*) It is precisely for this reason that his book was criticized, for having preserved several remnants of the conventional social sciences, like micro-macro or mind-action dichotomies. In a critical review, Robert Dingwall (2000: 904) pointed out that, although Matoesian (and others, like Conley and O'Barr, 1998) was interested mainly in cross-examination and the way in which it deals with competing evaluations of the credibility of evidence, the honesty or dishonesty of witnesses, and the coherence of arguments, his analysis demonstrated particular concern with the specifically biased nature of gender relations in rape trials. Dingwall (2000: 906) concludes – and we may use exactly the same terms in reply to Mir-Hosseini – that the difference between gender studies and the ethnomethological study of law is that the former knows in advance that courts where sentences are passed on rape cases are places of power and domination, while the latter insists that we must understand, first, what local phenomena take place before examining the potential relevance of other variables. It is necessary to highlight the contrast between a standpoint that starts by stipulating the existence and relevance of power and status within and between social entities, on one hand, and research that focuses on the many loci where the social order is manifested and produced, then describes how these entities orient, minute by minute, to temporally and locally situated questions that are relevant to their production.

> However well-intentioned and well-disposed towards the participants ... there is a kind of theoretical imperialism involved here, a kind of hegemony of the ... academics ... whose theoretical apparatus gets to stipulate the terms by reference to which the world is to be understood ... by those endogenously involved in its very coming to pass. (Schegloff, 1997: 167)

Respecification: Legal Work

Ever since the earliest work of Garfinkel and Sacks, law and justice have held a privileged position, with the practices of different legal actors – lawyers, police, prisoners, juries, judges, etc. – serving as a base for the study of activities and language in context. In this "radical" perspective (de Fornel, Ogien, Quéré, 2001), the point was not so much to identify the shortcomings of these practices by measuring them against an ideal model or a formal rule to which they were supposed to conform. Rather, it was to describe the means of production and reproduction, intelligibility and understanding, structure and public manifestation of law's structured nature and the different activities linked to it. Thus, rather than positing the existence of racial, sexual, psychological, or social factors, ethnomethodology and conversation analysis focused on seeing how activities are organized and how people orient to the structures of these activities, which are intelligible in a largely unproblematic way. As Alain Coulon emphasizes, the sociological hypothesis of norms being internalized, provoking "automatic", "spontaneous" behaviour, does not account for the way actors perceive and interpret the world, recognize that which is familiar and construct that which is acceptable, and does not explain how rules govern interactions concretely (1994: 648). As such, social facts do not impose themselves on individuals as objective realities, but as practical achievements.

Between a rule, or an instruction, or a social norm, and their implementation by individuals, an immense domain of contingency opens up, which is engendered by practice, and which is never the pure application or simple imitation of pre-established models. (*ibid.*)

We must therefore take law seriously, but law does not mean rules maintained in their formal abstraction, nor principles independently of their use context. Rather, it means law as practiced by legal actors, who are engaged on a daily basis in performing law. In other words, it is made up of the practice of legal provisions and their principles of interpretation.

As we have seen in the foregoing chapters, for ethnomethodology and conversation analysis, it is context – the legal context in our case – that provides the elements for its understanding and the action that suits it. Sharrock and Watson (1990: 238) thus give the example of the judge's replies to the remarks of the accused. For the accused, these replies constitute instructions allowing them to determine how to express themselves in court, but they may also instruct spectators as to the way in which the accused must generally behave. The context may thus be "self-explanatory", but it also provides the opportunity for relevance to emerge, in Schütz's words. In Sharrock and Watson's terms, this means that

> … the expression of a subsequent utterance manifests the meaning the second speaker gives to the utterances of the first speaker, and the latter can use the normative requirements projected by the former on his own expression to understand and assess the former's. (1990: 240)

Renaud Dulong (1991) arrives at similar conclusions when he shows how references to "official" law can intervene in ordinary interactions and exert a pragmatic effect on enunciation and action, which he calls "the law's reputation".

The attention paid by ethnomethodology and conversation analysis to practices and their context makes it possible to shed light on the nature, which is above all routine, of the formalization work in which law professionals engage. The work of lawyers and magistrates, especially the prosecutor's office, consists essentially of formalizing categories that are mobilized in the narration of facts undertaken by clients, defendants, and witnesses. To the contrary, the work of non-professional parties to a trial often consists of escaping the inference of guilt that results from this characterization work. Thus, as Watson demonstrates, the categorization processes that lie along the way to a legal ruling can be seen as means for those who are involved to ascribe motives to their actions, and thereby to allocate and negotiate incrimination, guilt, responsibility, and therefore causes for justification and excuse (see Chapters 8, 9, and 10).

These brief remarks concerning the ethnomethodological analysis of law and the judicial field aim to introduce the following section, which will focus on reviewing most ethnomethodological and conversationalist research into the various stages of the judiciary process, as well as the different legal acts and actions accomplished by law professionals and those who encounter the law in their daily lives.

Ethnomethodogical Studies of Law and Justice

Rather than attempting to provide an original presentation of ethnomethodological research into law and justice, we will review its characteristic works. This presentation fulfils three goals. First, we seek to present the most important works written on law in the ethnomethodological tradition. Second, this gives us the opportunity to develop the tools we will be using in the following parts of this book. Third, this presentation – which spans a gamut ranging from Garfinkel's use of jury meetings in criminal trials to ethnomethodological ethnography of legal work in a law firm, along with work on linguistic interaction in the courts – is organized in such a way as to allow a shift in observation. Attention may thereby be turned from ordinary practical reasoning as it may be observed in legal and judiciary interactions to a praxeological concern for legal work as such.

Practical Ordinary Reasoning in the Judiciary Context

Let us note from the outset that Garfinkel's first works already showed his interest in judiciary activity.[6] In his study of juries, Garfinkel examined the conditions in which practical reasoning is deployed and realized (1974b: 15). He wondered above all how juries knew what they were doing when they did the work of juries. And he stated:

> I was interested in such things as jurors' uses of some kind of knowledge of the way in which the organized affairs of the society operated – knowledge that they drew on easily, that they required of each other. At the time that they required it of each other, they did not seem to require this knowledge of each other in the manner of a check-out. They were not acting in their affairs as jurors as if they were scientists in the recognizable sense of scientists. However, they were concerned with such things as adequate accounts, adequate description, and adequate evidence. They wanted not to be 'common-sensical' when they used notions of 'common sensicality'. They wanted to be legal. They would talk of being legal. At the same time, they wanted to be fair. If you pressed them to provide you with what they understood to be legal, then they would immediately become deferential and say, 'Oh, well, I'm not a lawyer. I can't be really expected to know what's legal and tell you what's legal. You're a lawyer after all.' Thus, you have this interesting acceptance, so to speak, of these magnificent methodological things, if you permit me to talk that way, like 'fact' and 'fancy' and 'opinion' and 'my opinion' and 'your opinion' and 'what we're entitled to say' and 'what the evidence shows' and 'what can be demonstrated' and 'what actually he said' as compared with 'what you only think he said' or 'what he seemed to have said'. You have these notions of evidence and demonstration and of matters of relevance, of true and false, of public and private, of methodic procedure, and the rest. At the same time the whole thing was handled by all those concerned as part of the same setting in which they were used by the members, by these jurors, to get the work of delibarations done. That work for them was deadly serious. They were not about to treat those deliberations as if someone had merely set them an 'iffy' kind of task. For example, in the negligence cases they were handling up to $100,000 of somebody's business, and they were continually aware of the relevance of this (*id.*: 16).

In sum, Garfinkel was interested in jury activity because this activity allowed him to study recourse to common sense and its deployments, but also – and this is important – because it revealed how the members of a given social group are simultaneously constrained by the institutional context in which they interact and participants in the creation of this same context. What Garfinkel called a documentary method of interpretation is that capacity to resort to underlying schemes that produce a shared

6 One may cite his works on juries in the Deep South (1948) or Wichita (1984; the study began with what is known as the "Chicago jury study" of 1945), as well as those on the Los Angeles coroner's office (1997; this study began in 1957).

sense of social reality. Lawrence Wieder's work (1974) constitutes a remarkable example of how this method may be used. Based on a long field study in a halfway house for convicted narcotics offenders, Wieder shows how rules serve as a basis to observe, describe, and explain action. Rules – which he calls the "convict code" – in this case are a vague set of behavioural guidelines identifying a range of activities in which convicts must or must not engage. Wieder examined this code, not in order to judge its explanatory capacity, but to describe the explanatory uses that are made of it. He remarks that the code, as an interpretive system, allows convicts to identify and characterize events in the halfway house. In this manner, they can attach to the events they have qualified all the consequences specific to the event-qualified-as-such. Although the code is a powerful organizer of perceptions and actions for convicts and staff at the halfway house, however, this does not mean it has been incorporated. 'Its maxims did not relate antecedently existing situations to subsequent actions after the fashion required for the the rule-following model, nor did they "cause" these actions.' (Heritage, 1984: 206) Maxims, rather, are used as means of interpretation that make it possible to ascribe a particular relevance to new situations. They impose themselves not as preexisting rules, but because invoking and actualizing them convince actors of their preexisting nature and their generally constraining power.

Conversation Analysis of Law

Most works inspired by ethnomethodology and focusing on the law emerged from conversation analysis. The first of these studies to date was by Max Atkinson and Paul Drew (1979), who drew their material from transcriptions of court proceedings during an investigation of communal violence in Northern Ireland in the late 1960s. Apart from three chapters dealing with theoretical questions (what does ethnomethodology contribute to the study of law?) or methodological issues (analytical considerations related to the way the data was collected or suggestions for further research),[7] their work deals with questions of interest to conversation analysis, such as turn-taking organization, sequence, and the detailed description of speech acts that are typical of the judicial context: i.e. the way in which accusations are formulated and justifications or excuses presented. In a way that has since become classic for conversation analysis, the second chapter seeks to describe turn-taking in the context of judicial procedure against a background of ordinary conversation. In other words, the judicial system is only taken into consideration insofar as it brings a certain number of specific formal constraints to the conversationalist paradigm. We will return to the critiques that may be levelled against such a perspective. For now, suffice it to note, among these formal constraints: the limited and predetermined number of parties that can participate in judicial interaction; the predetermined and predefined nature of turn-taking in

7 Some of these considerations are particularly relevant in the context of our work, as long as they relate to the conditions in which a conversationalist study may be realized on the basis of written (and therefore not recorded) materials and in social contexts with which the analyst is unfamiliar. See Chapter 7.

conversation and the particular status of authorized interruptions (questions from the judge, objections from the lawyers). These specificities do not totally remove the participants' ability to manoeuvre intellectually, but they limit it drastically and force it to take tortuous paths. The third chapter focuses on a specific point in the proceedings: the beginning of a hearing and the means implemented to obtain the attention of those who are present on the site of judicial interaction. Evidently, chapters 3 and 4 are the heart of the book. The authors examine the way accusations are formulated in the course of the questions and answers of the cross-examination that was, until recently, restricted only to common-law legal systems. They emphasize first the fact that accusations are formulated in such a way as to produce strong expectations of denial. The conditional relevance of the second part of an adjacent pair in relation to the first means that its absence is not only remarkable but also inferential. In that sense, an accusation may be conceived in a progressive, prospective manner; its explicit formulation will intervene only at the end of the sequence. At the same time, the persons who are being cross-examined can easily perceive the inferential nature of questions, or in other words the particular force of implicit accusations, and construct their attitudes and responses in relation to that. Atkinson and Drew also show how descriptions of places and actions and classificatory systems of membership may be deployed in the judicial context. Their analysis suggests that

> The analysis suggests how the counsel can be heard to manage the production of descriptions in the question-answer sequences so as to be able … to formulate the upshot of those descriptions in such a way as to propose a judgement about the witness's action, where other descriptive work which could have been done might not have served that purpose. (Atkinson and Drew, 1979: 134)

Chapter 4 deals with the production of justifications and excuses by witnesses named in a cross-examination. We will return to these notions when discussing the grammar of causation in the judicial context (Chapter 9).

A second major study of discourse in the judicial context, by Douglas Maynard (1984) deals with plea bargaining, another specificity of common law. Maynard's goal is to describe the criteria implemented by participants in this procedure to determine what is essential in the course of their action. Clearly, Maynard was also seeking to replace normative positions on the benefits and drawbacks of plea bargaining with a detailed study on its modus operandi. To that end, he began by showing how a number of characteristics of plea bargaining are due more to its internal organization than to the effect of major factors external to interaction:

> … hidden decision making and rapid processing of cases are accomplishments of participants' specific interactional skills and orientations and are not the natural or necessary outcome of overloaded courts, urbanization, or other macrosociological processes stamping their imprint on particular settings of interaction. (Maynard, 1984: 52)

Maynard then introduced Goffman's notions of frames of analysis and footing to show how, in plea bargaining – a unique system of verbal exchanges – participants undertake various shifts in alignment that translate the diversity of organizational forms in which they are situated and the breadth of the questions they use to confront the structural constraints of the situation and derive practical benefit from it. In a fourth chapter, Maynard focused on the details of the negotiation sequence, which consists schematically of a turn unit where the speaker presents a position, and another turn unit in which the recipient of the first turn manifests his alignment or non-alignment with the first position. The construction of the plea sequence is the opportunity for many activities, such as exchange, compromise, and disagreement, with the common goal of arriving at a reasonable solution. Contrary to a widespread idea, the participants in a plea bargain do not necessarily deal with underlying questions, such as the facts of the case or the protagonists' profiles, before arriving at a mutually acceptable agreement. The fact remains nevertheless that the evaluation of these profiles is an important part of the negotiating sequence, in which it justifies the positions of the various protagonists. In the United States, research has focused massively on evaluating the impact on decision-making of the defendant's legal and extra-legal attributes, but Maynard pointed out that, in precise, empirically documented contexts, the characteristics attributed to the defendant are always part of a selection carried out in a situated way among a range of potentially ascribable characteristics. They are not "descriptively adequate" in any objective sense, but they are formatted as "facts" in a particular case, contextually, as arguments are produced (Maynard, 1984: 26). Maynard concluded by emphasizing the constraints specific to the institution of plea-bargaining. Far from considerations of "proper administration of justice", "equity", or "the just organization of exchange", this institution exerts procedural pressures towards a preference for the immediate resolution of a case, over going to trial.

Martha Komter (1998) has looked at interactions between judges and defendants in penal trials in the Netherlands. Her conversation analysis looks at the dilemmas and paradoxes that various parties to a penal procedure – accused and magistrates alike – must confront and resolve. Komter shows that the establishment of facts puts the accused in a situation where they have to choose between not contributing to their own incrimination and being perceived as having something to hide. Their interventions are therefore tightly constrained by dilemmas of interest and credibility. On one hand, they must preserve their personal interest by downplaying their specific "agency" in the event. On the other, they must preserve their credibility by showing their willingness to cooperate with the court. The various parties to a trial also face dilemmas of conflict and cooperation. On one hand, although the judges seek to obtain information from the suspects, they also imperil the latter's credibility when its aim appears too directly defensive. On the other, suspects know that appearing excessively defensive can undermine the credibility of their statements. A third type of dilemma – that of blame and sympathy – results from the fact that the production of accounts can be configured in such a way as to imply inferentially a moral condemnation (and therefore to aggravate the sentence) or, on the contrary, to attract sympathy and compassion (and therefore to attenuate the gravity of the case). At the same time, the mobilization of sympathy may be interpreted as being motivated by the intention of obtaining attenuation. Komter also explores what she calls dilemmas of morality and constraint, which the accused face when they seek to reestablish the moral equilibrium that their actions have thrown off kilter. Words generally appear insufficient to repair the harm suffered by the victim, and can additionally be perceived as self-interested, with the accused attempting to make a good impression. The accused is more likely to be taken seriously if he offers substantial compensation, but the spontaneous character of such an offer may be undermined by the persisting suspicion that the court imposed the compensation. As for promises not to repeat the offence, it is particularly difficult for the accused to convince a judge that such promises are sincere or even realistic, although the judge may sometimes be tempted to pressure the accused to do the honourable thing. In sum, this work, which emphasizes the moral dimension of the judicial game, describes the dilemmas facing the accused, who are encouraged to express remorse, tempted to downplay their responsibility, but also consistently suspected of acting in a self-interested and insincere manner (see also Komter, 1997).

Gregory Matoesian's work is certainly the most sophisticated version of what conversation analysis can produce on judicial interaction. It is simultaneously – and very strangely – accompanied by an analysis of domination and patriarchy that appears out of place, at best, and contrary to a conversationalist endeavour inspired by ethnomethodology, at worst (see above). *Reproducing Rape* (1993) examines the language used inside courtrooms during rape trials. Matoesian's starting point is clearly expressed in the book's introduction (1993: 1): 'This study offers a nuts and bolts view of the constitution of power and social structure as they live and unfold during the course of linguistic performance.' Language is therefore the medium through which social reality is interpreted; it is therefore a vehicle of power. Here, in the case of rape trials, power is the power of men over women – the power of patriarchy. Despite the fact that he aspires to provide overhanging interpretations through almost transcendental concepts and active forces that operate without social actors knowing it, Matoesian's work has value in that he focuses mainly on the linguistic details of judicial interaction. In that regard, he is not only a virtuoso, but also proves capable of detaching himself almost completely from this over-interpretive tendency. Thus, he demonstrates how

> … the facticity of social structure as an objectively constraining social fact stretching across time and space is achieved in mundane interactions through the categorization, routinization, and normatization of actions, actors, and relationships. (1993: 25)

After having emphasized the fact that the judicial process is not a question of justice or injustice, but rather, for the concerned parties, of winning or losing (1993: 64), and described the turn-taking process in normal conversation, Matoesian provides a detailed analysis of language in the judicial context, that of rape trials in particular. He deals with questions of turn-taking in conversation, reparation sequences, objection sequences, multiple turns and silence, the syntax of question-and-answer sequences, and the linguistic construction and implementation of power. He adopts the same perspective when discussing the Kennedy Smith trial. *Law and the Language of Identity* (2001) is a collection of articles in which Matoesian endeavours meticulously to deconstruct linguistic interaction in judicial debates during a well-known trial in the U.S. He starts by asserting that language is not simply a passive vehicle through which law is imposed and transmitted, but rather constitutes and transforms evidence, facts, and rules into relevant objects of legal knowledge (Matoesian, 2001: 3). Then he shows how linguistic ideology operates when it seeks to construct a witness's statements in terms of incoherence. This incoherence in testimony is constituted in interaction, through intertwined grammatical, sequential, and classificatory resources. This logic of incoherence, according to Matoesian, is based on gendered categories articulated on principles of identity and difference. These are organized linguistically through the poetic (meaning creative) properties of language. Matoesian, who is convinced that the social world in general and the legal world in particular is dominated by the male gender, nevertheless wonders through which mechanisms this domination is incarnated in powerful forms of legal-ideological practice, which are decked out in the colours of legal objectivity and rationality. He seeks to analyse the judicial techniques of cross-examination as closely as possible: these techniques consist of "detailing-to-death" and inflating the testimony while controlling it. In this way, Matoesian shows how the defence builds the evidence he wants to produce through the accumulation of successive questions that draw something unusual out of seemingly banal facts. Matoesian takes apart the method of "resumptive repetition" used by the defence lawyer, and shows – paradoxically, given his general thesis – that the outcome of rape trials cannot be analysed from the point of view of patriarchy, or the balance of power between the lawyer and the witnesses, alone. Instead, that outcome must be considered in light of shared knowledge of the relations that link the categories "women" and "rapists". The lawyer must bring this knowledge forward to compare it with the case at hand and draw conclusions from any incongruity (see also Matoesian, 1997). This leads him to caution that it is not sufficient for research to focus on the institutionalized distribution of asymmetrical options, on the characteristics of the cross examination, or even on variations in the format of the questions, as if these were the moving force operating backstage in the process of legal domination (2001: 102). Instead, it must seize the poetic work that is specific to the language of judicial interaction, if one wants to understand the particular force of different techniques mobilized during a trial. Matoesian also looks at two questions that are particularly important for the study of judicial interaction: intertextuality and expert testimony. Regarding the intertextual construction of legal discourse, in which textual events of current reporting and reported speech, he shows how a precise instance of interaction is articulated with a historically situated discourse and gives it its strength. Basing his analysis on Goffman, Bakhtin, and linguistic anthropology, he shows how 'complex interactions among grammar, prosody, and discursive style create a dense constellation of voices and footings and index multiple social contexts in the legal order.' (Matoesian, 2001: 7) All these interactional resources, through which the parties contextualize or decontextualize words and deeds, allow them to negotiate their own ascribed identities and moral classifications as well as those of others, and the hierarchical organization – and therefore the effectiveness – of textual sources. On the question of expert testimony, Matoesian endeavours to show that the identity and credibility of expertise are also constituted through the mobilization of linguistic resources. Here again, one may observe changes in footing that correspond to the mobilization of different identities and positions of authority, and to the need to solve diverse institutional and discursive dilemmas.

Conversationalist pieces that deal with law and legal interaction are legion. Briefly, we may cite a few contributions brought together in the work edited by Travers and Manzo (1997). Thus, an article by Drew (first published in 1992) examines the methods used by witnesses and lawyers in cross-examinations carried out in the context of rape trials. The close examination of certain exchanges is designed to explain how people resort to methods or devices to present contrasting versions of events. Drew thus offers us a classical demonstration of the ways in which ordinary (i.e. non-professional) skills and resources are used in the courts. Watson's article (first published in 1983) also deals with the way common-sense knowledge and reasoning are used in the penal judicial process. The way in which defendants describe their victim thus makes their motives clear, and occasionally attempts to shift the burden of responsibility, in whole or in part. These descriptive methods are very widely used, whether by the police, lawyers, or juries, to recognize aggressors and victims in a contextual framework. We may also cite two articles published in a special issue of *Droit et Société*. One of them, by Martha Komter (2001), is about the construction of evidence in police interrogations. She looks at the establishment of written reports, which are supposed to reproduce the suspect's words, and compares them to recordings of interrogations in order to show how the police must manoeuvre between legal requirements, a bureaucratic context, and the rules of ordinary conversation. The result is an elaborate endeavour to construct legal relevance, in which the suspect's voice is altered and the policeman's is obliterated. The other contribution, by Matoesian and Coldren (2001), looks closely at the police on the basis of an excerpt from a conversation about partnership between the police, academia, and neighbourhoods. The authors show how general notions, like that of "partnership", cannot be dissociated from the linguistic contexts in which they are used. They also show that the precise study of contextualized verbal interactions makes it possible to show that culture, far from being a pre-defined explanatory resource, is made up of a multitude of identifiable details to which the parties to the interaction refer even while they contribute to transforming them.

Returning to the study by Atkinson and Drew, it is important to note that it is worthy of rediscovery, in that it lays the foundations of most conversationalist analyses of discourse in the judicial field (Travers, 2001: 358). It is also important to emphasize that it bears some of the major distortions of the methodology. First, there is the idea underlying conversation analysis, that a detailed descriptive study of hearings tells us all there is to know about legal work in context. It is clear that conversation analysis contributed a great deal to our understanding of judicial interaction, but one must still be wary of reducing to the object of study to recorded sequences alone, since all that precedes or follows those sequences may be equally relevant to the analysis of the actions, gestures, words, and orientations of active and passive participants. There is a series of parameters that are simultaneously integral parts of legal activity and external to mere verbal exchanges and what may emerge from those exchanges. Another shortcoming results from the paradigmatic dimension bestowed upon ordinary conversation in relation to turn-taking in institutional contexts. David Bogen (1999: 83-120) rightly critiqued the tendency that causes conversation analysis to risk succumbing to the same foundationalism it denounces in advocates of formal linguistic analysis. Among the most harmful consequences, we may point out the risk of over-interpretation of aural or verbal manifestations, simply because the observer does not have access to the elements preceding the sequence under consideration. There is also a tendency to exaggerate the collaborative dimension of the verbal exchange, to the detriment of its agonistic dimension. In this way – and despite the systematic references to contextuality – conversation analysis is based on postulates it developed without paying sufficient attention to the local production of order, intelligibility, etc. (Bogen, 1999: 120; see Chapter 4 of this volume on context).

The Ethnomethodology of Law as Ordinary Reasoning

In line with this critique of conversationalist analysis of legal interaction, Lynch and Bogen (1996) analysed the Iran-Contra hearings. Although their book is not about a classical legal context, but rather a political and media episode – it offers a certain number of reflections that are relevant to the study of law in action. One of the interesting sections is related to the "ceremonial of truth". Here, Lynch and Bogen describe how procedural rules, although they never determine the exact course of activities that are supposed to follow their instructions, are nevertheless always relevant, from a practical point of view, for the way these activities are carried out. This is a good example of the idea that the rule cannot be understood outside of the way in which it is practiced, and, inversely, that no practical application – whether violation, subversion, or instrumentalization – of a rule is possible without prior identification of that rule. The authors also emphasize the importance of preserving the coherence of an affirmation in relation to the establishment of its justice, but this does not correspond to a sort of mystical call to rational coherence, as one might find in Habermas. Rather, it indicates the implementation of a practical ability to produce reasonable, convincing narrative accounts that contest the storyline imposed in an authoritarian way by the accusation. Lynch and Bogen are also interested in the intertextual production of a master narrative/document that provides a basis for subsequent evaluations; this product is an important object of conflict between the concerned parties. Other sections relate to the practical uses of memory in the context of hearings or interrogations. The authors show in a relevant way that disavowals of recall

> ... specifically obstruct an interrogator's attempt to exclude the middle when asking a yes or no question [although] it is often difficult to show unequivocally (or even plausibly) that these utterances reflect a witness's intention to obstruct or evade the operations of the truth-finding engine. (1996: 199)

The evaluation of claims to remember or not to remember occurs at the same time against background expectations of "what any normal person in this situation should remember", with the moral implications that might have with regard to the witness. If it were absolutely necessary to classify this book in a particular genre, one would say that it is a post-analytical conversationalist study, in the sense that it rejects the foundationalist tendency detected in conversation analysis. As the authors emphasize at the end of the work, 'the generic domain of conversation is not the only relevant backdrop against which singular events take on their specificity and sensibility.' (*id.*: 286) At the same time, because it relates to interaction that is methodically produced by the participants, this study is still largely conversationalist. The authors seek to describe the linguistic instantiation of cultural resources, which transcends classical conversationalist ambitions. They remain faithful to their ethnomethodological commitment, and do not attempt to interpret the video material on the basis of any abstract cultural framework, but rather to describe how a panoply of possible resources – legal, cultural, and discursive – were available and were actually used by the parties implicated in the hearings (*id.*: 266).

In a more phenomenological tradition, we have already mentioned Pollner's words. One has only to read the title of his book, *Mundane Reason* (1987), to agree that, like Garfinkel and his study of jury activities, what Pollner is interested in are the practical modes by which ordinary reasoning is deployed, more than legal activity in and of itself. The fact remains that the uses of mundane reason – among others, the postulates of coherence, determination, and non-contradiction of reality that we discussed earlier (see Chapter 2) – are subjected to an ethnographic study in the context of American traffic courts. Pollner's analyses thus show that disjunctions in descriptions of the same events are resolved not by adopting a post-modern and relativist point of view, which places multiple "narratives" on equal footing, but by pointing out the "exceptional" conditions for observation that prevailed at the time of the "contested" event. Hester and Eglin (1992: 214) sum up the different examples Pollner gives:

> Puzzle: how could a defendant claim that he did not exceed 68 miles an hour and an officer claim that he did? Solution: faulty speedometer. Puzzle: how could a defendant claim that the vehicle in front of him and not his camper held up traffic and an officer claim that it was the camper? Solution: The camper blocked the officer's vision. Puzzle: How could a defendant claim that drag racing did not occur at a specified time and place when an officer claims that it did? Is it possible

> that drag racing did and did not occur? Is it possible that drag racing did and did not occur at the same time? Are they both right? Solution: The officer was actually referring to a different time.

Furthermore, in his critique of Becker's model of deviance, Pollner points out precisely how difficult it is to take an interactionist position, which would refer to the "hidden face of crime" – people who are not classified as deviants, but who are objectively – and of "false accusation" – people who are classified as deviants, but who are not so objectively. This position is incoherent in the perspective of labelling theories, but it still corresponds to the typology of judges in traffic courts. This is the paradox Pollner identifies. He thus stresses that, for magistrates, violations of traffic regulations that come before them are only one part of the sum total of real violations that go undetected (the "hidden face of crime"). It is also clear that the judge "knows" that the police make errors of judgment, falsely accusing drivers. The judge's work is therefore based on the underlying idea of objective deviance from or conformity with the law. The judge is called upon to evaluate the relation between an alleged crime and "what really happened". What takes place in the courtroom – accusations, denials, testimonies, explanations, excuses, justifications, the search for extenuating circumstances – only has meaning if one admits that guilt and innocence are independent of the methods that make it possible to establish them. In that sense, a police officer may erroneously cite the objectively innocent behaviour of a driver, just as a driver who is objectively guilty of a violation may escape police detection (Pollner, 1975; 1979; 1987).

We may place James Holstein's book (1993) about involuntary commitment (the use of legal means to commit a person to psychiatric internment) in the same line as Pollner's work. Holstein clearly states that his book deals with interpretive practices, i.e. procedures through which people represent, organize, and understand reality (1993: 2). The aim of the work is specifically to explore the use of classifications like "mentally ill". At first sight, then, Holstein's perspective is largely interactionist and constructivist, since it sees mental illness as the result of a labelling operation. It departs from these genres, however, because of the attention the author pays to the labelling process. The ethnomethodological dimension of his work therefore, resides in his focus on contextuality and linguistic interaction:

> … interaction, in general, and, more specifically, talk and language use are not mere ways of conveying meaning [but rather] ways of *doing things with words* to produce meaningful realities and formulate the life world. (*id.*: 6)

In that perspective, Holstein seeks to identify the postulates on which judgments regarding people's mental health are based, as well as the constraints and intentions characteristic of the institution in which these judgments are passed. He thus shows how the examination sequence provides a structure making it possible to organize the questions for commitment hearings into medically informed legal proceedings. Furthermore, these hearings aim to put people on stage, to portray the circumstances specific to each case, and to make the achievement of "legality" and "justice" visible (Holstein, 1993: 87). Regarding legal decisions on psychiatric internment, the author describes the modus operandi of various underlying schemas that concern not only the conditions necessary to life outside a psychiatric institution, but also the various types of mental pathology and their practical consequences. In this way, he reviews a series of procedures that organize people's psychic competence or lack thereof, on the basis of the "normality" of their verbal expression, among other things; or that organize the description of the conditions for the internment of mentally ill individuals; or that organize the specific characteristics of credibility, "good" performance, and "appropriate action" in relations to the circumstances of the affair. In conclusion, Holstein attempts to reconcile his phenomenological-ethnomethodological approach with a Foucauldian vision of micro-controlling processes applying to all social spaces.

Analysing law through mundane reason provides us with many entrance points to practical methods of reasoning and judgment. At the same time, it does so in a constructivist way, which we may pause to examine. Lynch (1993: 37) points out that Pollner's approach tends to engage the ethnomethodological approach in a self-reflexive endeavour that is part of a radical constructivist struggle against objectivism. He goes on to say that such an attitude need not necessarily be anti-objectivist, however. In other words, Lynch considers that ultimately, Pollner, like many of those who oppose objectivism, has replaced one abstract foundation by another:

> In place of an independent 'mundane world' he installs the 'work of worlding': acts emanating from a subject that produce a world, acts the subject then 'forgets' by presuming the independence of that world. (Lynch, 1993: 37-8)

This type of constructivism bestows a founding status on social, textual, interactive, and rhetorical practices and systems. In consequence, it adopts a representational image of language: its adherents consider that "reality" is separate from language, and then accentuate the founding role of linguistic acts in realizing a simulacrum of reality (Button and Sharock, 1993: 12). They therefore fall back into the corrective trap by merely putting forth yet another sociological theory of reality, that aspires to correct different versions, whether they have been suggested by science or mundane reasoning itself (Button, 2001: 164). Button points out that correctivism hides part of the phenomenon it is supposed to be describing. Taking the example of a bridge that can be described as a means of transportation and a means of discrimination (it was built to prevent a given population from using it, since it is not accessible via mass transport, which is the way this population habitually moves around), he shows that these two readings cannot be carried out in parallel: the description of the bridge as discrimination depends on the description of the bridge as technique. In other words, describing the bridge as an agent of social control is a "re-description", which depends on the first description, of the bridge as bridge, being intelligible (Button, 2001: 168). In sum, to assert that describing the bridge as a means of discrimination is preferable to describing it as a bridge is tantamount to disregarding an essential part of the phenomenon – that of the bridge; extracting the phenomenon from the social world in which it is inscribed; and arbitrarily selecting elements relevant to the description instead. As for the social actor produced in the process, he is no longer Garfinkel's idiot, but rather a naïf, who believes that an "ordinary world" is normal when analysis repositions that world as the product of "social" practices that are accepted as normal (Lynch, 1993: 153). The immediate consequence is that we are back in the very same position of skepticism that ethnomethodology rejects.

The Ethnomethodological Ethnography of Legal Work

There is an important difference between resorting to legal material to develop our knowledge of interactive language and analysing legal procedure with the help of ethnomethodology. As Rod Watson points out,

> … some of the best ethnomethodology and conversation-analysis studies of law and legal reasoning come from analysts who do not regard themselves as having any special interest in 'the law' as a sociological specialism but instead simply conceive of themselves, like Garfinkel, as doing generic ethnomethodology/conversation analysis: there is a real distinction of focus, here. (personal communication)

Clearly, our method resorts to ethnomethodology and conversation analysis in order to respecify the object of socio-legal studies, but this does not mean that it is irrelevant to ethnomethodology in general – and particularly to the study of routine practices in an institutional context. This attitude corresponds to one of the tendencies prevalent in ethnomethodology: ethnomethodological ethnography, or the ethnomethodology of work. In that perspective, what is at the heart of the analysis is no longer so much the social production of order whatever the context than the study of the practical organization of a professional activity and the specialized production of order. In the legal field, this method finds an anchor in very old works, and is extended through recent research, even though it is necessary to recognize its paucity in quantitative terms.

Aaron Cicourel's research on justice for juveniles, though it is relatively old, emerged from this ethnographical concern, proceeding in a way we could describe as proto-methodological. Compared to the mobilization of the sociological (and particularly statistical) apparatus being carried out at the time, Cicourel (1968) showed marked interest in observing and describing the practices of groups and professionals who were responsible for implementing and administering the rights of juveniles, beyond the simple transcription of recorded verbal exchanges. This technique allowed Cicourel to show how police officers decided to arrest, accuse, or incarcerate juveniles on the basis of interrogation reports, according to organizational constraints and on the basis of a limited range of possibilities. But the truly pioneering study in this method allying ethnomethodological and ethnographic sensibilities was Sudnow's (originally written in 1965) on "normal crimes". Sudnow, who was interested in the process of legal qualification, showed how legal categories, far from being comprehensible exclusively thanks to compendiums of the main juristic principles, must be understood through the process of categorization itself. Sudnow's research was based on several months' continual observation of jurists at work, particularly in their plea bargaining, and he described in detail the methods they used to undertake negotiations starting from what appeared to be a "normal crime". According to Sudnow (1987: 158), formal legal categories are 'the basic conceptual equipment with which such people as judges, lawyers, policemen, and probation workers organize their everyday activities'. This signifies that once these categories are identified, it is still necessary to examine how people orient to them in practice. Here, Sudnow is establishing a distinction between necessarily included lesser offenses, and routinely included lesser offenses. The former are violations of the law that are implied by definition in the commission of more serious offenses, while the latter are only implied by the effects of the social actors' practices. The practical consequence is that

> … in searching an instant case to decide what to *reduce it to*, there is no analysis of the statutorily referable elements of the instant case: instead, its membership in a class of events, the features of which cannot be described by the penal code, must be decided. (Sudnow, 1987: 162)

It is precisely this category of events that Sudnow describes as "normal crimes". Normality here refers to the way people deal with a category of persons and events when they are dealing with certain types of criminal acts. Sudnow also shows that, in addition to lesser legal offenses, which are included by definition or situationally in the same category as graver offenses, some offenses are included simply because of the routine practice of professionals, since this routine associates certain offenses, as they are generally committed, according to the social criteria prevailing at a given moment.[8]

Along the same lines, we may cite an article by Sacks (1997; originally written in 1962) about lawyers' work, describing the way jurists are engaged, during their daily activity, in "managing routine" through their contribution to the stability of social life. At the same time, when carrying out their work before the courts, they are engaged in "managing continuity", and, for that reason, they deal with new cases as if they were instances of a prevailing legal category. As a result, non-legal practices are of primary importance in the administration of the law. As for Lynch, he wrote an article (1997; originally written in 1979) dealing with hearings before a Canadian legal tribunal, in which he examined the judge's visible, public work, ranging from the management of procedural constraints to the moral denunciation of the accused at the moment of sentencing. He points out that the public justification for judicial actions that are undertaken, and judicial reasons that are proffered, is an integral part of court hearings, which are therefore not limited to strictly legal procedures. An article by Albert Meehan (1997; originally published in 1988) examines the

8 For an implementation of Sudnow's idea in the Egyptian context, see Chapter 6.

modes by which the police produce interrogation reports and other documents in the policing of juveniles. Among these documents, he focuses particular attention on the running record, which includes all the knowledge collected about an individual, as well as past places and events, and which is used in sentencing. Maynard and Manzo (1997; originally published in 1993) also produced a detailed article about the way juries reach decisions, in which they show that the result precedes the decision. They also show that justice, far from being only the abstract notion of philosophers and, to a certain extent, sociologists, is something that exists empirically, i.e. in the words and deeds of ordinary society. Finally, we must cite the work of Stacy Burns (1997; originally published in 1996), which deals with legal education and describes how a teacher may emphasize the specifically practical dimension of a jurist's work. Stacy Burns is one of the rare individuals who followed Garfinkel's advice and sought to combine sociological training with professional qualification (as a lawyer), thus acquiring the double skill set that is ideally necessary to carrying out ethnomethodological research on work. Recently, Luisa Zappulli also carried out an ethnomethodological study of aspiring magistrates in Italy. In an article (2001) based on her research, she shows how institutional constraints, technical expertise, and ordinary knowledge mingle, as young magistrates are called on to develop their ability to master their new professional environment quickly, in order to start their career in the most advantageous manner.

There is only one monograph specifically devoted to legal work from an ethnomethodological point of view: *The Reality of Law* (Travers, 1997), which examines the activity of a firm specializing in criminal law. In the first part, he deals with the general question of the sociology of law, including its theory, subject, and method; and he tries to show, by way of contrast, what new and useful elements the ethnomethodological approach can offer in this regard. He evokes the "blind spot" in the sociological study of law, to wit, the failure to take into full account the organizational constraints and contingencies that affect lawyers' work. Lawyers must not only take these constraints and contingencies into account, they must also use them as resources to show that they have acted as fully as possible in practice. The ethnomethodological approach to law thus asks how to deal with legal activity as a social phenomenon. Travers then reviews a few ethnomethodological studies of legal activity. The second part of the book is devoted to fieldwork that the author carried out among criminal lawyers in the north of England. After a phenomenological description of the firm, Travers shows how its different nature, which makes this what he calls a "firm of radical lawyers", is made visible by those who work there through their way of speaking about their daily activities (*id.* chapter 3). In that sense, people are not simply members of a group; they are also the links to these categories, which always implies a degree of interpretation that is open to rectification. Furthermore, this membership is also translated by the promotion of a particular type of opinion on professional practice, and a form of self-presentation that highlights one's professionalism in carrying out that practice. The author also broaches the question of criminal lawyers' work strictly defined (chapter 4), in the specific context of this firm. Travers shows how law and procedure emerge first and foremost from a practical understanding that depends on the type of client, common-sense skills, and knowledge acquired through experience. This is particularly visible when we observe in detail how a lawyer persuades his client to plead guilty (*id.* chapter 5). The ethnomethodological perspective adopted by Travers aims to give weight to people's daily understanding of the social context, developed on the basis of shared methods, rather than adopting an overhanging point of view. Considered from this perspective, the lawyer is no longer only a cynical being who manipulates his client for reasons that have nothing to do with the client's welfare; he is also a professional who can carry out his activities as well as possible in the situation he is facing, using the limited resources available in that context. Travers also looks at the work that goes into preparing a trial for the Crown Court (*id.* chapter 6). In this part of his study, one sees how important simple routine is. Furthermore, one remarks the methods used to solve problems, among others the use of shop talk. All these methods display "routinized" legal knowledge, which mixes technical vocabulary and practical experience. In conclusion, Travers emphasizes the main advantages of ethnomethodology. He sees law as a social construct (a point on which he agrees with advocates of a realistic, critical vision), and shows why it is useful to analyse in detail all the specific episodes of legal work and the interaction between lawyer and client. He later adds, however, that the study of law in action shows that lawyers' constructivist stance cannot escape from the impact of the constraints they must face. The author agrees here with the critique some lawyers have leveled against legal sociologists, who blame them for not being able to explain the content of legal practice. Law is not an institution that fulfils a certain number of functions in society (like the reproduction of domination, for example), so much as it is a set of social practices that unfold in the context of complex societies. According to Travers, ethnomethodology is not unaware of the questions posed by critics of modernity, but it seeks to answer those questions through an empirical, rather than speculative, method.

Conclusion

This chapter looked at the idea of law in action. In order to show what sets the ethnomethodological study of law apart from classical legal sociology, we took the example of Islamic law and the way it is approached in the literature, which suffers from various defects, most importantly a strong essentialist tendency. We may also identify a propensity to set up a dichotomy between law on the books and law in action, to forget the phenomenology of law and to prefer general interpretations that shed no light on the description of situated legal practices. In contrast with this approach, the ethnomethodological study of law and justice allows for a respecification of the subject of research. In that perspective, the point is no longer to identify the shortcomings of legal practices in comparison with an ideal model or a formal rule, but rather to describe the modes of production and reproduction, the intelligibility, understanding, structuring, and public manifestation of the structured nature of law and the various activities related to it. This presentation of ethnomethodological research on the topic allowed us to lay the bases of the praxeological approach that follows our investigation of Egyptian law, undertaken in the following sections of this work.

PART II
Law in Context and in Action

Chapter 4
Law in Context: Legal Activity and the Institutional Context

We would like to begin the second part of this book with an empirically documented investigation of the entirely situated, contextual nature of legal activity. The foregoing chapters amply demonstrated that ethnomethodology rejects any attempt at formalization identifying the characters and properties of an action or a speech act independently of the context in which it is deployed and the infinite variety of configurations contained within that context. Now, we will show how law is produced and practiced in context, i.e. in a way that cannot be explained independently of contingencies related to time, place, membership, and the sequential course of the action under consideration. At the same time, the ethnomethodological requirement that action be contextualized creates a number of concrete difficulties. In this chapter, we will seek first to show how important it is to locate legal action in context. We will look at the institutional context of such action, and endeavour to emphasize that its occurrence must not be postulated, but rather described on the basis of empirically demonstrated manifestations of its relevance.

Context and Institutional Context of Legal Action[1]

It is possible to show how a series of legal concepts and categories only acquire significance if they are not abstracted from the context in which they were formulated. If we take the example of the notion of "natural person", we observe that it is narrowly constrained by the sequential, situational, and institutional context of its use (cf. Chapter 8).

To say that linguistic phenomena are inseparable from the context in which they are produced signifies above all that we must reject the dichotomy between speaking and acting. Discourse cannot be studied independently of the circumstances that give it meaning, and in which it is deployed (Sharrock and Watson, 1990: 234). An action and the account of that action are inseparable. People act and speak in order to be intelligible, and therefore it is the concrete, practical conditions in which intelligibility is produced that we must study. If we consider, for example, the social attributes that participants in interaction emphasize in discourse, we observe that they are not invariably attached to those to whom they are imputed. Rather, they depend on the particular environment in which the discourse takes place, and

1 For reflections on the notion of context in linguistic anthropology, see Duranti and Goodwin, 1992. On the notion of relevance, see Sperber and Wilson, 1995.

the discursive activities in which the speakers are engaged, in the "here and now" of their speech. John Gumperz (1982: 162) speaks of "contextualization cues" to indicate those aspects of the context that are relevant for the interpretation of what a participant means. In that regard, we may establish a parallel between such a notion and that of "frame" as developed by Goffman. According to him, behaviour, including discourse, must be interpreted in relation to the understanding that participants form of the frame in which they find themselves. The related notion of "footing" (Goffman, 1981) refers to the reflexive, fluctuating nature of frames, and to the constant re-evaluations and realignments in which participants may engage when shifting from one frame to another.

Whether we approach it through Gumperz or Goffman, then, it is clear that context may no longer be considered as a unitary, invariable thing. Contrary to the radical decontextualization that dominates the classic works of Austin and Searle – who, although they deal with relations between action, text, and context, tend to consider that meaning emerges from words themselves – it is necessary to remark that phrases and words, formed and conceived in order to be produced in particular sequential and social contexts, have a meaning derived from these contexts (Schegloff, 1984).[2] Words must therefore be evaluated in terms of whether they meet or depart from expectations specific to the language space in which they occur. There are two types of expectations. First, there are perlocutory expectations, established by a previous speech turn. For example, a question establishes the relevance of an answer; a salutation, the relevance of a returned greeting, etc. The fact that expectations are not fulfilled (a question is met by silence; a greeting is not returned) is, in that regard, significant, while a semantic approach cannot attribute meaning to the absence of speech. Second, there are expectations resulting from the general context of interaction, the social identity of participants, and the type of behaviour generally associated with a type of event. It is unexpected, for example, if a suspect speaks in familiar terms to the surrogate who is interrogating him. Here too, the fact that he does so will be highly significant, whereas a semantic theory of meaning could not account for this phenomenon (Drew and Heritage, 1992: 12-3).

Paul ten Have and George Psathas (1995: IX) refer to the concept of "situated order" to express the inextricable relationship between context and interaction. The social ordering of things is a local accomplishment, which can be analysed in terms of the participants' "work" as they seek to adjust their activities to the environment, or in terms of transformation and reorganization of the environment under the impact of that work. The relation between context and interaction is thus manifested at different levels. First, the various participants in an interaction manifest the fact that they orient to the particular context in which their interaction

---

2 The same idea brought about important modifications in the theory of acts of speech. According to Sbisà and Fabbri (1981), logical accounts cannot describe the way speech acts work. In practice, speech acts work not through the logical operation of necessary and sufficient conditions, but through the use and negotiation of these conditions in particular contexts of social interaction (cf. Jackson, 1995: 49).

occurs. For example, the fact that an accused party addresses the surrogate as "bey"[3] is not simply a mark of deference; it is also the sign that he recognizes the judicial context of the interaction. Next, it is possible to say that saying and doing are context shaped as well as context renewing. They are context shaped in the sense that what is said and done results from the preceding activity's configuration as well as from the wider framework in which people recognize that the activity is situated. Thus, the accused party's response proceeds from the surrogate's preceding question and from the framework of the Prosecutor's office, to which the parties refer explicitly. Saying and doing are also context renewing, insofar as they are the result of foregoing sequences and the basis for ulterior sequences, and therefore act to maintain, adjust, or modify the meaning of the prevailing context, to which participants in the interaction orient and direct their actions (Drew and Heritage, 1992: 18). In a Public Prosecution interrogation, for example, the surrogate's question may be formulated in such a manner as to imply that the accused is responsible. The accused party's response, in turn, may be formulated so as to anticipate the implied accusation, reposition the condemned action, and cause it to appear justified. This will cause the surrogate to realign himself at the next turn of speech. An act (of speech) and its context are so closely linked that, generally, the participants in an interaction find the resources and indications allowing them to understand their environment and to formulate the appropriate action from the context itself. One may then speak, like Pollner (1979; see also Sharrock and Watson, 1990) of a self-explicating setting, which refers to the ways in which some situations are arranged in order to manifest the familiarity and sense of routine it is appropriate to expect at that point. Pollner uses the example of traffic courts (see Chapter 3), which are organized as a series of hearings where presumed infractions are examined. These sessions present a regular, iterative structure, which allows the accused parties to prepare their own defense by aligning themselves on the way in which earlier cases were dealt with.

> Exchanges between judges, attorneys and accused persons, to which the person who waits his turn attend, do not represent for him a simple sequence of particular cases, but the manifestation, which develops in a cumulative way, of the specific organization of the sessions, a visible manifestation of the way things are done there, as required. [...] The judge's answers to the remarks formulated by the various accused persons constitute instructions for determining how to speak in a legitimate way before the court, what can be said to the judge, how he can answer his questions; yet, they can also be used by the spectators as instructions concerning the way accused people have to behave in general. This will in turn considerably help them behaving themselves, when their turn will come, in a standard way and defending themselves as it is usually done. This is how a particular accused person can incorporate in his own behaviour the "standard model" of defence before the court. (Sharrock and Watson, 1990: 238)

3 A term of politeness in colloquial Egyptian Arabic.

To act and speak in context means, among other things, to enunciate the context, make it visible and public; and these activities cannot be dealt with separately from the context itself. In that sense, context is not only that which an act (of speech) is projected into, but is also the product of that act.

Turning now to the institutional context, we may emulate Drew and Heritage (1992: 22-3) in identifying three main characteristics. First, discourse in this context is informed by its orientation to goals that are largely predetermined by insertion in this institutional context. Participants in institutional interaction, whether professionals or laypeople, generally manifest the fact that their behaviour is conceived and oriented to accomplishing institutional tasks or achieving objectives characteristic of that institution, even if that orientation is not subject to determinism, since orientations can fluctuate according to the temporary, local contingencies of interaction and the definition of the participants' status (see also Atkinson, 1982). Second, one remarks that in an institutional context, interaction is subject to a number of constraints that result specifically from this context and its functionality. These constraints, according to which participants shape their behaviour, may even be formal or legal, as is the case of procedure in the judicial context (see Chapter 5). Third, discourse in an institutional context is organized in inferential frameworks and procedures specific to that context. This means that inferences and implications drawn by participants in an interaction that is occurring in an institutional context will tend to follow patterns that are largely determined by their insertion in modes of reasoning specific to the institution in question.

These specific characteristics of institutional interaction have several important consequences. Among others, let us note that the turn-taking system in speech is institutionally structured and, in turn, strongly structures many aspects of behaviour for participants in the interaction. We might also remark that these participants organize their behaviour so as to manifest and realize its institutional character. As for the resources of action, they are more limited than in an ordinary context; options and opportunities for action are reduced and relatively specific. Furthermore, procedures are defined more precisely and failure to respect them is punished more strictly, so that one may observe their more systematic respect. The participants' lexical choices are also shown to be closely dependent on the institutional context, as is the allocation of speech turns, which expresses the selection of relevant actions (a procedural constraint; see Chapter 5) as well as their insertion in a framework of linguistic relevance (legal relevance; see Chapter 6). Sequences are thus substantively shaped by their institutional context – to such an extent, indeed, that they become characteristic of this context. One also remarks the existence of standard patterns of institutional interactions and professional practices aiming to manage the tasks specific to the interaction. Thus, professionals generally display a neutral position, and produce that neutrality precisely through lexical, procedural, and sequential choices. Finally, institutional interactions generally reveal an asymmetrical structure.

> In many forms of institutional discourse … there is a direct relationship between status and role, on the one hand, and discursive rights and obligations, on the

> other. [I]nstitutional interactions may be characterized by role-structured, institutionalized, and omnirelevant asymmetries between participants in terms of such matters as differential distribution of knowledge, rights to knowledge, access to conversational resources, and to participation in the interaction. (Drew and Heritage, 1992: 49)

We should emphasize the fact that the existence of such asymmetries cannot be postulated simply because the interaction is occurring in an institutional framework, however; it must be documented with elements that are endogenous to the interaction.[4]

At this point, it is interesting to give an example of an institutional constraint on action and language in the judicial context. The following example is drawn from the report of an interrogation led by the Prosecutor's surrogate in an attempted rape case. Here, the woman who claimed to have been the victim of this attempt – which the surrogate subsequently described as a violation of honour (*hitk 'ird*) is being interrogated.

Excerpt 1 (Case 5471, 1977, Muharram Bey, Alexandria)[5]

Surrogate's question: What happened

Victim's answer: I was in the street that day … when I met those two … and they told me come with us and they forced me to get in a taxi … and they went behind the Shipyard.

Q: What was their intention when they acted this way

A: They told me don't worry let's have a cup of tea together

Q: Why didn't you call for help when they took you …

A: I tried to shout and I rolled on the ground but the street was empty

Q: What is the number of the taxi they took you in

A: I don't know it happened in the street

Q: Why didn't you ask the taxi driver for help

A: The taxi driver was afraid of them and did what they told him to do

Q: What was their intention when they took you with them

---

4 Cf. the difference in perspective highlighted by Dingwall (2000) between the ethnomethodological approach and the approach incarnated by Conley and O'Barr (1998) on the question of relations between law, language, and power (see Chapter 3). We refer readers to the same chapter, and in particular to the presentation of the work of Atkinson and Drew (1979) with regard to the institutional specificities of action and discourse in a judicial context. It is also useful to refer to Martha Komter's article (1995) on the distribution of knowledge in judicial interaction.

5 We follow no specific system similar to that adopted by Gail Jefferson (1979: 287-9) in transcribing verbal interactions. We have attempted, however, to remain faithful to the mix of vernacular and technical language used by the participants. We have also decided to forego punctuating the material, for two reasons: one, these are translated transcriptions of oral testimonies, which are not punctuated; two, the original Arabic transcripts are also devoid of punctuation.

A: I think they wanted to violate my honor otherwise they would not have taken me to that place
Q: Did you know them before
A: No
Q: Do you have anything else to say
A: No

This exchange, while trivial, is interesting in more than one respect, with regard to interaction in a judicial context. First, it shows us how the surrogate seeks to present a narrative that makes the actions of all the parties involved mutually intelligible, by formulating "wh-" questions ("what happened", "what was their intention", "why didn't you", etc.). The surrogate's questions are also typically oriented to the search for a motivation or an intention, which he will then impute to the action. Here we see how fear and trust are combined in such a way as to provide a motive for the fact that the woman agreed to go with them ('Q: What was their intention when they acted this way; A: They told me don't worry we're going to have a cup of tea together') and that she did not try to resist ('A: They forced me to get in a taxi'). The woman's attitude, which wavers between voluntary behaviour and constraint, creates an ambiguity that could harm her credibility as a victim when heard in an institutional context, which is designed to assign responsibility. She seems to become aware of this when she shifts from a vocabulary of communication ('They told me…') and invitation ('let's have a cup of tea together') to one of force and constraint ('they made me get in a taxi'). We might also remark that the surrogate is continually looking for individual actions that are motivated ('Why didn't you ask the taxi driver for help'; see Chapter 9) and intentional ('What was their intention when they took you with them'; see Chapter 10). This very concretely expresses the fact that such actions are situated in relation to a practical goal, that of the legal characterization of facts (see Chapter 6). In general, one remarks the extent to which this excerpt reveals the contextual nature of characterizations and categorizations. Victimhood, for example, is not a predefined given, but may be observed in a process of (conflictually) negotiated deployment throughout the sequence. This sequence is particularly constraining since it is institutional and therefore reveals its specific aims. Institutional activities assign particular intentions and roles to people who participate in them, which in turn leads to a large number of inferential consequences.

Professional and Profane: Contextual Asymmetry

As we have noted, asymmetry is characteristic of interactions in the institutional context. This may be observed, as far as the judicial context is concerned, in the predominant pattern of question-answer interactions, the knowledge differential that separates professionals from laypeople (and that is often expressed through different lexicons), or in the contrast between the routine professional treatment of a case and its exceptional character for the layperson. At the same time, it is possible to emphasize the importance of cultural and communicational resources shared by laypeople and professionals. Most of their acts (of speech) are situated within a shared universe. Now, we will look at what is highly contextual in the distinction between professionals and laypeople.

First, like sociologists in relation to social knowledge, lawyers do not occupy a position that is totally distinct and distant from the social intrigues in which they must use their knowledge, or from the social knowledge that already comes to bear on these intrigues. This does not mean that we are incapable of grasping reality in the world, simply that we grasp it in a way that selects the relevant elements. As Schütz (1987: 10) points out, relevance is not internal to nature as such; it is the result of humanity's selective and interpretive activity in nature, or in nature as it is observed. Schütz also remarks that professionals and laypeople construct a world of typical elements on the basis of their biographical situation; the former aims to distinguish themselves from the latter thanks to their position and their mastery of a body of knowledge that is distinct and structured differently. And yet professionals and laypeople are socially involved, on the same footing, in producing knowledge. Professionals and laypeople do "sociology", use "ethnomethods", typify and characterize the world – in sum, they produce social visibility that allows itself to be acted upon. In consequence, what distinguishes professionals from laypeople has more to do with the context of their respective performances, and their membership in different "communities" engaged in different forms of "pragmatism".

The spontaneous classifications of sexual relations that Egyptian magistrates formulated in the course of seminars organized at the National Center for Judicial Studies may serve as a basis for the assertion that there is no radical disconnect between jurists and laypeople and, therefore, between the professional and profane meanings of law and justice. For these magistrates, who were all men, the basic reference for the evaluation of any sexual act was the category "permissible sexual relations", i.e. the category of relations that brings together a man and a woman of legal age within the framework of a legal marriage. The existence of consent or constraint never appeared as preponderant, as long as the permissible nature of relations could be established. In consequence, the idea of rape was excluded for a legally married couple. They referred to the Court of Cassation's definition of "permissible sexual relations" as 'the sum total of relations between a man and a woman in the framework of marriage through any insertion of the male organ or of an object held by the male into the woman's genitals.' Such a definition of the "legitimate sexual relations" paradigm implies that rape, which we may define as the accomplishment of illicit sexual relations through constraint, must necessarily be an action carried out by a man on a woman. In turn, this excludes any reversal of the protagonists' roles (a woman cannot rape a man according to this definition), any relation that departs from the strict definition provided above (like sodomy), and any homosexual relation (a man cannot rape a man).

Going through the media coverage of the circumstances and sentencing in the case of the "girl from Maadi" illustrates this point. Six young men, aged 18 to

30, were put on trial and accused of having kidnapped a young woman and her fiancé in Maadi, a Cairo neighbourhood. They were accused of having held and robbed the couple and of having raped the young woman. The media coverage featured a series of images that it is easy to describe as paradigmatic of feminine virtue, sexuality, the control of sexuality, and the repression of transgression. This is visible in the general heading foisted upon this morality play – the "case of the girl from Maadi" (*qadiyyat fatat al-Ma'adi*). In some of the headlines used by the media, the action seems to have been categorized systematically by attaching it to an archetype: that of the "repulsive crime" (*jarima bashi'a*), an archetype that seems to have validity for any case involving morality, from pornography to prostitution and rape. The way the Maadi affair was presented brought it within the sway of this category. One of the newspaper headlines thus featured the following statement from the young woman: 'I was faced with monsters, who tore me to pieces with their fangs (*wajahtu wuhushan mazzaqu adamiyiti bi anyabihim*).' The media coverage of another rape case, which occurred in March 1992, the case of the "girl from Ataba" confirms the way this category functions. In this second case, a young girl was subjected to a "repulsive attack" one evening during the "blessed month of Ramadan".

Among the elements that make up the category of "repulsive crimes", the question of virginity holds a preponderant place. For example, the fact that the forensic pathologist reported that the young woman from Maadi was still a virgin, despite the collective sexual attack to which she was subjected, is very clearly an incongruous element in the classification; only a detailed medical explanation was able to make up for this fact. The constant references made to the theme of virginity, furthermore, testify to the importance that such a concept, which is not a legal notion strictly defined, took on in the narrative of a crime against honour or a rape. The preservation of the young woman's hymen was certainly an enigma that had to be resolved in the application of the rape label, but the insistence one observes in this regard cannot have been due to simple technical considerations. We will see to what extent this sort of consideration organizes classifications carried out by protagonists as well as the rights and duties thereto appertaining. Here, we are referring to the linguistic, contextual, and indexical organization of meaning.

This type of classification, however, is not characteristic of journalists alone. While the press set the stage for "the young virgin" and the "six wolves" who raped her, the prosecutor's office and the judge used a dichotomous narrative organization that pitted the victim against her aggressors. One may also find articles written by jurists who draw parallels between the measures advocated by positive law and the rules attributed to Islamic *shari'a* with regard to rape. In that regard, we may highlight statements made by Ahmad Kamil Salama, a professor at Cairo University's Faculty of Law (*al-Gumhuriyya*, March 1985). In an article that dealt with rape from the point of view of *shari'a* and positive law, Salama introduced and concluded his article with a defense of the virtues and merits of marriage and a call for the need to enforce sanctions against any violation of the exclusively legal framework for sexual relations. From his presentation, it emerges that sexual morality is very clearly articulated, in its professional and profane dimensions, around the notion of matrimonial exclusivity. In this perspective, rape is simply the contradiction of an ideal, aggravated by the use of force. We may also observe here the intermingling of professional and ordinary understandings of law and justice.

Contrary to Alain Clémence and Willem Doise (1995), who claim that justice and law are not thought of in the same way by laypeople and professionals, and who assert that professional logic is rather analytical while profane logic is more representational, our work tends to show that it is unwise to divide the two spheres of thought too radically. Laypeople's knowledge is usually based on elements of technical knowledge while, conversely, professional knowledge includes an important profane substratum. Indeed, what is especially important is to note the extent to which the elements are intertwined, since both of these ways of sensing justice are based on shreds of shared knowledge. The essential difference may result from the ways in which the reference rules are articulated, rather than from the substance of these rules; from the pragmatic aspects of their enunciation, and not from their semantics.

Jackson (1994) developed a semiotic perspective on the notion of "professional" as an attribute, according to which the notions of narrative syntagm and narrative typification (see Chapter 1) can be applied to the content of a story or an action, but also to the very act of communicating that story or action. Using the metaphor of the football referee, Jackson shows that professionalism is borne by the transfer of certain modalities within the narrativised pragmatic of judging, rather than by the judge's deductive application of the rules of the game to the facts he encounters on a given field. This is a double transfer: it occurs both through the desire to "act like a good judge", and through the communication of the fact that the obligation appears to have been satisfied. The transfer, therefore, involves not only knowledge, but also – indeed, mainly – know-how. Professionalism thereby becomes the means whereby a client is persuaded that the know-how that has been transferred to him is "competent" (this is what Jackson calls the transfer of semiotic value: see Chapter 1). What is characteristic of the professional sense of law, therefore, is less the result of differences in typifications of the law than it is of the construction of modalities in legal activity. This approach, however, still relies too heavily on a dramaturgical understanding of professional action. In a sense, such action comes across as being aimed only at producing an impression on participants and spectators. By presenting it thus, Jackson dissimulates a fundamental dimension of professional action: to wit, the fact that this action is above all continuous, routine, bureaucratic, unproblematic, and non-dramatic.

In his article on lawyers' work, Sacks (1997) emphasizes that the performance of this profession relies on management of routine office work, on one hand, and continuous work before the courts on the other. In a well-known article, "On doing 'being ordinary'", 1989) Sacks also focuses on showing through which methods people manifest the normalcy of a situation and their personal normalcy. Taking up the same example, we will look at the methods whereby people who are involved in a legal profession act as judges, lawyers, court reporters, clerks, etc. This professional dimension of legal work may be manifested in a public way that can be recognized, described, and justified. To paraphrase Lynch, the legal professional we are describing does not react to secret, invisible motives; he is a professional who speaks, asks questions, acts, writes, listens, shows impatience, and a host of other things.

> It might be said that where Durkheim stresses the relationships between social facts and factors, Garfinkel urges us to investigate the *factories* that produce them. The *social*, for Garfinkel, is not a composite of variables in a regression analysis. It is not specified by measures of socio-economic status, gender, educational attainment, ethnicity, regional background, or any other social factor or combination of factors. Instead, social facts and social factors are uniquely, singularly, and routinely composed *in and through* the concerted production and competent recognition of actions on the 'factory' floor. Such performances *are* social, and their productin can be described praxiologically. If it can be said that there are lawful regularities to the organization of social affairs, the initial task is to describe the circumstantial production of such facticity. In the case of the *judge*, the facticity of the judge as a courtroom agency is a public issue for competent co-practitioners. The judge's place in a hearing is more than a role enacted by a person in an institutional setting. The metaphor of role is apt, in the sense that it differentiates the judge's ideal-typical actions from the judge's personality, but it too easily implies that the role of judge is somehow attached to or constructed by an individual actor. It may seem obvious that a judge is a person decorated with symbolic trappings of sovereign and impartial authority (robes, high-backed chairs, an elevated podium, honorary forms of address), a person who performs symbolic functions consistent with a spectacle of justice, but in this study I shall consider the judge as a configuration *in action* that is not, or at least not always, figured or expressed by a robed and bewigged person. (1997: 99-100)

The formal nature of the judicial procedure is one of the methods whereby the magistrate behaves as a magistrate and achieves his professional management of a case. The same may be said of the way an interrogation is organized when it is led by the Prosecutor's surrogate. The following excerpt from the report on the case of the "girl from Maadi" illustrates this statement. Note the formalism of the first and last paragraphs, the systematic, stereotypical description, and the orientation to questions of identity, fact, procedure, and legal qualification of the condemned actions.

> **Excerpt 2 (Affair 276, 1985, Ma'adi)**
> Taking advantage of the presence of the accused, who were being held outside the room where the investigation was taking place, we called them in and asked them to address the charges against them, after having informed them that the prosecutor was opening an investigation against them. They all admitted [that they had understood this information] and we asked them if they had a representative who would appear

> with them for the investigation. They replied in the negative. We made all the accused leave the room, apart from the first. In appearance, he is a young man in his 30s, around 1.70 meters tall, of average weight, with a dark complexion. He wore a blue suit with checks at the bottom and a blue pullover. We questioned him in detail and he replied as follows:
> A: Anwar Isma'il 19 years of age warehouse janitor resident of 'Izbat [?]
> Q: What are the details of what you admit [...] [the complete investigation follows]
> Q: You are accused of participating with others in a kidnapping and violent rape what do you have to say
> A: I said what happened
> Q: You are also accused of participating with others in the kidnapping and illegal confinement what do you have to say
> A: Yes it happened
> Q: Do you have a record
> A: No
> Q: Do you have anything else to say
> A: No
> End of the statement of the accused, Anwar.
>
> Next, we put this accused party aside and we called the second into the room where the investigation was taking place. In appearance, he is a young man in his early 30s, around 1.70 meters tall, with short black hair, an olive complexion, wearing a sweater that was originally yellow, lemon-coloured trousers, and black shoes. Next, we endeavoured to question him in detail about the following [...]

Nevertheless, we should not consider procedural formalism or professional routine as intangibles or factors in judicial activity of the sort that Lynch criticizes. Routine, to mention only one point, is also a circumstantial and contextual production: the temporary realization of a set of expectations regarding the ordinary character of work and the banality of the cases presented before professionals. When a given type of case becomes typified, and comes to belong to a category that is dealt with frequently, it is dealt with in a more routine way (Emerson, 1983: 433). It is only because carrying a homemade firearm or selling bango (a type of cannabis) are everyday activities in the rural judicial district of Shibin al-Qanatir, for instance, that the surrogate deals with a new case as a banal occurrence. He will only see a case as important if it escapes this practical geography of the penal mundane, as it were, that he has created for himself. The same surrogate, in the urban district of Bulaq, considers the sale of narcotic pharmaceuticals as routine, but would consider the carrying of a homemade firearm as exceptional.[6] The techniques implemented to manage routine, and particularly that which is presented as overtime or a judicial backlog, also testify to the contextual nature

6 On the concept of a practical geography of criminality, see Zappulli, 2001. On the geographical distribution of criminality on the basis of Egyptian judicial statistics, see Dupret and Bernard-Maugiron, 2002.

of professional activity. It frequently occurs that professionals devote particular attention to the first occurrence of a certain type of case, in order to be able to deal with subsequent cases of the same type in a repetitive way, and also in order to communicate with observers of the unfolding interaction the instructions that will allow them to situate themselves in anticipation of the moment when their own case will be dealt with. The attention devoted to a particular case must indeed also be justified. Any perceived excess attention is sanctioned as a waste of time. A surrogate who gives maximum attention to every case that comes before him will be told off by his boss. Symmetrically, the Head Prosecutor who micromanages each of the cases dealt with by his subordinates is seen as meticulous, obsessive, and even incompetent; his subordinates will be irritated that excessive time is being given to cases they perceive as banal.

> Under these circumstances, decisions as to how to allocate special commitments [to one case rather than to another] inevitably affect and implicate the workers' *reputations* as competent organizational members. (Emerson, 1983: 447)

The fact that routine itself is produced in a circumstantial, situated, and contextual way is made particularly clear when events come to disrupt this routine.

The Problems of Contextuality

The ethnomethodological study of judicial activity is concerned with context, and this concern raises a number of difficulties. Some result from a narrow understanding of the linguistic interaction under consideration, when this interaction and its context are limited to a fragmentary event stretching over a given period and integrated in a longer sequence. Others are due rather to the limited availability of material that researchers should ideally have in order to provide an adequate interpretation of a linguistic activity's contextual insertion, and here it is necessary to recall that research is limited by the realm of the possible. These remarks should not at all be taken to suggest that it would be appropriate to fill in the gaps left by the available material by replacing them with hypotheses on the incidence of factors whose relevance does not emerge from the object of empirical study. Instead, we must recognize the limits of what we may claim to observe and describe, and certainly not attempt to transcend these limits, formulate general hypotheses, or sketch out grand theoretical patterns.

It seems difficult to choose and work on a given fragment without taking into account the longer sequence in which it is located. Pollner (1979) thus shows that a number of explanatory transactions take place when the rules of a game that participants are about to play are more or less ambiguous, open to interpretation, and indeterminate. The margins of appreciation are subject to negotiations that aim at reducing uncertainty and allow the game to take place in conditions of sufficient stability. In the traffic violations that Pollner examines, these transactions take place at the beginning of the interaction pitting judges against violators. To observe excerpts of sentences without paying sufficient attention to the importance of these liminal moments, under the pretext that relevance emerges exclusively from the interaction under consideration, would present the risk of overinterpretation, as Bogen (1999: 108) shows very well in his critique of Schegloff's analysis (1989/90) of an interview Bush Sr. gave when he was running for president. Bogen points out that it is only because we did not have access to whatever preceded the transcript that we are forced to speculate on the factors relevant to the interaction. It is therefore impossible to avoid situating the interaction in a wider context, although we should still remember that one must be capable of demonstrating (albeit retrospectively) the relevance of this context in relation to the configuration of the interaction. Using a formulaic turn of phrase, we might say that the idea of a contextualizing context, i.e. a contextualization of the action that allows for the description of that action in all its specificity, does not allow us to disregard the fact that the context is already contextualized, i.e. integrated in interplays of longer sequences and background expectations that can only become public if the observer is also a competent member with the ability to cast a retrospective gaze on the configuration taken on by the event under study.

One consequence may be drawn from this notion of contextualized context: to wit, that the data of a judicial sequence should not be limited to a single segment of that sequence, but rather extended to the sum total of the sequence in which the segment occurs.[7] In other words, a single judicial operation must be considered as one segment in a longer sequence. In the perspective of analysing a single segment in the judicial sequence (point 1 in Figure 4.1), the interaction pits Q (the questioner) against R (the responder) in the initial phase, a. In a second phase, b, the questioner writes a report for recipient D. If, on the contrary, one resorts to the idea of an "overreading audience"[8] (point 2 in Figure 4.1), interaction a is no longer binary but rather ternary, by introducing the silent listener (A) to the verbal interaction in the interaction itself (Q-R-(A)). In the second phase, b, Q also writes his report to the recipient D, who, in the initial phase, a, was the third party to the interaction (D=(A)). The same goes for interaction between a police officer and an accused party, for example. Because the police officer must respect a certain

7 Concern for the sequential and intertextual insertion of various discursive elements may be found in elaborations on sequential analysis (Watson, 1997), intertextual analysis (Bakhtin, 1981), discourse network analysis (Kittler, 1990), and, more recently, dialogue network analysis (Leudar, 1995, 1998; Leudar and Nekvapil, 1998; Nekvapil and Leudar, 1998, 2002; see Chapter 13).

8 Paul Drew (1992; 1997) speaks of an overhearing audience to signify the silent audience whom the participants are addressing beyond their direct verbal exchanges. In the framework of the long sequence of a criminal trial, we will speak of an "overreading audience" to designate the silent, absent reader whom the participants are addressing beyond their direct verbal exchange; an "attending person" whose examination of the case is deferred in time.

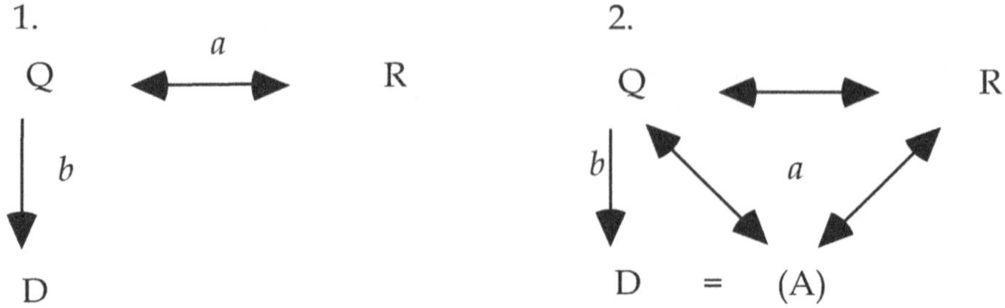

Figure 4.1 The contextualized context

number of formal rules, he leads the investigation with an eye to the objections that the Prosecutor's surrogate might raise. In fact, interaction with the third party functions on the basis of the absent third. Without being physically present in the interaction, the absent third party conditions it closely.

The figure, of course, can become more complex if it seeks to describe the judicial sequence in its entirety: the police investigation, relations with the surrogate (interview with an attorney), investigation led by the surrogate, relation with the court, hearing (lawyer's statement), court deliberations. It is therefore essential for our description to take into account all the participants in the long judicial sequence, whether or not they are physically present in every segment of the sequence.

To replace judicial interaction in context implies that we take into account the verbal and extra-verbal elements of the interaction. These elements may be visual, material, or related to the background expectations of the parties to the trial. Here too, we must be careful not to presume that these elements occur, but it is simultaneously possible to show how, in concrete cases, they exert a real constraint on the interaction. In the process, it is impossible to prevent our own background expectations and underlying patterns from forming; they will necessarily influence our description of interactions for which, nevertheless, we do not have the same type of information.

The vast majority of our sources are written. Besides legal and juristic texts, we have had access to complete judicial files including, among other things, forensic reports, evidence of all kinds, as well as transcripts of interviews with suspects, victims, witnesses, and experts carried out by the police, the prosecutor's office, and judges, in criminal and personal status cases for the most part. We were unable to work on audio recordings, simply because we never received the permission to record hearings. This dependence on written material is certainly problematic, given the type of analysis we seek to carry out. In a recent article, Komter provides a perfect summary of the type of relation between a recorded interrogation, on one hand, and the written report that transcribes such an interrogation, on the other:

> The [police officer's] work consists of a number of activities that are linked to each other: inviting [the accused] to give his version of events and recording them 'in his own words;' examining the consistent character of the version told

> [by the accused], which makes it possible to establish the credibility and 'truth' of his story; obtaining a coherent story, which includes choosing and recording the elements that follow the temporal order of the original events; seeking to obtain a 'recordable' version, which implies a piece-by-piece production of information; obtaining a legally relevant version that can be used as evidence in the criminal trial that will follow; establishing whether the version told [by the accused] is consistent or not with the other evidence; recording a version that displays its procedural rectitude; and, finally, producing a report that will be signed by [the accused].
>
> Two types of activities may be examined when we look at the way the interrogation is conducted: interrogation practices and routine activities related to typing up the interrogation. The story is requested stage by stage, with breaks in the questioning for the transcript to be typed up on the computer. These breaks signify that, for the time being, the story that has been produced can be recorded and typed in one go. An overview of the interrogation reveals that [the police officer] starts by asking open questions and questions about details, and then shifts toward the search for confirmation by [the accused] of what has been formulated. Finally, he places [the accused] before the information, which he already knows since he has read the reports, and partially recounts the story in his place. The story's coherence depends on the original temporal order of events. The narrative-until-now, like the recording-until-now, provide the impulse for the interrogation and the recording to be continued. To make up for the breaks in questioning, [the police officer] starts again, after having typed, where the story was interrupted, or where the report was interrupted. (2001: 383-4)

The word-for-word transcriptions of interrogations, therefore, are documents that have been subjected to considerable "editing" (Holstein, 1993), and that do not allow us to recreate, wholly and perfectly, all of the "conversational" operations leading to the production of the report. From experience, however – and here the reader will have to take our word for it – we can affirm that these transcriptions are generally faithful to the verbal exchanges that occurred, especially when these are exchanges of questions and answers. On the single occasion when it was possible for us to record an interrogation, we were even able to observe a perfect correspondence at this level.

Excerpt 3 (recording, June 2000, Bulaq)

Question from the surrogate: What do you have to say about what Captain N. al-B. recounted in his report dated the 14th of June 2000 according to which his secret informer called him and informed him that you are now present in front of your building your house and he led an auxiliary secret inspection force to see if you were sitting in front of his building and to arrest you is it true that he found you in front of your house

Answer from the accused [a woman]: No sir it's not true at all

The only difference that can be observed in the report of the interrogation consists of the elimination, in the response, of the word "sir" (*ya basha*). The written version therefore seems very loyal to the oral version. However, we should not minimize the importance of three things. First, this sort of detail (the elimination of "*ya basha*"), while marginal, is not insignificant in the study of judicial interaction. It indicates the identity that the participants grant each other publicly, the deference they may show, or the lexical gamut used in naming. Second, access to writing alone, no matter how faithful to the oral version that writing may be, necessarily causes us to lose a series of details from the interaction, the relevance of which should not be disregarded: silences, hesitations, stuttering, half-uttered words, slips of the tongue, corrections, changes in tone, overlaps, etc. Third, even though the text may be faithful to the literal verbal mode of expression, this must not hide the fact that the interrogation as a whole is a construct, which the surrogate orients to the production of procedural correctness and legal relevance (see Chapters 5 and 6). This may become clear through the transcripts, but only, we believe, if we have already developed an "ethnographic" familiarity with the context of the interaction. Having said all this, the fact remains that it is perfectly possible to obtain a great deal of information from this type of written material, as long as we do not seek to make it say more than it can, and we recognize its limitations. Following Atkinson and Drew (1979: 191), we should add that, if these transcription processes exist in the first place, it is 'on the assumption that they are adequate for lawyers and others to understand for the practical purposes of submitting or deciding appeals.' It would be astonishing were we to reject, on principle, material that professionals find adequate for their own purposes.

The physical environment of judicial interaction represents another element of the context to which we cannot have access on the basis of written documents or audio recordings. From that perspective, an ethnographic investigation is indispensable. The cases we were able to observe in an ethnographic way and those whose files we consulted are nevertheless distinct, which makes it impossible to pay due attention to the constraint imposed by the physical environment. At the same time, it is impossible to glance at the judicial interactions whose transcription we consulted and describe them while abstracting the background familiarity we have acquired with the Egyptian judicial environment. In general, in ethnographic terms and with no aim of providing a demonstration, we can present here a few moments selected among others, and occurring inside various buildings that shelter a number of different tribunals, bureaus, and judicial administrations (*mujamma' al-mahakim*).

Figure 4.2 is a diagram of the room where a session of the Court of First Instance, a single-judge summary tribunal was held in the Shubra al-Khayma courthouse. Below are the notes taken on the same occasion.

> Behind the seat of the sole judge, scales – the symbol of justice – hang on the wall, along with the motto 'Justice is the basis of authority' (*al-'adl asas al-mulk*). The walls of the room are covered with paneling to two thirds of their

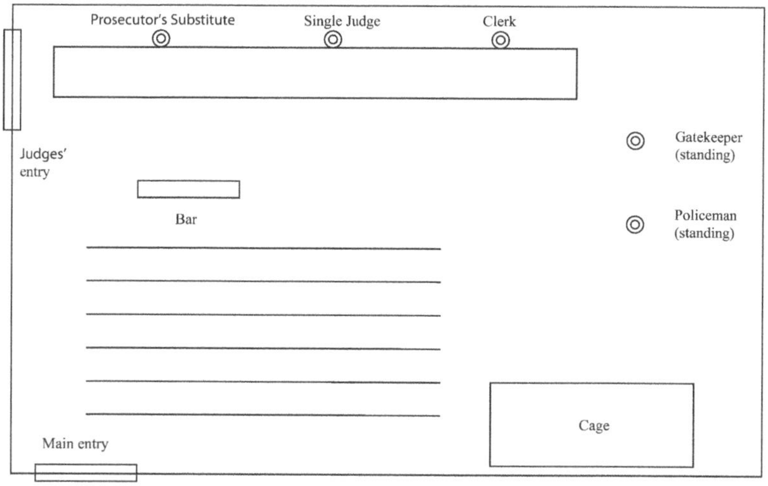

Figure 4.2 Shubra al-Khayma, Court of First Instance

heights and, above, painted in grubby white paint. In the courtroom, before the hearing begins, the registrar is seated and seems to be settling some trivial business with the lawyers, some of whom are wearing robes. The bailiff then comes into the room, calls for silence, and, when the judge arrives, shouts '*mahkama*.'[9] The judge takes his seat and says loudly: '*al-salamu 'alaykum*.' The assembly replies. Then the people who are to appear are called by name, and their names recorded with the court registrar. The bailiff frequently calls for silence. Many of those called by name are absent. There are so many that the registrar cannot keep up. The judge asks the attorney of the next accused party to stand aside and wait for the delay to be made up. The police officer takes the ID cards of the accused who are present. The Prosecutor's surrogate attends the hearing but does not intervene. He doesn't even seem to be following, and in any case there are no files in front of him. When attorneys do intervene, they literally stand between the court and their client. The accused are called only to verify their identity. After they have appeared, people who have been found guilty without any concrete measure being taken are sent to the back of the room until the end of the session (*akhir al-galsa*). A lawyer is holding a file containing paper printed with a letterhead that says 'Ibrahim the Lawyer.' The lawyers leave, having jotted down the date of the next hearing. A lawyer is called on to present his client's case, which is remarkable given how slowly cases are going on this hearing. The plea concerns a case of domestic violence. He makes the presentation loudly and demonstratively: the lawyer reproduces the gestures on his colleague of the opposite side. The latter tries to interrupt the presentation by

9 On the means used to obtain silence and the assembly's attention, see Atkinson and Drew, 1979.

> shouting even more loudly, but fails. Twice, a lawyer sitting next to us asks us to uncross our legs, since, as we are later told, this is a sign of disrespect toward the court. Over 200 cases were registered for this session. A man is standing to one side, better dressed than most of the accused. A policeman asks him for ID, but he refuses. The policeman asks him: 'Are you accused?' He replies: '*madani*' (a plaintiff asking for damages). The registrar organizes the files in three stacks: those that have yet to be dealt with, those that have already been dealt with, and problem cases. The lawyers and the accused do not stand at the bar, but approach the bench directly. Systematically, lawyers stick fiscal stamps on the documents presented to the court, before the registrar. Some of the accused, wearing peasants' clothing, are sitting on the floor at the back of the room. One of them is holding a bunch of paper in a plastic bag. He crouches and pulls the papers out suddenly. While the lawyers, when they stand before the judge, sometimes lean on the bench behind which he is seated, the policeman prevents the accused from doing the same. To a person who thanks him (*shukran*), the judge responds: 'Thank God' (*al-shukr li-l-Lah*). The sound of a glass at the back of the room angers the judge: 'What's that noise?' No response. The judge: 'Is this a coffee shop?'

Figure 4.3 is a layout of the room where a session of the Benha Criminal Court was held. This is followed by the notes taken on that occasion.

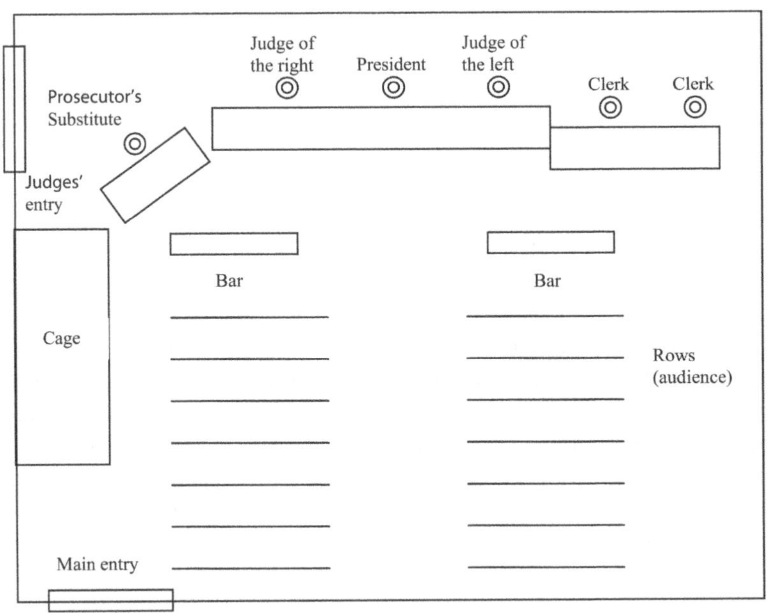

Figure 4.3 Benha, Criminal Court

> The room where the session takes place is small but fairly clean. At the back, on the left, is the cage where the accused are already waiting. The podium is raised, with three seats in the middle and two to the left and below the platform where the court will hold its session. There are two rows of wooden benches for the audience and the lawyers. The walls are panelled and the floor covered with tiles. There are three ceiling fans. The lawyers are already there and the registrars are busy behind the podium. Some trials are heard behind closed doors: the accused is called, taken from the cage, and, preceded by his lawyer, is led by a policeman to a room off the court. Later, the three judges who make up the criminal court, wearing green scarves, enter the room. The accused are summoned by name. Each case entails a plea. The defendants, after having been taken from the cage, stand before the judges. They are required to stand, facing the courtroom, without leaning on anything. A policeman makes sure they follow correct form.

As for the interrogations led by the surrogates, they take place in the prosecutor's offices, located in various courthouses:

> In Shubra al-Khayma, two surrogates share one of these offices. In Benha, it is shared among five of them. These offices are usually dilapidated, in contrast with the 'suit, tie, and polished shoes' worn by the surrogates. In general, each office has a bell to call a gofer and a soldier stationed in the hall. The first serves beverages, while the second carries messages and instructions, ushers in clients, lawyers, and other visitors, and imposes a semblance of order at the door. In Shubra al-Khayma, apart from the two desks and two high-backed chairs, there are two chairs for the surrogates' secretaries. A bench stands against the back wall for visitors; defendants are required to stay standing. There is fluorescent lighting, a fan, and, on the floor, two old carpets. There is a painting of flowers on one wall and a verse from the Qur'an on another. A clock with motionless hands hangs crookedly on a third wall.
>
> The alleged victim of a robbery is seated across from the surrogate, with the surrogate's secretary to the left. The surrogate asks the victim questions and dictates them to his secretary. The technique consists of echoing the statements made by the person being questioned while reformulating them in part. The surrogate concludes the victim's statement with the words 'By God Almighty, that is the truth' (*wa-l-Lahi al-'azim huwa al-haqq*). On another occasion, the mother of a young man who was poisoned with rubbing alcohol makes a statement. The prosecutor must open an inquest. The question is whether an autopsy is necessary. The woman expresses her pain and grief, accompanying the surrogate's interjections with prayers and gestures. The surrogate seems puzzled. He goes off to talk it over with his colleague. Later, he tells us that he doubted the credibility of the woman's testimony, since he found her demonstrations of grief inadequate for someone who had lost a son. According to him, she was not emotional enough. He consults a book, which turns out to

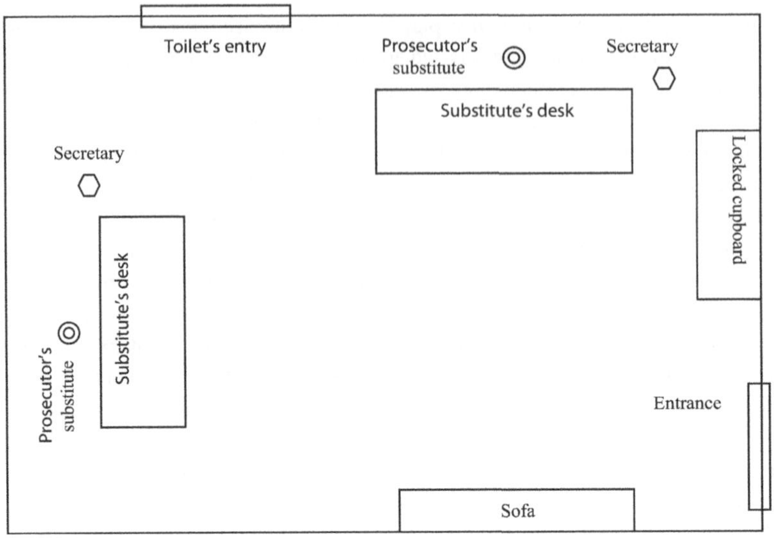

Figure 4.4 Shubra al-Khayma, Prosecutor's office

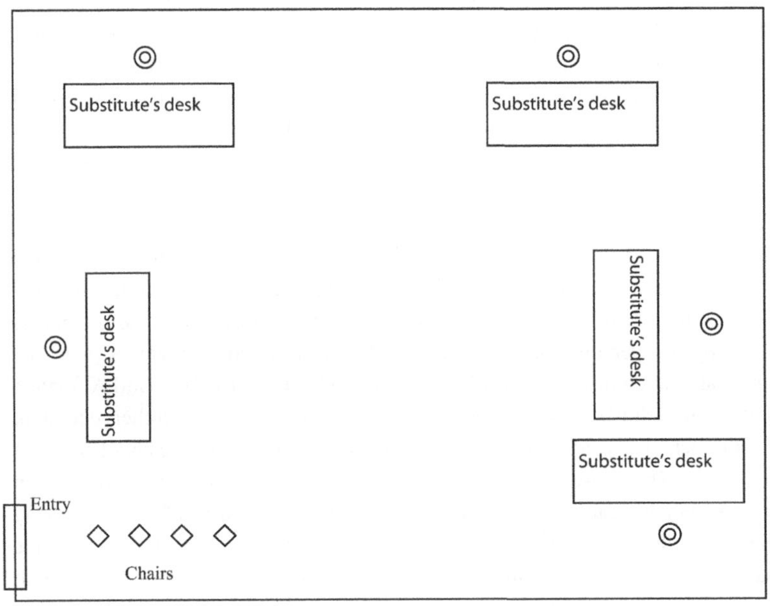

Figure 4.5 Benha, Prosecutor's office

> be the *Prosecutor's Instruction Manual*. A young woman later appears in a case of incestuous rape. She is pregnant. Relations lasted for six months. When we ask whether it is considered shameful to press charges in such a case, we are told that, since the young woman is pregnant but unmarried, it is better for her to appear as her father's victim than as a single mother. The questions seems to be organized in such a way as to detect potential lies (for example, cross-checking how long sexual relations lasted), to carry out the legal qualification of the facts (for example, emphasis on the question of whether the victim was a minor, whether or not the aggressor had legal guardianship), and to prepare for the interrogation of the defendant, who will have to respond to the incriminations contained in the victim's testimony. On the whole, work seems to take place in an extremely routine way. Sometimes, the surrogate seems somewhat insistent, as in the following example, taken from an interrogation session in a drug case: (surrogate) 'Are you a repeat offender;' (defendant) 'No;' 'You're a repeat offender you certainly are;' (defendant) 'No.'

Besides these elements of the visual and material context, which material made up mainly of transcriptions cannot include, it is also necessary to point out some of the parties' background expectations, access to which requires great familiarity with the Egyptian judicial environment. Cicourel (1968) points out that the most interesting observations in his study of justice for minors were gathered at the end of three years of fieldwork carried out in police stations and child welfare services, as a probation agent among other capacities. Many things would remain obscure if elements that are strictly speaking external to the material were not integrated in it. Let us take an example. Regarding drug dealing, prosecutors' surrogates are generally informed by the police, which send them a report on an infraction. It is well known, among the prosecution staff, that such reports narrate the facts according to a typical scenario that establishes the crime. Here is how a surrogate described these scenarios to me:

> In the rural areas, police have three types of stories. The first is when the policeman says he was on duty at a checkpoint (*kamin*) and saw someone coming towards him, who suddenly changed direction after seeing the policeman. When the policeman tries to catch him, the defendant takes something out of his pocket and throws it away, and the policeman picks it up and finds out that it's drugs. He chases the defendant, stops him, and asks why he had these drugs in his possession: for consumption or to sell? As we can see, the policeman is trying to create a situation that conforms to Article 30 of the Code of Criminal Procedure: first, he demonstrates that the defendant made himself suspicious by changing direction; second, he emphasizes that he did not arrest the defendant before having picked up what the defendant had thrown away and observed that it was a narcotic; third, he sticks to the limits of his prerogative because he is not questioning the defendant, he is simply asking him why he had the drugs in his possession.

> The second type of story also takes place at a checkpoint, but this time the defendant is not on foot. He is riding in a form of public transport, a minibus. The policeman specifies that the defendant was sitting next to the driver. While the junior officer is inspecting the driver's papers, the officer, who is in civilian clothes, sees the defendant throwing something into the street. He picks it up and finds that it is drugs. Then the story continues much as in the first scenario. Here, the defendant is always sitting next to the driver, to guarantee the credibility and validity of this type of story. The Court of Cassation has issued a statute on this type of situation, making the defendant's presence in the front seat of the minibus, next to the driver, a condition, because minibuses are so crowded in Egypt that it would be impossible to identify the person who threw the drugs outside the vehicle if that person was sitting in the back.
>
> The third scenario is when the police have received information that a drug dealer is about to make a delivery at 7:00 a.m. Since the policeman has not had time to ask the prosecutor for a warrant (which the Court of Cassation accepts only in case of plausible urgency, and even then rarely), the policeman arrives at 6:30 and hides in the grass. At 6:50 the defendant arrives, the police come out of their hiding place, and they arrest him with the drugs, although his accomplice has fled the scene.

We thus observe that, for the police, the point is not really to describe the facts that occurred, but rather to produce a narrative that establishes the crime according to the rules of the game. It is necessarily above all that the narrative be free of the very frequent legal infractions that would cause the case to be thrown out on procedural grounds if they were taken into account. The prosecutor's surrogate has this type of scenario in mind when a case is turned over to him. He will very infrequently question the police, however, at least directly. For researchers, this information cannot come from the documents, even if they are recorded or filmed. Understanding the context of judicial interaction requires the knowledge of elements that do not appear in the interaction itself, except when, in a retrospective posture, the researcher manages to give meaning to certain elements of the interaction in light of information he has learned elsewhere.

A last example comes from the *Diary of a Country Officer* (*Yawmiyyat Dabit fil-Aryaf*), by Hamdi al-Batran (1998).[10] This diary, made up of 200 brief pages, sounds spot on to whoever has had the opportunity to frequent ordinary Egyptian justice – not the big courts of Cairo, but the lower-level courts where plaintiffs come to make their statements jostle side by side with lawyers on the make, handcuffed defendants, bedraggled policemen, vendors of cigarettes and biscuits. All of them have come to meet the general prosecutor's surrogate for one reason or another. He is a young man, impeccably dressed in a suit and tie, his shoes shiny with polish, seated with authority behind a desk and assisted by a secretary, in a room he shares with several colleagues. The room, at this level, is often miserable, but attention is

10 The title was obviously chosen to echo Tawfiq al-Hakim's famous book (1942; El Hakim, 1974), *Diary of a Country Prosecutor* (*Yawmiyyat Na'ib fil-Aryaf*).

paid to a series of details that help to maintain hierarchies and the authoritarian administration of justice.

> I sat down in my huge office.
>
> At the door were two soldiers with their automatic weapons, along with a police auxiliary – a sergent major – who also had an automatic weapon.
>
> Next to me, a Kalashnikov-type automatic rifle hangs on the wall. It's excellent for shooting wildly. It shoots seven rounds in a single burst, and three bursts at a time. It can also shoot only one bullet, as one likes.
>
> I received this weapon as soon as I entered the district. A telephone operative called me and told me that the president of the municipal authorities wanted to greet me, congratulate me on my new position, and welcome me to town. He was coming by in half an hour. The district prosecutor called me to congratulate me, and told me of his sincere desire that my time in the district be one of sincere cooperation and trust between the prosecutor's office and the police (Batran, 1998: 8)

We must add to this the knowledge obtained through the study of cases that make up the prosecutors' daily bread – knowledge of what are often the most dramatic aspects of life for a population that remains rural in its majority. The detail of interrogations provides an ideal key with which to enter discourses of motive and justification. The only caveat is that these discourses may be invented wholesale, under the pressure of police brutality, for instance, in order to deflect or hide true responsibility. In that case, the book offers the advantage of documenting hypotheses that could not be demonstrated otherwise, for researchers tempted by a praxeological approach to judicial activity.[11]

Conclusion: What is the Relevant Context?

In this study of the context for judicial action before Egyptian courts, many difficulties arise from the fact that activity is always situated in a sequence that is longer than that available to the observer, and accessibility is limited in several ways. The problem of reducing the available context to a limited choice of

11 This is what Dusan Bjelic says (1999: 251) when recalling a personal experience as translator for Bosnian refugees arriving in the United States. He shows that a detail that changes the meaning of a situation is not available through the analysis of an "egalitarian" distribution in a video recording. Rather, this is a "privileged" detail that is only available through the self-referential analysis carried out by a producer of details in the conditions of the event. Furthermore, Bjelic correctly points out that, from the perspective of the reader (the television audience in his case, the lawyer or the judge in ours), the potentially fabricated or simulated character of the event cannot be perceived, unless someone takes it upon himself to inform the reader (the interpreter himself in Bjelic's case, one of the protagonists in our cases).

relatively short and isolated sequences of interaction appears even when analysing linguistic exchanges. It also appears at the level of analysis carried out on the basis of a written text – even when that text corresponds word for word to the verbal exchange – thereby dissimulating important data relevant to the context. This problem finally appears at the level of what interaction can reveal only to a competent observer, i.e. someone with prior knowledge of the background expectations harboured by the various parties to the interaction. To shed light on the nature of these difficulties, this chapter sought to compare first-hand material, ethnographic notes, and accounts that insiders have given of their own work.

This ethnography of legal communication has limits, of course. While recognizing them, however, it is also important to see their advantages. First, there is the fact of inserting speech acts in a long sequence, whereas conversation analysis would tend to isolate them and consider only the properties they produce in the extremely limited space of interaction. By showing that the context is contextualized in a longer sequence, it becomes possible to restore a wider framework of relevance, one that overflows the space of interaction, while refraining from extending it to elements that would appear to belong to the scene, from outside, although they escape the attention, interest, and orientation of the protagonists. This method therefore allows us to combine elements of relevance as they appear in the interaction, but also as they underlie and orient it. Those that are manifest in interaction are translated in indexical interplays (the way people address each other, for instance), behaviour (posture and the attention it implies), and lexicon (the choice of which makes the register of interaction public and explicit). The elements underlying the interaction result from the total background knowledge necessary to the protagonists for acting in a given context and imbuing the situation with significance. The elements that orient interaction result from the specific end of that interaction, without which people would conceive of time as myriad discontinuous points and not as a succession of events.

Which context – Egyptian, local, judicial, or case-specific – is relevant? The question remains open. Indeed, it cannot be asked as a general question. The relevant context is the context that is important at a given time and place, in the protagonists' perspective, as they carry out their actions. It is therefore necessarily variable, although it is not necessarily multiple. Essentially, it is not opaque. Among the elements visible on a snapshot taken by an outside observer, the ones that are considered relevant by those present are usually quite easy to see, as long as one is willing to abandon the ironic gaze of the critical social sciences, and adopt the endogenous position of a normally competent person, acting in a more or less familiar world.

Chapter 5
Procedural Constraint: Sequentiality, Routine and Formal Correctness

Legal action is inscribed within an institutional context. This produces a number of constraining effects on the way that action is deployed, in its sequential organization and its orientation toward procedural correctness. Through the documents produced during the prosecutor's interrogations or the sentencing, as in interactions that take place during the investigation or the testimony of witnesses, it is possible to identify the ways that different parties to the trial manifest the particular dimension of the process in which they are engaged and the care they take in displaying its formal correctness. In that sense, procedural correctness refers to a series of achievements that are empirically observable and explicitly produced by the multiple parties to a trial.

We will discuss procedural constraint in three stages. First, we will examine the judicial sequence, its organization, and its effect on the accomplishment of legal activity (Dingwall, 1976). Second, we will focus on the way judicial clutter and the routinization of work can exert constraints on the performance of professionals engaged in administering a trial. Third, we will look at the methods utilized to produce correct procedure, in judicial interaction and in the production of different written documents that contribute to the formation of a sentence.

Orienting to the Sequentiality of a Trial

As Holstein (1993: 60) emphasizes, trials are inscribed in a sequence that acts as a framework; in it, the participants speak and act for all practical legal purposes, and in such a way as to manifest their competence. This sequence, far from being limited to a single judicial interaction, like a witness hearing for instance, spreads through a succession of stages, to which participants orient prospectively – in that they await, count on, and anticipate the accomplishment of these stages – and retrospectively – in that the accomplishment of these stages is a matter that participants must be able to corroborate, and whose non-occurrence they must be able to justify.

Thus, it is significant to examine judicial interactions in the context of Egyptian law, which may be attached schematically to continental legal traditions of the civil or Roman-Germanic type. In such systems, formal procedure is generally distinct from that followed in the common law system. In that sense, Paul Drew (1992: 470) might assert that, in the Anglo-American penal system, cross-examination is essentially contradictory; but in the civil system, one is forced to observe that the very principle of cross-examination does not really exist. This difference in procedural organization has enormous consequences on the forms of verbal expression and the ways in which such expression may be exploited. In matters of criminal law, the Egyptian judicial system follows the procedure of inquisition that is specific to legal systems in the continental tradition. This means that a deed with possible penal consequences is immediately referred to the prosecutor's office, which is the institution responsible for leading the investigation and the trial. In this context, the punishable act is, so to speak, withdrawn from the victim, who is no longer a party to the trial, and is replaced by the prosecutor's office. The victim is then no longer necessary, except as a witness. After the prosecutor has heard the various protagonists in the case, he establishes the facts and emits an initial judgment with regard to admissibility. It is therefore up to the prosecutor's office to file the case or, on the contrary, to refer it to trial. In theory, the prosecutor's representative (the prosecutor-general's deputy or substitute) provides for a verbatim transcription of the statements made before him by the various protagonists he has summoned for the trial. On that basis, he writes up a memorandum (titled "Inventory of the evidence" when he transmits it to the court). The court hears the prosecution and the defense, using this document as a reference, then deliberates and finally issues a sentence. The procedure is public at this stage, apart from the deliberations. According to the case, the court is made up of one or three judges. The court sessions are not transcribed. The sentence, on the other hand, is issued in writing.

Studying the process by which legality is produced therefore depends closely on the very nature of the procedure followed before judicial bodies. In the case at hand, two particularly important points deserve emphasis: the essentially written nature of the judicial process, and the very specific organization of auditions led by the prosecutor's office.

In penal law, the role of lawyers consists, first and foremost, of structuring the narrative of the client-protagonist in order to make it legally relevant. It is necessary to take into account the minimally interactive character of this operation. Initially, the lawyer may ask the client a number of questions that will allow him to construct a relevant narrative – which implies a reflexive form of interaction; but afterwards, the lawyer produces a global written and oral narrative that has been subjected to legal restructuring, and which makes it possible not only to orient the client but also to replace him before the magistrate. The lawyer intervenes only marginally, when his client is being questioned, in order to correct a point. We should also note that a criminal sentence is not delivered, in the Egyptian judicial system, by a judge and jury. This structural difference is essential to the analysis of the legalization process, for it implies that the conclusions reached in conversation analysis as applied to common law procedures must be adapted completely. Among other things, this implies that the study must be oriented to specific materials, which to our knowledge have not been used in conversationalist research. In addition, we can only use the conclusions reached in studies of cross-examination techniques and jury trials – to cite only two types of well-known research – indirectly and with circumspection. In the Egyptian judicial process, verbal interaction is quite weak on the whole: sometime, a precise question is directed at the defendant, the victim, or a witness; sometimes a plea is solicited from the lawyer, but generally such interaction is reduced to its simplest expression, due to the extreme overload on the courts (there are rarely fewer than 200 points of law to be dealt with during a single session, and sometimes more than 500). Deliberations are generally carried out on the basis of a draft decision drawn up by a magistrate and rarely discussed in detail among colleagues.

Furthermore, because the formal rules that organize his work, the prosecutor's deputy is obliged to carry out an interrogation whose content is transcribed verbatim by his secretary. It is important to note nevertheless that he generally does not proceed in exactly this manner. In most of the auditions we were able to attend, the interrogation was carried out in two stages. First, the deputy, after having confirmed the identity of the suspect, the victim, or the witness, requests a global narrative based on a general question like "What are the details of what you have admitted you did?" After having heard the narrative as a whole, without it being transcribed, the deputy then goes over it point by point, organizing it around a series of questions he is obliged to ask, according to the rules of his profession. This reconfiguration of the narrative around legally relevant questions is a fundamental element in the legalization process (see Chapter 7). Note that the interactive aspect of these auditions is more important than at the earlier (lawyer) and later (judge) levels of the judicial sequence. Also note the absence, at this stage and others, of any "overhearing audience" (Drew, 1992; 1997), i.e. of any silent audience addressed by the parties to the interaction beyond their direct verbal exchange. The different protagonists in the audition do not interact while simultaneously addressing a silent listener, as is the case in the cross-examination, which seeks to capture the jury's attention. As we were able to show in the preceding chapter, however, this remark must be nuanced if we agree to relocate the interaction in the framework of the criminal trial's long sequence. Indeed, we may consider that the protagonists – and especially the prosecutor's deputy, even more than those he is called upon to interrogate – are indirectly addressing a judge, who will later become acquainted with the facts as they are laid out in the investigation report, and who will pass the sentence on that basis. It would be more appropriate, therefore, to speak of an "overreading audience", i.e. a silent, absent reader whom the participants are addressing beyond their direct verbal exchange; a listener whose review of the case at hand is postponed to a later time.

Whether we regard it as part of the long or short sequence of judicial interaction, procedural constraint is a point to which actors orient when producing legality. The judge takes into account its inscription in the long sequence, as we see when we contrast, for example (cf. Dupret, 2000), the exceptional case of a magistrate who refused to apply Egyptian law under the pretext that it ran counter to *shari'a*, with the frequent situations where provisions specific to the *shari'a* are mentioned without challenging the positive provisions of Egyptian law and therefore opening the possibility to overturn the judgement on appeal for formal or legal reasons.

Excerpt 5 (Court of First Instance, 'Abdin, 8 March 1982, cited in Ghurab, 1986)

[...] Regarding the general application of laws, the theory of nullification means that, among the rules elaborated from positive law, all types combined, only those that agree with the texts of the *shari'a* will be applied. The [rules that] contravene these must be set aside completely; we must ignore them entirely, and restore to their rightful place, immediately and unreservedly, the rules of *shari'a*.

Regarding the application of *shari'a*, the nullification of positive law texts contrary to the *shari'a* means that the courts apply *shari'a* law texts with no need for intervention on the part of the legislative organ. On the contrary, nullification means that the People's Assembly is limited to the penalties restrictively defined by the *shari'a* in the new laws that it promulgates [...].

It is expected that the court will refer to the preceding rules [...] to establish the nullity of every law that contradicts the Divine Laws, foremost among them the penal provisions specific to this case. They are all absolutely null. They are void of reference to Divine Law [...].

The court considers that the Islamic penalty for inebriation is applicable, by virtue of what God revealed and what He transmitted through His Messenger (may God's blessings and peace be upon him). The guilt of the accused has been established in a convincing manner [...].

For these reasons,

1. The court, after a hearing, condemns the guilty party to 80 lashes of the whip. This is a binding sentence [...].
2. The court is in favour of conducting an equitable constitutional referendum carried out by the concerned parties and bearing on draft laws for penalties that are restrictively defined by the *shari'a* (*hudud*), the *lex talionis*, blood penalties, and the prohibition on usurious interest.
3. Anticipating the day when all judges will be discouraged from applying the laws that God revealed, the court demands that the President of the Republic promulgate laws on penalties restrictively defined by the *shari'a* (*hudud*). It also requests that the legislative authorities and anyone responsible for legislation in the country institute these as the laws that judges must follow and that the executive must apply.
4. We request that al-Azhar, the Ministry of Pious Endowments (*waqf*), the Institute for Islamic Legal Research (Dar al-Ifta'), and the media, each in its own field, petition the concerned parties to promulgate these laws. We ask that all draft Islamic laws be instituted, brought out of anonymity, and made perceptible, visible, binding, and applicable.
5. We ask the prosecutor-general to bring an authentic copy of this sentence, its articles and its provisions, to the attention of all those mentioned in the two preceding paragraphs.

It is reasonable to surmise that, when he emitted this sentence, which is contrary to the provisions of the Egyptian penal code, Justice Ghurab was seeking either to force acceptance of the primacy of *shari'a*, or to underline the Egyptian government's opposition to *shari'a* law. In all likelihood, he anticipated the possibility of seeing his verdict reversed in a court of appeal due to a legal deficiency, as manifested in the very form he gave the expected results (which resemble a political manifesto just as much as they do a judicial sentence). The following excerpt from an interview the judge granted to a newspaper called *al-Umma al-Islamiyya* in August 1983 confirms this expectation.

Press excerpt 6 (al-Umma al-Islamiyya, August 1983, cited in Ghurab, 1986)
Calmly and firmly, the judge added: 'First, I must tell you clearly that the idea never crossed my mind, as I was writing up this verdict, that it would be applied. I know very well that the verdict will not be applied. This is why I said that I was placing the burden of non-implementation on the qualified authorities. It is not my duty to execute the judgment. My duty is to promulgate that which will satisfy God…'

For the record, the sentence was indeed overturned on appeal. Justice Ghurab was subjected to disciplinary sanctions and transferred to a non-litigious administration.

Excerpt 6 (Judicial remonstrance 5-81/1982, cited in Ghurab, 1986)
In the name of God, the Merciful, the Compassionate

[…] It emerges from an examination of the verdict passed in case 165 of 1982 that the prosecutor-general held the accused guilty of having been apprehended in a state of manifest inebriation in public, and asked that he be punished according to articles 1, 2, and 7 of law 63/1976. In this case, dated 8 March 1982, you uttered a binding sentence after the hearing, condemning the guilty party to 80 lashes. Among the motives for this verdict, after the accusation was qualified and the prosecutor-general requested the sentence according to the abovementioned articles, we may note that 'the guilt of the accused has been established by virtue of his confession […] and the sum total of repressive provisions are absolutely null and void. They are devoid of references to Divine Law. Judgment will be issued not in implementation of [these repressive provisions], but in implementation of articles 1, 2, and 324 of the draft law submitted by the High Commission of the Ministry of Justice regarding penalties restrictively defined by the *shari'a* (*hudud*), and applying to the consumption of alcohol, presented to the People's Assembly on 17 June 1976.'

The following criticism is levelled against this judgment:

It is established that no punishment may be pronounced without a law, that a crime only exists if the act was committed after the law was promulgated, and that penalties are limited to that period. This is not the case in the sentence passed inflicting a whipping on the guilty party. The sentence therefore contravenes the law, and this renders it null and void.

The First Commission […] has decided as follows:

The issuing of a judicial remonstrance, in the abovementioned form, against the president of the Southern Cairo court of first instance, Mahmud 'Abd al-Hamid Ghurab.

The anticipation of subsequent control, of an "audience looking over your shoulder", is particularly clear in this type of attitude, which seeks precisely to depart from legality. Against the backdrop of this disruptive attitude, it is easier to see in the decisions invoking the existence of the *shari'a* but refraining from using it to replace positive law, the orientation of professional actors to this virtual audience and to the later stages of the judicial sequence. This, indeed, was Justice Ghurab's position on several decisions that pre-date his 1982 verdict, where he exposed the contradictions between the brand of Islamic law he was advocating and the type of positive law he was criticizing, while still opting, *in fine*, to apply positive law.

> **Excerpt 7 (Summary Court, Sanuris, 17 May 1979, cited in Ghurab, 1986)**
> [...] Seeing as the last of God's Prophets and Messengers said 'all alcohol is wine and any wine is forbidden'; and since the accused put alcoholic beverages on public sale at a time and in a place that are specified in the file, thereby contravening God's religion and illustrious law; and given that the penalty in such cases is 50 to 70 lashes of the whip [...];
> Seeing as the court has asked repeatedly and persistently for this binding Islamic penalty to be applied, and has never failed to advise that the penalties restrictively defined by the *shari'a* be codified [...],
> Since this is the situation, and since article 2 of the Constitution stipulates that Islam is the state religion and that the principles of Islamic *shari'a* are a main source of legislation [...],
> For these reasons,
> The court condemns the accused, in his presence, to six months' prison with forced labour, a 200-pound fine, and 200 pounds in compensation.

The parties to the judicial action also situate their actions in a short sequence. Thus, the inquiry carried out by a prosecutor's deputy or a police officer always begins by the secretary asking the accused, the victim, or the witness, who has been shown into the office, to present his or her ID. In the interrogation report, this brief interaction takes the following form:

> **Excerpt 8 (Prosecutor's office, case 6953, 1997, Sahil, Cairo)**
> [...] and, taking advantage of the presence of the witness Muhammad Fadil Mahmud al-Wakil outside the interrogation room, we called him in and undertook to question him in the following manner.
> He replied:
> My name is Muhammad Fadil al-Wakil, age 67, retired and residing at 41 'Abd al-Khaliq Wasfi Street. I have a family ID, number 20081 civilian al-Qanatir al-Khayriyya.
> (oath)

Next, the deputy – although some delegate this task to their secretary – undertakes to provide a summary description of the physical appearance of the accused and the clothes he or she is wearing.

Excerpt 9 (Prosecutor's office, case 3459, 2000, Zaqaziq 2)

[...] we called [the accused] in and, having examined him, found a man of 40, of average height, with a golden complexion, black hair, white shoes, a light moustache and beard, wearing western (*ifrinjiyya*) clothes: an olive sweater over a dark blue shirt, black jeans, brown shoes[1] and white socks.

Finally, the deputy begins the interrogation proper with a formula like "What are the details of the act you have confessed to committing?"

Excerpt 10 (Prosecutor's office, case 3459, 2000, Zaqaziq 2)

My name is Mu'min Sa'd al-Din Muhammad Hamdi, age 38, engineer and owner of a computer store on Mugamma' al-Masalih al-Hukumiyya Street, residing in Kafr al-Zand, Mansur Street, Block 60 B, first district of Zaqaziq, type B driver's license number 22264, Sharqiyya Traffic Department, expiring on 23/7/2007.
Question: What do you have to say with regard to what you are accused of, i.e. that you forced the victim, Amir Sabir, to sign two blank pieces of paper [...]?

This stereotypical organization by which the interrogation is launched manifests the orientation of the deputy (or the policeman) and his secretary to the accomplishment of a set legal task, where it is important to mark the beginning in order to single it out from the multitude of other interactions that may be carried out in the same office where this interaction is taking place. The sequence that consists of recording the identity of the accused, describing him, and asking him an initial, standard question indicates to the participants that what will now be said is written down and granted legal value. The transcription of the operation targets a future reader of the case, and demonstrates that the required procedures have been carried out properly.[2]

Constraints of Judicial Routine and Clutter

The routine character of judicial activity exercises a constraint on a magistrate's ability to do his work. Work overloads increase this constraint further. Here, we find echoes of what Emerson (1983) calls the holistic effects of the decision-making process, i.e. that which, in the participants' orientation to judicial interaction, refers a case under examination to a "whole" that is larger than just the case at hand, but is at the same time specific to the organizational context in which that case is situated.

Professionals tend to accumulate know-how and develop expectations as to the specific attributes of the different types of cases they encounter. Once these cases are subjected to categorization, once they are considered typical, they are dealt with in a more routine manner. Even cases that seem particularly important enter into this routine, and their "serious" character is in turn made part of a routine. The

1 Sic! It was just said the line before that the shoes were white.
2 On the structure of the interrogation, see also Chapter 12.

following text, in which a prosecutor's deputy accounts for the modes of acquisition of magistrates' professional behaviour, will illustrate this point (Rady, 2000):

> At the beginning of his professional career, the prosecutor's deputy is not required to know anything about the way the prosecutor's office works or the applicable laws. This is a well-known fact for the prosecutor-general's staff in Egypt. Recruits have no professional qualification, apart from those among them who have already worked as policemen for a year or two, and thereby gained knowledge of a number of procedures that relate to the organization of police stations and the transcription of reports [...]. Furthermore, we must note that all the deputies need, in terms of substantive legal knowledge, is limited to the provisions of the Penal Code, the Code of Penal Procedure, and the Instructions to the Prosecutor-General. After a year in the prosecutor's office, the new deputy will have realized that everything he learned in law school was useless as far as being a good deputy is concerned. This is because most of the prosecutor's work has to do with procedural, rather than substantive, rules. To shed light on this, we may divide up the different activities that constitute the deputy's work, and examine, for each, the rules he must know. First, there are the interrogations. Here, the deputy only needs to know the penal provisions that allow him to suggest a correct legal qualification of the crime. Second, he must attend court sessions. This is just a matter of correct behaviour, because the prosecutor's report no longer exists. Third, there are relations with the police. Only procedural rules that affect oversight of work in the police stations and the transfer of cases from the police to the prosecutor are at stake here. Fourth, there is the examination of trials. Here again, procedural and professional rules dominate. Fifth, there is the need to submit cases to the relevant courts of law. This is probably the only time when knowledge of criminal law is necessary, since it is important to characterize an action correctly, but on the whole there are few of these rules [...]. Although the deputy's jurisdiction gives him access to different legal authorities, he generally does not waste his time investigating, except rarely, if he is preparing a report or dealing with a new and complicated case. There are actually specific decisions for each type of crime, and the deputy systematically bases his accusations on these. He keeps a written copy of them so as not to waste his time in pointless investigations. In most cases, former deputies pass down these decisions, which means that they are not necessarily new or even adapted to the problems that new magistrates have to deal with. Therefore, deputies often make do with the experience of their predecessors [...]. All the references cited (Penal Code, Code of Penal Procedure, Instructions to the Prosecutor-General) are insufficient when measured against the practical problems that arise in the course of work. This is where professional norms appear: norms that emerge from practice, making it possible to deal with new situations. These are rules on how to write up an interrogation, questions relevant to each type of interrogation, and procedures to follow in order to close a case.

Generally, the way of dealing with cases has a lot to do with the available means and the caseload. In all likelihood, changes at this level result in modifications to the categorizations carried out by professionals. Thus, a drop in resources or an increase in the overload generally leads to a shift in the threshold above which a case is reviewed substantively and with closer attention. The account of the same deputy refers to this type of phenomenon (Rady, 2000):

> Before, the head of the prosecution office to which the new deputy was assigned used to play a major role in his career and professional training, so much so that the deputy would be marked for his whole life by the personality of his first boss. Today, this role has been greatly reduced, and as a result the knowledge acquired at the beginning remains superficial and insufficient to launch one's career properly. This trend is due to the fact that the prosecution no longer has time to devote to new deputies. The number of trials has increased, as has the load of administrative work. We might add that in the 1960s and '70s, the prosecution had no more than four deputies to organize, whereas now there are a dozen. The consequence is that the prosecution must increase its supervision work.

Another result of the judicial overload is that the attention given to a case is estimated not according to the case's intrinsic importance, but rather in relation to what seems reasonable relative to the other cases the prosecution has before it. This is what Emerson (1983: 439) calls the specific effects of the workload. Note that this is not a factor whose relevance is supposed beforehand, but rather a constraint to which professionals orient explicitly (Garfinkel, 1967). In another account, regarding the empirical differences in the content of verdicts issued by first and second instance judges when dealing with the same case, Rady (2002) accounts for the way a professional understands workload-specific constraints.

> The question is not whether a judge has superior legal knowledge to his colleagues; in any case, this is very exceptional. The empirical difference in the content of decisions has to do with two main factors. First, second-tier jurisdictions are normally made up of four judges, while first-tier jurisdictions have only one. The numerical superiority of second-degree formations can partially explain the fact that they do a better job of administering justice. Each judge's knowledge completes that of the others. Each, through his professional experience, has acquired knowledge that his colleagues do not share. They exchange information during deliberations, before handing in the verdict. This type of consolidation of legal knowledge is not accessible to the single first-tier judge, who has only himself to rely on. Furthermore, second-tier judges are specialized in reviewing cases that have already been judged. Their work therefore always consists of verifying the validity of sentences rendered in the first instance, and this is why they have experience detecting irregularities that can invalidate these sentences. There is also the enormous number of cases that a judge in a court of first instance must deal with. Sometimes he sees over 200 cases in a single session. This can prevent him from examining the cases for which he is responsible correctly. This certainly contributes to increasing the number of verdicts that can be overturned on appeal. On the other hand, this is

> not the case in jurisdictions of the second instance. The agenda for an appeal court with regard to misdemeanours ranges from 70 to 100 cases, and the burden for reviewing each is shared among several judges. The overload factor is independent of the judges' legal knowledge, but it contributes directly and effectively to the problem of jurisdictional dysfunction.

As Emerson points out (1983: 442), the fact that a professional brings up consequences of a work overload fulfils several objectives. It can serve to recognize the gap between what should be done in such a case and what was actually done. In so doing, the agent testifies to the primacy of organizational objectives precisely as he is violating their specific provisions (Zimmerman, 1970; Emerson and Pollner, 1976). This can also serve to justify measures that have already been taken. In that sense, if someone has followed inappropriate provisions, he has done so for "good reasons" or "rational" reasons.

Emerson also speaks of the partial effects of the workload. Typically, professionals orient to segments of their total workload, according to the immediate relevance these segments might have in relation to a precise, urgent organizational task (Emerson, 1983: 442). Rady (2000) identifies this constraint when he brings up the problem of bringing in new deputies at a time when judicial statistics are being compiled.

> Finally, we should emphasize that most of the substitutes are given their appointments in May or June, the period when biannual judicial statistics are compiled, and when neither the prosecution nor the senior deputies have "the time to look under their feet".

Finally, we should point out that the acquisition of legal knowledge is largely a matter of professional routine, as Rady's account (2000) proves:

> A question that sometimes preoccupies new deputies has to do with the fact that different professional norms are not codified. They are passed on from one generation to the next as a function of the confidence that newbies have in their elders. This raises the problem of how to find the norm. Furthermore, norms are sometimes based on erroneous principles, which does not prevent their being passed from one deputy to the other, without being verified. Then they become a practical reality. It happens that senior substitutes might doubt the validity of information they are passing on, but, rather than revealing their ignorance and risking their reputation, they persist and assure the new deputy that this is indeed the correct rule. Another difficulty arises from the disparities between these norms. If the new deputy asks one colleague, he will get one answer; if he then asks another, he will get a different one [...]. As a counsellor said, the prosecution's work depends a great deal on the street smarts (*fahlawa*) of the deputy [...].

> In Egypt, a deputy who has just been assigned a post has to attend a hearing in a correctional tribunal once a week and in a criminal court once a month. Officially, he does so to represent the prosecution and uphold the accusation. The main reason, however, is to strengthen the deputy's legal knowledge. During the hearings, he listens to the lawyers' defense and sees them challenge charges or accusations. This gives the deputy the opportunity to discover the mistakes the prosecution can make, especially when the judge confirms the lawyer's point of view. Sometimes, he can also hear about a rule of law or a jurist's decision he didn't know about [...]. Let's take an example: a rape trial with charges brought by a deputy. Before the court, the defendant's lawyer accuses the deputy of having brought an incomplete case, without having questioned the victim or any witnesses. The judge acquits the defendant. In this case, the deputy realizes the mistake he's made. He won't make it again, because he's embarrassed himself. Here's another example, which Samih Midhat, a new deputy, recounted: "A lawyer is defending his client in the case of a check. During the trial, he submits to the judge a new jurisprudential decision that voids all handwritten checks prior to the adoption of the new Commercial Code. The judge verifies the decision and immediately acquits the accused. I didn't know about this jurisprudence, and when I went back to the prosecution I talked about it with my colleagues. They didn't have the faintest idea about it either. After a week, that jurisprudence had spread among the deputies like wildfire."

In conclusion, we should emphasize everything that the accomplishment of a professional's legal work owes to its insertion in a bureaucratic, routine setting. In that sense, it is not possible to account for a decision in isolation. On the contrary, every decision is integrated in a wider framework, which includes a number of other cases to deal with and certain empirically developed techniques to deal with them. It is impossible to examine a decision independently of the way in which those participating in the procedure orient to the constraints specific to the acquisition and implementation of their knowledge.

Procedural Correctness

A professional who is engaged in routine professional work orients, very generally, to the public production of the fact that he is carrying out his work correctly. This is expressed in his search for a dual form of procedural correction: writing down the accomplishment of the various procedures, on one hand, and writing the judgment, on the other. Affirming that procedure is important in law may seem trivial to a jurist. This, however, does not dispense us from examining closely the way people manifest their practical understanding of this importance. Our examination must necessarily take place through a detailed description of the praxeology of the production and manifestation of contextualized procedure, because such procedural constraints, to which actors orient explicitly, do not correspond neatly to a set of abstract rules drawn from an external, historical, overhanging legal system. Rather, they correspond to the routine, bureaucratic performance of the legal professions (Dingwall, 1976; Lynch, 1997).

Most of the documents in a judicial dossier translate the orientation of judges, prosecutors, and other professionals to procedural correctness. This seems to be linked directly to the general sequence of judgment, in which the participants address people who are not necessarily physically present in the room, but constitute an audience that overhears or oversees, so to speak, and that is virtually capable of invalidating a procedure on an irregularity ("overreading audience"; see above and Chapter 4). Take the example of a rape case brought by the prosecution. Among other things, the file contains interrogations carried out by the deputy, the report reconstituting the crime, and the forensic assessment. This set of documents is synthesized in an "Inventory of Evidence".

Excerpt 11 (Prosecution, case 276, 1985, Ma'adi)

Opening of the report today 20/1/1985, noon, general office of the prosecution.

In the abovementioned position, including the secretary of the investigation, Tag al-Din Hasan.

Given that it emerged from annex 40 dated 19/1/1985, written up by Colonel 'Abd al-Mun'im Radwan, police inspector in Masr al-Qadima, that after speaking with the victim, he undertook to order an initial investigation and carry it out and that, when officers occupied the buildings in which the garages of the Digla and New Ma'adi areas are located, they found a Renault taxi with five people inside it, bearing the number 54990-Cairo Taxi, near Road 216, in Digla; they walked towards the car and were surprised when they tried to flee the scene. The officers undertook to make them exit the car after having observed that one of them corresponded to Salah Shawqi 'Ali Halawa, on police file for dangerous burglary, who was carrying a knife while attempting to flee. They undertook to summon the five individuals. It came about that the abovementioned was wearing a wristwatch corresponding to the characteristics of the one whose theft the victim reported. Asked where it came from, he admitted that he and his four colleagues had committed the acts. They then undertook to arrest them [...].

An examination of the records of the suspects in the files of the criminal police showed that the first was classified "dangerous" while the other accused had records. The stolen objects presented in consignment reports 1/9, 2/9, 3/9, and 4/9 were seized.

Object 1/9 [...]

Taking advantage of the defendants' presence, as detainees, outside the room where the investigation was taking place, we called them in and asked them to respond to the accusations against them, after having informed them that the prosecution was opening an investigation against them. They all admitted [having taken cognizance of this] and we asked them if they had a representative appearing with them for the investigation procedure. They replied in the negative. We made all the detainees leave the room, apart from the first. Upon examination, he was revealed to be a young man in his 30s, around 1.70m in height, of average girth, dark-skinned, and wearing a blue suit with checks at the bottom and a blue pullover. We undertook to question him in detail and he replied:

A: Anwar Isma'il 19 years of age warehouse janitor residing in 'Izbat (?)
Q: What are the details of what you admit to having done [...]
Q: Did you agree to pick up any woman on the road [...]
Q: What are the details of what you admit to having done [...]
Q: Did you agree to pick up any woman on the road [...]
Q: What are the sexual acts you committed upon the (female) victim [...]
Q: Was the girl in this situation of her own volition [...]
Q: Did the (female) victim go with you to the place where the (female) victim was attacked of her own volition [...]
Q: You are accused of participating with others in kidnapping and rape with use of force what do you have to say [...]
Q: You are also accused of participating with others in the abovementioned rape with use of force what do you have to say [...]
Q: You are also accused of participating with others in kidnapping and illegal detention what do you have to say [...]
Q: Do you have a record [...]
Q: Do you have anything else to say [...]

End of the interview with the accused Anwar.

Next we put aside this suspect and called the second into the room where the investigation is being carried out. Upon examination, we found a young man in his early 30s, around 1.70 m high, with short black hair, a golden complexion, wearing a windbreaker that was originally yellow, lemon-yellow trousers, and black shoes. Then we undertook to interrogate him in detail about the following:

A: My name is Salah Shawqi 'Ali Halawa 20 years of age driver residing in Digla in Ma'adi at number 23 in the Officers' Buildings in Ma'adi
Q: What are the details of what you admit having done

There are two parts to this document. The first summarizes the conditions in which the police became aware of the facts, led an investigation, drew up a police report, and transferred the case to the prosecution, which opened its own investigation, consisting of reviewing the police report and any evidence joined to it. The second part is a word-for-word transcript of the interrogation of the suspects. The first demonstrates that all the operations carried out by the police were procedurally impeccable: complaint filed, approved police operation, suspects apprehended due to abnormal behaviour, external signs of guilt, confessions, detailed description of the facts resulting from the confessions, and seizure of stolen goods. The second aims to prove that the interrogations were produced in conformity with the rules; as Sharrock and Watson (1990: 236) emphasize, 'if one wants the recording to serve showing that one has proceeded as required, one must act so as to make the recording satisfy the requirements any justification before a court may impose.' Hence the concern with carrying out an interrogation articulated around the questions of "who" (identity of the suspect), "what" (the facts), "how" (the modalities), and "why" (the motives), as well as the explicit enunciation, in the conclusion, of the charges ("you are accused of..."), while respecting the rights of the defence ("do you have anything else to say") (cf. Mellinger, 1992).

As for the "Inventory of Evidence", it is a document that summarizes the investigation led by the prosecution, the means by which the accusation is founded, and the case against the accused. The prosecution asks the criminal jurisdiction to reach a decision based on this document.

Excerpt 12 (Prosecution, case 276, 1985, Ma'adi)
In the name of God, the Compassionate, the Merciful
Southern Cairo Prosecution
Miss [...; identity, age, status, residence] testifies that [...; date, circumstances, facts (rape + theft + beating and bodily harm)]
M. [...; identity, age, status, residence] testifies to the content of the testimony of the first (female) witness and adds that [...; additional facts (theft + beating and bodily harm)].
Observations
The first suspect recounted [...] that he had agreed with the second, third, fourth, and fifth suspects that they would kidnap any woman they met and rape her [...].
The second suspect recounted [...] the same as the first [...]. He admitted [... facts (theft + sexual aggression)].
The third suspect admitted [...] the same as the first and added [...; facts (sexual aggression)].
The fourth suspect admitted [...] the same as the first and added [...; facts (sexual aggression)].
The fifth suspect admitted [...] the same as the first and added [...; facts (sexual aggression + premeditation)].
The sixth suspect admitted [...] that he knew that [... collusion ...] and that he received [...; payment for his collusion].
[...; stolen goods] were seized from the sixth suspect, and [...; evidence] was seized in his home.
On the first suspect, at the time of his arrest, [...; weapon, stolen object, sum of money] were seized. On the second suspect, at the time of his arrest, [...; weapon, sum of money] were confiscated.
It emerged from the medical report concerning the (male) victim [...] that the examination he underwent resulted in a diagnosis of [...; lesion showing beating and wounding].
The forensic expert's report concludes that the examination of the (female) victim shows [...] the existence [...; lesion showing beating and wounding]. It also emerges objectively from the examination that she [...; virginity, medical justification]. Analysis of [...; exhibit] belonging to the (female) victim as well as [...; exhibit] as [...; material evidence] confirms [...; sexual aggression].
The female doctor [...], coroner, testified [...] that [...; likelihood of sexual aggression despite there being no physical traces].

> It emerges from the initial medical report that [the second] suspect [...] is over 18 years of age.
> Written on 12 February 1985
> Head of the Southern Cairo Prosecution [...]

This document, too, shows how the deputy produces a narrative organized around the testimony of the main victim, completed by that of the second victim, that of the suspects, and that of the forensic expert, for a later reader: the judge. These testimonies, together, are organized in such a way as to testify to the correct accomplishment of procedural requirements related to, among other things, identity, age, status, residence, date, circumstances, facts, the action or participation of each protagonist, stolen goods and their characteristics, exhibits, evidence, and even justifications for the possible lack of evidence.

Producing a procedurally impeccable document therefore clearly constitutes one of the priorities to which law professionals orient, and this is expressed to all practical and public ends in the production of accounts (police reports, prosecution investigation reports, medical reports) and in the organization of interrogations or, retrospectively, in the sentence itself. Let us take an example drawn from judging practices in a personal status case.

In Egypt, personal status matters are organized through a series of laws, essentially laws 25/1920 and 25/1929, both amended by laws 100/1985 and 1/2000. In the absence of explicit legislative provisions, law 1/2000 stipulates that the judge must refer to 'the leading opinion in the tradition of the Imam Abu Hanifa'. In practice, given the prevailing uncertainty, many judges still use the unofficial codification carried out by Qadri Pasha (1347 A.H.), a compilation of provisions inspired by the Hanafi school, or by other works explaining the laws and systematizing jurisprudence. Ever since Egypt's courts and tribunals were brought together in a centralized national system, personal status has been subject to rules of procedure that are common to all civil and commercial matters. Cases are initially examined by summary tribunals (*mahkama guz'iyya*) or courts of first instance (*mahkama ibtida'iyya kulliyya*), according to the nature of the dispute and the sum of money involved. Tribunals are made up of divisions, among them the personal status division (*da'irat al-ahwal al-shakhsiyya*), which has jurisdiction over financial matters (*wilaya 'ala al-mal*) as well as non-financial ones (*wilaya 'ala al-nafs*) related to personal status (marriage, divorce, inheritance, paternity). This is the case in our example, one of judicial divorce on grounds of prejudice, ruled on according to article 6 of law 25/1929. This article stipulates:

> If the wife claims that her husband mistreated her in such a way that it becomes impossible for people of their social status to continue marital relations, she may ask the judge to separate them, after which the judge will grant her an irrevocable divorce if it is established that reconciliation is impossible. If, however, he [i.e. the husband] refuses her request and she subsequently repeats her allegation without

> prejudice having been established, the judge will designate two arbitrators and rule according to the provisions of articles 7, 8, 9, 10, and 11 [of the same law].[3]

Whether or not a lawyer represents her, once a woman submits a request to the judge requesting that he pronounce a divorce on the grounds of the prejudice inflicted upon her by her husband, the judge's work is constrained – at least formally – by the various elements of this legislative provision. A sequential process is begun, and through it the judge goes through a series of stages before arriving at his decision. This appears in the way the sentence is constructed.

Excerpt 13 (Court of First Instance, case 701, 1983, Personal Status, Giza)
"In the name of God, the Compassionate, the Merciful"
In the name of the people
Court of First Instance, Giza, for personal status in cases involving persons
Sentence
During the public session held in the courthouse on Monday [...]
His Excellency Mr. [...], president of the tribunal, presiding
With the participation of Mr. [...], president of the tribunal, and Mr. [...], judge
In the presence of Mr. [...], deputy for the prosecution
In the presence of Mr. [...], secretary
The following sentence was issued
In case 701 of 1983, plenary, Giza personal status, submitted by
[...] against [...]
The court
After having heard the complaint, examined the documents, and deliberated:
Given that the cause and the means, as they appear to the court from the evidence, [show] that the plaintiff has presented a form signed by a lawyer and registered with the secretary of this court on [...], and has legally requested a judgment finalizing an irrevocable judicial divorce, which prevents her husband from forcing her to return [to the marriage], on [the basis of] prejudice resulting from 1) impotence, which cannot satisfy the aims of marriage; 2) the violence he [exercises] against her through beatings, insults, mistreatment, and accusations [...] [1]
Given that the request was suspended as indicated in the minutes of the hearing; during the session held on [...], this court handed in a judgment asking the forensic expert to examine the defendant, and the court made the forensic expert's report public in its judgment. [2]
Given that His Excellency the forensic expert carried out the medical examination of the defendant and his report was attached to the case file; it is dated [...] and it concludes that [...] [3]
Given that the parties appeared [in court] after the report was submitted and introduced as evidence; neither of the parties objected to the report or opposed it. [4]

3 On the notion of prejudice in personal status law, cf. Naveh, 2002.

Given that the case was heard at the following sessions. On […], the court handed in a judgment requesting that every means of proof be used to reexamine the existence of the moral prejudice that [she suffered]; the defendant must oppose this [judgment] by the same means. [5]

Given that the court undertook to carry out the investigation, after which it heard the plaintiff's two witnesses […]

The court also heard the defendant's two witnesses […] [6]

Given that the court, after hearing the witnesses […], postponed the arguments to the session of […] [7]

Given that the court offered reconciliation to the parties several times; that the plaintiff's representative refused while the defendant accepted. [8]

Given that the prosecutor-general, represented by its deputy, who attended the hearings, has presented an opinion to the court. [9]

Given that the parties requested sentencing; the court then set the sentence for the session of […] and decided to defer explanation of the motives for the sentence to today's session, in order to complete its deliberation. [10]

Given that, when the court offered the parties reconciliation […]; this was interpreted by the court as meaning that reconciliation was impossible. […] [12]

Given that, in light of the above, the plaintiff's representative refused reconciliation; the court was then led to proceed. [13]

Given that, as is clear in article 6 of binding decree 25 of 1929 concerning certain provisions specific to repudiation, Egyptian legislators demand, in order for the judge to be authorized to pronounce a sentence of judicial divorce on grounds of prejudice, that […] [14]

Given that Egyptian legislators took (*naqala*) the rule for judicial divorce on grounds of prejudice from the doctrine of Imam Malik […] [15]

Given that Hanafi doctrine makes the acceptance of testimony concerning the rights of believers conditional upon its concordance with the plea […] [16]

Given that, with regard to the first means of plea, the forensic expert established that […] [17]

Given that, with regard to the second means of plea, to wit the violence exercised against her through beatings and insult, her two witnesses [those of the plaintiff] testified that […] [18]

Given that, in light of the preceding, the court is aware that to pursue their conjugal life […] would be to commit an injustice against her, […] the court has no choice but to grant her judicial divorce. The prosecutor-general does not oppose this and, on the contrary, rendered an opinion identical to that of the court. [20]

Given that, in light of the preceding, the court pronounces a verdict of judicial divorce for the plaintiff from her husband on grounds of prejudice. [21]

Given that expenses […] [22]

Given that, with regard to urgent execution, […] [23]

For all these reasons,

> In [the parties'] presence, the court pronounces the judicial divorce of [...] from her husband [...], [in the form] of an irrevocable divorce, and requires the defendant to pay expenses [...] and rejects other demands.
> Secretary
> President of the tribunal

The legislative rule formulated in article 6 constrains sentencing in a judicial divorce case on grounds of prejudice to follow a pattern of "request – establishment of prejudice – attempt at reconciliation – judgment". The sentence, however, reveals an internal structure, which may be summarized schematically as follows:

1. introduction
2. request [given 1]
3. procedure followed by the tribunal [givens 2 to 10]
    - expert opinion [2-4]
    - proof of prejudice [5]: witness testimony [6]
    - pleas [7]
    - attempts at reconciliation [8]
    - prosecution's opinion [9]
    - fixing and issuing of the sentence [10]
4. examination of legal means [11-16]
    - reminder of the means invoked by the plaintiff [11]
    - attempt at reconciliation and failure [12-13]
    - concept of prejudice in Egyptian law [14-15]
    - testimony in personal status cases [16-17]
5. application of law to the facts of the cause [18-21]
    - first means: impotence [18]
    - second means: violence [19]
    - conclusion of the court [20-21]
6. expenses and associated demands
7. sentence

Although the judge formalizes this sequence in the form of a judgment, it reflects the real procedural constraints under which he operates. One of his main tasks, as a professional engaged in his activity in a routine manner, is to manifest publicly the correct accomplishment of his work. The production of a procedurally impeccable judgment is one of these priorities, and this is demonstrated publicly through the recapitulation that the judge carries out of all the stages that must necessarily be carried out and that have been effectively accomplished. At this procedural level, it is clear that the judge orients exclusively to the technical aspects of Egyptian procedural law. These aspects might include a reference to provisions that are explicitly connected to Hanafi or Maliki jurisprudence, but, as our example shows, with regard to witnesses in cases of judicial divorce on grounds of prejudice (givens 15 and 16), this always occurs through the provisions of Egyptian law, possibly as interpreted by the Court of Cassation.

Excerpt 14 (Court of First Instance, case 701, 1983, Personal Status, Giza)
Given that Egyptian legislators took the rule on judicial divorce on grounds of prejudice from the doctrine of Imam Malik – may God be pleased with him. It is not permitted, when establishing [prejudice], [to refer] to this doctrine, from which it is imported, and no rule has been stipulated for its establishment. In such a case, in order to prove prejudice, we must return to the majority opinion in the school of Imam Abu Hanifa al-Nu'man, in accordance with article 280 of the Regulations for *Shari'a* Tribunals, to which article 6 of law 462 or 1955 refers (Cass., Personal Status, appeal 11, 48th judicial year, session of 25 April 1979). In consequence, prejudice is established by proof through testimony (*bi-l-bayyina*): to wit, the testimony of two men or of a man and two women. Oral testimony is not acceptable to establish it, even though it is authorized in certain matters other than repudiation on grounds of prejudice (appeal 65, 52nd judicial year, session of 12 March 1984; cf. also the Compendium of Personal Status for Muslims by Counselor Nasr al-Gindi, ed. of the Judges' Association, commentary on article 6 of legal decree 25 of 1929).

Most of the documents in a judicial file show this orientation of judges, prosecutors, and other professionals to procedural correctness. This is due to the way the process is inscribed in a long sequence, and oriented to silent or absent audiences (cf. above; cf. also Chapter 4 and Drew, 1992 and 1997). The potential invalidation of a judgment that such an audience could subsequently effect is directly taken into account by the participants, and translated in the very conditioned attitude they adopt relative to the procedures they are required to follow. These procedural constraints are not considered elements imported from some external, historical, or overhanging legal system. Rather, they represent the direct, evident, real, practical dimensions of the daily bureaucratic routine for persons in today's Egypt, engaged in a variety of professional legal activities. This is perfectly well illustrated by the general structure of the forensic scientist's report.

Excerpt 15 (Forensics, case 701, 1983, Personal Status, Giza)
In the name of God, the Compassionate, the Merciful
Ministry of Justice
Giza Forensics Department / 84
Forensic report
Case 701, Giza Plenary, year 84
By virtue of the decision taken by the personal status tribunal (persons [i.e. the chamber with jurisdiction over matters affecting the administration of persons]), I examined the case file transferred to us by [the court] in this case. I also examined the defendant [...] in order to show whether he suffers from impotence preventing him from carrying out his matrimonial duties, and to evaluate such impotence, if exists, determining when it began and whether it can be treated. I report the following:

> First: circumstances of the case […]
> Second: procedures
> We have examined the case file transferred to us by the court in this case and set the date of […] for the appointment intended to accomplish it. We informed the parties to the litigation of this by registered letter, which I sent before the legally stipulated deadline.
> On the set date, the plaintiff […] was present […].
> The defendant […] was also present.
> The two expressed mutual recognition at the session. We reported this.
> Third: the forensic examination […]
> Opinion:
> In light of this, we consider that:
> The examination of […] reveals that he seems in normal health […]
> His medical examination does not show that he suffers from any pathological […] problem […]
> We consider that the defendant […] might suffer from […] psychological impotence […]
> It is well known that […] it is not possible to predict a time frame for a cure. [….]
> Handed in on […]   High representative of forensic experts

Besides the substantive foundation of prejudice, to which the physician is supposed to testify (cf. Chapter 6), the general structure of this document shows different things:

1. The report is an achievement in and of itself. In this report, the forensic expert produces all the characteristics that manifest the fact that he is acting as an expert and that he masters the formal, procedural, and medical technical aspects allowing him to produce a document titled "Forensic Medicine Report".
2. This report is part of a global procedure. It mentions the fact that it is integrated in a wider procedure, followed in the trial of a case that the court referred to the forensic expert, asking him to give an expert opinion on the subject of the husband's presumed impotence, on the basis of which the court is going to issue its sentence.
3. This report anticipates future uses that the court may make of it. It broaches all the questions the judge might consider relevant, to wit: the defendant's general health, his medical record, etc. More importantly, it gives the judge the possible qualification of a state that cannot be subjected to clinical examination: the husband's "psychological impotence". It is interesting to note that the forensic physician suggests this qualification as a possible explanation, without concluding that it is proven unambiguously, and yet the court goes on to base its verdict on this opinion as if it were a scientifically established fact. This leads us to discuss legal relevance, the topic of the following chapter.

Chapter 6

Legal Relevance: The Production of Factuality and Legality

Legal relevance refers to a characterization process that consists of making a factual situation correspond to a formal legal definition. Professionals' work is very largely made of the formalization of categories that are enunciated in the narratives of facts elaborated by the parties to a trial. In other words, writing up a trial responds to a formal requirement – the ascription of legal consequence to an action – that does not necessarily corresponds to the protagonists' orientation. In this chapter, we seek to describe the process of legal abstraction in which professionals are engaged, and the implied transformation of factual statements as formulated by lay participants in a judicial interaction.

Judicial Syllogism

Legal interpretation has attracted a great deal of attention from researchers. Jacques Lenoble and François Ost's work (1980) deserves special mention in this regard, since it deconstructs the mechanisms of judicial syllogism according to which the judge's work consists mainly of applying a legal rule to facts that are presented to a given jurisdiction. The two authors show that this thesis is based on three representations: the judge applying law to facts which are assumed to be presented in their "reality"; legal language considered as adequate to the reality submitted to it and intelligible as such; no distortion in the process linking fact to law. By virtue of the transformation carried out on reality by its apprehension as part of the law, and of the semantic shifts that affect legal terminology, however, the law functions in a tautological manner: a rule deals only with what it has already assimilated and interpretation ultimately concerns only some substance that was pre-determined by legal language. This leads the authors to conclude that, once we accept the polysemic dimension of the words used by the text of the law, it is absolutely necessary to contextualize interpretation (Lenoble and Ost, 1980: 133-49). The same holds true for Hart (1961: 123) when he notes: 'Even when verbally formulated general rules are used, uncertainties as to the form of behaviour required by them may break out in particular concrete cases. Particular fact-situations do not await us already marked off from each other, and labelled as instances of the general rule, the application of which is in question; nor can the rule itself step forward to claim its own instances.' According to Hart, this does not mean that interpretation is purely a matter of social convention. An "internal point of view" also exists that makes people follow rules out of habit, use them as a basis for decisions or even refer to them as a model for behaviour. Moreover, for a limited number of cases requiring a real interpretation of the applicable rule, there is a multitude of situations where people do not interpret but simply follow the rule, simply because its meaning is unproblematic. In that sense, Hart takes a position close to the one we described in the discussion of Wittgenstein and the controversial interpretations of his stance on rule-following (cf. Chapter 2). The open texture of law does not mean the absence of any texture; it is also a constraining framework to which practitioners orient. This is reflected in their anticipation of the future usages that can be made of the documents they produce, and in their reluctance to see their decisions nullified and their preference for conformity.

Jackson shows clearly how the theory of judicial syllogism – that is, the operation through which law is deductively applied to facts – supposes a conception of reference that reflects a theory of truth based on correspondence. The praxeological study of judicial reasoning, however, reveals that this is not the way adjudication functions. According to Jackson's narrative perspective, judicial syllogism is a discourse of justification that gives special status to a discourse of decision-making. In this type of syllogistic reasoning, the major and the minor have a narrative character and their relationship is established in terms of coherence (Jackson, 1988: 58-60); this coherence operates after the fact as a way of justifying decisions. Decisions, in the adjudication process, proceed from the comparison between the narrative unit constructed from the facts of the case and the explicit or implicit narrative pattern underlying the legal rule. In consequence, Jackson (1988: 101) argues: 'The more abstracted the latter has become from its narrative foundations, the more likely difficulties will appear in the "application of law to fact", notwithstanding the apparent clarity of the legal rule, and the apparent subsumability of the "facts" within it'. This narrative conception applies to both rules and facts (Bennett and Feldman, 1981). According to these two authors, the construction of reality, in the judicial process, is a question of the general narrative plausibility of the story that is told, and this plausibility is in turn a function of the decision-making authority's stock of social knowledge (itself largely organised in narrative terms). The structure of the stories that are constructed exerts a direct impact on their credibility. Moreover, this structure is biased in many ways, among them the fact that social actors may or may not possess the cognitive routines allowing them to present information in accepted narrative forms, and may or may not share norms, experiences, and presuppositions with other participants in the judicial interaction (Bennett and Feldman, 1981: 171). However, these authors' perspective is flawed by their exclusive focus on the semantic level of the characterizing operation, to the detriment of its pragmatic level (cf. Jackson, 1988: 70-6).

A Substantialist Conception of the Rule and its Re-specification: The Example of Harm in the Egyptian Law of Divorce (1)

If we examine the literature focusing on the notion of harm (*darar*) as grounds for judicial divorce, in Egyptian law, we observe the tendency to deal with practical cases in a very abstract and homogenized way, so that the notion of harm or harm is transformed into a concept having a substantive definition outside the practice that makes it real. Often, this definition is associated with the Islamic lineage of the concept and therefore the *shari'a* as a theoretical, formal, trans-historical, and trans-geographical corpus.[1] This appears clearly when reading the chapter Ron Shaham devotes to judicial divorce at the wife's initiative in his book on family and courts in modern Egypt (1997). From the very first sentence, we get the impression that social phenomena take place against the immutable background of Islamic law and Islamic legal doctrines (1997: 112):

> In Islamic law, a marriage may be dissolved either through *talaq* or through *faskh*. Each method of dissolution has specific legal and financial consequences, and each may be carried out either judicially or extrajudicially. Muslim jurists differentiate between *talaq* and *faskh* on the basis of the grounds on which a dissolution is sought, about which there is considerable disagreement among the schools.[2]

However, when discussing the different conceptions of *faskh* and *talaq* according to the various schools of jurisprudence, Shaham himself illustrates the inanity of the distinction between legal concepts and interpreting practices: Hanbalis consider *faskh* the rule and *talaq* the exception; Malikis consider the opposite; and Hanafis do not care.[3] However, no sooner has Shaham opened the door to a sociological perspective on legal practices than he closes it again, writing: '[B]eyond [the limited cases in which the Hanafites allow a woman to apply for a judicial dissolution of her marriage], she has no means of freeing herself from a prejudicial union, apart from negotiating a divorce by mutual agreement.' (1997: 112-3) It is clear that he is referring to doctrine and not to practice, and this is precisely the point: why should practice be considered against the backdrop of legal doctrine? The production of legal doctrine is an interesting topic *per se*, but it creates confusion when the study of doctrine serves as a framing device for the study of practice.

This lack of concern for practice is also obvious in the neglect of technical and procedural issues. The codification of personal status – the laws of 1920 and 1929 – is presented as the culmination of the modernist call to offer women more

1 On the notion of harm before the Egyptian Court of Cassation, see also Naveh, 2002.

2 Put in this way, it becomes difficult to account for the provisions on *khul'* (unilateral divorce on the wife's initiative without her husband's or the judge's consent on condition that she renounces the financial gains resulting from the marriage contract) in Law No. 1 of 2000. *Khul'* can be considered neither as repudiation, i.e. unilateral divorce by the man, nor as judicial divorce (the judge has no power of evaluation), nor as grounds for annulment of the marriage. Using Islamic law as a background model, legal transformations must necessarily be considered as conforming to or deviating from the "pure paradigm". However, this completely fails to address the question of what people do and say when confronted with *khul'*.

3 Shafi'is, Hanbalis, Malikis, and Hanafis are the members of Islamic schools of jurisprudence that follow the Imams al-Shafi'i, Ibn Hanbal, Malik, and Abu Hanifa respectively.

grounds for the dissolution of marriage, but nothing is said about the considerable technical and procedural consequences that codification certainly had in courtrooms. Without speculating, it can safely be said that they must have changed the ways in which facts, evidence, and legal arguments were presented and, hence, the practice of personal status in general. When Shaham undertakes to review the four additional grounds for judicial divorce that the new laws granted women (illness or infirmity of the husband, non-provision of maintenance, absence, or harm), his argument follows a general pattern that consists of referring the new provision to the Islamic jurisprudential background. For instance, Shaham states, with regard to defects and disease, that these provisions are based on a minority opinion of the Hanafi school and the majority opinions of the three other schools (Shaham, 1997: 114). Although this statement looks true from a panoptical and retrospective view of the historical development of Islamic law, it is also symptomatic of the dynamic of legal Orientalism. It assumes that law is constructed along the lines that are followed for constructing scholarly discourse on law. In this case, when Shaham talks about minority Hanafi opinion and majority Maliki, Shafi`i, and Hanbali opinion, he is suggesting that we must infer that the provisions of the law of 1920 are based on this shared understanding. This implies that, all possible practices notwithstanding, Egyptian personal status law is a mere replica (with some methods for selecting preferred solutions) of the substantive corpus of preexisting Islamic legal rules. Besides the fact that, historically speaking, matters are certainly more complex, this approach has the effect of inverting the practical modes of reasoning that are followed for drafting and passing laws. Instead of assuming that the Islamic provisions existed first and that subsequently the legislators made their choice among the many possibilities Islamic law offers, we argue that these legislators determined their preference first and only then looked back at the corpus of *fiqh* so as to find the legitimate justifications. Here again, something has been lost in this quest for the historical and religious "roots" of legal provisions: the sense of what is done when codifying and practicing Egyptian personal status law.

Shaham commits the same mistake when addressing harm (*darar*) to the wife as grounds for judicial divorce. First, he states that Hanafi law 'does not recognize harm caused to the wife by her husband as a ground for dissolution.' (Shaham, 1997: 116) Second, he stresses (*ibid.*) that Article 6 of the 1929 Law, based on Maliki doctrine, allows a wife who alleges that her husband mistreated her in such a way as to make it impossible to continue the marriage to request that the judge separate them. Third, he states that, according to the explanatory memorandum, this reform was necessitated by public interest. Fourth, he explains that, because of imprecision in the definition of what constitutes *darar*, judges were obliged to consult Maliki literature in which harm is interpreted in a manner favourable to the wife. Finally, he asks whether one must speak of judicial dissolution, with the meaning the Malikis gave this expression, or of judicial divorce, the term used by Egyptian legislators. What is the point of establishing connections between, on one hand, Egyptian personal status law as codified in the laws of 1920 and 1929 and subsequently amended in the laws of 1985 and 2000, and, on the other, the various opinions formulated by jurists from the four schools of Islamic law? Although these connections are obvious in some ways, there seems to be limited practical purpose in searching for their precise origins. Worse, this approach creates confusion. First, to posit a connection does not imply that there is a causal relation. As mentioned above, the line of argument may easily be reversed: Maliki law was not the source from which the new legislations proceeded but the resource used to justify the new orientation of the law. Second, Shaham's presentation gives the impression that legal change can occur only in some interstitial space left open by the vagueness of the law. Nevertheless, Shaham invokes the general model of Islamic law and its many schools, despite the ambiguities of the various sources and of the references to these sources, as the background against which the notion of *darar* must be evaluated in Egyptian personal status law. Finally, we remain as far as ever from knowing what people do when practicing personal status law.

Only after this long introduction does Shaham turn to the study of Egyptian judicial practice in personal status matters in pre-revolutionary Egypt. He offers a review of the many circumstances in which a woman could ask a judge to be judicially divorced from her husband on grounds of harm or harm, and under which circumstances the judge would or would not grant such a divorce. Unfortunately, Shaham presents these cases in a totally abstract manner, as a kind of compendium of case-law principles similar to the compendia that summarize rulings issued by the Court of Cassation (*Majmu'at al-ahkam allati qarraratha mahkamat al-naqd*), and aim at extracting general, abstract principles from these rulings. Although these compendia, which constitute the basis on which precedents of the Court of cassation are constituted, published, and referred to, may serve as practical guides for the interpretation of statutory legal provisions, they can never account for the characterization process of which they are the outcome. When presenting these summarized cases as a reflection of Egyptian judicial practice in matter of divorce on grounds of harm, Shaham is still trapped in the straitjacket of legal syllogism, according to which facts are presented objectively to judges who, in a mechanical way, must identify the applicable law and apply this law to the facts. However, it is clear that things do not happen this way empirically. Facts are never raw facts, applicable law is itself a (potential) object of interpretation, and the legal characterization of facts is not an abstract and objective operation (although this should not be taken to mean that everything is a pure construct). As Pollner (1974: 37) has shown, even though deviance is created by the social characterization of an act as deviant, the fact remains that members of society see themselves as confronted with a situation whose deviance is assumed to be independent from society's response. In other words, although sociologists might consider rules and deviance as artifacts, they are conceived and lived by social actors as meaningful objective categories. People therefore tend to objectify facts and legal categories, and, following Sudnow (1987: 158), we must consider these categories 'as constituting the basic conceptual equipment with which such people as judges, lawyers, policemen, and probation workers organize their everyday activities'. All this means that the mere identification of legal categories cannot suffice: we still need to examine and describe how people practically orient to them.

In the first section of his article, Sudnow distinguishes between "necessarily-included lesser offences", i.e. offences that are definitionally included in the commission of other more encompassing offences, "situationally-included lesser offences", i.e. offences whose inclusion in more encompassing offenses depends on the manner in which they were committed, and "routinely-included lesser offences", i.e. offences that are neither situationally nor necessarily included, but which prosecutors and attorneys normally associate with certain types of crimes. In the course of plea bargaining, lesser offences are often negotiated between the protagonists. Although a statutorily designated lesser crime is not always necessarily included in a more encompassing one,[4] there often exists some situationally- or routinely-situated lesser offence.[5] In other words, 'in searching an instant case to decide what to *reduce it to*, there is no analysis of the statutorily referable elements of the instant case; instead, its membership in a class of events, the features of which cannot be described by the penal code, must be decided.' (Sudnow, 1987: 162)

The rule that makes it possible to describe the transformation from the statutorily described offence to the reductions routinely made must therefore be sought elsewhere, in the character of the non-statutorily defined class of offences, which Sudnow calls "normal crimes". Such normal crimes correspond to the ways in which people typically characterize the offences which they encounter in the performance of their routine activities. It includes 'the knowledge of the typical manner in which offences of given classes are committed, the social characteristics of the persons who regularly commit them, the features of the settings in which they occur, the types of victims often included, and the like.' (Sudnow, 1976: 162) The term "normal", in the expression "normal crimes", refers to the way people attend to a category of persons and events when dealing with a certain type of crime. This normalcy has some general features: it concerns offence types rather than particular individuals; its attributes are often non-statutory; its features are specific to the specific community in which the offence has been committed; its features are shared because they are routinely encountered in the courtroom; this normalcy is ecologically specified, i.e. it is constituted according to the locales within which offences are committed; it mainly consists in what we might call professional how-to guides. The close observation of actual legal encounters reveals that plea bargaining often results in the co-selection of lesser offences (in exchange for pleading guilty) that are neither

4 As Sudnow explains, 'if any of the statutorily required components of drunk behavior (its *corpus delicti*) are absent, there remains no offense of which the resultant description is a definition' (Sudnow 1976: 161).

5 For instance, for drunkenness, there is an offence typically and commonly associated with the way that drunk persons are seen to behave, i.e. "disturbing the peace". Although disturbing the peace is not definitionally associated with drunkenness, it is considered as an alternative offense to offer in return for guilty pleas. The same holds true for "molesting a minor" and "loitering around a schoolyard" or "burglary" and "petty theft".

statutorily nor even situationally included in the more encompassing offence, but that are routinely associated by professionals with the crime as it is normally committed according to prevailing social standards.

If we draw a parallel between Sudnow's "normal crimes" and Shaham's approach, we conclude that what is missing in the latter is the practical operation by which Egyptian judges substantiate the concept of harm as grounds for granting judicial divorce. Apart from its formal definition, in fact, we cannot understand the concept of harm. For instance, we know that some judges interpreted Article 6 of the Law of 1929 by referring to Maliki sources, 'because the article does not explain in detail which types of harm make a divorce mandatory.' (Shaham, 1997: 130) However, this suggests that judges, in their attempt to define the notion of harm, were constrained by its formal definition in the sources of Maliki legal doctrine. This could be partly the case, although we have no means of finding out. But, at least, this is the case only partly, for the features related to the case at hand and the routine of the judges' work certainly contributed to the definition of what counts as "normal harm". Once again, following Shaham's account, the judge seems to proceed syllogistically from the broad Maliki definition of harm to the facts of the case, although everything that counts as harm normally, routinely, and situationally in these many Egyptian legal settings is hidden behind the judge's quest for a satisfactorily formal justification of his decision. Sudnow (1976: 167) has successfully shown, however, that it is not the statutorily conceived features of harm but its socially relevant attributes that give it its status as a characteristic instance of the class "normal harm".

A Substantialist Conception of the Rule and its Re-specification: The Example of Harm in the Egyptian Law of Divorce (2)

One of the main tasks of professionals engaged in a legal procedure consists in giving facts a legal substance and giving legal categorizations a factual basis. As for laypeople, they engage in practices aimed at corroborating or invalidating characterizations produced by the professionals. In the case of judicial divorce on grounds of harm, two questions must be dealt with: what counts as harm and what is the cause of this harm? The two questions appear to be closely related to each other, and all the participants in the judicial process orient to them.

Article 6 of the Law of 1929 defines harm in broad terms. It refers to the wife's allegation that her husband mistreated her in such a way as to make it impossible for people of their social standing to continue the marriage relationship. Hence, it is up to the judge to characterize the facts which are under review so as to make them correspond to the definition of Article 6. Here, the judge is constrained by the definitions given by the Court of Cassation, as is clear when we read the following excerpt:

Excerpt 16 (Court of First Instance, Case 701, 1983, Personal Status, Giza)

Given that, as shown in the text of Article 6 of Legal Decree 25 of 1929 concerning certain provisions on repudiation, the Egyptian legislature requires, so as to allow the judge to rule for judicial divorce on grounds of harm, that the harm or harm come from the husband, to the exception of the wife, making life together impossible. Harm here is the wrong done by the husband to his wife by means of speech or action or both, in a manner that is not acceptable to people of the same status, and constitutes something shameful and wrongful that cannot be endured (Cassation, Personal Status, Appeal 50, 52nd Judicial Year, session of 28 June 1983); the standard here [applied by the Court of Cassation] is the non-material standard of a person, which varies according to environment, culture, and the wife's status in society (Cassation, Personal Status, Appeal 5, 46th Judicial Year, session of 9 November 1977, p. 1644). Harm also has to be a specific harm resulting from their dispute, necessary, and not subject to cessation; the wife cannot continue marital life; it must be in the capacity of her husband to stop it and to relieve her from it if he wishes, but he continues to inflict it, or he has resumed it (Cassation, Personal Status, Appeal 5, 47th Judicial Year, session of 14 March 1979, p. 798; Cassation, Personal Status, Appeal 51, 50th Judicial Year, session of 26 January 1982).

The formal definition provided by the court does not totally lift the uncertainty the judge faces when characterizing the facts. This does not mean, however, that the judge's work is particularly problematic or arbitrary. On the contrary, the categories to which the judge refers have an objective nature for him, even though it is his characterization that objectifies them. Moreover, the legal process of characterization is thoroughly supported by the sociological process of normalization, i.e. the operations through which the judge routinely selects some of the features of a case resembling a common, normal, usual type of case (cf. Sudnow, 1987). It is to these "normal" categories, which have, beyond their legal definition, a commonsense dimension,[6] that the judge, like the prosecutor, the attorney, the victim, the offender, the witnesses, or the experts, orient.

In the case we are looking at here, the wife mobilized two types of reason in order to substantiate the category of harm: (1) the husband's alleged impotence and, (2) the violence from which the wife allegedly suffered:

Excerpt 17 (Court of First Instance, Case 701, 1983, Personal Status, Giza)
[The wife required] a ruling [that would] judicially divorce her [in the form of] an irrevocable divorce, with no right for him to [reverse it], on [grounds of] harm resulting from 1) impotence, which cannot satisfy the aims of marriage; 2) his violence against her by means of blows, insults, abuse, and accusations against her. …

---

6 Things that might be pointed to as having "common-sense" status are not thereby awarded any universal and generally incorrigible character. '*Analytically speaking*, talk of "common sense" merely intends the fact that *amongst any given collection of persons organized into anything that can meaningfully be called a collectivity*, there will be a corpus of matters which those persons will find "obvious", a "going without saying" and as "beyond doubt and investigation". What those matters will be will vary, of course, from one collectivity to another' (Sharrock and Anderson, 1991: 63-64).

Neither impotence nor violence is explicitly mentioned in Egyptian law. However, on the one hand, impotence is traditionally assimilated with either permanent illness (Article 9 of the 1920 Law) or harm (Article 6 of the 1929 Law), while violence is considered as the exemplary type of harm. Hanafi law, however, recognizes impotence as a ground for the dissolution of a marriage (Shaham, 1997: 125), and this is confirmed in our case by the judge:

> **Excerpt 18 (Court of First Instance, Case 701, 1983, Personal Status, Giza)**
> Abu Hanifa and Abu Yusuf allowed separation on grounds of a permanent defect that impedes intercourse between a man and a woman, for example if he is impotent, emasculated, or disabled, because the goal of marriage is the preservation of procreation, so that, if the man is not capable of this, it becomes impossible to implement the provision of the contract and no good can come of upholding it. Upholding [a marriage contract] despite this [constitutes] harm for the woman whose perpetuation cannot be accepted and nothing can resolve it save separation (*The Personal Status of Imam Abu Zahra*, p. 414, par. 297, ed. 1957).

But it is important to emphasize that this reference to Islamic law is made to substantiate a positive-law provision, i.e. Article 6 of the 1929 Law. Impotence and violence are not presented in the ruling as Islamic-law provisions that must be directly implemented by the judge, but as two forms of harm from which the wife might be suffering and on the basis of which the judge can grant a judicial divorce according to Article 6 of the 1929 Law:

> **Excerpt 19 (Court of First Instance, Case 701, 1983, Personal Status, Giza)**
> Given that, with regard to what precedes, the court rules for the judicial divorce of the plaintiff from her husband on the grounds of harm [which he inflicted upon her].

The judge seeks to substantiate the legal category of harm, and what counts for him as harm does not depend entirely on provisions defined statutorily (the 1920 and 1929 laws) or Islamically (the rules formulated by Abu Hanifa and Abu Yusuf), even though these can play an important role. This legal category also varies according to the judge's conception of "normal harm", i.e. the way he typically characterizes a certain type of behaviour he encounters in the performance of his routine activities. As mentioned above, what counts for the judge as harm includes his knowledge of the typical manner in which a wife may suffer harm, the social characteristics of given classes of male offenders and female victims, the specific social and physical features of the settings in which such a situation can take place, etc. The judge's conception of harm functions reflexively: he orients himself to a conception that he thinks he shares with, other people participating in the judicial process. In turn, these other participants confirm his conception. Inversely, the other participants base themselves on the judge's conception, which they are asked to confirm, and produce reports that in turn serve as the basis for the judge's final ruling. Unfortunately, beyond the intertextual relations of expert reports and witness testimony with the final ruling, it is difficult to document this process empirically, since most of the judge's work happens while he is deliberating, reaching his decision, and writing up the sentence, and none of these processes are accessible to the public. What can be stated with some certainty, on the other hand, is that there is a gap between the formal representation of documents like the ruling and the facts these representations claim to document (cf. Chapter 7). The ruling operates in a justificatory way, orienting to a body of procedural and substantive rules while hiding the practicalities of its own constitution. This justificatory character appears in the conclusion of the ruling:

> **Excerpt 20 (Court of First Instance, Case 701, 1983, Personal Status, Giza)**
> Given that, with regard to what precedes, the court realizes that the continuation of their marital life ... would be an injustice (*zulm*) against her [the wife]. It is the judge's responsibility, as protector of justice, to put an end to it. Although repudiation is the most hated of permitted acts in God's eyes, it is equally forbidden to keep a wife tied by marital bonds to a husband when he causes her injuries that make it impossible for women of her status to pursue their conjugal life. The court takes into consideration the words of the Almighty: 'But do not take them back to injure them' [Qur'an 2: 231]; and the words of the Almighty: 'Then, the parties should either hold together on equitable terms, or separate with kindness' [Qur'an 2: 229]; and the words of the [Prophet] – may God bless him and give him peace: 'Neither harm nor counterharm [viz., a harm inflicted to counter another harm]'. It was not incumbent upon the plaintiff to request repudiation if she found life with her husband enjoyable. However, she turned to the court, made her public statement and refused reconciliation on the grounds that it is impossible for them to live together. The court has no choice but to grant her a judicial divorce. The General Prosecution does not object to this; on the contrary, it gave an opinion identical to that of the court.

A number of elements that concur in constituting the ruling as a disengaged textual document can be identified through the close examination of the many steps and procedures that supported the judge's work (although these steps are themselves transformed into partly disengaged textual documents). In this case, two evidentiary techniques are mobilized so as to establish the types of prejudice that result in harm. With regard to the husband's impotence, the forensic physician is asked to give a medical report, while the husband's violence is established through the oral testimony of witnesses. As we saw before, the forensic physician's report is very much oriented to the accomplishment of its procedural correctness. However, this report is equally oriented to the production of categories of legally relevant facts and people. The forensic physician's medical examination is largely directed at the construction of the report, which in turn is largely directed at its future readers. Paraphrasing Martha Komter, this record looks backward to establish the medical circumstances of the case and to show its procedural correctness, and it looks forward to its use as evidence in the judicial process, 'not only containing "the facts", but also displaying those elements that are legally required' (Komter, 2001: 384-5), i.e. by establishing that the necessary conditions have been met for some physical situation to be assimilated with the legal category of 'male impotence'. This orientation towards legal relevance is reflected in the fact that, despite the absence of any physical disability and of any psychological examination, the report concludes that psychological impotence is a probability, even while acknowledging that psychological impotence is hard to establish scientifically.

> **Excerpt 21 (Forensic Medicine, Case 701, 1983, Personal Status, Giza)**
> Expert opinion
> In light of this, we consider:
> – The examination we conducted on [...] indicates that he seems to be in normal health, that his growth and constitution are natural, and that he exhibits normal masculine characteristics (*'alamat al-dhukura*).
> – The medical examination does not show that he suffers from any pathological or congenital state, whether general or objective, that would cause him permanent physical impotence.
> – Even though from the forensic medical point of view he is free from the causes of physical impotence (*'unna 'udwiyya*), the defendant may well be affected at the same time by psychological factors which could cause him psychological impotence (*'unna nafsiyya*), although we realize that the existence of this kind of impotence cannot be deduced decisively from the clinical examination.
> – It is well known that psychological impotence lasts as long as its causes last. It is therefore impossible to predict a precise term or date of recovery, considering that the necessary period of time depends on the extent of the psychological factor, its type and the effectiveness of the therapy; it also depends on the wife's readiness to help and assist in the therapy in particular. If the wife lacks attachment to her husband, respect for him and readiness to assist him in the therapy, this therapy will either be exceptionally long and arduous or simply impossible.[7]

The second evidentiary technique is oral testimony, intended to document the alleged mistreatment of the wife by her husband. As mentioned above, this is one of the few sections in the ruling that refers to Islamic law, although here again it is mediated by positive-law mechanisms, in this case the Court of Cassation's case-law:

> **Excerpt 22 (Court of First Instance, Case 701, 1983, Personal Status, Giza)**
> Given that the Egyptian legislature has taken (*naqala*) the rule of judicial divorce on grounds of harm from the doctrine of Imam Malik [...] It is not allowed, in establishing it [harm], [to refer] to the same doctrine from which it is imported, and no particular rule has been stipulated to establish it. In such a situation, to prove that harm has been inflicted, one must go back to the majority opinion in the doctrine of Imam Abu

7 We must note the authoritative character conferred upon medical expertise. Indeed, the judge deduces the existence of the husband's impotence as one of the two sources of harm, although the physician only speaks in terms of probability. On the use of terms expressing probability before the judiciary, see Lynch and McNally, 2003.

Hanifa al-Nu'man, in accordance with Article 280 of the Shari`a Courts Regulations, to which Article 6 of Law 462 of 1955 refers (Cassation, Personal Status, Appeal 11, 48th Judicial Year, session of 25 April 1979). In consequence, harm is established through testimonial evidence (*bi-l-bayyina*), i.e., the testimony of two males or one male and two females. Oral testimony is not accepted […].

Given that Hanafi doctrine makes the acceptance of testimony regarding the rights of believers conditional upon its congruence with the petition for which it has been solicited, therefore no contradiction is acceptable here. Congruence is complete when what the witnesses testify to is exactly what the plaintiff has claimed; congruence is implicit when testimony bears on part of the case. This is taken as acceptance. The judge considers the witnesses' testimony as evidence of what was established by the plaintiff. There need be no literal congruence; congruence in meaning and intentions suffices, whether the expressions used are the same or different (Cassation, Personal Status, session of 23 November 1982, published in the *Judges' Review*; Appeal 2, 53[d] Judicial Year, session of 20 December 1983).

In accordance with this point of view, the court decided to collect the testimonies of the witnesses designated by the plaintiff and the defendant. Although these testimonies are written documents,[8] they bring us closer to the interactional details of the practice of judging.

Excerpt 23 (Court of First Instance, Case 701, 1983, Personal Status, Giza)
[First witness]
1- The court called the plaintiff's first witness and he said:
2- My name is […] oath
3- Q: What's your relationship to the two parties
4- A: My workplace is close to the post office where the plaintiff works
5- Q: What are you testifying to
6- A: The plaintiff is the defendant's wife by virtue of a legal marriage contract there were disputes between them and I saw the plaintiff's husband whom I know although I don't know where he lives he was speaking to her sharply in front of the post office where she works calling her I heard him addressing her as you whore you're disgusting and other words of this kind for nearly two years and one month ago he called the police against her because something happened between them I don't know what
7- Q: For how long have you known the plaintiff's husband
8- A: For nearly two years
9- Q: Does he live in your neighbourhood
10- A: I don't know
11- Q: For how long has the defendant addressed insults to the plaintiff
12- A: For nearly two years

8 Legally speaking, these testimonies made in front of the court are considered as written testimonies.

13- Q: What are the words he used against her
14- A: He you're a whore you're disgusting and similar things and this was in front of the post office
15- Q: Did any harm befall the plaintiff because of this
16- A: Yes she broke down while working at the post office
17- Q: Anything else to say
18- A: No
[Second witness]
19- The plaintiff's second witness was called and he said:
20- My name is [...] oath
21- Q: What's your relationship to the case
22- A: The neighbour of the plaintiff
23- Q: What are you testifying to
24- A: The plaintiff is the defendant's wife by virtue of a legal marriage contract there were disputes between them and I saw him hitting her more than once in front of their home and I also heard him calling her things like you're a whore you're disgusting
25- Q: Did you see the defendant hitting the plaintiff
26- A: Yes I saw him hitting her in front of their house
27- Q: Why are you testifying
28- A: Because I'm their neighbour and I saw him hitting her
29- Q: Did you hear the defendant insulting the plaintiff
30- A: Yes I heard him calling her you're a whore you're disgusting and other things
31- Q: Did any harm befall the plaintiff because of this
32- A: Yes harm befell the plaintiff because of this because she's young and a civil servant at the post office
33- Q: Anything else to say
34- A: No
[Third witness]
35- The defendant's first witness was called and he said:
36- My name is ... oath
37- Q: What's your relationship to the two parties
38- A: The defendant lives with me at home
39- Q: What are you testifying to
40- A: The plaintiff is the defendant's wife by virtue of a legal marriage contract and the defendant lives with me and he's lived in my home for one year and eight months and nothing like a misunderstanding happened between them and he didn't assault her and he didn't hit her and he didn't insult her and the policeman came and took the defendant and locked him in the station
41- Q: Did you see the defendant assaulting the plaintiff
42- A: No
43- Q: Did you hear the defendant insulting the plaintiff
44- A: No
45- Q: The plaintiff's two witnesses reported that he insulted her and hit her in front of her workplace

46- A: No it didn't happen
47- Q: Anything else to say
48- A: No
[Fourth witness]
49- The court called the defendant's second witness and he said:
50- My name is [...] oath
51- Q: What's your relationship to the two parties
52- A: The neighbour.
53- Q: What are you testifying to
54- A: The defendant is the plaintiff's husband by virtue of a legal marriage contract and he lives close to me and she for one year and a half and he didn't hit her and he didn't insult her except once when the policeman came and took her and took him I don't know the cause
55- Q: Did the defendant hit and insult the plaintiff
56- A: No
57- Q: The plaintiff's two witnesses reported that the defendant had hit her and insulted her
58- A: No I didn't see him hitting her
59- Q: Anything else to say
60- A: No

Even though testimonies are supposed to be transcribed in the witnesses' own words, they clearly appear to have been, at least partly, reformulated by the judge (and his clerk). This is why the witness is always reported to have begun his testimony by stating that the plaintiff and the defendant are spouses "by virtue of a legal marriage contract". In addition to this re-writing operation, the overall stereotypical nature of the testimony organization and the pre-allocated sequence of turns in the testimony production are noteworthy. Both depend on the institutional context in which these testimonies are given. As noted by Atkinson and Drew (1979: 35), 'the talk in each stage of court hearings shares the feature that although it occurs in a multi-party setting [...], the parties who may participate are limited and predetermined.' Moreover, the participants necessarily manage whatever is done in this context within the constraining framework of this pre-allocated turn-taking organization. In other words, unlike ordinary conversations, turn order in judicial settings is fixed, as is the type of each speaker's turn.

Within this system of turn allocation, both the judge and the witnesses are oriented to the production of legally relevant information and to the credibility of this information. On the judge's side, the credibility of the information provided by the witness is tested by questions directed at the credibility of the witness himself. This is why the interrogation always begins with a question about the witness's 'relationship with the two parties' (turns 3, 21, 37, 51). This credibility can be further investigated by asking the witness to produce a first account of his testimony (turns 5, 23, 39, 53) and then by assessing the reliability of this global narrative by asking the same witness to confirm his statements piecemeal (turns 7-14, 25-30, 41-44, 55-56).

Some of the judge's questions are clearly directed at challenging the witness's version of the facts by confronting him with another witness's testimony (turns 45 and 57: 'The plaintiff's two witnesses reported that the defendant had hit her and insulted her'). Clearly, the judge also seeks to extract some elements of information – nature of demeanour (insulting and hitting: turns 25, 29, 41, 43, 55), temporal dimension of the behaviour (for how long: turn 11), content of the behaviour (words used by the husband: turns 13, 16, 32), responsibility (who did it: turns 11, 25, 29, 41, 43, 55), nature of the harm caused by the behaviour (what effect on the wife: turns 15, 31) – that are the features constituting the legal category of harm. Put together, the spare parts of this quest for information are congruent with the many conditional elements of the notion of harm as defined, in the ruling and according to the Court of Cassation, as 'harm caused by the husband to his wife by means of speech or action or both, in a way that is not acceptable to people of their status, and constituting something shameful and wrongful, which cannot be endured.'

For their part, the witnesses attempt to establish credibility by giving elements of information that can be reasonably considered to qualify them as reliable – vantage point (turn 4: workplace; turns 22, 38, 52: neighbourhood), time span during which he witnessed given types of behaviour (turns 8, 12: nearly two years) – or that appear very plausible – exact wording of the insults (turns 14, 30: whore and disgusting), effects of these insults (turns 16, 32: her breaking down at the post office). With regard to the content of his testimony, the witness clearly orients to what appears to him as the constitutive element of the harm, either denying or confirming its having occurred. Interestingly, the witnesses who deny the existence of any harm directly orient their first global narrative, the elements of which were not elicited by the judge, to the question of the husband having neither insulted nor hit her. Accordingly, we may easily conclude that the normal conception of harm is made of either blows or insults, or both, in a manner largely independent of any formal legal definition.

To the judge's question confronting them with the plaintiff's witnesses, who testified that harm had occurred (turns 45 and 57: the plaintiff's witnesses reported that the defendant had hit and insulted her), the defendant's witnesses respond by categorical denial. This is an indirect way of addressing the challenge to their testimonies and defending themselves against the aspersions this challenge casts upon their credibility. However, this total denial produces quite a paradoxical picture: on one hand, two spouses living in perfect harmony (turn 40: 'nothing like a misunderstanding happened between them and he didn't assault her and he didn't hit her and he didn't insult her') and, on the other, a policeman coming and taking them to the police station (turns 40 and 54). One of the witnesses apparently tries to repair the contradiction by saying that he does not know the cause of this police intervention, but he thereby acknowledges that this intervention occurred, in contrast to his former claim that the two spouses lived in harmony. The judge seems to have detected this problematic paradox. Even though he does not directly challenge the sincerity and honesty of the defendant's witnesses, he simply does not take their testimonies into account his final ruling.

Excerpt 24 (Court of First Instance, Case 701, 1983, Personal Status, Giza)
Given that, with regard to the second argument of the petition, which is the assault inflicted upon her by means of blows and insults, her two witnesses testified to the fact that they heard him insulting and slandering her in the street; moreover, one of them saw him hitting her more than one time and testified that the words with which he slandered her cannot be accepted. Life together became impossible and she suffered harm because of this. In light of the above, the testimony of her witnesses is congruent with the petition and is acceptable.

The Production of Factual and Legal Relevance

The inventory of the elements of proof concerning the case of the "girl from Ma'adi", written up by the chief prosecutor of South Cairo Plenary Court Prosecution, is a document illustrating one of the steps of the legal process of characterization.

Excerpt 25 (Prosecution, Case 276, 1985, Ma'adi)
In the name of God, the Compassionate, the Merciful
South Cairo Prosecution
Miss [...], aged 17 years, a student at the Music Institute, residing at 95A, Abd al-'Aziz Al Sa'ud Avenue, Misr al-Qadima district, testifies to the fact that on 17 January 1985, she was in the company of her fiancé, Ahmad Hamdi Hasan Imam, and that, while they were stopped in the car on Canal Street in Ma'adi, the suspect Salah Shawqi 'Ali Abu Halawa threatened them by showing a knife (gazelle horn[9]) and ordered her fiancé to get out of the car. [...] They forced them to get in the taxi driven by the fifth suspect and they left for another place [where the first suspect undertook to rape her] [...] when gunshots were heard. [They] hastened to get into the car [...]; they then proceeded to an inhabited area and stopped in front of a building at the foot of which was a garage in which there was no car. The first suspect got out and met the sixth suspect; he then returned to the car and told the female victim to enter the garage. She obeyed the order while the sixth suspect looked on. The first accused then took out a blanket and a cushion and put them in a room adjoining the garage into which the suspects, with the exception of the sixth, entered. Each then undertook to remove his clothes and lie on her [...] But she made every effort to resist them and was injured on her left hand as a result of her resistance. She added that the first accused, when he led her into the room adjoining the garage, took possession of two rings she was wearing.
Mr [...], aged 24 years, director of a company of textile products, residing at 95A, 'Abd al-'Aziz Al Sa'ud Avenue, Misr al-Qadima police district, testifies to the content of what the first [female] witness testified to and adds that, while he was being held by the suspects on the public road, the first suspect seized a bracelet with golden clasps, while the second suspect seized his watch as they were heading with him to the cab. Each of the two suspects threatened him with a knife in presence of the rest of the suspects, with

9 This is a reference to the shape of the blade.

the exception of the sixth. He adds that the first suspect struck him with the knife when he and the [female] victim were brought into the car that the fifth suspect was driving.

Observations

1. The first suspect said [...] that he had agreed with the second, third, fourth, and fifth suspects to abduct the first woman they met and to rape her. [...]

2. In the report from the arrest, the second suspect said the same thing as the first suspect had reported. He admitted [...] that the first, third, fourth, and fifth suspects had stolen from the two victims by force, that he had stolen the watch of the [male] victim on the public thoroughfare by threatening to use the knife he carried, and that he had kissed and embraced the [female] victim.

3. In the prosecution's investigation, the third suspect admitted [...] the same thing as the first suspect and he added that he had seized the female victim by force, had lain on her, and had kissed her.

4. In the prosecution's investigation, the fourth suspect admitted the same thing as the first suspect and he added that he had seized the [female] victim, had embraced and kissed her. In the report for renewal of his detention, he also admitted [...] that he had participated in the rape of the [female] victim, kissed her, and nibbled her breasts.

5. In the prosecution's investigation, the fifth suspect admitted [...] the same thing as the first suspect and he added that he had seized the [female] victim, had embraced and kissed her. In the report for renewal of his detention, dated 21 January 1985, he also admitted that he had agreed with the first four suspects to abduct the [female] victim, to rape her, and to steal what she possessed by force.

6. In the report for renewal of his detention, dated 21 January 1985, the sixth suspect admitted that he knew the [female] victim had been abducted and that he had received the two rings and gold chain in return for providing the place where the suspects raped the [female] victim.

7. A golden keyring belonging to the [male] victim and one of the two rings belonging to the [female] victim were found on the sixth suspect. The blanket he offered the first five suspects when they undertook to fornicate with the [female] victim was likewise found at his home.

8. A knife (gazelle horn), the [female] victim's watch, and a sum of money amounting to 3.10 EGP were found upon the first suspect's person at the time of his arrest. A knife (gazelle horn) and the sum of 48 EGP were confiscated from the second suspect at the time of his arrest.

9. It appears from the medical report concerning the [male] victim [...] that the examination to which he was subjected found a wound to his right pinkie finger and traces of medical care going back to less than 21 days, with no complications.

10. The forensic physician's report deduces from the examination of the [female] victim, daughter of [...], the existence of a slight bruise on the rear of the left hand caused by a blow inflicted with a small, hard object at the moment of the event. It also appears objectively from medical examination that she is a virgin, her hymen is intact and devoid of any old or recent tear, and her orifice is narrow, which does not permit penetration without tearing. At the same time, external sexual contact does not leave any mark that can testify to it, and analysis shows sperm on the shirt and underwear

> belonging to the [female] victim, as well as on the blanket seized in the fifth suspect's room [...], which confirms the occurrence of sexual aggression on the [female] victim resulting from external sexual contact alone.
> 11. The [female] doctor [...], forensic physician, testified in the general prosecution's investigation to [the fact] that the partial penetration does not destroy the hymen, and leaves no trace that can testify to it; it is plausible that one of the suspects made part of his penis penetrate in the victim's vagina without leaving any trace that can testify to it.
> 12. It appears from the initial medical report that the suspect Ashraf Hasan Gamil is over 18 years old.
> Written on 12 February 1985
> Head of the Southern Cairo General Prosecution

Without analysing the document in detail, we can identify many interesting points. First, this report is made up of two distinct parts, the first presented as the objective rendering of facts by the victim of the sexual aggression and the second presented as a list of annotations originating from the other parties who witnessed or participated in this aggression and completing the first narrative. Facts are therefore established on the basis of the statement made by the principal victim. What the secondary victim reports is only subsidiary, whereas what the aggressors say takes the form of admissions that corroborate and complete the principal narrative. Moreover, it clearly appears that the narrative statement does not unfold clearly, but is on the contrary structured by the legal classifications in which it must be embedded. It makes sense to think that the public prosecutor re-organized what the principal victim narrated, directly (by re-writing) or indirectly (through the conduct of the interview). A close look at the other protagonists' additional considerations supports this point. Since criminal trials are organized as interrogations, what conditions the presentation of facts and the ascription of responsibilities is the need to punish the criminal, not reparation or compensation for the harm inflicted. Thus, greater emphasis is placed on each suspect's subjective implication than on the harm experienced by the victims. Hence the importance of each suspect's admission of his personal role in the crime: the first five confess to 'having lain on the victim', while the sixth only assisted them knowingly. In the same way, because criminal intent transforms characterization, the mention of circumstances preceding the performance of the crime has special importance: the first five suspects had decided to 'abduct the first woman they met and rape her'. The same holds true of the protagonists' age, which also modifies the characterization and therefore the punishment: the principal victim was 17 (i.e. a minor) and the medical report indicates that 'the accused Ashraf Hasan Gamil [was] over 18' (i.e. legally an adult). It can also be added that, even though the true nature of the crime is not in itself modified, the triple characterization of facts (abduction and confinement, armed robbery, rape) makes it possible to ascribe aggravating circumstances to the suspects' responsibility and to go beyond the maximum penalty stipulated for rape. Komter (1994) uses the term hyper-accusation to designate the prosecution's perspective, encompassing the transaction positions the defendant could adopt as well as the possibility he has of confessing to selected accusations, in order to avoid confronting the judge with questions that have not been dealt with preventively.

On the basis of the inventory of the elements of proof, the judge has at his disposal a series of facts – "what happened" and "what role each person played" – that have been fitted to a legal format. It is his responsibility to characterize them. This characterization is prejudiced, since the organization of the narrative depends on the legal classifications to which he must fit the case. This characterization is the product of interactions that bring together the various parties to the trial, and intertextual relations that these parties establish between the factual narrative and the applicable laws. As an example, we may look at the notion of sexual assault, as defined by Egyptian doctrine and the Court of Cassation's jurisprudence. In doctrine (Hasan, n.d.), such an affront is 'a grave and deliberate assault on the victim's propriety, affecting his or her body and generally involving the genitals.' This generic crime is divided into two distinct sub-crimes, depending whether or not force or threats have been used. The law stipulates a penalty, which may be increased if the victim is a minor or incapacitated. It varies according to whether or not force and/or threats were used, and whether or not the assault was premeditated. It also varies according to whether the victim is a random person or a descendant of the accused. The definition implies that it must be 1) an act aimed at seizing the victim's body and 2) a serious attack. This distinguishes "sexual assault" as a category from that of "public indecency" (*fi'l fadih*). This definition of sexual assault, however, fails to provide strict criteria for identifying what is meant by "genitals", and this opens the door to casuistic on the part of the Court of Cassation.

Applications in jurisprudence of the criterion for "genitals" (*mi'yar al-'awra*): jurisprudence considers the following acts as sexual assaults due to the fact that contact occurs with the sexual parts of the body: the accused lays the [female] victim on the ground and ruptures her hymen with his finger; pinching a woman's posterior; the accused grasps the breast of the [female] victim; pinching the [female] victim's thigh; the accused lays the [female] victim on the ground on her back, lies on top of her, and puts his finger in her anus; embracing the [female] victim; the accused squeezes the [female] victim with his hands; the accused tears the garments of the [female] victim and penetrates [...] her vagina; the accused lies on top of the [female] victim after having lain her on the ground; to tear the garments from part of the [female] victim's body, exposing the genitals to look at them; the accused places his hand on the vagina of the first [female] victim, palpates the stomach and breasts of the second, and seizes the knees and stomach of the third. When applying this criterion, jurisprudence does not consider the fact of kissing a young woman on the cheeks or kissing a young man on the neck and biting him at the site of the kiss as a sexual assault on either of them. (Hasan, n.d.: § 84)

From this list, we may draw the evident conclusion that sexuality, and the various crimes and misdemeanours attached to it, are not subject to substantive definitions; rather, they are the product of interaction and intertextuality, in which the different parties to the judicial process participate. As Holstein (1993: 150-1) emphasizes, facts and people are not the raw data of the trial, but rather the products of descriptions by multiple people engaged in various tasks, with different, potentially conflicting interests, aiming at certain precise goals (which have to do, among other things, with their respective positions in the ongoing activity), in institutional contexts that impose a number of constraints, with background expectations that define normalcy and mark the incongruity or conformity of the situation being described in relation to that normalcy, and situated in a prospective orientation to the subsequent possible uses of the documents produced by institutions like the court, for example.

Turning, now to the questioning of suspects by the public prosecutor's deputy, we notice that the factual narrative is achieved in interaction. On one hand, the deputy seeks to emphasize legally relevant elements. Thus, the aggressors' intention is made manifest, and has implications for the characterization of the facts. In the same way, the detainees' age is a topic for concern, because it affects the invocation of an extenuating factor and the applicable law. Another possibility is that the element of constraint is actively sought.

Excerpt 26 (Public Prosecution, case 276, 1985, Ma'adi)

[Anwar Isma'il]

Q: Did sexual relations with the girl occur with her consent

A: No

Q: Did the [female] victim go willingly with you to the place where Salah attacked her

A: No we took them and we made them get into the taxi we had and we told them we're taking you to the station

As for the suspects, they resort to different strategies allowing them to try and evade or at least attenuate their responsibility. The suspect may provide alternative descriptions. In the Ma'adi case, for example, the statement made by one of the suspects emphasizes the role of another suspect in the crime committed, while the deposition made by the latter places greater weight on the collective nature of the crime.

Excerpt 27 (Public Prosecution, case 276, 1985, Ma'adi)

[Anwar Isma'il]

Q: Did you agree to pick up the first woman you met on the road

A: We agreed that we would kidnap a woman and *Salah would take her from us*

[Salah Shawqi]

Q: Did you have a conversation about looking for a woman

A: Yes *we agreed* that we would look for a woman

Another possibility is to provide motives for an act. Observe, for example, the argument made by one of the aggressors, who claims he suggested to the fiancé that they "share" (*shirka*) the victim, and alleges that the fiancé accepted. One might think that this is a bid to attenuate the aggressors' guilt by presenting the case as one in which the victims almost consented, or at least by spreading out responsibility.

Excerpt 28 (Public Prosecution, case 276, 1985, Ma'adi)
[Salah Shawqi]
Q: What did you do when you went up to him
A: I went to help him change the tire and when he was about to get in the car I said we can all have the girl who's with you
Q: And what was his response
A: He said ok

Other motives are also put forth, such as the one that attempts to explain the decision to organize a "woman hunt" by tricking another suspect after the woman he was flirting with left with another man.

Excerpt 29 (Public Prosecution, case 276, Ma'adi)
[Anwar Isma'il]
Q: What did you talk about during this time
A: When Salah got in he said there was a girl with me just now and a cop took her and I gave him five pounds we sat down to chat and Salah said I'm going to get you a woman

In general, the suspects seem to answer questions not only according to their factual content, but also according to their moral implications. This is the case, for example, of the suspect who admits having gone into the room to rape the young woman, but explains that, because the woman reminded him that he was behaving reprehensibly, he left the room without having had intercourse with her.

Excerpt 30 (Public Prosecution, case 276, 1985, Ma'adi)
[Anwar Isma'il]
Q: What are the sexual acts you carried out on the [female] victim
A: When I went in I found her sitting on the cushion I went to have sex with her I kissed her and held her around the waist and took her in my arms and then when she said shame on you (*haram 'alayk*) I left her and I left.

The interrogation, rather than the unveiling of objective facts, is a cooperative accomplishment that is both situated and oriented. It is cooperative in the sense that the positions one participant adopts in the interrogation only have meaning in relation to the positions adopted by another participant. It is situated because the context for the interaction defines, to a large degree, the nature of relations between the parties, their discursive rights and obligations, and the vocabulary that they mobilize. Finally, it is oriented because all the parties are turned to the uses that may later be made of their statements and of the descriptions of people, facts, words, and gestures that their statements contain. This has professional implications for some of the parties, and "existential" implications for the others.

PART III
A Practical Grammar of Legal Concepts

Chapter 7

From Law in the Books to Law in Action: Egyptian Criminal Law between Doctrine, Case Law, Jurisprudence and Practice

According to Cicourel (1968: 17), 'The use of a dictionary for the analysis of written reports or documents assumes the researcher can legitimately impute the abstract or disengaged meanings of the dictionary to the text, thus suspending the relevance of meanings in their situational context.' In other words, a ruling goes through a formalization and disembodiment process, the final result of which hides the many negotiations, compromises, re-writings, omissions, over- and under-determinations that were necessary to its production. Consequently, even though people involved in a judicial process are oriented to a single legal system, one cannot observe or describe their actual orientations on the basis of a formalized and polished document, which reflects only the narrative process that gave the facts their legal relevance, that is, their characterization. This chapter will present formal law, i.e. law on the books, on one hand, and, on the other, will emphasize the severe limitations the study of this type of texts alone necessarily imposes.

Following a brief introduction to Egyptian law, roughly situating it in relation to codified legal systems of the Roman Germanic type,[1] we will sketch out the broad outlines of current criminal law as laid out by Egyptian jurisprudence and the case law of the Court of Cassation. Both present themselves as a form of rationalization and exegesis of the law. We will consider them in the context of a retrospective and prospective rationalization of the criminal legal system, before analysing them as texts that erase the practical modalities of their constitution and therefore as documents incapable of accounting for the specifically praxeological dimension of legal work.

Detour: An Overview of the Egyptian Legal System

The Egyptian legal system as we observe it today is the outcome of an enterprise that is over 200 years old. During the nineteenth century, Ottoman governors, viceroys, and khedives strove to give the legal and judicial system a "modern" tone largely inspired by Western models (Hill, 1987; Reid, 1981; Ziadeh, 1968;

1 Although such a presentation is not particularly justified in the perspective of this study.

Botiveau, 1989; Brown, 1997; Dupret and Bernard-Maugiron, 2002). In less than a century, this system gradually evolved 'into a much more complex and sophisticated type of justice administered by a fully-fledged judiciary' (Peters, 1999), before being replaced by a French-type court system. From the late 1870s onward, mixed courts (*mahakim mukhtalita*) and national courts (*mahakim ahliyya*) operated, together with religious courts (*mahakim shar'iyya*) for matters related to personal status. However, the latter were progressively stripped of their jurisdiction and were finally absorbed in 1956 by a unified system of national courts. Following the French practice of separating civil and administrative law, the State Council (*majlis al-dawla*) was created in 1946. In 1969, the Supreme Court (*al-mahkama al-'ulya*) was established with jurisdiction on constitutional matters. It was replaced in 1979 by the Supreme Constitutional Court (*al-mahkama al-dusturiyya al-'ulya*).

The nineteenth century was also a time of intense codification. In Egypt, decrees and laws regulated criminal matters as early as 1829. Although in 1852, a new penal code was promulgated that was largely identical to the Ottoman Penal Code of 1851 (Peters, 1995), French law massively suffused Egyptian law at the time of the promulgation of the mixed and national codes of 1876 and 1883. Other codifications, written up by French and Italian jurists for the most part, followed the same trend. Only the new Civil Code – drafted by 'Abd al-Razzaq al-Sanhuri, the most prominent figure in Egyptian law, and promulgated in 1948 – constituted an attempt to establish a civil law that took the systematic form of a code, but asserted its adherence to Islamic legal principles. Of course, new laws were passed continually and judicial institutions, crowned by the Court of Cassation, the Supreme Constitutional Court, and the Supreme Administrative Court, produced an impressive body of jurisprudence. In this process, law, originally imported from France and elsewhere, became without contest Egyptian – that is, a national law, whose formal structure brings it into the family of Roman and Germanic civil law from a technical point of view.

Main Principles of Egyptian Criminal Law

The general theory elaborated by Egyptian jurists defines crime (*al-jarima*) as 'an illegitimate action produced by a criminal will for which the law stipulates a sanction or precautionary measures.' (Husni, 1989: 40)[2] This definition may be deconstructed as follows: (1) Crime supposes that an action (*fi'l*) be committed either actively (commission) or passively (abstention); (2) This action must be illegitimate (*ghayr mashru'*) with regard to an explicit provision of criminal law and must not be committed under circumstances that can excuse it; (3) This action must originate in a "criminal will" (*al-irada al-jina'iyya*), i.e. a human will that is capable of distinction

2 We draw most of the information concerning Egyptian criminal jurisprudence from Husni, 1989, which Egyptian jurists unanimously consider the most authoritative reference in the field.

and free to choose, yet that sought to perform this action and is therefore responsible for it; if this will intended the consequences of this action, jurisprudence speaks of "criminal intent" (*al-qasd al-jina'i*), whereas it speaks of "unintentional fault" (*al-khata' ghayr al-'amdi*) when the will did not intend the consequences of this action; (4) The law must stipulate a sanction (*'uquba*) or precautionary measures (*tadbir ihtirazi*).

Three basic elements therefore make up a crime: the legal element (*al-rukn al-shar'i*), the material element (*al-rukn al-maddi*) and the moral element (*al-rukn al-ma'nawi*). First, the legal element, made up of three components: action (commission: 'a tangible material component [...] expressed by the author through the movements of his limbs to achieve precise material effects' (Husni, 1989: 374); or abstention: 'refraining from achieving a positive action which the legislator expected from him in precise circumstances' (Husni, 1989: 376)); the consequence of this action (simultaneously 'the transformation that occurred in the external world as a result of the criminal behaviour' (Husni, 1989: 380) and 'the offense that harmed an interest or a right which the legislator considers worthy of penal protection' (Husni, 1989: 381)); the causal relationship (*al-'alaqa al-sababiyya* or *'alaqat al-sababiyya*) linking the act and its consequence ('the link that unifies the action and the result and establishes that the action led to the result' (Husni, 1989: 385)). Second, there is the moral element, i.e. the will that accompanies the action, in the form of either criminal intent (the results of the action were intended) or unintentional fault (the results were not intended). The moral element conditions the infliction of a penalty to the commission of an offense by a human being. As Husni (1989: 501) points it, 'nobody is accountable for an offense in which the material and psychological aspects do not combine.' Third, there is the legal element, which refers to the illegitimate status of the action and implies that there must be a text criminalizing this action, providing for the punishment of its perpetrator. The legal element also implies that there must be no justification or extenuating factors (*sabab al-ibaha*). In addition, specific elements distinguish crimes from each other. In the case of theft, for instance, the material element is the seizure of goods belonging to someone, while the moral element is the intent to take possession of these goods, and the legal element is included in Article 318 of the Penal Code. The law also takes into consideration certain features subdividing the category of theft and individualizing situations (e.g. nighttime theft, theft committed by someone acting under duress). These last features, not defined by the law, are left to the judge's discretionary power.

Legal Personality, Criminal Liability, and Criminal Intent

The moral element of the crime is the major constitutive element of criminal liability (*al-mas'uliyya al-jina'iyya*), as its establishment presumes that the legal and material elements of the crime have also been determined, and since it conditions the establishment of criminal capacity (*al-ahliyya al-jina'iyya*), i.e. the capacity to be criminally liable. In Egyptian jurisprudence, the system of criminal liability rests on a combination of the philosophy of free will (*hurriyyat al-ikhtiyar*) and the philosophy of determinism (*jabariyya*). According to the former, the offender is presumed to have had the freedom to abide by the law or to contravene it; if he chose the latter, he is considered to have expressed a criminal will for which he is liable. According to the latter, human actions are subject to natural laws, including the criminal nature of man; crime is the result of internal factors that depend on the physical and mental constitution of the offender and on external factors related to the social environment. In other words, a human being enjoys limited freedom (*hurriyya muqayyada*), with the consequence that liability is based on free will, though will and liability can be limited or excluded on the basis of various factors, which must lead to the adoption of precautionary measures protecting both the offender and society. Although Egyptian law recognizes the principle of free will, it also admits that a person might have no choice, i.e. no free will, or lack consciousness, i.e. the faculty of distinction (*tamyiz*).

Criminal intent is the fulcrum of this doctrine. It is defined as an intention based on violating an explicit provision of the law. Since, according to this logic, only human beings are endowed with will, only they can be criminally liable. There are, however, various impediments to the enactment of criminal liability: these are defined as 'situations in which the will is devoid of legal value, which the law does not take into consideration, which do not provide any place for such a characterization, and in which the moral element of the crime is not constituted.' (Husni, 1989: 521) The law requires two conditions to establish will: the faculty of distinction and free will. If either or both are missing, the impediment to liability is constituted. Husni explains distinction as follows: 'The law incriminates the offender because he has oriented his will in a way that contradicts its provisions, and this orientation can only be ascribed when [the offender] had the opportunity to know the many orientations his will could take and the orientation it actually took.' (Husni, 1989: 522) As for free will, he defines it as 'the offender's capacity to delineate the orientation his will takes, i.e. his faculty to push his will in a specific direction among the different orientations it could have taken.' (*ibid.*) Since offenders have only limited control over the many factors surrounding their acts, their liability may be precluded by two types of cause: external causes, like duress or necessity, and internal causes, which depend on their mental and psychological state (Article 61 of the Penal Code).

Law 12/1996 on children, which replaced Law 31/1974 on juveniles (itself a replacement of the Penal Code articles on minors), stipulates in Article 2: 'Within the scope of the provisions of this law, one means by "child" a person who has not attained the age of 18 years.' Eighteen is therefore the age of legal majority in criminal matters. Chapter 3 outlines the criminal aspects of legal minority. Article 94 stipulates: 'Criminal liability is denied to the child who has not attained the age of seven.' This text echoes Article 64, now abrogated, of the Penal Code. Jurists justify it by reference to the presumption that seven years is the age of discernment (*sinn al-tamyiz*). Article 95 stipulates: 'In compliance with Article 112 of this law [to wit, that juveniles between 15 and 18 years of age are given lesser penalties], the rules stipulated in this chapter apply to persons not having attained the age of 18 at the time when the crime was committed, as well as those found in one of the situations that expose children to delinquency.' Children above the age of seven and under the age of 15 may be submitted to various measures: reprimand (*tawbikh*), delivery (*taslim*), remanding to vocational training (*ilhaq bi al-tadrib al-mihani*), assigning to certain duties (*ilzam bi-wajibat mu'ayyana*), judicial control (*ikhtiyar qada'i*), placement (*ida'*) in social care or in a hospital, etc. (Article 101). These measures expire when the child attains the age of 21 (but judicial control can be extended for two years, and psychiatric treatment can be extended as long as deemed necessary). Under the age of seven (Article 98) or if the child suffers from mental deficiencies (Article 99), no measure can be taken except to refer him to specialized hospitals. Article 99 defines a mentally deficient child as 'the victim of a mental or a psychological disease or a mental deficiency, and who has been judged as lacking, totally or in part, the capacity to understand or to choose, so that one fears for his security and the security of others.' If the child is between 15 and 16 years of age, the penalties of capital punishment and hard labour are reduced respectively to prison and custody (or placement in social care, at the judge's discretion); penalties for misdemeanors may be reduced to judicial custody and placement. If the child is between 16 and 18, capital punishment is reduced to prison for at least 10 years; life at hard labour is reduced to prison for at least seven years; temporary hard labour is reduced to prison (Article 112). Finally, Article 119 stipulates: 'A juvenile who has not attained the age of fifteen may not be held in protective custody.'

The combination of the two elements of majority and consciousness can be schematized in the following picture, which depicts the four different possible states of legal personality in Egyptian criminal law:

(a) majority / consciousness (d) majority / no consciousness

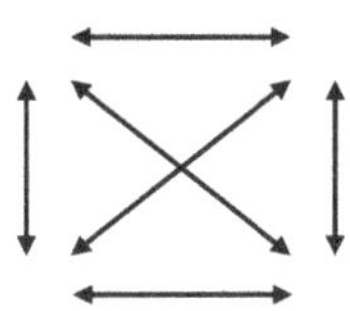

(b) minority / consciousness (c) minority / no consciousness

Figure 7.1 Types of legal personality

Different types of criminal liability correspond to these different forms:

- Full liability is presumed for people who have attained the age of 18 years of age and do not lack consciousness.
- Minors above the age of seven and not lacking consciousness are

distinguished from minors above seven and under 15 years of age (b') and minors above 15 (b"). Both are partially liable, but they are treated differently. Whereas no punishment can be imposed upon children under the age of 15, who can only be subjected to precautionary measures, alleviated punishment can be imposed on children above the age of 15, with a further distinction between children younger than 16 (b"1) and children between 16 and 18 years of age (b"2), the former receiving a more lenient penalty than the latter.

- Minors lacking consciousness, either because they are under seven years of age or because they suffer from a mental deficiency, can neither be punished nor subjected to the abovementioned measures.
- Adults lacking consciousness cannot be condemned to any penalty and can only be referred to a medical institution.

In sum, we can list six states of legal personality, corresponding to three types of liability: full liability, no liability, and limited liability. This can be schematized as shown in Figure 7.2.

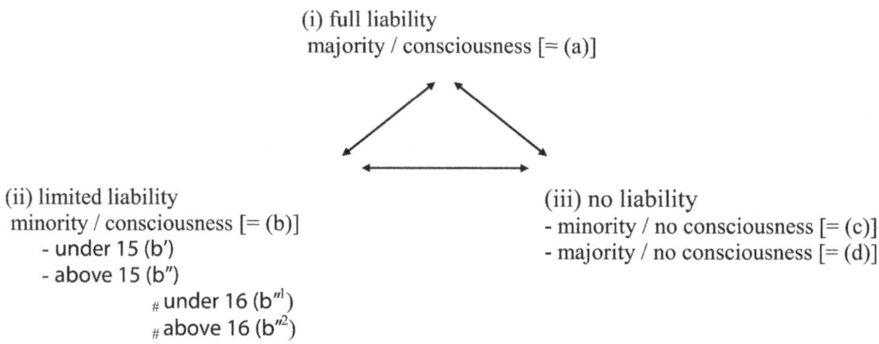

Figure 7.2 Types of legal liability

b) Case-law:

Although the Penal Code identifies two different types of mental deficiency, from which different types of legal capacity and criminal liability follow, it does not define what mental deficiency is. Here again, we must turn to the jurisprudence of the Court of Cassation, even though it does not seem able to answer this question in a satisfactory manner. Here follow some of the principles it established in the field of mental health.

According to the Court of Cassation, not all mental illnesses lead to an impediment of criminal liability.

Excerpt 31 (Court of Cassation, Compendium of Principles)
It is established that mental illness, which is characterized as insanity or mental disorder and by virtue of which there cannot be any legal liability, is an illness that in itself impeaches consciousness and awareness. Most psychological illnesses and states in which people do not lack consciousness and awareness cannot be considered as a cause for the absence of liability. The court is not obliged to appoint a technical expert in this case to define the extent of the illness from which the accused is suffering and its effect on his criminal liability, except in purely technical questions where its [power of] appreciation is impossible (Case 3, 33rd judicial year, session of 26 March 1963, Folio 14, p. 254; Case 986, 33rd judicial year, session of 22 October 1963, Folio 14, p. 678).

Reference can only be made to insanity and mental disorder:

Excerpt 32 (Court of Cassation, Compendium of Principles)
Non-punishment due to the criminal's lack of consciousness or ability to choose his action at the time when the act was committed concerns only the reference to this state of insanity or disorder of the mind (Case 216, 24th judicial year, session of 13 April 1964, Folio 15, p. 295; case 243, 38th judicial year, session of 25 March 1968, Folio 19, p. 350).

Other types of mental illness must be defined before determining the extent to which they fit the categories of insanity and mental disorder:

Excerpt 33 (Court of Cassation, Compendium of Principles)
A person suffering from the state known as 'psychotic personality', which, from the scientific point of view, is considered as a psychological illness, is not deemed in the realm of law as suffering from insanity or disorder of the mind, in which case he may have been considered as lacking consciousness or choice in his action (Case 2313, 31st judicial year, session of 28 November 1961, Folio 12, p. 942).

Idiocy is a disorder of the mind that stops the growth of intellectual capacities before the stage of natural maturity is achieved. Mental disorder does not require that the person suffering from it lack awareness and free will at the same time, only that he lack one of the two (Case 438, 36th judicial year, session of 23 May 1966, Folio 17, p. 674).

Violent emotions and stress do not constitute mental disorders in and of themselves (cf. references given by Husni, 1989: 532, n. 1). Even insanity and mental disorder do not preclude criminal liability; it is the lack of consciousness and choice of action that precludes liability (cf. references given by Husni, 1989: 533, n. 1).

As for recourse to medical expertise, the Court of Cassation asserts the judge's discretionary power:

Excerpt 34 (Court of Cassation, Compendium of Principles)
It is established that the court of merits is responsible for evaluating the opinions of experts, assessing their reports, and adjudicating in objections that these reports may arouse. This court has complete freedom to evaluate the evidentiary force of the

expert reports presented to it, without being obliged either to appoint another expert or to return the question to the same expert, provided that the opinion on which the expert bases his decision is valid and does not oppose reason and law (Case 91, 45th judicial year, session of 3 March 1975, Folio 26, p. 207).

Causal Relationship

Both jurisprudence and legal doctrine consider that causal relations constitute a pillar of criminal liability. The establishment of a causal relation aims at showing the role of an action in the production of harmful effects. Causality here is taken to mean the existence of a necessary relation between two realities, the first being the cause of the second. However, things rarely have single causes. In this respect, Husni (1989: 301-25), following John Stuart Mill, defines a cause as a set of positive and negative factors whose realization entails the occurrence of the result in a necessary way. Nevertheless, this definition raises legal difficulties, since it extends the scope of causation beyond the boundaries of human agency. How can we give something the status of a cause if it is not one of many factors contributing to a given result? Two theories of jurisprudence offer contradictory answers to this question: on one hand, the theory of the equivalence of conditions defines a cause as either the sum total of the chain of events having concurred in effecting damage (*sine qua non* conditions) or any one of these conditions; on the other, adequate cause theory defines a cause as a fact that modifies the normal course of events.

The Egyptian Court of Cassation acknowledges the legal function of causal relations and makes them one of the components of crime. A ruling that fails to mention any causal relation is deemed deficient (*qasir al-tasbib*). The Court requires that a cause be a material relationship that began with the action of the causing agent (*fi'l al-mutasabbib*):

Excerpt 35 (Court of Cassation, quoted by Husni, 1989: 303)
Morally, [a causal relationship] is linked to the usual results of the causing agent's action, which he should have foreseen if he committed this action wilfully; or, with regard to what he committed mistakenly, to his inability to foresee the usual obstacles to his conduct and anticipate that his actions would entail harm to a third party.

The criterion used by the Court of Cassation in assessing the existence of a causal relationship is grounded in two elements: material and moral. The material element means that the action is linked to the factors that contributed to the result, i.e. that what happened would not have happened if this action had not been initiated. The moral element is the difference between intentional and unintentional crimes. It means that, with regard to intentional crimes, the criminal result must be normal and the offender capable of foreseeing it. The Court issued several rulings supporting this idea. For instance, it declared a physician responsible for the death of his patient, which occurred 58 days after treatment began, if the physician had the capacity to foresee the result. In the same way, it considered that someone who was accused of wilful battery was liable for his victim's death even if factors like geriatric weakness, medical history, or complications concurred in this result. With regard to unintentional crimes, the moral element of the causal relationship requires that the offender was unable to foresee the normal consequences of his action. On the whole, therefore, the Egyptian Court of Cassation appears to have adopted the criterion of adequate causality.

Mitigation of and Exclusion from Criminal Liability

Penal doctrine establishes a major distinction between justifications, excuses, and attenuating circumstances. Herbert Hart defines these notions in the following way:

1. 'In the case of "justification", what is done is regarded as something which the law does not condemn, or even welcome' (Hart, 1968: 13);
2. In the case of excuse, '[w]hat has been done is something which is deplored, but the psychological state of the agent when he did it exemplified one or more of a variety of conditions which are held to rule out the public condemnation of individuals' (*ibid.*: 14);
3. In the case of mitigation, 'a good reason for administering a less severe penalty is made out if the situation or mental state of the convicted criminal is such that he was exposed to an unusual or specially great temptation, or his ability to control his actions is thought to have been impaired or weakened otherwise than by his own action, so that conformity to the law which he has broken was a matter of special difficulty for him as compared with normal persons normally placed.' (*ibid.:* 15).

Egyptian positive law, as it appears in legal texts, jurisprudence, and doctrine, precludes criminal liability when the causes of an action make it justifiable. Further, criminal liability cannot be implemented when the causes of action make it excusable. Finally, punishment for criminal action can be aggravated or mitigated according to the circumstances surrounding its occurrence.

Article 60 of the Penal Code stipulates: 'The provisions of the Penal Code do not apply to any *bona fide* act committed in pursuance of a right established according to the *shari'a*. No penalty can be inflicted on a person who has committed a crime if he was incited by the need to preserve (*darurat waqaya*) himself or others from serious, life-endangering harm (*khatar jasim*), or if he suspected that his life or that of others could be endangered, provided his will had no role in the occurrence [of this crime] and he was unable to prevent it in another way.' Justifying causes (*asbab al-ibaha*) are defined in Egyptian law as the features of an action that foreclose the existence of the legal element of the crime, i.e. that negate the criminal nature of the act. Two types of justification obviate the criminalization of an action: direct justification (for instance, an authorized medical action justifies violating the right to bodily integrity) and indirect justification that make one right superior to another (for instance, homicide is justified in self-defense on the basis that the victim's right to life is superior to the aggressor's).

'No penalty can be inflicted on someone who was unconscious (*faqid al-shu'ur*) or had no choice (*faqid al-ikhtiyar*) at the time when the act was committed, whether because of insanity or mental disorder, or because of a loss of consciousness (*ghaybuba*) resulting from the ingestion of drugs, whatever their kind, if he was forced to take them or did not know that he was taking them.' Excuses (*a'dhar*) are therefore linked to the existence of impediments to criminal liability (*mawani' al-mas'uliyya*). Excuses negate the moral element of the crime and therefore exclude the imposition of a penalty on the perpetrator; Husni defines them as 'causes that impose themselves upon the perpetrator of an act, preventing his will from being expressed legally, since his discernment or free will was absent.' (Husni, 1989: 160)[3]

Egyptian criminal legislation deals with the question of the circumstances surrounding a crime as part of general penal theory. These circumstances, which concern how the crime was committed and not whether it took place, affect the severity of the punishment. Thus, the question of circumstances is related to the application of the penalty. According to Husni (1989: 805), '[legislators] cannot adapt [every] penalty to each individual committing a crime, since they cannot know every individual's personality in advance, and it is impossible for them to determine all the circumstances (*zuruf*) surrounding [a crime] and to know the considerations determining a fair and suitable punishment for each [criminal].' This is why the legislature defines the penalty which it thinks is fair and suitable for 'an ordinary person [acting] in ordinary circumstances' (*shakhs 'adi dhi zuruf 'adiyya*), although it assumes at the same time that the perpetrator acted under circumstances that are not ordinary, and gives the judge the discretionary power (*al-sulta al-taqdiriyya*) to assess these circumstances and to adapt the rough legislative definition to various concrete situations.[4] Two types of cause can modulate a penalty: aggravating causes (*asbab tashdid al-'iqab*)[5] and mitigating causes (*asbab takhfif al-'iqab*).[6] Mitigating causes are divided into two categories:

3 Discretion means here 'the ability to understand the significance of an action and its nature, and to anticipate the consequences that could follow because it was carried out.' Free will means 'the offender's ability to outline the orientation his will takes, i.e. his faculty to push his will in a specific direction among the different orientations it could have taken.' (Husni, 1989: 522)

4 The judge's discretionary powers are defined as 'his capacity to ensure that the sentence he determines with regard to the situation submitted to him fits the actual circumstances of this situation, i.e. simply the ability to move between the maximum and minimum limits of the [stipulated] penalty.' (Husni, 1989: 807)

5 'Situations in which the judge may or must punish the crime more severely than the law stipulates or increase the maximum penalty stipulated by the law for this crime.' (Husni, 1989: 830)

6 'Situations in which the judge may or must punish the crime with greater leniency than the law stipulates or reduce the minimum penalty stipulated by the law.' (Husni, 1989: 816)

excuses (*a'dhar*) that the law obliges the judge to consider, either preventing him from punish the offender altogether (absolutory excuses, *a'dhar mu'fiyya*),[7] or imposing the lightest possible penalty stipulated by the law (mitigating excuses, *a'dhar mukhaffifa*);[8] and circumstances that are not defined by the law and which the legislature leaves to the judge's discretion, allowing him to mitigate the penalty (attenuating circumstances, *zuruf mukhaffifa*).

The case law of the Court of Cassation seeks to interpret this set of notions. It has elaborated a theory of justification that distinguishes between personal and real causes (Sidqi, 1986: 404). The former include duress (*ikrah*), necessity (*halat al-darura*), insanity (*junun*), mental deficiency (*'aha 'aqliyya*), unconsciousness (*ghaybuba*), inebriation (*sukr*), and *force majeure* (*quwwa qahira*). The latter include the use of a right established in pursuance of the law (*isti'mal haqq muqarrar bi-muqtada al-qanun*), like a husband's right to discipline his wife or parents' right to discipline their minor children, a civil servant's execution of an action which the law commanded him to perform, legitimate self-defense (*difa' shar'i*), the practice of medical and surgical professions, and the practice of sports.

The Court of Cassation has formulated a number of principles that abrogate criminal liability and can be summarized as follows:

- Duress is an incident originating from an involuntary event in which the accused played no part and which he had no capacity to prevent. A father's order to commit a crime therefore does not constitute a case of duress.
- Necessity is a situation in which the crime committed was the only way of protecting oneself against imminent danger; it corresponds to circumstances that push an individual to commit a crime in order to protect himself or a third party from a serious and imminent threat to their survival.
- Insanity and mental frailty refer to states that deprived the offender of his consciousness or will at the time when the crime was committed. The judge is not compelled to heed expert advice in these cases.
- Inebriation is only accepted as an excuse if the offender did not consume alcohol of his own volition. As for lethargy or loss of consciousness, it must result from the consumption of a narcotic under duress or in ignorance. Wilful inebriation does not preclude liability for wilful homicide.
- Force majeure is linked to situations where the offender could not prevent the occurrence of harm or was incapable of forbidding it. (Qabbani, 1988: 391-8; 521-42)

7 Example: a man who abducts a woman will be exempted from punishment if he marries her legally (Penal Code, Article 312, abrogated).

8 Example of a general mitigating excuse: repeat offenders who are minors aged 15 to 18 receive a lighter penalty. Example of a particular mitigating excuse: a husband who unexpectedly comes upon his wife committing adultery and kills her and her partner on the spot (Penal Code, Article 338).

With regard to real justification, the Court of Cassation has formulated the following principles:

- The excessive use of a right established pursuant to the law constitutes a crime (the excessive use of the right to discipline is thus constitutive of the crime of battery).
- The practice of medical and surgical professions is limited to duly registered professional practitioners and to the respect of professional rules, among them therapeutic intent.
- A civil servant who obeyed the orders issued by his superiors must have been acting in good faith and in the conviction that his action was legitimate.
- Legitimate self-defense does not authorize violence but must be aimed at protecting oneself against aggression. It is not necessary for a real threat to be proven; it is sufficient that the accused was convinced of its reality. Nor could the threat have been foreseeable. (Qabbani, 1988: 367-91; 400-520)

The Court of Cassation formulated different principles concerning mitigating excuses and mitigating and aggravating circumstances.

- Egyptian law does not treat anger as a mitigating excuse ('udhr mukhaffif), except in the case of a husband who discovers his wife committing adultery and kills her and her partner – as long as the killing was not premeditated. Legal minority is also seen as an attenuating excuse when the normal penalty is death or forced labour.
- Attenuating circumstances (zuruf mukhaffifa) cover everything related to the material conditions surrounding a crime, including the personalities of the criminal and the victim. Evaluating the incidence of this set of factors and circumstances is left to the judge's absolute discretion. As examples of mitigating circumstances, one can point to legal minority, when it does not constitute a mitigating excuse as defined by the law; provocation; unreasonable fears that do not count as legitimate self-defense, etc.
- Among aggravating circumstances (zuruf mushaddida), the Court mentions, with regard to homicide, premeditation and ambush, or, with regard to theft, the use of force or the carrying of a weapon. (Sidqi, 1988: 213-7; Husni, 1989: 822-30; Qabbani, 1988: 615-44)

What Law Books Say and Do Not Say

Having provided a summary presentation of penal law, we will now undertake to analyse it. In this section, we shall show how jurisprudence and case law constitute effective instruments in the hands of professionals who orient to "law in the books" for all practical purposes. Then we will focus on the fact that the same law cannot be taken as an account of the legal practice that led to its transcription. In other words, while law in the books allows professional actors to orient their actions, it does not retrospectively account for these actions.

Law in the Books, for All Practical Purposes

Law professionals use jurisprudence and case law, not as accounts of past legal actions, but rather to orient their future legal actions. In other words, jurisprudence and case law serve as prospective guidebooks or milestones for action and not as retrospective descriptions of action. To mistake them for sources that allow for the reconstitution of a factual truth implies that one has committed a triple error: first, by omitting to consider that documents of doctrine and jurisprudence were written for the practical purpose of their future use; second, by neglecting the fact that these documents take the modalities of their elaboration into account only to ensure procedural correctness and legal relevance (cf. above, Chapters 5 and 6); and third, by forgetting that these documents constitute legal "generalizations" and not factual "singularizations".

In the present sociological endeavour, which seeks primarily to describe the activity of judging, law in the books functions as a milestone according to which people orient themselves. It is necessary to assess its nature if we are to grasp a number of features that make up the background of people engaged in judicial activities. In this sense, law in the books can be considered the point of origin from which law professionals undertake the process of legal characterization. It is therefore one of the sources to which judges, among others, refer intertextually in order to give ongoing procedures the form of a judicial ruling. Law in the books can thus be considered as an intertextual support through which judicial work explicitly incorporates current action within the authority of legal, doctrinal and jurisprudential texts. The idea of intertextuality refers to the work of Bakhtin (Voloshinov, 1973; Bakhtin, 1981; 1986) and to the claim that texts generally have dialogical and polyphonic dimensions. As Matoesian (2001: 108) puts it, a text can 'incorporate the interpenetration of multiple and shifting voices, ideologies, and historical contexts when contextualized to fit the discursive relevancies of a current performance.' By way of illustration, if we take the text of a standard sentence, as in the two preceding chapters, we may observe how legal, doctrinal, and jurisprudential sources are mobilized to underpin judicial authority. The following excerpt also illustrates our point about legal authority:

> **Excerpt 36 (Court of First Instance, Case 701, 1983, Personal Status, Giza)**
> Given that, as evidenced by the text of Article 6 of Legal Decree 25 of 1929 concerning certain provisions on repudiation, in allowing the judge to rule for judicial divorce on the basis of harm, Egyptian legislators require that harm or prejudice come from the husband, and not from the wife, so that their life together has become impossible.

In the same clause, the Court of Cassation's authority is also mobilized:

Excerpt 37 (Court of First Instance, Case 701, 1983, Personal Status, Giza)
Harm here consists of the wrong done by the husband to his wife by the means of speech or action or both, in a manner that is not acceptable to people of similar status, and constitutes something shameful and wrongful that cannot be endured (Cassation, Personal Status, Appeal 50, 52nd Judicial Year, session of 28 June 1983; the standard applied here [by the Court of Cassation] is the non-material standard of a person, which varies according to environment, culture, and the wife's social status: Cassation, Personal Status, Appeal 5, 46th Judicial Year, session of 9 November 1977, p. 1644).

Since the sentence concerns personal status, the authority of the different schools of Sunni law (*madhhab*) is also invoked, albeit through legislative and jurisprudential provisions:

Excerpt 38 (Court of First Instance, Case 701, 1983, Personal Status, Giza)
Given that the Egyptian legislature has taken (*naqala*) the rule of judicial divorce on grounds of injury from the doctrine of Imam Malik [...] It is not allowed, in establishing it [injury], [to refer] to the same doctrine from which it is imported, and no particular rule has been stipulated to establish it. In such a situation, to prove that injury has been inflicted, one must go back to the majority opinion in the doctrine of Imam Abu Hanifa al-Nu'man, in accordance with Article 280 of the Shari'a Courts Regulations, to which Article 6 of Law 462 of 1955 refers (Cassation, Personal Status, Appeal 11, 48th Judicial Year, session of 25 April 1979).

Reference can also be made directly to the most prominent scholars in Islamic law (*fiqh*):

Excerpt 39 (Court of First Instance, Case 701, 1983, Personal Status, Giza)
Abu Hanifa and Abu Yusuf allowed separation on grounds of a permanent defect that impedes intercourse between a man and a woman [...]. Upholding [a marriage contract] despite this [constitutes] harm for the woman whose perpetuation cannot be accepted and nothing can resolve it save separation (*The Personal Status of Imam Abu Zahra*, p. 414, par. 297, ed. 1957).

Finally, the intertextual game can even be extended to the Qur'an or the words and deeds of the Prophet Muhammad, which sometimes seem to be invoked in an almost superfluous manner (Dupret, 2000):

Excerpt 40 (Court of First Instance, Case 701, 1983, Personal Status, Giza)
Given that, with regard to what precedes, the court realizes that the continuation of their marital life ... would be an injustice (*zulm*) against her [the wife]. It is the judge's responsibility, as protector of justice, to put an end to it. Although repudiation is the most hated of permitted acts in God's eyes, it is equally forbidden to keep a wife tied by marital bonds to a husband when he causes her injuries that make it impossible for women of her status to pursue their conjugal

life. The court takes into consideration the words of the Almighty: 'But do not take them back to injure them' [Qur'an 2: 231]; and the words of the Almighty: 'Then, the parties should either hold together on equitable terms, or separate with kindness' [Qur'an 2: 229]; and the words of the [Prophet] – may God bless him and give him peace: 'Neither harm nor counterharm [viz., a harm inflicted to counter another harm]'.

Beyond the intertextual nature of rulings, we may also show how they partake of a process of formal abstraction that aims at endowing practitioners with guidelines that will allow them to orient themselves in cases that are considered to belong to the same type. In that sense, texts of law, jurisprudence, and doctrine show no concern for history but rather correspond to a practical desire to use them as references for all future legal practical purposes. Using Jackson's semiotic language (1988: 97-111), we can say that the practical purpose of these texts is to be used as underlying schemes of interpretation and evaluation of new cases submitted to the attention of law practitioners. In this way, they set the conditions for the possibility of certain types of interpretation while foreclosing others (Umphrey, 1999: 404).

To illustrate the point, we will use a case taken from the Compendium of the Court of Cassation's rulings. It shows how case-law texts are prospectively organized to serve as interpretive schemes in cases that future judges will preemptively characterize as medical errors. First, note the form taken by the narrative of events (*waqa'i'*):

Excerpt 41 (Court of Cassation, 1973, Case 40, 1983, Claim 1566, 42nd Judicial Year)

The civil petitioner directly introduced his petition before the Azbakiyya Court of misdemeanors against the first defendant, claiming that the latter, during the month of December 1964, in the district of Azbakiyya, caused an error (*khata'*), due to his negligence (*ihmal*), lack of care (*'adam ihtiraz*) and precaution (*'adam ihtiyat*), and failure to observe medical principles that must be followed (*'adam mura'atihi li-l-usul al-tibbiyya al-wajib ittiba'iha*), all of which resulted in the petitioner's complete loss of eyesight. This is because [the defendant] conducted a surgical operation on both [the petitioner's] eyes simultaneously in order to remove cataracts, without previously carrying out the medically necessary measures and examinations. [The defendant] conducted the operation on the petitioner without notifying him and without obtaining his consent, without the assistance of an anesthetist and outside a hospital. Furthermore, he did not compel [the petitioner] to rest and obtain medical follow-up after the operation. Rather, [the defendant] abandoned [the petitioner] in the middle of the street without assistance, and this led to the inflammation of his eyes [...] and the occurrence of complications that weakened his eyesight. He [the civil petitioner] asked that [the defendant] be condemned pursuant to Article 224/1-2 of the Code of Penal Procedure and that he be compelled, together with Misr Petroleum Company, which is liable for civil obligations, to pay compensation [...] as well as expenses and retainers [...]. The [the civil petitioner] then amended his petition and requested [double] the

> amount. On 26 June 1969, pursuant to the provision [stipulated] in the accusation, the abovementioned court [decided]: (1) to condemn the defendant to payment of a fine [...]; and (2), with regard to the civil petition, to reject the defense invoked by the company responsible for civil obligations, according to which the petition was inadmissible with regard to anyone other than a person acting on his own behalf, and to declare the petition admissible, thereby compelling the defendant together with the abovementioned company to pay the civil petitioner [...]compensation, expenses, and [...]retainers [...]. The defendant, together with the company responsible for civil obligations, introduced an appeal against this ruling. The Cairo Court of First Instance, in its appeals circuit, ruled on 30 April 1972, admitting the appeal with regard to its form, confirming the ruling against which the appeal was lodged as to penalty [viz., the fine], and amending the ruling as to compensation, limiting it [...], besides the expenses corresponding to both degrees of jurisdiction and [...] retainers. Both the defendant and the party responsible for civil obligations decided to appeal this ruling in cassation.

This presentation, which follows the summary of the legal grounds for the sentence in the compendium of the Court's rulings, clearly reflects the prospective orientation of the text. The factual aspect is reduced as much as possible, in order to standardize the summary, making it easy for a virtual future judge to find relative similarity between the case he will be hearing and the precedent constituted by the case at hand. The description of the error that led to the condemnation is not bogged down in detail; instead, it concentrates only on the facts that might have legal relevance: here (a case of medical responsibility), the elements constitutive of a medical act and the conditions surrounding it. Doctrine, jurisprudence, and legislation (Qayid, 1987) define the medical act (*'amal tibbi*) as 'any action necessary or desirable for the exercise by a physician of his right to practice the medical profession' and make such acts subject to three conditions: that the individual performing them be legally authorized to dispense care (*tarkhis qanuni bi-muzawalat al-'ilaj*); that the patient expressed consent (*rida' al-marid*); that there be a therapeutic intent (*qasd al-'ilaj*). The description of facts, carried out in our case by the Court of Cassation, is clearly organized around the issue of determining whether or not these elements are present. The case at hand here has been stripped of its singularity and serves as the basis for a generalizing process, which some future virtual judge will use in order to characterize a new factuality.

Even before the enunciation of the facts, however, the Compendium of the Court of Cassation's rulings enumerates a list of keywords referring to the formulation of rules concerning legal questions raised before the Court. This summary enumeration proceeds in two steps. First, the enumeration in its most condensed form:

Excerpt 42 (Court of Cassation, 1973, Case 40, 1983, Claim 1566, 42nd Judicial Year)
(a) appeal [...]
(b) criminal responsibility – civil responsibility – fault – unintentional injury – medicine – trial court – "its jurisdiction regarding the assessment of the fault that is required to engage responsibility"
the trial court's jurisdiction regarding the assessment of the fault that is required to engage criminal and civil responsibility – example: from surgery on both eyes simultaneously, resulting in the loss of eyesight
(c) causes for authorization (*asbab al-ibaha*) – "the physician's work" – criminal responsibility – fault – unintentional injury – medicine
authorization of the physician's work – on condition that his work corresponds to the basic principles of the operation – to forego these basic principles or to breach them engages criminal responsibility
(d) authorization of error (*ibahat khata'*) – crime – "to commit a crime" – criminal responsibility
only one of the faults enumerated in article 244 of the Code of criminal procedure suffices to open the possibility of penalty for the crime of unintentional injury
(e) evidence (*ithbat*) [...]
(f) link of causality [...]
(g) civil responsibility [...]

Then, the same enumeration in a more expanded form:

Excerpt 43 (Court of Cassation, 1973, Case 40, 1983, Claim 1566, 42nd Judicial Year)
1 – [...]
2 – The trial court, when assessing the fault engaging the criminal or civil responsibility of the person who committed it, considered that the petitioner, who is a specialist, made an error when carrying out surgery on both eyes simultaneously, although expediency was not required given the circumstances [of the case] and the considerations indicated in the technical reports. The petitioner did not take all the general precautions necessary to guarantee the outcome and did not heed suitable obligatory precautions in the method he chose. Consequently, [the petitioner] exposed the patient to complications in both eyes simultaneously, a situation that led to the complete loss of his eyesight. [If the trial court considers this,] the degree established for this error is sufficient to make the petitioner liable at [both] criminal and civil levels.
3 – It is established that authorization for working as a physician is conditional upon the fact that the physician's activity corresponds to established scientific basic principles; if he deviates from observing these ground principles or breaches them, criminal responsibility is ascribed to him according to the intentional character of the deed, its result, or its insufficiencies, and the lack of precautions taken in its implementation.

> 4 – To determine that unintentional injury has occurred, it is sufficient for only one of the errors enumerated in article 244 of the Code of Criminal Procedure to have been committed.
> 5 – [...]
> 6 – [...]
> 7 – [...]

Only at the last stage is the structure of the Court of Cassation's ruling integrally reiterated, adding only a few elements to what was summarized previously. This structure, incidentally, is not reproduced in another type of publication: the compendia of rules formulated by the Court (*Majmu'at al-Qawa'id allati Qarrarataha Mahkamat al-Naqd*). It appears explicitly from the way the publication of these rulings is organized that their presentation is intended for future users. In that sense, the Court of Cassation's case law belongs more to the genre of legal principles for future practical purposes than to that of the detailed accounting of past facts.

Formal Abstraction and the Dissimulation of the Practical Conditions of Constitution

There is a manifest gap between facts and their formal rendering in documents like a court ruling. This gap is produced by 'the transformation of locally accomplished, embodied, and "lived" activities into disengaged textual documents.' (Lynch, 1993: 287) The transformation process includes a conditional reduction of information. By reduction, we mean that only some of the available information is selected so as to produce an "authorized" account of facts. By conditional reduction, we mean that this selection depends on formal legal categories to which factuality will be assigned. Basing an analysis totally on the formalized and polished text of court rulings means running the risk of missing the very phenomenon one seeks to study: i.e., judicial practice in general and modes of reasoning in judicial settings in particular. These rulings are merely the *ex post facto* formalization of earlier practices, and not the description of these practices. Using only the example of medical responsibility described above (excerpts 40 to 42), we observe that facts are presented as speaking in and of themselves, in a totally unambiguous way. The intertextual authority of medical expertise is never questioned; nor is the victim's point of view presented. Witnesses' credibility and thus the veracity of their testimony are not assessed. The whole set of practical and contingent aspects, background expectations, people's orientations, and situational constraints is thus erased in the process of producing a retrospective account that satisfies the requirements of its prospective use for all practical legal purposes. As Lynch (1993: 289) puts it, summarizing an anecdote recounted by Garfinkel in an unpublished paper, 'the *transformation* that is achieved from the rendering of the case is itself hidden whenever the case report becomes the relevant analytic datum.'

However, legal activity is mainly a linguistic activity. This signifies not only that language is the means of implementing law, but also that it is the means through which facts are transformed into relevant legal objects (cf. Chapter 6), evidence is endowed with the authority to establish the veracity of facts, and rules are interpreted so as to encapsulate facts in legally relevant categories. Gregory Matoesian (2001: 212) writes the following about a rape trial:

> ... language use actively and reciprocally shapes and organizes legal and cultural variables into communicative modes of institutionalized relevance. It constitutes the interactional medium through which evidence, statutes, and our gendered identities are improvisationally forged into legal significance for the trial proceedings. And it represents the primary mechanism for creating and negotiating legal realities, such as credibility, character, and inconsistency; for ascribing blame and allocating responsibility; and for constructing truth and knowledge about force, (non)consent, and sexual history.

In other words, when concentrating exclusively on formalized documents, we neglect the tortuous path followed by legal activity before it takes its definitive aspect. We forget that legal reasoning, not to mention other examples, is a social process during which people ascribe reasons, motives, and explanations to various words and deeds, in a way that depends not only on the "objective historicity" of these facts, but also – and no doubt essentially – on the contextual, situational, institutional, interactional, and artifactual contingencies of fact production itself. This does not signify that formalized legal documents do not deserve attention, quite the contrary. Nor does it mean that legal reasoning, as it appears from the examination of these documents, cannot be studied in and of itself. As we saw, such documents constitute the basis on which later judicial decisions will be taken, a basis that practitioners consider reliable; as such, these formalized rulings, in their own right, constitute legitimate research topics. However, they cannot be taken as either the main or the sole source of judicial activity and reasoning in general. The need for praxeological re-specification intervenes at this level: instead of producing accounts of accounts and documents abstracted from the concrete lived conditions of the process through which they were produced, and instead of dissociating documents from the activity that produced them, the ethnomethodological study of judicial work seeks to consider both the document and the documentary activity at the same time, as indispensable to and inseparable from each other, for the adequate understanding of the phenomenon under consideration (cf. Livingston, 1987; Lynch, 1993: 287-99). This approach obviously runs counter to the semiotic perspective, which considers formal accounts to be equivalent to the activity in which they originate, when in fact we must focus on formal accounts as local, reflexive activities conducted for purposes that are legal, practical, and forgetful of their own historicity. This is the incommensurable relationship in which we find testimonies and rulings, *ex post facto* formalizations and synchronic transcripts, Court of Cassation rulings and Prosecution interrogations, conventional historical narratives and situated stories. (Lynch and Bogen, 1996: 164)[9]

We will illustrate this point by comparing different documents from a single trial, the case of the Ma'adi girl (cf. above). On one hand, we have the Court of Cassation's ruling, as recorded in the *Compendium of the Court of Cassation's Rulings*; the opinion issued by the Mufti of the Republic; and the ruling of the Criminal Court. All these narrate the facts in a certain way. On the other hand, we have the Prosecution's interrogation transcripts, in which we can observe the practical modalities of enunciation, negotiation, and contestation of the same facts. In this way, we can see the asymmetrical disjunction (Garfinkel, unpublished, as quoted by Lynch, 1993: 290) that arises between these documents when they have to account for the activity of judging.

Without repeating earlier points, suffice it to note here that the case is recorded in the *Compendium of the Court of Cassation's Rulings* under a series of keywords allowing for the indexing of the legal principles. At this stage, it is thus clear that the ruling is oriented mainly to future users.

Excerpt 44 (Court of Cassation, 1986, Case 20, 1983, Claim 4421, 55th Judicial Year)

a. Cassation "appeal memorandum – and presentation of motives" "delay" [...]
b. General Prosecution – death penalty – sentence "death penalty – presentation" – Court of Cassation "its authority" [...]
c. evidence "confession" [...]
d. evidence "by general way" "confession" – defence "defense of null and void confession [due to duress]" – sentence "its motive – motive invalidated" – Cassation "motives for appeal – what is accepted" [...]
e. death penalty – connection – sentence "its motive – motive invalidated" – Court of Cassation "its authority" [...]

In contrast, establishing the facts requires revealing the sentence's orientation toward a factual past. Let us take different examples, starting with the beginning of the paragraph devoted to the facts of the case in the Court of Cassation's ruling, which followed the appeal against the Criminal Court's first ruling of 6 April 1985.

9 On this relation between narratives and narrative accounts and the contingent transformation of stories into history, much ethnomethodological work exists. We may cite Garfinkel (1974) on medical reports, Cicourel (1968) on police records, Zimmerman (1974) on construction of facts as practical achievement, Meehan (1997) on police documentary activity, and Komter (2001) on the construction of evidence in police interrogations.

Excerpt 45 (Court of Cassation, 1986, Case 20, 1983, Claim 4421, 55th Judicial Year)
The General Prosecution accused the petitioners of the following: (1) all the accused collectively: of having abducted the [female] victim [...], to which is added the misdemeanour of non-consensual intercourse with the abducted person, since the first five suspects had agreed to abduct and rape any woman they encountered on the road. In accordance with this agreement, they got into a cab driven by the fifth suspect and drove around until they met the [female] victim, who was sitting with her fiancé in his car on the public thoroughfare. Each of the first suspects drew a gazelle-horn knife and threatened to attack the [female] victim and her fiancé. They forced her (*arghamuha 'unwatan*) to get out of her fiancé's car and into the cab driven by the fifth suspect. They travelled some distance with her to another place on the public thoroughfare until the first suspect started threatening her with his knife and stripped her of her clothes. He undressed, lay upon her, and penetrated her vagina partially with his penis. Then the second suspect began undressing [...]

The Court of Cassation's enunciation of the facts explicitly repeats the General Prosecution's. There are no special factual developments. It must be said that, technically speaking, the Court of Cassation does not examine the substance of the case, but only procedural issues. Consequently, special attention is given to legal principles. The court's jurisdiction also explains the particularly bald style used to describe the facts.

Following the Court of Cassation's ruling, which reversed the Criminal Court's first sentence, the case was sent before a second Criminal Court (in fact, the same Court with different judges). The latter, in turn, reviewed the facts of the case:

Excerpt 46 (Criminal Court, South Cairo, 12 May 1986)
... on 17 January 1985, the second suspect, Ashraf Hasan Gamil, the third suspect, Anwar Isma'il Salim, and the fourth suspect, Mitwalli 'Abd al-Munsif Muhammad, got into a cab driven by the fifth suspect, Ahmad Sayyid Ahmad. On the road, they met the first suspect, Salah Shawqi 'Ali Abu Halawa, who is a friend of the second suspect and who got in the car with them. They all agreed to look for any woman with the aim of having sexual intercourse (*irtikab al-fahsha'*) with her. To this end, they drove around Ma'adi until, at 4:30, they saw a private car stopped on the public thoroughfare near one of the villas [in the neighbourhood]. Ghada Muhammad Kamal Sulayman and her fiancé, Ahmad Hamdi Hasan, were in the car. They were discussing their engagement party. The suspects found in the [female] victim the prey they sought to execute the nefarious (*athim*) aims on which they had agreed previously. The first suspect walked toward the car where the [female] victim was sitting and pulled out a knife, while the third and fifth suspects hid among some nearby trees in order to encourage the first accused and to intervene if necessary, and the second and fourth suspects remained in the cab and observed the situation. When the first suspect reached the [female] victim's car, he ordered her to get out and, when she did not obey, began to slash the left front tire of the car with his knife. Then he repeated [the operation] on the rear left tire in order to prevent the [female] victim from escaping.

> Despite this, the [male] victim, Ahmad Hamdi, managed to start the car and drive it to a nearby street. He got out to change the front tire so as to be able to drive. [...] The first suspect demanded the sum of 50 L.E. [...] The [male] victim asked his fiancée to hand over her gold bracelet, asserting that its value exceeded the 50 L.E. he was asking for. However, the first suspect refused and the [female] victim became convinced of his wicked (*athim*) and forbidden (*haram*) intentions. [...] The other suspects [got out of the cab] and surrounded the [female] victim. The second suspect told them that his father was a policeman at the Ma'adi station and that he had to bring them before him. Then the first suspect stabbed the [female] victim on her right hand, causing the wound indicated in the medical report. Then they forced them to approach the cab and the second suspect pushed the [female] victim inside [...] and they left with them [...] to a dark desert zone outside the Ma'adi neighbourhood. [...] When they arrived at that place, the second, third, fourth, and fifth suspects got out and took the [male] victim with them, leaving the first suspect in the car alone with the [female] victim, a virgin (*bikr*), who was 17 years old. The [male] victim opposed this, imploring (*mutawassilan*) the accused, telling them that his fiancée was a virgin, and begging for mercy (*mustarhiman*), but his requests for clemency were like a call for prayer that went unheard, meeting only cruel hearts that did not react. The [male] victim stood among the suspects, who were threatening him. He could not oppose them and could do nothing for his fiancée, whom the first suspect had isolated in the car, forcing her to strip at knifepoint and paying no heed to her supplications (*tawassulatiha*), implorations (*isti'tafatiha*), weakness (*du'fiha*), young age (*sughr sinniha*), and disgrace (*qillat haya'iha*). On the contrary, he met all this with cruelty (*qaswa*). He addressed her with coarse words (*alfaz wa 'ibarat badhi'a*) and accompanied this with grotesque noises. When the [female] victim was totally naked, he forced her to lie down in the back seat and lay on top of her to rape her. He began embracing her, grasping her breasts and kissing her, ignoring the [female] victim's continuous supplications. He succeeded in parting her legs despite the resistance of the [female] victim, who was defending her virtue (*'ird*) and he partially penetrated her vagina with his penis. [...] Then, the second suspect headed to the car and forced the [female] victim to lie down in the back seat [...]

The Criminal Court's narrative appears far more detailed than the Court of Cassation's. However, we must take note of the moral considerations riddling it. The terms used by the Court are sufficient indication of this moral bias: wicked (*athim*), forbidden (*haram*), implorations (*isti'tafat*), weakness (*du'f*), disgrace (*qillat haya'*), cruelty (*qaswa*), coarse (*badhi*), grotesque (*qami'*), virtue (*'ird*), etc. It is also important to note the insistence on the victim's virginity (*bikr*). Equally noteworthy is the prominently intertextual character of the Criminal Court's narration, which largely matches the account given in the victim's testimony as presented by the General Prosecution (Chapter 6, Excerpt 25), while amplifying it further. As we saw, nevertheless, the inventory of the elements of proof through which the Prosecution presents the narrative of facts is itself a homogenized compilation of various narratives collected during the investigation and the interrogations conducted as part of the process. The Criminal Court's amplified version accentuates this homogenizing effect by totally erasing the suspects' voices. Although the Criminal Court's ruling, contrary to the Court of Cassation's, is mainly oriented to past factuality, it operates through versions of events mediated by intermediary instances, located between judicial action – interrogations and testimonies – and procedurally correct, legally relevant narratives. This process of homogenizing and duplicating earlier narratives may also be found in the opinion submitted by the Mufti of the Republic, in conformity with the Code of Penal Procedure, regarding the application of the death penalty to a given case. In this opinion, the mufti, who was giving his opinion for the second time on the same case, also used the facts as they had been iterated by the second Criminal Court (Excerpt 44):

Excerpt 47 (Mufti of the Republic, Opinion 31 C/2, Crimes, 7 May 1986)
[The Criminal Court] examined this case, dated 1/4/1986, for the second time, and adjourned [its ruling] to the session of 15/4/1986. During that session, the Court amended the charges brought against the first five suspects in the following manner:
1. They forcibly kidnapped the [female] victim, a crime compounded by the offense of non-consensual copulation with the kidnapped [person]. This is by virtue of the fact that the first five suspects agreed to [...]

This process of occultation of the practical conditions and circumstances in which legal work is carried out, a process specific to the polished, homogenized, and formalized versions produced by the different judiciary authorities we have just reviewed, is largely absent from transcripts of interrogations, even though we are perfectly aware that, as Komter points out (2001), an interrogation report is not a word-for-word transcript of the verbal exchanges that take place during the interrogation, but already an interactional construct. The fact remains that a multitude of elements specific to verbal interaction and the practical implementation of judicial activity appear through the transcripts of interrogations, and that these elements are entirely absent from the texts edited, in the strict sense, by official bodies. The following excerpts illustrate this point:

Excerpt 48 (General Prosecution, Case 276, 1985, Ma'adi)
We asked all the accused to leave the room, with the exception of the first. He is a young man in his 30s, around 1.70m tall, of average girth, with a dark complexion, wearing a blue suit with checks at the bottom and a blue pullover. We questioned him in detail and he replied:
A: Anwar Isma'il, 19, warehouse janitor, residing in 'Izbat (?)
Q: Tell us the details of what you have admitted
A: I left my house and met Ashraf and Mitwalli and we agreed to go to the movies. We went to the Thakanat Cinema and after we left at around 3 in the afternoon we met Ahmad, the driver, who is a friend of Ashraf. We told him drive us to Basatin so he said yes and we got in and drove for a while then we met Salah Abu Halawa

> who knows Ashraf and he said he was with a woman but a cop took her and took five pounds off him. He got in with us and while we were driving for a bit he said I'm going to get you any woman and a little later we found a parked car with a man and a woman in it. Salah got out and went over while me and Ahmad the driver were watching to see what he'd do and to help him if the guy in the car hit him. Salah had a knife on him and he took it. He talked to the guy in the car and slashed the front tire of the car with the knife and then the guy tried to drive off and Salah hit the second tire of the car. [The guy] started the car and me and Ahmad headed back to the taxi and got in and Salah got in and said let's catch up with him again. We went after them and stopped behind the car and [Salah] was holding the knife. We went with him and made them get out of the car and get into the taxi. We took them to Qattamiyya and we all got out and Salah stayed in the car with the girl and made her get naked then we heard her screaming a bit and after a while Salah came and said it's over I did her and Ashraf got in [the car] and then after a while we saw a guard coming towards us and we ran back and got in the car. We went to Basatin to finish with the girl and drove around looking for a place but we couldn't find one so we went to Ma'adi with the car and stopped and [Salah] went into the garage. He came back and took the girl and the guy and Ahmad got out (?) and me and Mitwalli stayed in the car and we went into the room and Salah went to have sex with her and Ashraf went to have sex with her but she was sick and then (?) and Mitwalli went in and bit her. I went in and kissed her and put my arms around her waist and she said don't you have sisters and I left her [...]

This excerpt presents the summary of the testimony that the person interrogated by the prosecutor is supposed to have produced at the beginning of the interrogation. Komter's remark is particularly apt with regard to this summary: direct observation of interrogations shows that witnesses never produce such continuous narratives, but rather always offer a version of the facts that the prosecutor endeavours to reformulate, in part, while dictating it to his secretary. This, however, does not prevent the words and expressions used by the witness to appear in the report (as evidenced, for example, by the presence of several direct speech utterances or a number of lexical choices).

The initial summary of the facts is followed by an interrogation that systematically takes up each of the previously evoked points. While it is clear that the prosecutor has full control over the way the interrogation unfolds – we refer here to earlier remarks about institutional context and sequential judicial interaction (see Chapters 5-7) – it is reasonable to think that the witness's statements are subject to minimal reformulation. This at least is what we were able to observe directly in cases we were able to follow. This is also due to the simple fact that speech turns are relatively short and articulated around simple questions, which leaves little room for massive intervention on the prosecutor's part in formulating responses. Here is the following section of the interrogation of Anwar Isma'il:

Excerpt 49 (Prosecution, Case 276, 1985, Ma'adi)

Q: When did this happen

A: Thursday 17 January 1985 at 3:30 in Ma'adi

Q: What are the ties between you and the other suspects
A: Ashraf and Mitwalli are buddies of mine
Q: What about the other suspects
A: Don't know 'em
Q: How did you meet them shortly before the events
A: Me and Mitwalli and Ashraf left the movies and we took the cap that belongs to a driver who's a friend of Ashraf and we met Salah while we were driving and he got in with us
Q: What conversation did you have at this time
A: When Salah got in he said there was a girl with me and now a cop took her and he gave him five pounds and we sat down to talk and Salah said I'm going to get you a woman
Q: Did you agree to take any woman on the road
A: We agreed to take a woman and for Salah to take her
Q: What means did you employ to carry out what you agreed on
A: We started driving the taxi around Ma'adi to find a woman
Q: What led you to do this
A: We saw a parked car and inside there was a guy and a girl and we stopped near it and Salah got out for them
Q: Who was in the car with you
A: Me and Ahmad the driver and Mitwalli and Ashraf and Anwar
Q: Which of you had a weapon
A: Salah had a knife on him and Ahmad had a knife (gazelle horn) switchblade
Q: Was the suspect Salah carrying the knife when he walked to the place where the young man and the girl were sitting in the parked car
A: Yes he had the knife in his hand
Q: What was your intention when you sent Salah to attack the young man and the girl
A: He went to take the girl
Q: What happened when he reached their car
A: Salah broke the window with the knife and told him give me 50 pounds and the guy tried to start the car to get away and then Salah started to stab the tire with the knife
Q: Where were you
A: We were near them, waiting behind a tree
Q: What made you stop there
A: In case the guy from the car tried to hit Salah, we would have gone
Q: Was the young man able to leave the place where he was parked
A: He drove the car forward a little way
Q: What did you do at this time
A: We got in the cab and started looking for him
Q: Under what circumstances did you meet him the second time
A: We found him changing the tire
Q: Which of you went to him
A: Salah
Q: What happened then

A: We made them get out of the car and get in the cab with us and then we headed for Qattamiyya in the desert
Q: In what state were the young man and the girl in at this time
A: They were both scared and the girl was crying and Salah was threatening the guy and she was crying and saying help me
Q: What happened when you got to the desert
A: When we got to the desert Salah told us get out and we all got out and he kept the girl with him in the car
Q: Then what happened
A: [He wanted] to have sex with her
Q: What did he do to her
A: He made her take her clothes off and we were sitting a little further away
Q: How's that
A: When Salah got out of the car Ashraf got in and after a little while a guard came and we ran to the car and she was naked and we left in the car
Q: What state were the two suspects, Salah and Ashraf, in at this time
A: When Salah got out of the car he put on his shorts and socks outside and his clothes outside and Ashraf was dressed
Q: Where was the [male] victim at this time
A: He was with us not far from the car
Q: Could he have run away
A: We were with him
Q: What did you do to him during this time
A: Salah took his chain and Ashraf took his watch
Q: Where did you go after that
A: We got in the car and we took them to a place near Basatin
Q: What was your intention
A: To keep going with the girl
Q: Were you able to take her there
A: We drove around to find a place but we couldn't
Q: Then what happened
A: We went to Ma'adi and stopped near a garage and Salah got out but I don't know what he did
Q: How did you meet the suspect Muhsin
A: When Salah came out of the garage he took the guy and the girl and they went into a room and when we went to the garage we met Muhsin
Q: What happened inside the garage
A: Salah took the girl and went into a room and had sex with her and after he was done Ashraf went in with her and after that Mitwalli went in with her and then I went in last and I didn't do anything
Q: What did the other suspects do with her in the room
A: I don't know but when they went in with her they closed the door
Q: What was the position of the victim, Ahmad, at that time
A: Salah was threatening him with the knife

Q: What sexual acts did you commit with the [female] victim
A: When I went in I found her sitting on a cushion and I went to have sex with her. I kissed her and put my arms around her waist and hugged her and then she said shame on you (*haram 'alayk*) so I left her and went out
Q: What role did each of you play in the theft of the money, the key ring, the [female] victim's two rings, and the watch
A: Salah is the one who took the two rings and the chain and the 25 pounds, and Ashraf is the one who took the watch
Q: Where were these items stolen
A: Salah took the money when we were in the street in Ma'adi and the key ring when we were in the desert and the two rings in the garage
Q: Were you with him when he took these things
A: Yes all four of us were with him
Q: Under what circumstances did they take these things
A: Salah was threatening them with the knife
Q: Did sexual relations take place with the girl's consent
A: No
Q: Did the [female] victim go with you to the place where Salah attacked her of her own volition
A: No, we took them and we forced them to get in the cab that we had and we told them we're taking you to the police station
Q: What is the role of the suspect called Muhsin 'Atiyya Ibrahim
A: When we took the taxi to the building where he walks he gave us the blankets and the cushion and opened the room where we had sex with the girl
Q: Did the abovementioned person have sexual relations with the [female] victim
A: No
Q: What made him help you
A: He was obviously scared of Salah
Q: What time did these events occur
A: Between about 4 and 9:00 p.m.
Q: You are accused of participating with others in a kidnapping and rape with coercion, what do you have to say
A: I said what happened
Q: You are also accused of participating with others in theft with coercion of the abovementioned, what do you have to say
A: I said what happened
Q: You are also accused of participating with others in an act of illegal kidnapping and detention, what do you have to say
A: Yes, it happened
Q: Do you have a record
A: No
Q: Do you have anything to add
A: No
End of the statements made by the suspect named Anwar

When we read these excerpts, we can see that what the transcript of Anwar's interrogation makes it possible to document from a praxeological point of view has been erased from the factual narratives produced by the prosecution, the Criminal Court, the Mufti of the Republic, and the Court of Cassation. Let us focus on two elements in particular. First, at the end of the interrogation, Anwar's assertion that he did not have sex with the victim (Q: What sexual acts did you commit with the [female] victim; A: When I went in I found her sitting on a cushion and I went to have sex with her. I kissed her and put my arms around her waist and hugged her and then she said shame on you (*haram 'alayk*) so I left her and went out). No trace of this attempt on the suspect's behalf to defend himself subsists in the formalized texts. Next – and even more blatantly – Anwar's tendency to accuse the first suspect, Salah, systematically. His name is repeated 27 times. He also puts direct speech in his mouth, thus bringing his role to the fore (A: When Salah got in he said there was a girl with me and now a cop took her and he gave him five pounds and we sat down to talk and Salah said I'm going to get you a woman). Without it being possible to determine here whether or not Salah was the prime mover of the case as a whole, it is clear that Anwar, throughout the interrogation, massively emphasized Salah's leading role, while reducing his own involvement to give the impression that his presence was a matter of chance and his participation was accidental, if not nonexistent.

The contextual negotiation of legal and moral responsibility, like the prosecutor's perfectly clear concern for organizing the interrogation with the practical aim of establishing the legal qualification of the facts, can in no way appear through texts of jurisprudence. In that respect, the Court of Cassation's ruling – to cite this example only – is a retrospective sentence on past facts, not an account of activities that presided over the constitution of the judgment. In that sense, formalized texts and raw transcripts, law in the books and law in action, are indeed in a relation of asymmetrical disjunction as described above.

Chapter 8

The Natural Person: The Contingent and Contextual Production of Legal Personality

In this chapter, I am interested in the notion of natural person and the way people orient to it in the judicial context of law in action. The notion of natural or physical person, which is closely associated with the concept of mental capacity and incapacity, is organized as an artefact with a moral and normative character, resulting from its association with a "natural order" of things. By observing the contextualized usages of a category like that of the person, it is possible to describe the deployment of mechanisms through which nature becomes a normative referent, by virtue of appearing to impose itself objectively.

A category like that of the person is necessarily contingent and situated. In other words, it depends closely on the context of its mobilization. In this chapter, I intend to focus on these two dimensions, the contingent and the contextual. First, I will examine the notions of norm and normality, arguing that it is through these notions that the category of the person takes its local and contextual meaning. Second, I shall examine the notion of context, particularly the institutional context, using as an example a case in which a person was accused of having intentionally murdered a woman, and claimed to have been possessed by spirits. I shall thereby document the influence of the institutional judicial setting in the production of the person as a signifying category.

The Category of the Person

In this section, I shall focus on the notion of the person as articulated in its legal treatment. Using examples taken from Egyptian criminal law, I shall show that this category is both normative and contextual. The person, in the specific context of Egyptian legal practice, does not correspond to something whose characteristics can be identified *a priori*. It is a type or a category and functions as such normatively.

It is not to praxeology that we owe the first claim that the person and the concepts associated with it are embedded in a social context. This was already the position taken by Marcel Mauss (1938), according to whom different conceptions of the person existed, with trajectories and genealogies it was possible to identify. Mauss's conception, however, was radically evolutionist, which led him to conclude the existence of 'a modern world in which the person becomes a sacred being, the possessor of metaphysical and moral value and of moral consciousness – the bearer of rights and responsibilities, the source of autonomous motivation and rational decision, valuing privacy and capable of self-development.' (Lukes, 1985: 294) In this overview, which seeks to reconstitute the trajectories of the category of the person, the end-point is found in 'modern Western cultures' (*ibid.*: 298) and their specific mode of thinking, articulated around the notions of will, autonomy, freedom, consciousness, and intentionality: all notions that we find in the discourse specific to law in the books. The will, which is defined as the capacity to freely determine that one will act, or abstain from doing so, constitutes the cornerstone of this discourse. The subject is established as the causal principle of action, which is itself an intentional process. The subject thereby becomes an autonomous instance ascribing objectivity to objects of the world – a meaning that is not determined once and for all, as such, but is always the expression of the subject's intentionality in his actions and interactions (Stockinger, 1993: 48). If we stick to a strictly formal reading of Egyptian jurisprudence and case-law, in the criminal field (Chapter 7) as elsewhere, it is at this type of conclusion – relating to the philosophy of history – that we inexorably arrive.

However, the praxeological re-specification I have undertaken implies that the person, in the specific context of Egyptian legal practice, cannot be identified and defined *a priori*, independently of the circumstances in which people orient, through their words and deeds, to something that resembles this notion. The person and everything associated with it is a category and therefore functions as such normatively. In what follows, I would like to explore some of the theoretical implications that may follow from my assertion that the person is produced, reproduced, and transformed by people as a normative category.

Instead of considering that actors encounter situations to which sets of learned or "internalized" rules apply and, hence, instead of analysing their actions as guided or caused by these rules, we will adopt a more Wittgensteinian approach and consider that "following a rule is a practice" (Wittgenstein, 1961: § 202; see Chapter 2). In the legal field, as Hart has stressed, this means that

> ... particular fact situations do not await us already marked off from each other, and labeled as instances of the general rule, the application of which is in question; nor can the rule itself step forward to claim its own instances. (...) Canons of 'interpretation' cannot eliminate, though they can diminish, uncertainties; for these canons are themselves general rules for the use of language, and make use of general terms which themselves require interpretation. They cannot, any more than other rules, provide for their own interpretation. (1961: 123)

This means, as Heritage paraphrases it, that

> ... legal rules cover an indefinite range of contingent, concrete possibilities. The rules must, in short, be applied, and to specific configurations of circumstances which may never be identical. (... The) precedent having been established, there

> must still be a judgment as to whether the next occasion is sufficiently similar to fall within the scope of the prior judgment.[1] (1984 : 121-122)

Following a rule can be understood as a typifying practice. Husserl argued that one could observe typical pre-knowledge of things, underlying any predicative judgment. Translated into sociological terms, this means that people immediately grasp things, events and persons as belonging to a kind and endowed with typical properties, within 'a horizon of familiarity and pre-acquaintanceship which is, as such, just taken for granted until further notice as the unquestioned, though at any time questionable stock of knowledge at hand.' (Schütz, 1990: 7) In other words, 'events have "normal patterns" and "usual causes" of occurrence that can be relied upon.' (Heritage, 1984: 77) These ideas, of course, are indeterminate and indistinct, but members initially display their perception of the normality of events, and it is only in a situation of incongruity that they look for explanations for this threat to normality. It is in that sense that people are (made) morally accountable for any breach in what is perceived as the normal course of events.

Nor are legal categories excluded from this system of naturalness and normality. Thus, the idea of a normal person and, in its wake, the related ideas of volition and cognition, constitute a reference point for practical legal reasoning. As such, the conscious, intentional person, far from being an abstract and inaccessible category, is publicly constituted through the methodical deployment of public, i.e. linguistic, resources, in social interaction (Watson, 1998: 213). As Douglas Maynard (1984: 138) puts it, 'when persons are talked about in any conversation, descriptions are selected and produced according to what activity is being done [...] Who a person officially is, for others, depends on what activity is being accomplished in their talk.' The person is a category produced in the public domain and, as such, is a thoroughly public phenomenon. The realization of this category is, in such a perspective, oriented and constrained by the scheme of the natural and normal person, as in Garfinkel's seminal study of the case of Agnes, in which sexual identity is conceived as a produced and managed feature of ordinary social interactions and institutional workings. The category of personhood is deployed 'as an invariant but unnoticed background in the texture of relevancies that comprise the changing actual scenes of everyday life.' (Garfinkel, 1967: 118)

In this perspective, the realization of personhood as a category is oriented to the scheme of the natural, normal person, conscious and endowed with an autonomous

---

1 However, one must remain cautious and not consider that every application of the rule implies its interpretation. Wittgenstein draws our attention to the difference between following a rule and interpreting it. In various circumstances, we know perfectly that we follow a rule without interpreting it, i.e. without trying to reformulate it verbally. According to Andrei Marmor, the distinction established by Hart between simple cases (that do not require interpretation) and hard cases (that require it) is based on the non-confusion between the implementation of a rule and its interpretation (cf. Jackson, 1996: 237-8, quoting Marmor, 1992, and Wittgenstein, 1967).

will, at the same time as it is constrained by it. This background is constantly mobilized, though it remains largely unexplained or loosely defined. Hence, being defined as a person largely depends on the capacity to present a normal appearance and to expect people to treat one on such grounds. As Harvey Sacks puts it, 'persons using public places are concurrently expected by others to present appearances which can be readily so used, and expect others to treat their own appearances at face value.' (1972: 281) We do not deal with naturally conscious and wilful persons, therefore, but with the naturalization of the person's consciousness and will, so as to assess the conformity of any instance to the general category, with all the rights and duties that are attached to membership in this category – something that ethnomethodologists call a "membership categorization device" (cf. Introduction).

We now turn to the production of the normal person in the Egyptian judicial context. The first excerpt, which we have encountered before (Excerpt 1, Chapter 4), is the account of a young woman who was allegedly the victim of attempted rape, subsequently characterized by the public prosecution as indecent assault (*hitk 'ird*).

Excerpt 50 (General Prosecution, Case 5471, 1977, Muharram Bey, Alexandria)
Surrogate's question: What happened
Victim's answer: I was in the street that day … when I met those two … and they told me come with us and they forced me to get in a taxi … and they went behind the Shipyard.
Q: What was their intention when they acted this way
A: They told me don't worry let's have a cup of tea together
Q: Why didn't you call for help when they took you …
A: I tried to shout and I rolled on the ground but the street was empty
Q: What is the number of the taxi they took you in
A: I don't know it happened in the street
Q: Why didn't you ask the taxi driver for help
A: The taxi driver was afraid of them and did what they told him to do
Q: What was their intention when they took you with them
A: I think they wanted to violate my honor otherwise they would not have taken me to that place
Q: Did you know them before
A: No
Q: Do you have anything else to say
A: No

Besides what was said previously with respect to this excerpt, we might make a remark or two with regard to the implications the use of direct and indirect quotes can have on the production of personhood as a category. Twice, the victim uses direct quotes in her answers to the prosecutor's questions ("They told me come with us"; "They told me don't worry we'll have a cup of tea together"). The use of direct speech is a central device in talk activities. As Gregory Matoesian and James Coldren put it,

> Direct quotes are a type of reported speech which minimizes the gap in the decontextualization and recontextualization of prior talk. They make the words being spoken here and now appear as an exact replica of the words spoken in historical context. They make the performed words appear close to previous words and, in so doing, make those historical words come alive – giving them an aura of objectivity and authority. In this way, direct quotes provide a rigid boundary between the quoting and quoted voices which maintains the historical authenticity and integrity of the reported speech, as the reporting speaker purports to represent the reported speaker's exact words. (2001: 404)

Foregrounding the voice of one of her aggressors, the victim's narrative appears much more reliable, with her own voice being relegated to the background. The authenticity of her statement becomes harder to challenge and the whole drama much more lively. However, there are detrimental implications as well. While it might be credible that the two young men invited her to join them, it is also credible that she consented to flirt with them. This, however, is not something young women are supposed to do. Consequently, her narrative, although it takes the form of direct quotes, is harmful to her moral standing. It creates a disjuncture between the legal characterization of the facts and the way in which they are reported.

The role played by the institutional function of the parties (offender, victim, witness) in their discourse and in the general construction of the narrative clearly emerges from the following excerpt from the interview with one policeman in the same case:

> **Excerpt 51 (Prosecution, Case 5471, 1977, Muharram Bey, Alexandria)**
> Question from the Prosecutor: What information do you have
> Answer from the policeman: Today, when I was on patrol with my colleague Ahmad Hasan al-Shinnawi in the first zone of the police station of Muharram Bey, where 'Izbat Nadi al-Sayd is located, we were behind the Arsenal and heard a woman calling for help. The noise was coming from behind the Arsenal and my colleague and I started searching for its origin. We witnessed a girl and two boys holding her. They attempted to escape but my colleague and I hurried to catch them and to make inquiries about the girl. It turned out that her name was Magda al-Sayyid Muhammad Qasim, and she reported to us that the two boys had met her at Alexandria Prison and brought her by force in a taxi to this place and attempted to assault her.

The very detailed categorization of events and people is organized here so as to be useful for all subsequent legal purposes: date, actors, place, circumstances, action, and accounts. Moreover, we should note that this account provides the professional character of its authors (Jackson, 1994). As noted by Sacks (1972: 293), one basis for this professional status seems to be the concern of the police to develop means for establishing their job 'as business-like, i.e. impersonal, code-governed, etc.' Both the actors' actions and their accounts are institutionally organized with reference to some accounting framework (Wieder, 1974). This has consequences for the definition of the person, whose circumstances are presented so as to fit the requirements of a proper accomplishment of legal characterization. 'Here, the categories of the criminal law [...] are seen as constituting the basic conceptual equipment with which such people as judges, lawyers, policemen, and probation workers organize their everyday activities.' (Sudnow, 1965: 255)

The two former accounts should be contrasted with the accounts given by the two alleged offenders. First, 'Abd al-Hafiz Ahmad:

Excerpt 52 (Prosecution, Case 5471, 1977, Muharram Bey, Alexandria)

Question of the Prosecutor: What do you have to say about what concerns you

Answer of the suspect: Nothing happened. I was walking on Muharram Bey Bridge and I met Mahmud Basyuni walking on the bridge and this girl was with him. He asked me don't you know a place where I can take this girl and I told him I don't know I'm on my way to pick up a tip from someone at the Arsenal. He told me take me along, my foot hurts. I hailed a cab and he and the girl got in with me. She was crying and when the cabdriver heard the girl crying he tried to make her get out of the cab at a used oil garage. I headed for the place for the tip behind the Arsenal, and Mahmud Basyuni and the girl were behind me. Then I suddenly realized that the cops had caught me.

Q: Where and when did it happen

A: Today around 3 o'clock, on Muharram Bey Bridge Mahmud Basyuni met me and the woman who was with him

Q: Did you know one of them from before

A: I knew Mahmud Basyuni because he lives on our street but I don't know the girl

Q: What was the situation in which you witnessed the aforementioned Mahmud Basyuni and the girl

A: The girl was walking along with Mahmud Basyuni and he was holding her hand and she was crying

Q: Didn't you ask why she was crying

A: No

Q: What did the aforementioned Mahmud Basyuni tell you when you met him

A: He told me have you got a place where we can take the girl and I told him I don't

Q: What do you have to say concerning what the two policemen and the victim reported

A: What they said didn't happen as God is with us

Q: Why did the two policemen arrest you

A: I don't know I was just walking and going to pick up a tip

Q: The victim declared that the taxi driver refused to take you anywhere and started to push you out of the car at the Matchstick Company on the Suez Road when he saw that she was asking for help

A: He saw the girl and started to push her out

As for Mahmud Basyuni Muhammad:

Excerpt 53 (Prosecution, Case 5471, 1977, Muharram Bey, Alexandria)
Question of the Prosecutor: What do you have to say about what concerns you
Answer of the suspect: It didn't happen
Q: How do you explain the statement made by the two plain-clothes policemen
A: I don't know. What happened is that I was coming back from running an errand today and this girl met me and I knew her from before. We walked together and we were talking and we met 'Abd al-Hafiz Ahmad in Yasir b. 'Amir Street and he walked with us. Afterward 'Abd al-Hafiz said that he was going to pick up a tip from someone at the Arsenal and the girl and I went with him. Afterwards the policemen caught us while we were walking like that
Q: Where did you meet the victim
A: On Suez Street at the Industrial Gas Company. She and I were walking toward Yasir b. 'Amir Street and afterward we met 'Abd al-Hafiz
Q: How did you arrive at the rear of the Arsenal
A: We walked
Q: What do you have to say with regard to what the victim reported
A: It didn't happen the policemen are the ones who persuaded her [to make her statement]
Q: What do you say with regard to what the aforementioned 'Abd al-Hafiz Ahmad reported
A: None of what he said happened
Q: Why did he make that statement against you
A: I don't know

In both accounts, the alleged offender attempts to present himself as a normal person, i.e. a man who behaves in a way that does not appear incongruous to others. To be considered normal, people exhibit and display what seems to be, according to them, normal behaviour. Hence, 'Abd al-Hafiz's repeated claim that he was 'on my way to pick up a tip from someone at the Arsenal', or Basyuni's presentation of a normal way to spend one's time ('I was coming back from running an errand today and this girl met me and I knew her from before. We walked together and we were talking and we met 'Abd al-Hafiz Ahmad in Yasir b. 'Amir Street and he walked with us'). The presentation of oneself as a normal person is reinforced by the description of a banal sequence of events in a familiar environment: '(I met the victim) on Suez Street at the Industrial Gas Company. She and I were walking toward Yasir b. 'Amir Street and afterward we met 'Abd al-Hafiz'. Conversely, it is by damaging this self-presentation that people's behaviour is presented as abnormal, and becomes behaviour for which they can be held personally (and even criminally) responsible or accountable. This is why the prosecutor asked 'Abd al-Hafiz: 'Didn't you ask why she was crying?' Indeed, there is a discrepancy between the presentation of his behaviour as normal and the abnormal character of meeting a girl who is crying. In Basyuni's case, the discrepancy between his account and the others' makes it abnormal, and he tries to repair this anomaly by providing an alternative account of events ('Q: What do you have to say with regard to what the victim reported; A: It didn't happen the policemen are the ones who persuaded her [to make her statement]'), though he fails to provide acceptable reasons for these diverging accounts, as evidenced by his repetitive answers ('It didn't happen;' 'I don't know').

Turning now to cases in which people suffering from mental illness are involved, several observations can be made regarding the concept of the person. We will use examples taken from a case in which a man was accused of having perpetrated indecent assault on a mentally deficient boy.

Excerpt 54 (Prosecution, Case 7158, 1993, Sahil, Cairo)
Sahil Prosecution
In the name of God the Merciful the Compassionate
Investigation report
Report opened on 28 July 1993
Sharif 'Abd Allah, deputy-prosecutor
Sharif al-Shishtawi, investigation secretary
Given what was presented to us in report 7058 of 1993, felonies (*junah*), Sahil, issued on 27 July 1993 at 1:30 a.m. (*masa'an*) by adjudant Diyab Hamid al-Sayyid of the police station of al-Sahil. Given the establishment, after examination of the report issued by first lieutenant 'Atiyya 'Abduh on the organization of the patrol in the northern sector, of the information that a sexual assault had been reported on someone in building 51, Nasr 'Abd al-Mawla Street, Sahil District. The aforementioned officer proceeded to the location and met with Sami Hamid Ahmad, who works as a police sergeant in the Khayyala administration and lives in building 51, Nasr 'Abd al-Mawla Street. The latter informed him that the aforementioned Ayyub As'ad Tadrus attempted to carry out a sexual assault on the aforementioned Ayman 'Abd al-Khaliq 'Uthman, who is mentally retarded (*mutakhallif 'aqliyyan*) and lives in the same building. The aforementioned officer accompanied the man who conveyed the information, the victim, and his mother, who is called Rasmiyya Muhammad Nabhan, to the department of the Sahil police station to take the necessary measures (*li-ittikhadh al-lazim*) and to question Sami Hamid Ahmad in a report collecting all the evidence. He reported that, during his stay in his home, 51 Nasr 'Abd al-Mawla Street, he heard the noise of a quarrel on the ground floor. When he arrived at the location, he found the aforementioned Rasmiyya Muhammad Nubhan crying, holding her son, and claiming that the aforementioned Magdi Ayyub As'ad had sexually assaulted her son, Ayman 'Abd al-Khaliq 'Uthman. He added that he did not witness the facts of the sexual assault on the victim, but that he witnessed the victim's mother. who was holding the accused and claiming that he had tried to sexually assault her son, who has no kinship relation to the offender. When she was questioned, Rasmiyya Muhammad Nabhan reported that the aforementioned Magdi Ayyub had tried to call her son into his house, and that a girl living in the house came and informed her that the aforementioned Magdi had taken her son into his room and locked the door. She went to this place

and she banged on the door of the room and she witnessed him sexually assaulting her son. Upon questioning, the accused Magdi Ayyub As'ad Tadrus denied what was attributed to him and explained the accusation of the aforementioned Rasmiyya Muhammad Nubhan by the fact that, when she saw her son coming out of his room, she claimed what was mentioned, whereas he was trying to expel the aforementioned Ayman from his room, which he had entered on his own. The report is made up of two foolscap documents, plus another document including the patrol officer's report on the information. We indicated all the information relevant to the report. Today, with the suspect present outside the interrogation room, we asked him to enter and questioned him about the accusation directed against him, after having informed him of it, the punishment associated with it, and the Public Prosecution's responsibility for conducting an interrogation with him. He denied the accusation and we asked him whether he had an advocate representing him in the investigation proceedings [?] and he replied in the negative. Then, we proceeded to hear the testimony of the police sergeant Sami Hamid Ahmad and left him to one side in the investigation room. We summoned the aforementioned Ayman 'Abd al-Khaliq 'Uthman, the victim, into the interrogation room. He was introduced to us, with his mother Rasmiyya Muhammad Nabhan accompanying him. We asked her to stay outside the investigation room and we kept the victim with us. He is an adolescent (*sabi yafi'*) exhibiting the signs of mental retardation (*al-takhalluf al-'aqli*). We asked him what had happened but could not understand his response, except that he pointed his index and uttered the 's' sound (*sin*), pointing at his neck, i.e. he had a knife to his throat. We asked him once more about what happened and he pointed at the suspect in the investigation room and then pointed to his rear and pointed at him another time and uttered the 's' sound again, but we found it difficult to understand the rest of his answer.

First, the victim is never characterized by the technical legal terms of "insanity" (*junun*) or "mental deficiency" (*'aha 'aqliyya*). These terms characterize the offender's liability, not the victim's personality. Furthermore, the only aggravating circumstances of sexual assault are the use of force (Penal Code, Article 268) and the victim's minority (Penal Code, Article 269), defined here as less than eighteen years of age. Hence, the victim's mental retardation should not play a role in this case; and yet the parties and the prosecutor systematically mention it. The following is an excerpt of the interview with the victim's mother:

Excerpt 55 (Prosecution, Case 7158, 1993, Sahil, Cairo)
Then we asked his mother to enter the interrogation room again and we asked her the following question. She replied:
Answer of the witness: My name is Rasmiyya Muhammad Nabhan [...]
- oath -
Question of the Prosecutor: What information do you have
A: What happened is that I was sitting in my flat on the third floor and my son Ayman went out to go to the workshop he works in at 10:00 in the morning and a few minutes after he left a girl called Wizza Muhammad 'Abd al-Razzaq and whose actual name

is Umm Hashim who lives with us in the house came and said help me Auntie Umm 'Aziza it's Magdi he made Ayman enter in the room and he locked the door I was scared and I said [?] and I went down immediately to Magdi's room which is under the stairs but I found the door closed so I broke it down and went in and I found Magdi tearing my son Ayman's clothes and bunching up the gown he was wearing. He was lying down on my son so I screamed and Magdi got off Ayman and then the neighbours gathered when they heard my voice and he began to insult the neighbours and he went to inform the police. When the police came to find out what had happened I went to the police station but afterward he denied that this is what happened [...]

Q: What's your relationship with the victim

A: He's my son

Q: What's his age exactly (*tahdidan*)

A: He's 17 or 18, and he has been mentally backward since birth [...]

Q: From the facts you witnessed [can you say whether] your son consented to the assault or resisted

A: My son is mentally backward and he doesn't know anything and he didn't say a word [...]

Characterizing the victim as mentally deficient has a number of implications, which emerge clearly from this excerpt. First, the characterization is directly associated with his age ('He's 17 or 18, and he has been mentally backward since birth'). Second, the characterization is invoked so as to assess his consent to the alleged sexual relations ('My son is mentally backward and he doesn't know anything and he didn't say a word'). In other words, being mentally backward allows for the absence of consent to be presumed.

All these consequences are even more manifest when we contrast the preceding excerpt with the following, taken from the offender's interview:

Excerpt 56 (Prosecution, Case 7158, 1993, Sahil, Cairo)

Question of the Prosecutor: How long have you known the victim

Answer of the witness: I have known him since I went to live in the building in 1978

Q: At first glance is he a sentient person (*shakhs mudrik*)

A: He speaks in a jerky way

Q: Is he mentally backward

A: I don't know

Q: You have seen the victim since 1978 and you don't know whether he's mentally backward or not despite the fact that it is obvious that he's mentally backward

A: I don't know

This excerpt can be considered at different levels. First, we note that the prosecutor uses another term for characterizing the state of the victim ('At first glance, is he a sentient person?'). Then, we can observe the manner in which the offender avoids using damaging characterizations. On the one hand, he engages in rhetorical understatement or euphemism ('He speaks in a jerky way'). On the other hand, he refuses to adopt the characterization provided by the prosecutor ('Q: Is he mentally backward? A: I don't know'). Finally, the prosecutor's last question raises several basic points and provides very interesting clues allowing us to understand what role background assumptions, consequential inferences, and institutional settings play in the construction of personhood as a category in Egyptian law.

All these excerpts and the last one in particular demonstrate that participants in legal interactions share a background understanding of the nature of legal inquiries, so that they know it is often not in the interests of a defendant to co-operate beyond a minimum level. (Levinson, 1992: 77) This is what Komter (1998: 129) calls the dilemmas of conflict and cooperation: 'The dilemma of the suspects is to produce defenses that are not heard as defenses but as cooperation and to show cooperation without foregoing opportunities for mitigation.' We also see that the sentence "I don't know" is uttered so as to avoid confirming knowledge of something that would further the blame-implicative nature of the facts (Drew, 1992: 480ss.).

The excerpt also underlines the function of questions in criminal prosecution, which is mainly to extract from the interviewee 'answers that build up to form a "natural" argument for the jury.' (Levinson, 1992) This creates the kind of incongruity that has already been referred to above. From the sense of normalcy that is mobilized and the discrepancies that are identified in relation to this normalcy, many inferences can be drawn. As Matoesian puts it in his study of a sensational rape trial, the Kennedy Smith case:

> Through a myriad of linguistic and sequential resources, the defense attorney creates a turn-by-turn disjunction between category bound activities/states and the rapist category, drawing attention to the abnormality of rapists, the normality of his client, and the irrationality of the witness's actions if he were a rapist (or the rationality of her actions with a non-rapist). There is no way the witness can do 'normal' things with someone who is supposed to be an 'abnormal' person. In this way, we can see how social structure is mapped onto categorization work, and how categorization, in turn, is harnessed as an interpretative resource in the constitution of grammatical sequential structures. (Matoesian, 1997, with reference to Watson, 1997, Jayyusi, 1984, et Matoesian, 1995)

Finally, the same excerpt points to the goal-oriented nature of all these activities that together make up a judicial setting. These teleological activities (cf. for instance Meehan, 1997) are consequential for the definition of the person in the sense that the goals to which people orient define the strategies that are used to achieve these goals, and these strategies, in turn, imply the characterization of the person in specific ways. In other words, legal interaction is a language game, in the sense Wittgenstein gives to the notion, i.e. an activity that in part determines the role language will play and the particular strategies or procedures used within this activity (Levinson, 1992: 92). In sum, the use of language is dependent on the context of its use, and in particular on its institutional context.

The Person in the Judicial Context

In this section, I endeavour to show how personhood and its definitions, as we might encounter them in a study of the Egyptian legal setting, are shaped and transformed by the procedural and structural context of their utterance. I base my observations on a case involving conflicting conceptions of the person.

I discussed the issue of context in general, and institutional context in particular, in Chapter 4. To summarize briefly, following Drew and Heritage (1992), three features are characteristic of an institutional context: participants' orientation, in the organization of their conduct, to institutional tasks or functions; the incidence of constraints linked to institutional goals on the participants' behaviour; inferences and implications are also shaped by their embeddedness in an institutional setting. All this has important consequences for the turn-taking system, the room left open to initiative, the subjective perception of experience and its expression, the definition of procedures and the sanction that any departure from them attracts, lexical choices, the configuration of the sequence, standard patterns of interaction, the production of a professional attitude, and the asymmetrical nature of interaction.

Returning to the person, relative to this notion of context, we should note that interacting people are very actively engaged in characterizing each other, i.e. in ascribing identities or attributes to one another. When they speak to each other, members of a group characterize, identify, describe, refer to, and conceive of people. These category terms are organized in collections, some of them adequate to categorize any member of any population, some of them usable only on already specified populations. Among all these categories, people choose those that are appropriate to them so as to categorize others, and this choice is relevant for producing and interpreting the conduct of participants in an interaction (Sacks, 1972; Schegloff, 1992). In other words, it is on people's actual characterizations of personhood that we must rely, not on our assumption of their belonging to any given category. The analysis must demonstrate the relevance of any characterization in its actual setting. Bearing this in mind, we can conclude that any categorization, characterization, or qualification of personhood is context-sensitive, and that this context proves very constraining when it is of an institutional nature. Institutional activities assign particular roles and specific types of intentions to people participating in them, and this in turn allows for consequential inferences.

The following case will help illustrate what has just been said. We begin with the Cairo Criminal Court's narrative of the facts in its ruling of 15 October 1997.

Excerpt 57 (Criminal Court, Case 2783, 1997, Cairo)

Considering that the facts of the claim, to the extent of the court's conviction and the confirmation of their veracity, indicate that the accused, Twingir (???) […], knew the victim, Qiddisa […], who was related by marriage to the widow of the suspect's brother and who lived in the same building. After visiting her, he advised her that a demon had taken possession of her and declared that he had knowledge of these things and knew that the demon, which was dressing in her clothes, would harm her children, whose lives were thereby exposed to danger. The victim lived in anxiety and feared for her children so, when the accused convinced her to entrust her case to him and she submitted to his will, he convinced her that he could exorcise this devil from her. He arranged to meet her for this confrontation, [telling her] he would take her somewhere to attempt this exorcism. He warned her not to mention anything to anybody about this appointment. The victim was convinced and accepted so as to ward off the alleged danger to her children that the accused had suggested. On the day of the appointment, she left her house, after having informed her granddaughter of this appointment, and warned her not to mention anything to anybody about it. She met the suspect, who accompanied her to 10th of Ramadan City, and took her into a building in an uninhabited and remote area; he had decided secretly and persisted with the idea of isolating himself with her in this distant place. His intention was to get rid of her so as to dispose of the money and jewels and whatever else he found on her. To this end, he put a handkerchief on her mouth and nose and pressed hard; he suffocated her and left only an inanimate body. He then put the corpse in plastic bags he had prepared previously and rolled them in a carpet that was in the house. He dragged her downstairs and threw her into a deep pit close to the house where he had killed her. Then he returned to his lodging in the Zaytun neighbourhood and stayed put, keeping quiet as if he had not done anything. Later that night, the victim's children realized she had been absent all day, and her granddaughter told them what she had said about her appointment with the suspect. They grew afraid for her. As for the suspect, he persevered in his denial from the day of her murder, on 8 August 1996, until 19 August 1996, when he went to the Zaytun police station and confessed that he had accompanied the victim to a flat in 10th of Ramadan City, alleging that he would exorcise the demon from her. He said that while he was performing some prayers the victim fell to the ground, and he realized that she had died; he then found some plastic bags and he put her corpse in them, then threw it in a pit. He indicated the place where the body was buried …

In this narrative, we may note the existence of conflicting conceptions of the person.[2] On one hand, the judiciary's conception seeks to establish the criminal liability of the accused for premeditated wilful homicide. As the Court puts it, referring to the Prosecution's report:

Excerpt 58 (Criminal Court, Case 2783, 1997, Cairo)
Given that the Public Prosecution accused the aforementioned of having intentionally murdered (*qatala 'amdan*) Qiddisa on 17 August 1996, in Zaytun District, Cairo Governorate, … with premeditation (*ma'a sabq al-israr*). He acted with care and determination in order to kill her, and consequently tricked her into entering his son's

2 For another example of possession and separation between bodily and spiritual agency, see the case of Schreber, the German doctor whose family sought to interdict him in the 19th century, and the opinion of the psychiatrist who had carried out the expert investigation.

house and succeeded in murdering her intentionally. She was injured in the way described in the forensic report, and this led to her death in the manner documented in the file.

On the other hand, the accused claimed not to have been acting intentionally, nor to have been mad, but to have been possessed by a devil. As the Court put it:

Excerpt 59 (Criminal Court, Case 2783, 1997, Cairo)
It emerges from the statements of the accused during the investigations and in his cross-examination during the session that he and his defense agree that he accompanied the victim to an unfinished flat owned by his son in 10th of Ramadan City in an uninhabited area, so as to exorcise the demon that lived in her and caused her suffering …

… the accused went to the police station and informed them that the victim suffered from headaches and nightmares, that he had accompanied her to his son's house in 10th of Ramadan City, that he had begun to pray to free her from her ailment, claiming that a demon had possessed her, that she was injured as a result, that she had spasms and that she lost her life…

What the defense means is that it is the demon who killed her because the accused was unable to exorcise it, since it was more powerful than him.

These are not so much conflicting conceptions of the person as they are common conceptions to which people orient differently. Indeed, the Court never denies the existence of spirits and demons or of possession. To the contrary, it explicitly acknowledges them, even while contesting the consequentiality the defense would like to attach to such recognition.

Excerpt 60 (Criminal Court, Case 2783, 1997, Cairo)
The attempt of the defense to attribute the crime to the demon by claiming that it killed the victim when the accused tried to exorcise it, because of the demon's power exceeding the power of the accused, is contradicted by all divine revelation, according to which demons, while able to inflict bodily harm upon human beings, cannot harm their souls or threaten their lives. This is because, as revealed in the Holy Quran, 'They will ask you about your soul. Say: The Soul is among my Lord's matters' (XVII, 85), and also as revealed in the Holy Gospels: 'And do not be afraid of those who kill the body but cannot kill the soul; rather, be afraid of the one who can destroy both soul and body'.[3] Furthermore, as revealed in the Torah, in the first part of Job's journey, God Almighty permitted to the devil to tempt Job, but ordered him not to touch his soul.[4]

---

3 Matthew, Chapter 10 Verse 28: 'And do not be afraid of those who kill the body but cannot kill the soul; rather, be afraid of the one who can destroy both soul and body in Gehenna' (Amercian Bible, Vatican website).

4 Revised Standard Version: 1:6 'Now there was a day when the sons of God came to present themselves before the LORD, and Satan also came among them. 1:7 The LORD

In other words, each party's position within the organization of adjudication has strong procedural consequences for the definition of the person. This has much to do with assumptions as to normal or abnormal behaviour. Consider the following extract:

> **Excerpt 61 (Criminal Court, Case 2783, 1997, Cairo)**
> Present with the accused, Mr. Nabil [...], advocate,
> He said that the victim died of natural causes, in which the accused played no part [...] Is it natural that people, if they face a crime whose penalty is strengthened in such a way, turn themselves over [to the police] after having prayed on the Muqattam hills? [...] If the accused had wanted to steal from or rape the victim, he would have chosen a young girl or a rich one.

Here we find an attempt to show that there is a discrepancy between normal criminal behaviour and the actual behaviour of the accused. The disjunction between criminal abnormality and the normal and natural behaviour of the accused suggests that he must be innocent. This categorization gives us important clues for understanding what the concept of the person represents in Egyptian law. It is a category whose normalcy is continuously produced and reproduced by interacting people, such normalcy bearing normative consequences and being used as a yardstick in the evaluation of any situation. At the same time, the context here contributes greatly to the definition of normalcy, in the sense that people look for characteristics that seem to be more significant and more relevant in this precise frame. This can be deduced from the cross-examination of the accused by the judge:

> **Excerpt 62 (Criminal Court, Case No 2783, 1997, Cairo)**
> The Court considered the cross-examination of the accused. The defense of the accused, the accused, and the parties claiming damages agreed to the Court's cross-examination of the accused.
> Question of the Court: Why did you take Qiddisa [...] to 10th of Ramadan
> Answer of the accused: At the request of the victim, because nobody knew that she was possessed by a demon and she feared that people would find out

---

said to Satan, "Whence have you come?" Satan answered the LORD, "From going to and fro on the earth, and from walking up and down on it." 1:8 And the LORD said to Satan, "Have you considered my servant Job, that there is none like him on the earth, a blameless and upright man, who fears God and turns away from evil?" 1:9 Then Satan answered the LORD, "Does Job fear God for nought? 1:10 Hast thou not put a hedge about him and his house and all that he has, on every side? Thou hast blessed the work of his hands, and his possessions have increased in the land. 1:11 But put forth thy hand now, and touch all that he has, and he will curse thee to thy face." 1:12 And the LORD said to Satan, "Behold, all that he has is in your power; only upon himself do not put forth your hand." So Satan went forth from the presence of the LORD'.

Q: How did you know that the victim had a demon (*shaytan*) or foul spirits (*arwah najisa*) in her
A: She told me that that she had a headache (*suda'*) and nightmares (*kawabis*) and I told her there's a demon in you
Q: Did you observe other symptoms
A: She told me that she had choking spells (*khunaq*) and headache
Q: What clothes was the victim wearing
A: A black gown (*jalbab*) and a shawl and a veil (*tarha*) under the shawl and shoes
Q: What happened to the victim when you prayed for her
A: I was shocked (*hasal liyya dhuhul*) and disturbed (*irtibak*) and I lifted the veil she was [unclear] and she did not answer I didn't know what to do
Q: Did you move the corpse by yourself to its position below the building
A: There was nobody to help me and I don't know how I lifted her
Q: The forensic physician established that the victim was in her underwear
A: She had all her clothes on
Q: How did her clothes get torn
A: I don't know
Q: Describe the veil she wore on her head
A: It was black and I don't know whether it was tied or not
Q: What was the position in which you placed her in the well
A: I don't know
Q: What do you think of the forensic physician's report according to which the victim died as a result of asphyxiation
A: I don't know
Q: Was there anybody with you while you were praying over the victim
A: No there was nobody during the prayer and she died by herself
Q: Was the victim wearing any gold jewellery on her ears or on her breast
A: No
Q: The victim was wearing gold jewellery on her ears and her breast
A: She had no jewellery on her
Q: Was it made possible through prayer to know the wicked spirit she had inside her
A: She didn't speak nor did the wicked spirit
Q: For how long have you known the victim
A: My sister's daughter is married to her son
Q: Was there any other relationship
A: No there's no relationship except kinship
Q: How much time elapsed from the time of the prayer over her
A: Approximately five minutes
Q: What conversation took place between you and the victim before the prayer
A: There was no conversation
Q: What means of transportation did the victim take to the 10th of Ramadan
A: [unclear]
Q: Is the housing unit completed

A: There's a door to the flat and the cement structure and there are interior walls but the flat is not completed
Q: What was she sitting on and what was her position before the prayer
A: She was seated
Q: You mentioned in the investigation that she was standing
A: I didn't mention it
Q: Have you ever prayed and exorcised evil spirits from anyone before
A: Yes
Q: Did you suggest to the victim that she was possessed by an evil spirit
A: Yes
Q: The victim's son says that she was normal (*tabi'iyya*)
A: No she didn't speak to anybody else
Q: Was there any material compensation in exchange for this
A: No that would have been crazy
Q: The forensic physician says that you strangled her
A: No she died of natural causes

Many features observed in previous sections of this chapter are confirmed in this excerpt. There is, firstly, the frequent use of the "I don't know" pattern of response. As shown by Drew, this is clearly used to avoid confirming. The accused may be anticipating that what he is being asked to state will turn out to be prejudicial to his situation (Drew, 1992: 481). A claim of ignorance may be interpreted as a strategic avoidance of potentially damaging information. But, at the same time, claiming not to know or remember makes it unnecessary to negate what is proposed in the question, and therefore makes it possible to avoid posing a direct challenge to the judge's interpretation. Finally, claiming not to know or not to remember is a strategy used to highlight the insignificance of a detail. It appears to be much more beneficial for the accused to rebut the judge's versions of events, 'not by directly challenging his versions, but by implying a different characterization of events' (Drew, 1992: 486) (Q: The forensic physician says that you strangled her. A: No, she died of natural causes). Following Komter (1998: 129), we can argue that 'the dilemma of suspects is to produce defences that are not heard as defences but as cooperation and to show cooperation without foregoing opportunities for mitigation [...] Suspects manage their dilemma by offering partial admissions or qualified versions that downplay or camouflage their participation in the events or by confirming the morals while dissociating themselves from negative inferences about their guilt and moral character.' The description of a person in terms of his moral character seems to be of great importance in the process. This is why, as shown previously, one advocate stresses the normal, hence moral, character of the accused who went to pray in the Muqattam hills. This also explains why the accused denied receiving any material compensation for performing the exorcism (Q: Was there any material compensation in exchange for this? A: No, that would have been crazy).

Parties are oriented to the specificities of the setting in which they are embedded. This can lead them to anticipate a great deal with regard to the morally damaging potential of some of the judge's questions. For instance, in response to the question about his relationship with the victim, the accused emphasizes that he had only kinship bonds, thereby implying that there were no sexual relations between the victim and himself (Q: How long have you known the victim? A: My sister's daughter is married to her son. Q: Was there any other relationship? A: No, there's no relationship except kinship). This is confirmed by his denial that the victim was in her underwear (Q: The forensic physician established that the victim was in her underwear. A: She had all her clothes on). Another example is his denying that the victim had any jewellery on her; the question clearly anticipates the possibility that he will be accused of stealing from the victim (Q: Was the victim wearing any gold jewellery on her ears or on her breast? A: No. Q: The victim was wearing gold jewellery on her ears and her breast. A: She had no jewellery on her). Obviously, the accused is aware that he may be accused of stealing (as in fact happened).

The goal orientation of the parties vis-à-vis the context and its procedural implications means that the parties are sensitive to the issue of personal involvement and intentions. As we shall see in the following chapter, on one hand, the definition of intention must be inferred from actual interactional circumstances and data. As was shown in the former chapter, on the other hand, they cannot be deduced or induced from jurisprudence, law or case law. The meaning of intention emerges from actual judicial settings and interactions, not from the logic of goals and motives as developed by textual law.[5] In the case that we used to illustrate this argument, we observe a complex game of intention, purpose, personal participation, etc. At the risk of repeating myself, I maintain that it is from this information in particular that we can infer the, local, limited contextual meaning of personhood and its characteristic features. We can review different themes:

- Motivation and initiative (Question: Why did you take Qiddisa […] to 10th of Ramadan? Answer of the accused: At the request of the victim, because nobody knew that she was possessed by a demon and she feared that people would find out/Q: Did you suggest to the victim that she was possessed by an evil spirit A: Yes): On one hand, the judge seeks to attribute precise motivations to the circumstances, so as to characterize them properly (e.g. willful homicide vs. unintentional manslaughter). On the other, the accused seeks to demonstrate that he had no personal interest in initiating the interaction between the victim and himself, without however damaging his credibility. This is what Komter (1998) calls the dilemma of interest and credibility.
- Intention and agency Q: What happened to the victim when you prayed for her? A: I was shocked (hasal liyya dhuhul) and disturbed (irtibak) and I lifted the veil she was [unclear] and she did not answer. I didn't know what

5 As, for instance, in the work of the famous Egyptian jurist 'Abd al-Razzaq al-Sanhuri (Arabi, 1997).

to do.): Here again, the judge is interested in knowing whether the accused acted with purpose or not. The accused is interested in making his personal agency disappear, while not appearing a fool and/or damaging the credibility of the demon possession narrative. In fact, the accused is claiming that the responsible agency was that of the demons, not his own; that the demons have a personality that inhabited the woman, attacked him when he tried to exorcise them, and killed her in a way he cannot remember. In other words, the accused tries to displace the question of agency and to state its reassignment from himself to the devils – hence, to underplay his active participation in the events through the formulation of an alternative version implying the participation of a third actor. By so doing, he is confirming shared conceptions of what is moral and immoral (e.g. killing is immoral), while avoiding negative inferences about his own moral character. Moreover, although his moral character could be compromised by placing emphasis on his lack of mental capacity, in the narrative, the accused makes himself completely disappear from the scene, with the consequence that he claims to be neither personally responsible nor mentally irresponsible (Komter, 1998).

- Excuses, consciousness and agency (Q: Did you move the corpse by yourself to its position below the building? A: There was nobody to help me and I don't know how I left her.): The judge is interested in proving the suspect's personal and intentional involvement in the crime, hence denying the relevance of any excuses the latter produces. On the other hand, the accused seeks to produce excuses for what he did, including the action of an external constraint obliterating his intentional agency. Here again, both the judge and the accused seem committed to the production of narratives that could account for the personal role, i.e. the intentional and motivated participation of people involved in the case. We may say, following Ferrié (1995; 1997), that they show solidarity in identifying the relevant issues of the case, although no consensus is possible with regard to defining the parties' role in it. In other words, they share an understanding of what features are relevant to the characterization process and they disagree, asymmetrically, on how to fulfil these features in the case under scrutiny.
- Normality and agency (Q: Was there anybody with you while you were praying over the victim? A: No, there was nobody during the prayer and she died by herself/ Q: The forensic physician says that you strangled her. A: No, she died of natural causes): Agency and normality seem to be inextricably interwoven. Each situation is characterized according to what is considered to be the normal behaviour of the actors involved. In the case of death, "normal" and "natural" are defined with regard to the non-intervention of human agency in its production. Thus, if someone dies due to the action of wicked spirits, this cannot be considered abnormal, since it is not the consequence of any human agency. In contrast, suicide is deemed abnormal, since it is the result of the victim's own agency. This shows that the definition of normality can differ from place to place and from time to time.

It is interesting to contrast the accounts given by the accused with the following account by the plaintiff's advocate:

Excerpt 63 (Criminal Court, Case 2783, 1997, Cairo)

Present with the parties claiming for damages, Mr. Samih [...], advocate,

He said that the accused performed this heinous crime, that there were ties between the accused and the victim; the victim helped everybody; that is why the accused chose to tell the victim, as the witness mentioned in the former session, that her children were in danger; the victim had gold and money with her; hence, the goal was to steal from the victim, the proof being that he brought her far away from her family and her neighbours, to a building in the 10th of Ramadan, far from everything; if he really intended to exorcise the demon, as alleged, he could have done it in front of the family and neighbours [...].

This excerpt clearly shows how an advocate can contribute to the production of a normal pattern of behaviour (e.g. the victim being known to all and helping everybody) that should have led to normal consequences (he could have performed the exorcism in the presence of the family and neighbours), the violation of which must therefore be accounted for (why did the accused take her to this remote place?), which in turn moralizes the case ("a heinous crime"). Furthermore, it gives a direct account of the suspect's possible motivations (to steal from the victim) and the strategies he used to achieve his aim (frightening the victim to lure her into the trap of such a remote place). In sum, the production of normalcy makes it possible to infer normative consequences from congruence with, or divergence from, what is supposed to have happened.

Ultimately, the defence only claimed that the accused was insane in a subsidiary manner, in order to avoid his criminal liability. However, the Court rejected this argument, largely on the basis of the impression he gave during the cross-examination.

Excerpt 64 (Criminal Court, Case 2783, 1997, Cairo)

Considering that the defence asked [...] for the accused to be transferred to a hospital for psychiatric diseases [...]

The Court rejects this request for the following reasons:

First: [...]

Second: The Court is convinced that the accused was in full possession of his mental capacities at the time when he committed the crime and that he is criminally responsible for his deeds, because the Court's cross-examination of the accused [...] contradicts [his alleged insanity], since his answers to the Court's questions were logical [...]. On the basis of the above, the Court considers that the accused was conscious and capable of discernment when he committed the crime, and that makes him responsible for his deeds, because the disease characterized as mental disorder, which diminishes responsibility, according to article 62 of the Criminal Code, diminishes consciousness and discretion. In contrast, all the other psychiatric states that do not diminish the

> person's consciousness and discernment are not considered to diminish responsibility. The defence did not prove that the accused is affected by insanity or mental disorder.

As noted earlier, the accused did not claim insanity as an excuse for his behaviour and what happened. However, since the parties to the trial are entirely oriented to the legal consequences produced by characterizing the facts, and are also constrained in their statements and actions by the institutional context in which the case is situated, insanity appears as a convenient way to mitigate the implications of incrimination, in the case that the Court rejects demon possession as a justification. In other words, this can be analysed as a shift from justification (the accused acted under constraint) to excuse (the accused is insane). For the Court, however, accepting insanity would mean that possession is not an acknowledged state of the person, and can only be seen as a manifestation of mental disorder. This was obviously not its opinion (cf. excerpt 60). If spirit possession could not be considered as the expression of mental disorder, the Court had no choice but to convict the accused for wilful homicide. Indeed, it could not break free of the procedural constraints that allow a condemned person, among other things, to appeal to another jurisdiction. In other words, it was forced consider the existence of a kind of 'overreading' audience (cf. Chapters 4 and 5), an instance that could eventually invalidate its initial ruling. If this ruling was based on unsubstantiated grounds (and it must be said that Egyptian law recognizes neither the legal personality of devils and other spirits, nor any kind of possession by them), the Court ran the risk of its ruling being overthrown, and even of a possible sanction.[6] This definitely constitutes a procedural constraint on the judge's work.

Conclusion

I have attempted in this chapter to demonstrate that the meaning of categories is not substantial and essential, but is context-sensitive, i.e. this meaning is shaped and oriented according to the setting within which it arises. Given that this context is mainly institutional, we might add that the meaning given to categories is related to the institutional circumstances of their use. This, of course, is also true of law and judicial institutions. I documented this argument with the help of examples concerning the category of the person. One of the main benefits of the praxeological approach as used here is its ability to show how an exclusive focus on law in the text[7] conceals the major significance of institutional contexts of discourse and action, even while a category like that of the person can only be accounted for in the description of its practical grammar.

6 As occurred in the case of Justice Ghurab, mentioned in Chapter 5, excerpts 5 to 7.

7 As, for instance, the perspective taken by Arabi (2004), according to whom "Egyptian law" pays less tribute to the "Islamic conception" of insanity than Ottoman (*Majalla*) or Iraqi law.

Chapter 9
The Production of Causality: A Praxeological Grammar of the Use of Causal Concepts

In this chapter, I intend to examine causal concepts as they function within the situated context of Egyptian judicial institutions. Causation has been the topic of much research in legal philosophy and theory. I will argue, however, that this was achieved to the detriment of the situated examination of its practical grammar. This grammar, which aims at bringing out the variations and ambiguities of epistemological expressions in common usage, makes it possible to show how such causal concepts acquire a singular relevance according to the contextual conditions of the activities in which they are embedded. Causal ascription then departs the field of nominal coherence and enters that of the deconstruction of the mechanisms whereby people come to identify an activity as part of "the search for causes", without it being possible to tell in advance that the local, time-bound realization of such an activity will fall under a "general theory of causation". I therefore intend to treat cause as an epistopic (cf. Introduction; Lynch, 1993: 265-308).

The chapter will proceed in two stages. Referring to the analysis in Chapter 7 on Egyptian jurisprudence and case law concerning causation (and the associated notions of excuse, justification, and circumstance), it will immediately present the main contributions of Hart and Honoré's (1985) analytical approach. These authors offer a kind of inventory of the forms taken by causation in commonsense reasoning and map out the logical categories that law professionals use to determine whether something has a causal relationship with something else. Their perspective goes beyond purely formal categories and underscores the close relationship between causal reasoning in law and causation in ordinary reasoning, as well as the sensitivity of both types of reasoning to the context of their formulation. However, it fails to transcend either the level of thought experiments of a hypothetical nature on commonsense categories or the level of polished and formalized case-law texts, and therefore obfuscates the essentially practical dimension of the question of causation. This is precisely what the praxeological approach seeks to analyse. In the second part of this chapter, I show its contributions through the study of the grammar of causal concepts in the context of Egyptian judicial practice. On the basis of cases in the field of good morals, I show that causation – far from being a purely logical and mechanical system for discovering facts and establishing a relationship between actions and their authors – constitutes a thoroughly moral phenomenon, the grammar of which can be contextually observed. I seek to show how people describe, categorize, ascribe (by aggravating or mitigating) a responsibility, or give explanations therefore orienting toward a moral order, producing and reproducing it in what I call a normalization process.

Commonsense and Legal Reasoning on Causation

In this section, I will proceed in two stages, first offering a brief synthesis of Herbert Hart and Tony Honoré's major contribution to the understanding of causation in the law (Hart and Honoré, 1985), and then focusing on two rulings emitted by the Egyptian Court of Cassation in order to illustrate their approach.

Following Hart and Honoré's Footsteps

Where classical philosophy constructed a model of causation intended for use in the natural sciences, Hart and Honoré formulated a realistic three-stage approach. Their demonstration shows that classical legal philosophy has failed to make sense of causation in the law; traces the paths that causation follows in common sense; and describes the links between ordinary and legal modes of causal reasoning.

Classical European philosophy analysed the concept of cause in terms of generalizations or laws that assert an invariable connection between types of events. For Hume, the notion of cause raised two general questions: the truth and character of the principle that every event has a cause, and the notion of necessary connection between a cause and its effect. He insisted that we make causal statements only after experiencing the constant conjunction of pairs of events in nature and after getting the feeling of 'a determination of the mind to pass from one object to its usual attendant.' (Hume, 1969: book I, part III, chapter 14) This doctrine was passed down to us through John Stuart Mill, who replaced the psychological argument with the logical form of counterfactual inference: what would the case have been if some event, which in fact happened, had not happened? Unlike Hume, who holds that a consequent necessarily has one single antecedent, Mill (1886: book III, chapter 5, section 3) recognized the complexity of causal connections, though he still made causality a relation of necessity. According to him, the cause of an event is, philosophically speaking, 'the sum total of [its] conditions' and 'we have philosophically speaking no right to give the name of cause to one of them exclusively of the others.'

In their remarkable analysis of causation in the law, Hart and Honoré stress that the way philosophers discuss this issue fails to address the specific and practical aspects lawyers face in their occupational work:

> Their [viz., the lawyers'] characteristic concern with causation is not to discover connections between types of events, and so not to *formulate* laws or generalizations, but is often to *apply* generalizations, which are already

> known or accepted as true and even platitudinous, to particular concrete cases. In this and other respects the causal statement of the lawyer [...] are like the causal statements most frequent in ordinary life: they are singular statements identifying in complex situations certain particular events as causes, effects, or consequences of other particular events. (Hart and Honoré, 1985: 10)

One difficulty lawyers face in applying known or accepted generalizations to particular cases is making a distinction between an occasion, a condition, and a cause. This distinction has little to do with generalizations and laws asserting invariable causal connections, 'but very much to do with the particular context and purpose for which a particular causal inquiry is made and answered.' (*id.*: 11) Stating that people make context-sensitive choices from among a variety of causal explanations does not mean that the choice is arbitrary or haphazard. It means that such a choice does not follow purely logical and natural rules; rather, it is the product of a combination between the particulars of a case and a set of possible commonsense, professional, and expert explanations. The philosophical approach to causation scarcely addresses the main question that lawyers face: 'are there any principles governing the selection we apparently make of one of a complex set of conditions as the cause?' (*id.*: 17) According to Hart and Honoré, rather than one single concept of causation, there are common conceptions of causation with features that vary from context to context, there are different types of causal inquiry, and there are clusters of related causal concepts, all of which are practically relevant in these causal inquiries. Hence, we reach the conclusion that the generalizations involved in commonsensical and legal causal statements are of a broader and less specific nature than those generalizations sought by the classical philosophy of causation. In its practical and contextual legal form, causal inquiry is about what made the difference between the accident occurring and normal functioning. This is what Hart and Honoré call "explanatory causal inquiry", which is often paralleled with an "attributive inquiry" that seeks to determine whether some harm, whose occurrence has been successfully understood, can be attributed to someone's action as its consequence (Hart and Honoré: 24).

Stating that an ordinary person masters causal concepts in their daily use and acknowledging the sensitivity to context of these numerous causal notions, Hart and Honoré stress how difficult it is to produce a full and comprehensive formal picture of causation in general. Instead, they propose to select 'standard examples of the way in which causal expressions are constantly used in ordinary life,' examples that form 'a core of a relatively well-settled common usage.' (*id.*: 27) According to the two authors, there is not one single concept of causation but a cluster of concepts that share what Wittgenstein calls a family resemblance. For instance, the term consequence 'is typically used of what emerges as the culminating phase or outcome of a process which is complex and consciously designed' (*id.*: 28), whereas the effect is perceived as 'the desired secondary change' and the cause as 'our action in bringing about the primary change in the things manipulated or those primary changes themselves.' (*id.*: 29) Contrary to Mill's theory of causation, they show that, in simple cases,

> ... where we speak of a deliberate human intervention or the primary changes initiated by it as the cause of an occurrence, we rely upon general knowledge and commit ourselves to a general proposition of some kind; but this is something very different from causal 'laws' or general propositions asserting invariable sequence which Mill regarded as essential to causal connection. (*id.*: 31)

A commonsense conception of causation is organized around a certain idea of the normal, natural, state of things and, conversely, of their abnormality. Common experience teaches us that things have a nature and would persist in their "natural" state if not manipulated; such manipulation is the cause that interferes with, or intervenes in, the "normal" course of events.

> There is a presumption, normally fulfilled but rebuttable, that when we deliberately intervene in nature to bring about effects that in fact supervene, no other explanation of their occurrence is to be found. Hence to make this type of causal statement is justified if there is no ground for believing this normally fulfilled presumption not to hold good. It is, however, a feature of this, as of other types of empirical statement, that exceptionally they are not vindicated in the result and have to be withdrawn. (Hart and Honoré: 32)

The commonsense concept of cause as a breach of the natural course of events extends far beyond the mere idea of human manipulation: '[I]t is also generally used whenever an *explanation* is sought of an occurrence by which we are puzzled because we do not understand why it has occurred.' (*id.*: 32) It is here that a distinction is commonly made between a cause and mere conditions, generally through the use of two devices contrasting between, on one hand, normal and abnormal conditions and, on the other hand, voluntary and involuntary human action.

Abnormality is defined as what makes the difference between an accident and things going on as usual. In this sense, normality is relative to context and perspective. What is deemed normal in one context is deemed abnormal in another, but what somebody considers merely a condition for the occurrence of an event in one and the same case, somebody else might see as the cause of this occurrence. Moreover, normality is not only the ordinary course of nature unaffected by human intervention; it may also correspond to the way things must happen thanks to human intervention or man-made norms to which people are expected to conform. Hence, abnormality can occur if one omits to do something or fails to comply with a norm. The causal explanation (and this is part of the difference between cause and condition) does not consist in looking for the cause of a normal consequence in a normal sequence of events but for the "Why did this happen when normally it would not?" – a breach to normality that calls for an explanation (Hart and Honoré: 33-41).

Voluntary actions occupy a special place in causal inquiry. It remains necessary to point out that people make various distinctions between voluntary, involuntary, and partially voluntary actions. A human action will be said not to be (fully) voluntary: 'if it is done "unintentionally" (i.e. by mistake or by accident); or "involuntarily" (i.e. where normal muscular control is absent); "unconsciously", or under various types of pressure exerted by other human beings (coercion or duress); or even under the pressure of legal or moral obligation, or as a choice of the lesser of two evils, which is often expressed by saying that the agent "had no choice" or "no real choice".' (*id.*: 41) Each time, human agency occupies a central place in the causal inquiry, and indeed often serves as an end point for such inquiry. Thus, for instance, 'The causal explanation of the particular occurrence is brought to a stop when the death has been explained by the deliberate act, in the sense that none of the antecedents of that deliberate act will count as the cause of death.' (*id.*: 42)

In attributing responsibility, a cause is generally considered to be the necessary condition without which something would not have occurred. The cause is the event without which the subsequent event would not have come about, while the consequence in the event that would not have occurred if a previous event had not taken place. There is therefore a "chain of causality" linking a consequence to the event that initiated it, with the latter operating as an end point in the causal regression. In simple cases, such an event is generally an intentional action. The causal chain thus created is broken by the intervention of an external or abnormal element, such as an excuse, a justification, or a circumstance, which modifies the responsibility that would otherwise be attached to the authors of the act that led to the event. In that case, the action is no longer considered as the product of an informed choice, accomplished without anyone's intervention (*id.*: 75).

The relations between causality and responsibility are multiple and testify to the close connections between commonsense and legal reasoning in this area. This holds true with regard to demands for compensation. In the moral judgments of ordinary life, we may blame people because they have caused harm to others and insist that they are morally bound to compensate those they have harmed (for instance, we ask a child who hit his friend to ask the friend to forgive him). According to the law, liability to receive punishment or pay compensation generally depends on whether an action has caused harm. In other respects, common sense accepts the idea that moral blame should be ascribed to someone who cheats or lies or breaks promises, even if no one has suffered particular harm. In the legal domain, failed attempts to commit crimes are punished, as is the illegal possession of certain kinds of weapons, drugs, or counterfeiting materials. The causal connection is also, in common sense as in the law, central to the establishment of liability. We blame people for harm "directly" caused, but also for harm that arises from or is the consequence of their neglect of common precautions, even if harm occurred when another human being deliberately exploited the opportunities provided by neglect. Finally, common sense blames people for the harm we consider to be the consequence of their influence over others. As for the law, it represses instigation of criminal behaviour and incitement to crime.

To conclude, returning to the notion of the causal chain and its incidence on the attribution of responsibility in criminal law, the question that the courts most often have to address is that of knowing whether a human act or omission caused specific harm. Crimes, felonies, and misdemeanours are defined as acts that caused specific prejudice. In that regard, the establishment of responsibility (i.e. the establishment of the fact that a particular crime was committed and that its author is liable to be punished) requires that one demonstrates that a causal relation exists between the action of the accused person and the harm that has occurred. Furthermore, criminal liability is often limited by recourse to causal distinctions embedded in ordinary thought, and that highlight the occurrence of abnormal events or coincidences (*id.*: 84; 325).

Causation in the Egyptian Court of Cassation's Rulings: Two Cases

One of the merits of Hart and Honoré is to have removed inquiry into causation from the domain of legal theory and jurisprudence and introduced it into the field of applied legal reasoning. Two examples drawn from the doctrine of the Egyptian Court of Cassation allow us to see how a set of causal notions is expressed in a non-random manner (see also Chapter 7, excerpt 35). In the first of these examples, cited previously (excerpt 41, Chapter 7), the Court of Cassation adjudicated in a case of medical responsibility.

> **Excerpt 65 (Court of Cassation, 1973, Case 40, Petition 1566, 42nd Judicial Year)**
> The civil petitioner directly introduced his petition before the Azbakiyya Court of misdemeanours against the first defendant, claiming that the latter, during the month of December 1964, in the district of Azbakiyya, caused an error (*khata'*), due to his negligence (*ihmal*), lack of care (*'adam ihtiraz*) and precaution (*'adam ihtiyat*), and failure to observe medical principles that must be followed (*'adam mura'atihi li-l-usul al-tibbiyya al-wajib ittiba'iha*, all of which resulted in the petitioner's complete loss of eyesight. This is because [the defendant] conducted a surgical operation on both [the petitioner's] eyes simultaneously in order to remove cataracts, without previously carrying out the medically necessary measures and examinations. [The defendant] conducted the operation on the petitioner without notifying him and without obtaining his consent, without the assistance of an anesthetist and outside a hospital. Furthermore, he did not compel [the petitioner] to rest and obtain medical follow-up after the operation. Rather, [the defendant] abandoned [the petitioner] in the middle of the street without assistance, and this led to the inflammation of his eyes [...] and the occurrence of complications that weakened his eyesight. He [the civil petitioner] asked that [the defendant] be condemned pursuant to Article 224/1-2 of the Code of Penal Procedure and that he be compelled, together with Misr Petroleum Company, which is liable for civil obligations, to pay compensation [...] as well as expenses and

> retainers [...]. [The civil petitioner] then amended his petition and requested [double] the amount. On 26 June 1969, pursuant to the provision [stipulated] in the accusation, the abovementioned court [decided]: (1) to condemn the defendant to payment of a fine [...]; and (2), with regard to the civil petition, to reject the defense invoked by the company responsible for civil obligations, according to which the petition was inadmissible with regard to anyone other than a person acting on his own behalf, and to declare the petition admissible, thereby compelling the defendant together with the abovementioned company to pay the civil petitioner [...] compensation, expenses, and [...] retainers [...]. The defendant, together with the company responsible for civil obligations, introduced an appeal against this ruling. The Cairo Court of First Instance, in its appeals circuit, ruled on 30 April 1972, admitting the appeal with regard to its form, confirming the ruling against which the appeal was lodged as to penalty [viz., the fine], and amending the ruling as to compensation, limiting it [...], besides the expenses corresponding to both degrees of jurisdiction and [...] retainers. Both the defendant and the party responsible for civil obligations decided to appeal this ruling in cassation.

In the body of the ruling, the Court of Cassation addresses different procedural and substantive issues. Among other things, it examines the meaning of criminal liability, civil responsibility, and involuntary battery (*isaba khata'*). Moreover, it addresses the issue of the performance of surgery as a cause of justification (*sabab ibaha*), its conditions, and the breach to these conditions that makes the physician criminally liable for the results. It furthermore examines the causal link (*rabitat al-sababiyya*) that must exist between medical malpractice and its effect on the victim's health. The Court stipulates that authorization to perform a medical activity is conditional upon the fact that what the physician performs corresponds to scientifically established principles. If the physician deviates from the observance of these principles or damages them, he will be considered criminally liable according to the action's intentional character, its result or defects, and the lack of precaution taken in its execution.

The point the different courts had to decide was whether it was the way the physician (the petitioner) had performed the surgical operation that caused the harm, i.e. the victim's loss of eyesight, or some factor extraneous to the operation that was beyond the physician's capacity to anticipate. In reaching their decision, the courts examined different forensic reports, according to which the victim did not urgently need the operation, and nothing justified the physician's precipitation. These reports concluded that internal functional examinations should have been conducted before the operation; that operating on both eyes at the same time exposed the patient to complications that could result in the loss of his eyesight; that the physician should have advised his patient to take the rest necessary for his recovery after the operation; and that a physician who is a specialist has a greater duty to take precautions than a generalist. The Court of Cassation quoted the report of eminent specialists:

Excerpt 66 (Court of Cassation, 1973, Case 40, Petition No. 1566, 42nd Judicial Year)

What the accused person has done, as indicated formerly, is recognized by the medical art and does not constitute a professional fault in the strict sense; however, we join the three experts appointed earlier in affirming that the choice made by the accused of this therapeutic method and the decision to carry out the operation on both the patient's eyes in a single session, in these circumstances, without taking all the precautions necessary to secure the result, proceeded from an unusual feeling of self-confidence (*shu'ur za'id 'an al-ma'luf bi-l-thiqa bi-l-nafs*). Thus was he blinded to the need to take all the precautions corresponding, in such circumstances, to the nature of the method chosen to obtain the practical result he expected from the patient, i.e., the preservation of his eyesight, thereby exposing the patient to complications in both eyes simultaneously, and leading to the complete loss of his eyesight. Thus, the accused is liable for the result, i.e. the loss of the patient's eyesight, not because of a scientific mistake, but as a consequence of a lack of personal foresight on his behalf (*'adam tabassur shakhsi minhu*), and this is a question of abstract evaluation that does not depend on a particular criterion.

On the basis of these medical reports, the courts declared the physician criminally liable and civilly responsible for the harm caused to the patient, and these rulings were uphold by the Court of Cassation.

The Court's dealing with the question of causation is organized as follows. First, the cause of justification that makes the exercise of medicine and surgery legitimate is conditioned upon its performance according to the accepted scientific principles; if these are neglected or violated, the accused is liable according to the intentional character of the action (*ta'ammudat al-fi'l*), its result (*natija*) or defects in its accomplishment (*taqsir*), and the absence of precaution (*'adam taharruz*) in the performance of his profession. Second, there must be a causal link between the shortcoming due to the physician's fault and the harm that resulted for the victim. This is established, according to the Court, since the permanent loss of the victim's eyesight would not have occurred had the physician, first, made the necessary preliminary examinations and, second, not operated on both eyes at the same time. Finally, professionals and specialists have a specific duty with regard to precautions and foresight. This means that negligence on their part is especially punishable.

The second example is a case of wilful homicide and sexual assault. The facts as the Court of Cassation summarized them read as follows:

Excerpt 67 (Court of Cassation, 1988, Case 6, Petition 4113, 57th Judicial Year)

The General Prosecution has accused the petitioner: (1) Of having willfully killed (*qatala 'amadan*) … [victim's name] by striking her (*inhal ta'n*) with a sharp weapon (*silah had*) with the aim (*qasdan*) to kill her. She was struck down by the blows described in the autopsy report, from which she died. Another crime is linked to this [viz., the willful homicide]: the accused person had sexual intercourse (*waqa'a*) at the same time and in the same place with the aforementioned victim without her consent (*bi-ghayr*

> *rida'iha*), forcing her to lay down on the ground as a result of his assaulting her with the aforementioned sharp weapon, pulling off her clothes and undergarments, exposing her pudenda (*'awratiha*), then introducing his reproductive organ forcefully into her genitals (*mawdi' al-'iffa*) until he ejaculated. Furthermore, the accused also attempted, at the aforementioned time and place, to steal the belongings of the aforementioned victim and was stopped in his crime by a cause unrelated to his will (*sabab la dakhl li-iradatihi*), i.e. his fleeing for fear of being caught. The crime is therefore *in flagrante delicto* (*fi halat talabbus*); (2) of having, without authorization, purchased a knife. [The General Prosecution] referred him [viz., the petitioner] to the Cairo Criminal Court to be punished according to the act [of which he is accused] and the characterization defined in the act of transfer. This Court unanimously decided to refer the documents of the case to his Excellency the Mufti of the Republic to obtain his opinion, and set the session of … [date] for the discussion of the ruling. At the designated session, the Court decided unanimously, pursuant to Article 45, 47, 234, 267-1, 316 (II), 316 (III) and 321 of the Code of Criminal Procedure, Article 1-1, 25-1 (II) and 30 of Law 394 of 1954, amended by Law 165 of 1981 and Article 10 of the first addendum to this law, in pursuance of Article 32 of the Penal Code, to condemn the accused to the death penalty.
>
> The condemned person has lodged a petition against this ruling by cassation and the Public Prosecution has presented the case to the Court in an advisory memorandum.

Besides procedural questions, the Court of Cassation addresses several substantive issues in its ruling. First, it examines the constitutive elements of the crime of fornication, which it defines as 'subjection [to sexual intercourse] through the use of any means denying the victim's will.' According to the Court, this means conversely that the woman must have had freedom in her sexual relations, and this is possible only if she was still alive at the time of the assault. Second, it examines the link between the crime of wilful homicide and the two related offenses of fornication and theft. Since it cannot be established that sexual intercourse happened before the woman's death, it appears to the Court that the crime of wilful homicide cannot be associated (*iqtiran*) with the crime (*jinaya*) of rape, although it is linked (*irtibat*) to the misdemeanor (*junha*) of theft. The consequences are important, since the law – today amended – provided that the crime of wilful homicide was to be punished by the death penalty when associated with another crime, whereas it was to be punished by the death penalty or perpetual forced labour when linked only to a misdemeanour.

The Court of Cassation's reasoning is expressed as follows:

> **Excerpt 68 (Court of Cassation, 1988, Case 6, Petition 4113, 57th Judicial Year)**
> [Considering the Criminal Court's ruling and considering that] the text of Article 267/1 of the Penal Code, as formulated in Chapter IV concerning crimes of indecent assault (*hitk 'ird*) and immoral offences (*ifsad al-akhlaq*), which is part of Book III of the same code concerning felonies and misdemeanours against persons, stipulates: 'Whoever has sexual intercourse with a woman without her consent shall be punished by perpetual forced labour.' It indicates explicitly and in the clearest sense that the crime of fornication is conditional upon the fact that criminally sanctioned sexual

> intercourse occurred without the consent of the female victim. This can only be the case, as established by this Court's jurisprudence, when the accused person, in carrying out the crime, resorted to what [the Court] designates as force, threat, or impact (*yu'aththir*) on the victim, denying her the [free exercise of her] will, and preventing her from resisting. It means only that the victim enjoyed freedom of sexual relations, and this could only be so if she had the will, i.e. if she was alive. Thus, freedom is linked to will, with regard to [its] existence and [its] denial, as a cause is linked to the consequence and a reason to an effect. Since the faulty judgment, as it appears from the record, omitted to ask whether the victim was alive at the time of the assault [...] it is affected by a flaw that nullifies it and it must be overruled and returned [to another criminal court].

The Court of Cassation's ruling suggests some remarks on the topic of causation. In the statutory definition, lack of consent is the main constitutive element of the crime. It is duress, constraint, or menace that constitutes the cause of the woman's subjection to undesired sexual intercourse. However, according to the court, the causal relationship between recourse to duress, constraint or menace and the lack of consent to sexual intercourse on the woman's part must be direct; that is, she must have been denied the expression of her consent by the offender who precisely sought to deny her the expression of her will. It cannot be indirect: for instance, if menace and duress aimed at forbidding her to cry or to escape, and she was killed in the course of this first interaction, this means that the offender did not seek to deny the expression of her will with regard to sexual intercourse. It then follows that the post mortem failure to consent to intercourse was not the direct result of his denying the expression of her will, but only the indirect result of a first assault that was not sexually motivated. It could be argued that the first assault caused the last effect, i.e. the offender's attack with a knife finally made sexual intercourse possible without the victim's consent. However, the Court of Cassation adopts a very narrow interpretation of the concept of proximate cause, according to which it is not enough to show that one event was a necessary condition of the other; it must still be shown that this event was directly linked to the other.

Causation in Context: A Praxeological Perspective

The preceding paragraphs have shown the contribution made by Hart and Honoré's analytical approach to causation in the law. Causation is no longer equated to the normative propositions of legal theory, as it is the case in Husni's criminal law treatise or in the compendium of the Court of Cassation's principles, and is more fully articulated with commonsense and legal-practical modes of reasoning. In the two cases I discussed above, the Court of Cassation followed basic patterns of causal reasoning and used a cluster of causal concepts, to which it is impossible to attend without contextual elements provided here by the court's rulings. However, Hart and Honoré's demonstration suffers from essential flaws related to, first, the type of material upon which they rely and, second, the basic epistemology underlying their treatment of this material (cf. Chapter 7). At present, I will adopt a determinedly praxeological perspective to look at the literature on legal causation and thereby answer the problems identified above. I ground my demonstration in a series of real cases taken from Egyptian judicial practice.

Causal Reasoning

To re-specify the question of causation means to focus the analysis upon causal reasoning as a form of praxis in its own right. In the second chapter, I applied this re-specification to ordinary reasoning, concluding that causal reasoning is a public phenomenon (Watson, 1983: 43) mainly directed at establishing a relationship between an "action" and its "author", and the nature of such a relationship. Thus, the description of an action and the characterization of its causes – e.g. deliberate, hazardous, accidental, fortunate, negligent, and the like – have major direct consequences in terms of the ascription of responsibility. This is very clear in the following excerpt, where a judge examines the accused in a case of possession, with the accused claiming the ability to perform exorcism while facing accusations of premeditated willful homicide.

> **Excerpt 69 (Criminal Court, Cairo, Case 2783, 1997)**
> Question of the Court: Why did you take Qiddisa […] to 10th of Ramadan
> Answer of the accused: At the request of the victim, because nobody knew that she was possessed by a demon and she feared that people would find out

This categorization game may be observed empirically in the judicial process. This is due, among other things, to its insertion within an institutional framework in which people tend to orient toward specific inferential ends and frameworks (Drew and Heritage, 1992: 22). It is reflected first in the lexical choice, through the selection of technical terms and/or use of descriptive terms corresponding to the role ascribed to a person and therefore highlighting or downplaying his personal agency.

> **Excerpt 70 (General Prosecution, Case 7158, 1993, Sahil, Cairo)**
> Question of the Prosecutor: At first glance is he a sentient person (*shakhs mudrik*)
> Answer of the accused: He speaks in a jerky way
> Q: Is he mentally backward
> A: I don't know

Second, it is reflected in what conversational analysts call "turn design" and sequentiality. The institutional role of participants often exerts a constraint on their positioning within the sequence, on the argumentative opportunities the sequence offers them, and accordingly on the design of causal reasoning.

Excerpt 71 (General Prosecution, Case 5471, Muharram Bey, Alexandria)
Question of the Prosecutor: What happened
Answer of the victim: I was in the street that day ... when I met these two ... and they told me come with us and they made me get in a cab ... and they went behind the Arsenal

Furthermore, one can observe the interaction's orientation toward relatively specific goals. This is what I have called the issue of procedural correctness in the judicial setting (Chapter 5, excerpt 72) and legal relevance (Chapter 6, excerpt 73).

Excerpt 72 (Court of Cassation, 1973, Case 40, Petition No. 1566, 42nd Judicial Year
The court called the plaintiff's first witness and he said:
Answer of the witness: My name is ... oath

Excerpt 73 (General Prosecution, Case 276, 1985, Ma`adi)
Question of the Prosecutor: Did sexual intercourse with the girl occur with her consent
Answer of the accused: No

The asymmetrical nature of the parties' roles in the judicial encounter must be emphasized. There is a direct relationship, in judicial interactions, between the status and role of participants, on the one hand, and their discursive rights and obligations, on the other. This can have a direct impact in terms of causal reasoning, as professionals engage mainly in soliciting legally relevant accounts (cf. excerpt 73), whereas laypeople seek to produce least damaging accounts (cf. excerpt 74), victims seek recognition of their victimhood (cf. excerpt 75), witnesses the admission of their credibility (cf. excerpt 76), etc. (cf. Drew and Heritage, 1992: 29-53)

Excerpt 74 (General Prosecution, Case 7158, 1993, Sahil, Cairo)
Question of the Prosecutor: At first glance is he a sentient person (*shakhs mudrik*)
Answer of the accused: He speaks in a jerky way
Q: Is he mentally backward
A: I don't know

Excerpt 75 (General Prosecution, Case No. 5471, Muharram Bey, Alexandria)
Question of the Prosecutor: What was the purpose of them taking you along
Answer of the victim: I think that they wanted to assault my honor otherwise they wouldn't have taken me to that place

Excerpt 76 (General Prosecution, Case 5719, 1996, Rud al-Farag, Cairo)
Question of the Prosecutor: Why haven't you testified to all this before
Answer of the witness: I thought it's just kids talking, we don't know for sure

The production of descriptions constitutes a first level in the analysis of causal reasoning in legal settings. As Atkinson and Drew (1979: 117) point out, '[b]ecause the description which can be given of a person, a group, an action, etc., is indefinitely extendible (that is, there is always more that might be added to the description), any empirical description is in principle a selection from alternative ways of describing the "same" person, etc.' Such a selection accomplishes an interactional task, e.g. providing co-participants in the interaction with a causal explanation of "what happened" and the inferences that can be drawn from it.

Excerpt 77 (General Prosecution, Case 5719, 1996, Rud al-Farag, Cairo)
Question of the Prosecutor: Did the child suffer from psychological or nervous diseases
Answer of the witness: No she was very normal and lively
Q: Was she wearing items of value
R: No we're poor God knows

Following Drew (1992), we may also observe that descriptions have often a maximal inferential property, i.e. the capacity to indicate that some event implicates "nothing more than" or "nothing less than" x or y.

Excerpt 78 (General Prosecution, Case 7158, Sahil, Cairo)
Question of the Prosecutor: From the facts you witnessed [can you say whether] your son consented to the assault or resisted
Answer of the witness: My son is mentally backward and he doesn't know anything and he didn't say a word [...]

Moreover, the descriptive process is closely linked to procedures of membership categorization through which people are attributed authorship of certain types of activities and, consequently, the whole set of rights and duties conventionally bound to these activities. Among other things, descriptions can warrant inferences about people's identity, the nature of events, and the relationship between people and events. The close examination of actual interactions allows us to observe the use of various techniques contributing to the production of such descriptions and categorizations. There are, on one hand, techniques by which people disengage themselves from situations incriminating them. Memory lapse, for instance, is frequently used to avoid confirming accounts whose nature seems consequential in terms of legal culpability. "Not remembering" or "not knowing", in this respect, can be a means for avoiding the moral and legal consequentiality of accounts one is asked to produce, and it can also be used to display the unimportance of a detail.[1] People frequently anticipate the implications of their testimonies on their and their stories' credibility.

---

1 On the role of memory in truth ceremonies, memory loss, partial memory, and the construction of "plausible deniability", see Lynch and Bogen (1996), who analyse Oliver North's testimony in the Irangate affair.

Excerpt 79 (General Prosecution, Case 7158, 1993, Sahil, Cairo)
Question of the Prosecutor: Is he mentally backward
Answer of the accused: I don't know

We also observe, on the other hand, techniques of reformulation, through which others' accounts are not denied but amended. Among these techniques, modified descriptions and selected details are often devised alternatively to produce less implicative causal explanations or to re-qualify impressions or implications enclosed in the first version of events. All the techniques of disengagement and re-formulation are clearly operating when people, while confronted with the many dilemmas they face in the course of judicial interactions, must produce causal accounts. For instance, there is the dilemma of personal interest and credibility, which makes it necessary for the accused to preserve his or her interests by reducing personal implication in the event where the trial originates, while maintaining credibility through cooperation with the court (Komter, 1998).

Excerpt 80 (General Prosecution, Case 276, 1985, Ma`adi)
Question of the prosecutor: What sexual acts did you commit with the [female] victim
Answer of the accused: When I went in I found her sitting on a cushion and I went to have sex with her I kissed her and put my arms around her waist and hugged her and then she said shame on you (*haram 'alayk*) so I left her and went out
Q: What role did each of you play in the theft of the money and the key ring and the [female] victim's two rings and the watch
A: Salah is the one who took the two rings and the chain and the 25 pounds and Ashraf is the one who took the watch

Motivation

Motive ascription occupies a central situation in the judicial process, whether at the level of intentionality (see Chapter 9) or of causality. Invoking and ascribing motives is part of the activity of formulating grounds, reasons, and causes of action. All these are closely linked to operations of categorization:

> [T]hrough the procedure of establishing category-boundedness, one can, in the first instance, establish a temporal order to the offense, and then establish a commonsense causality to the offense, or rather to the generation of the ill effects of the offense, particularly for the victim. Such imputations can straightforwardly begin when the offender initiated the offense and therefore initiated the ill effect or outcome. However, society-members also possess procedures for mitigating and, on rare occasions, even reversing such imputations. Moreover, the commonsense imputations made on the basis of membership categories are not relevant simply to interpretative work; these imputations also work to establish *moral* rights and responsibilities. (Watson, 1976: 64)

The way people are categorized has consequences on the motives imputed. With regard to causation, this means, for instance, that the victim can be categorized in such way as to become part of the causal explanation, with all the moral and legal blame-implicative consequences (the "apportionment of the quantum of blame": cf. Hart, 1963, and Watson, 1976). Notions such as victim-precipitated or victim-induced offenses are extensions of this category-bounded character of descriptions. Categorization has also consequences for causation on the side of the offender: as we saw previously (Chapter 2), "killing John" and "pulling the trigger", though formally equivalent, have different implications and meanings according to context. Such differences can proceed from the way the offender is categorized and the normative implications it has. A policeman is supposed to know how to manipulate weapons. A physician is supposed to know how to administer drugs. Their membership in a category transforms the nature of their participation in the deed. The physician who made a mistake in the proportion of anaesthetic he prescribed to his patient can be said to have caused his patient's death, whereas the woman who pumped poisoned water from the well cannot be said to have caused her child's death (see Jayyusi, 1984).

Generally speaking, motive ascription is supported by background expectations. With regard to law and judicial settings, this means that assumptions about the types or categories to which parties in a judicial process belong are heavily implicative in terms of motives, reasons, and causes for their actions. In the case of commitment proceedings, for instance, the assumption of mental illness serves as a scheme of interpretation for the judge and 'imposes a particular *context* upon all other information regarding the candidate patient, embedding knowledge of and judgments about the person and his or her behaviour in a particular body of commonsense knowledge about mentally ill persons.' (Holstein, 1987: 155) It operates in a reflexive manner, i.e. the underlying pattern providing the basis for interpreting actions, and actions so interpreted serving to document the underlying pattern. Assumptions about types and categories also have consequences on people's capacity to provide the judge (and other participants) with credible accounts of the motives, reasons, and causes of their actions. In other words, credibility assessments play a fundamental, though indirect, role in causal reasoning. '"Truthfulness" (or its lack), Brannigan and Lynch (1987: 117) argue, is reciprocal to legal practitioners' attempts to elicit testimony and expose its accountability.' Credibility is by and large an interactional accomplishment resting on background expectations and membership categorizations. In turn, credibility will affect the acceptance or rejection of causal accounts given by participants, even though there is no direct evidence as to the "true" or "false" character of such accounts. Causal reasoning and causal construction are situated processes through which participants in the judicial interaction retrieve, reformulate, and juxtapose utterances and endow them with a kind of logical order.

The case of divorce on the basis of harm that I analysed earlier (excerpts 13-24) will help illustrate the argument concerning the use of categories in recourse to motives. It clearly emerges from various excerpts of texts produced in this framework that the legal conception of harm (non-procreation) and its cause (impotence) is closely linked to the commonsense conception. At the same time, these conceptions vary according to the position people occupy within the judicial proceedings. This does not mean that these conceptions of harm have any substantial existence or that they are based on objective reality. They are most certainly constituted in an intersubjective way. However, as shown by Pollner (1974, 1975, 1979, 1987), people ascribe an objective and substantial definition to harm, and consider that definition natural. In commonsense reasoning, harm is something that exists independently from subjective points of view. As long as life is considered generally non-problematic, only deviance from what is perceived as "normal" must be accounted for in terms of causes. In our case, we can observe that the petitioner (cf. excerpt 81) as well as the judge (cf. excerpt 82) orient toward marriage as an institution endowed with normal aims.

Excerpt 81 (Court of First Instance, Case 701, 1983, Personal Status, Giza)
The petitioner is the defendant's wife by virtue of a legal marriage contract; she was married to him and suddenly discovered that her husband, the defendant, was affected by a constitutive defect: namely, he was totally incapable of having conjugal relations with her, which consequently prevented her from procreating. This has disturbed their life and made her psychologically sensitive, and her life became deeply sad as it became clear that this kind of marriage would not realize the aims of the conjugal relationship.

Excerpt 82 (Court of First Instance, Case 701, 1983, Personal Status, Giza)
Considering that [...] the forensic doctor established that the defendant [...] suffers from psychological impotence [...]. Abu Hanifa and Abu Yusuf allowed separation on grounds of a permanent defect that impedes intercourse between a man and a woman [...]. Upholding [a marriage contract] despite this [constitutes] harm for the woman whose perpetuation cannot be accepted and nothing can resolve it save separation (*The Personal Status of Imam Abu Zahra*, p. 414, par. 297, ed. 1957).

In the terms of membership categorization analysis, as developed by Sacks, we can observe that husband and wife form a pair belonging, by virtue of marriage, to the membership categorization device of the family, whose many components (i.e. the family, the husband-wife pair, each part of the pair, and other possible elements) are endowed by commonsense with a normal way of functioning from which expectations, rights and obligations follow. The many parties engaged in this case and its resolution consider that the absence of marital relations and inability to procreate constitute a discrepancy that disrupts the marriage's normal course. This is precisely what must be accounted for. A causal factor – impotence in this case – is highlighted to remedy this discrepancy. Impotence is elevated to the status of main causal source from which all the others (blows, insults, public shaming) follow. Impotence is thus considered the cause of harm in a teleological way: the feature that makes it impossible to realize the goals of marriage. The argument presents itself in the form of a succession of intertwined factors, in the sense that each one seems to be necessarily entailed by the other. In this case, the wife risks committing infidelity because antipathy is born between her and her husband, because marital life became unbearable, because the wife is compelled to live under conditions of moral constraint, because she is the target of blows, insults, and false accusations from which she suffers, because her husband is consumed with bitterness, because he is impotent.

Excerpt 83 (Court of First Instance, Case 701, 1983, Personal Status, Giza)
For the same aforementioned reason, the defendant's reproductive impotence and his incapacity to achieve the aims of marriage led him to pour out his rage [in the form] of revenge and hostility against the petitioner, by insulting her, hitting her, and finally accusing her of dishonesty and telling the police, in a wrong, aggressive and erroneous way, that the petitioner, who is his wife, stole 1,500 pounds and jewels (golden bracelet, chain and ring), so as to compel her to live with him under [the effect of] moral constraint. Then, he denounced her because she was calling for the restitution of her marital belongings. The continuation of marital life became impossible, because there exists antipathy and enmity between them, she is still young, she fears becoming unfaithful, and she fears God Almighty.

Note that, as shown by Hart and Honoré, there is actually a close relation between causation and liability, in the sense that legal consequences are attached to the fact that someone's action has caused harm to someone else. Such a relation is variable (direct or indirect harm, omission, negligence) but necessary: there can be no harm without an author. No harm can be accepted as a cause of divorce if no responsibility, no matter how indirect, that underlies it. In other words, participants to the judicial process consider causation as "agentive".

There are also other background expectations with regard to factors disrupting the normal features of married life. The testimony of the petitioner's witnesses insists, for instance, on the fact that insults were uttered publicly, that these insults physically affected the petitioner, and that her young age made her more sensitive than other people to this kind of moral constraint.

Excerpt 84 (Court of First Instance, Case No. 701, 1983, Personal Status, Giza)
[first witness]
Question of the Prosecutor: Did any harm affect the petitioner because of this
Answer of the witness: Yes she broke down while working at the post office
[second witness]
Question of the Prosecutor: Did any harm affect the petitioner because of this
Answer of the witness: Yes harm affected the petitioner because of this because she's young and a civil servant at the post office

Excuses, Justifications, and Circumstances

Turning now to excuses, justifications, and mitigating circumstances, we note that they occupy an important place in the praxeological study of causal reasoning in judicial settings. On the whole, justifications, excuses and circumstances are invoked in order to qualify an action in a way that reduces the agent's role in its production. In other words, they participate in causal reasoning by modulating the definition of personal agency for people engaged in an interaction.

In a non-legal perspective, Austin (1970: 176) differentiates between justifications, where persons accept responsibility for their actions but deny their "bad" character, and excuses, where persons admit that the actions and their consequences are "bad" but deny their responsibility in committing these actions: Reformulated by Rod Watson (unpublished) in more praxeological terms, this idea suggests that 'excuses – as sequentially relevant next actions following an allocation of blame, in the form of for instance, an accusation – can achieve two things. First, they themselves can achieve a lodging of blame and thus are often addressed to the *relocation* of blame, guilt or responsibility. [...] The second aspect of excuses as moral discourse is that they are addressed to issues concerning what Hart calls the *quantum of blame* to be allocated.' From a more legal point of view, Hart (1968: 13-5) makes a difference between justifications (regarding actions the law does not condemn or even encourages), excuses (for something that is deplored, but not condemned publicly because of conditions surrounding its commission), and mitigating circumstances (a good reason for administering a less severe penalty if the situation or mental state of the convicted criminal is such that conformity to the law was a matter of special difficulty for him as compared with normal persons in normal conditions). Practically, we may offer the following examples of justifications (excerpt 85), excuses (excerpt 86), and circumstances (excerpt 87).

Excerpt 85 (Cairo Criminal Court, Case 2783, 1997)
Question of the Court: Why did you take Qiddisa [...] to 10th of Ramadan
Answer of the accused: At the request of the victim, because nobody knew that she was possessed by a demon and she feared that people would find out

Excerpt 86 (Vice Squad, Case 2677, 1983, Heliopolis)
Question of the police officer: How many times did you practice prostitution
Answer of the suspect: More than once but I don't do it a lot just once or twice a month because I don't like doing that

Excerpt 87 (Cairo Criminal Court, Case 2783, 1997)
Question of the Court: What happened to the victim when you prayed for her
Answer of the accused: I was shocked (*hasal liyya dhuhul*) and disturbed (*irtibak*) and I lifted the veil she was [unclear] and she did not answer I didn't know what to do

In verbal exchanges, excuses, justifications and mitigating circumstances often operate at the level of alternative descriptions, which are mobilized to create a discrepancy between the type of incriminated action and the type of accused person. By furnishing substitute interpretive schemes, the re-characterization of an action (by presenting an alternative description) or a person (by presenting reasons motivating action) solves the problem that stemmed from the lack of congruence between background expectancies and the scene observed.

Excerpt 88 (Cairo Criminal Court, Case 2783, 1997)
Question of the Court: Was the victim wearing any gold jewelry on her ears or on her breast
Answer of the accused: No
Q: The victim was wearing gold jewelry on her ears and her breast
A: She had no jewelry on her [...]
Q: You mentioned in the investigation that she was standing
A: I didn't mention it [...]
Q: The forensic physician says that you strangled her
A: No she died of natural causes

We can observe that, often, further information contains biographical information about the individual concerned (Jayyusi, 1984: 142).

Excerpt 89 (Cairo Criminal Court, Case 2783, 1997)
Question of the Court: The victim's son says that she was normal (*tabi'iyya*)
Answer of the accused: No she didn't speak to anybody else

Moreover, contrary to justifications, excuses – let alone circumstances – do not deny the "badness" of the act, but they can work 'to cut off the inferential extrapolation of the "seriousness" or "badness" from the act to the person.' (Watson, unpublished)

Excerpt 90 (Vice Squad, Case 2677, 1983, Heliopolis)
Question of the police officer: What have you to say about what is said against you
Answer of the arrested person: I'm guilty of everything that happened and you if you knew the circumstances of my life you'd excuse me because my mother is sick and she's got cancer and I'm responsible for her and I work like that exploiting myself

In their chapter on the production of justifications and excuses by witnesses in cross-examination, Atkinson and Drew (1979) focus on the ways in which these are interactionally and collaboratively produced in situations where their production as an answer to a formal accusation is not necessarily explicitly elicited. At a general level, one can observe that it is often important for parties in a judicial process to anticipate and neutralize other people's capacity to question their moral nature and judgment. Causal accounts and, in particular, justifications, excuses, and circumstances are oriented to what appears to members as the predominant morality, which they generally seek to confirm in a way that preserves the possibility of qualifying or withdrawing their participation in its violation.

Excerpt 91 (General Prosecution, Case 5471, Muharram Bey, Alexandria)
Question of the Prosecutor: What do you say with regard to what the victim reported
Answer of the accused: It didn't happen the policemen are the ones who persuaded her [to make her statement]

More specifically, it is observed that witness's replies are often designed to manage projected blame allocation (Atkinson and Drew, 1979: 138).

Excerpt 92 (General Prosecution, Case 5471, Muharram Bey, Alexandria)
Question of the Prosecutor: You've seen the victim since 1978 and you don't know whether he's mentally backward or not despite the fact that it is obvious that he's mentally backward
Answer of the accused: I don't know

One of the strongest implications of this is that the production of justifications and excuses is not formally determined by legal provisions but closely constrained by the design of conversational practices in an institutional setting. Often, it is observed, justifications operate in a prior position in blame sequences (cf. excerpt 93), while excuses occur in a subsequent position (*id.*: 141; excerpt 94). Both have a prospective-retrospective character in that they seek to answer already (even though indirectly) formulated accusations with a simultaneous view to the projected sequences.

Excerpt 93 (General Prosecution, Case 5471, Muharram Bey, Alexandria)
Question of the Prosecutor: What do you have to say about what concerns you
Answer of the accused: Nothing happened I was walking on Muharram Bey Bridge and I met Mahmud Basyuni walking on the bridge and this girl was with him and he asked me don't you know a place where I can take this girl and I told him I don't know I'm on my way to pick up a tip from someone at the Arsenal [...]

Excerpt 94 (General Prosecution, Case 276, 1985, Ma'adi)
Question of the prosecutor: What sexual acts did you commit with the [female] victim
Answer of the accused: When I went in I found her sitting on a cushion and I went to have sex with her I kissed her and put my arms around her waist and hugged her and then she said shame on you (haram 'alayk) so I left her and went out

As a conversational device, defenses must solve interactional dilemmas, among which the dilemma between blaming oneself and overtly disagreeing with the position of the questioning party (cf. Komter, 1998). Accounts reformulating the scene that is under scrutiny are often preferred to direct rebuttals of blame-implicative questions. This reformulation often consists of citing localized factors that exerted a constraint on witnesses and prevented them from satisfying this or that requirement completely.

Excerpt 95 (General Prosecution, Case 468, 1997, Rawd al-Farag, Cairo)
Question of the Prosecutor: What are your comments given that both of them state and it's been established by Adjutant Sami Ghunaym in a report dated 9/10/1996 that when the first accused met you he realized you had run away from home and were looking for a shelter and he asked to accompany you and you walked together until you met the third accused whereupon he asked to have sexual relations with you and they were able to achieve what they wanted with your consent
Answer of the victim: What they said never happened and the two of them took me by force (*bi-l-'afiya*) after threatening me with force and they slept with me and I was afraid they'd kill me

In this language game of causal accounting, parties struggle to make their argument convincing (more than accurate), while their opponents try to undermine their credibility through the description of their inconsistency, even though such inconsistency has little to do with the issue at stake. This means that causal arguments are always constructed with an eye toward the interactional work they must accomplish (Matoesian, 2001: 228). Persuading, justifying, excusing, explaining, motivating are, in this sense, operations closely associated with the activity of presenting oneself as a victim (cf. excerpt 96), defending oneself against an accusation (cf. excerpt 97), testifying in a conflict (cf. excerpt 98) or adjudicating this conflict (cf. excerpt 99).

Excerpt 96 (General Prosecution, Case 468, 1997, Rawd al-Farag, Cairo)
Question of the Prosecutor: What is the cause of your presence at that moment and in the aforementioned place
Answer of the victim: I suffer from a psychological disease and depression and during the night I heard a voice while sleeping and it told me go out go on the Corniche and I left my family asleep and I dressed and I went out [...]
Q: In what state was the first accused Hasan Faruq when you met him and what did you talk about
R: He was walking on the Corniche and he stopped me and said come here you where are you going and what are you doing and I asked him what about you and he said I'm with the police and I told him about the voice I heard and he told me come I'll take you home because you shouldn't be walking alone now and I walked with him [...]

Excerpt 97 (Vice Squad, Case 2677, 1983, Heliopolis)
Question of the police officer: What have you to say about what is said against you
Answer of the arrested person: I'm guilty of everything that happened and you if you knew the circumstances of my life you'd excuse me because [...]

Excerpt 98 (General Prosecution, Case 5719, Rawd al-Farag, Cairo)
Question of the Prosecutor: What was the nature of her relations with the family and did she fight with anyone

Answer of the witness: She was a good girl with everybody and with us and nobody ever complained about her
Q: Do you have disagreements with anyone
A: No I'm a quiet guy and I've no problem with anybody […]

Excerpt 99 (General Prosecution, Case 276, 1985, Ma'adi)
Question of the Prosecutor: You're accused of participating with others in abduction and rape with [the use of] force what do you have to say
Answer of the accused: I said what happened
Q: You're also accused of participating with others in theft with [the use of] force what do you have to say
A: I said what happened

It can be added that in an interactional framework that pre-allocates speech turns and strictly limits the parties' capacity to take the initiative during questioning, control over the course of interaction is a sensitive issue, since it allows or forbids people to produce descriptions, justifications, excuses and circumstances to their actions in a satisfactory way. Thus, the fear of not being asked questions allowing them to justify themselves, make excuses or produce mitigating circumstances can induce these parties not to wait for "why" questions before foregrounding their own causal argument.

Excerpt 100 (General Prosecution, Case 5471, Muharram Bey, Alexandria)
Question of the Prosecutor: What do you say with regard to what relates to you
Answer of the accused: It didn't happen
Q: How do you explain the statement by the two plainclothes policemen
A: I don't know what happened is that I was coming back from a trip today and this girl met me and I knew her from before we walked together and […]

Conclusion

In this chapter, we went further in our inquiry into the practical grammar of criminal concepts and focused on causation. In comparison to Hart and Honoré, who set the outlines of an exploration into causal reasoning in the law, we suggested a re-specification of the material on which the analysis is grounded and, by the same token, of its building blocks, so as to resituate the practical, contextual and situated dimension of causal reasoning. We also saw that legal and commonsense reasoning are practically and contextually articulated on notions like cause, reason, motive, intention, excuse, justification or circumstances, all notions toward which people orient all along the judicial sequence. People's orientation is articulated, in this case, to underlying schemes of normality and naturality from which multiple inferences are drawn. This orientation depends closely on its positioning in the judicial sequence and on the interactional task it seeks to achieve.

Chapter 10

Intention in Action: The Teleological Orientation of the Parties to Criminal Cases

In criminal matters, intentionality constitutes one of the central criteria in the work of legal characterization. This chapter shows how magistrates, and more particularly public prosecutors, practically organize their activity around the establishment of this component of the crime. I shall start by giving a summary of the literature in legal theory pertaining to this question. The essentially semantic nature of these approaches will be noted as they attempt to comprehend intention as a philosophical notion independent of the institutional context of its use. In a second step, I shall propose a praxeological approach in which intentionality is viewed as the result of interactions integrated in the judicial institutional context, which obliges professional actors to orient themselves toward the production of a legally relevant decision. This leads us, in conclusion, to observe that lay actors adjust themselves to this constraining institutional context, influenced by the inductive reasoning of professionals and by their own anticipation of the means which enable them to obtain from the place and the persons with whom they are confronted the most favourable, or the least damaging, solution for themselves, or simply the solution best adapted to the routine accomplishment of their work.

Intentionality: A Classical Perspective

Let us begin with a detour via what may be described as a classical approach to the question of intention, in legal theory and philosophy, in order to put this approach in perspective compared to the praxeological process I am proposing.

Marcel Mauss's study by the notion of person (1938) can conveniently serve as a starting point for a classical description of intention in law. Mauss describes a broad evolutionary movement from a simple masquerade to the mask, from a personage to a person, a name, an individual, from the latter to a being with metaphysical and moral value, from a moral conscience to a sacred being, and from that sacred being to a fundamental form of thought and action that results in this primordial category of contemporary understanding: the person.

It is from this perspective that a few recurrent notions of Kantian and Freudian discourse, such as autonomy, liberty, will, conscience, and intention, are classically designated as markers of the modern conception of personhood. Along with autonomy, the will, defined as the "faculty to freely determine to act or to abstain", constitutes one of the cornerstones of modern philosophy and epistemology.

According to Kantian thinking, the subject has become a causal principle of a certain force termed action or intentional process:

> The subject, the Kantian 'cogito', is an *autonomous instance* ascribing a certain objectivity to objects in the world – objects as such, only becoming knowable in terms of the very subject who gives them a certain meaning, a meaning which is never determined once and for all, in itself, but which is always an expression of the *intentionality* of the subject in its actions and interactions. (Stockinger, 1993: 48)

Liberty is also classically associated with will: 'Human beings can only judge what is proper through the use of the faculty called will; for the idea of will assumes the existence of other faculties through which the will can express itself.' (Pufendorf, quoted in Arnaud, 1993: 345) The legal principle of the autonomous will, a veritable basis of the law of contract, probably best expresses the importance of this philosophical concept in law. Will, autonomy, liberty, and intentionality thus form the very foundations of the philosophical economy of modern law and one immediately perceives all the implications that the concept of the subject acting freely and autonomously can have in terms of responsibility, imputation, premeditation, decision or judgment, all notions that are seen to be very much present if we merely glance at many legal codes.

The place occupied by responsibility in the philosophy of law originates in the Kantian philosophy of causality and imputation, by virtue of which one must consider oneself as the unique and ultimate point of what happens to oneself, with the notion of fault as the point of articulation. While one cannot fail to observe at which point the theory of responsibility underwent a very considerable evolution in the course of the twentieth century, which not only saw it being substituted for a principle of solidarity in certain areas, and led to its break-up in other areas (for example, with the notion of hazard in labour law), but also marks the passage from a philosophy of individual fault to a philosophy of collective reparation,[1] it is nevertheless important to note that this extension in space and prolongation in time of the legal philosophy of responsibility does not occur in the sense of a de-individuation, but indeed in that of a reinforcement of the exigency of forethought and of the collectivization of reparation. It is, in fact, not only a question of the imputation of fault, but also, upstream, of exigency of precaution and prudence

1 One speaks of the crisis of responsibility, 'with as starting point a shift in accent formerly placed on the presumed author of the wrong and today preferably on the victim whose suffering puts him in a position to demand redress' (Ricœur, 1995: 58), moving 'from individual management of fault to socialized management of risk' (Engel, 1993). Ricœur stresses the enormous paradox of a 'society that speaks of solidarity only to reinforce electively a philosophy of risk', and 'the vindictive search for the culprit, tantamount to condemning anew the identified perpetrators of damages.' (Ricœur, 1995: 59).

and, downstream, of assumption of responsibility for the potential effects of each person's acts.

Herbert Hart has proposed very interesting developments regarding the questions of responsibility, causality and intentionality, particularly in his works *Causation in the Law* (1985, written with Tony Honoré) and *Punishment and Responsibility* (1968). In both works, the author undertakes to examine legal reasoning closely and to view it from the common-sense perspective. By briefly presenting Hart's demonstration, I believe it is possible to identify a problematic. The means he employs to affirm the meaning assumed by certain notions in law and in common sense, and the manner in which one ties up with the other, however, do not receive an entirely satisfying response. It is precisely at this level that the praxeological perspective can shed new light on the matter.

The problematic of intention, the only one that concerns us here, is in part subsumed, at least in the philosophy of law, under the broader question of causality and its relation to will. Intentionality is a property of the cause of harm necessary to establish criminal responsibility in a number of important crimes. In other words, it is because the activation of the trigger (cause) is wilful (intention) that the death of the victim is defined as voluntary homicide and sentenced as such. Intention may also be seen as the moral quality of a physical act that has caused harm. This does not mean that contemporary criminal law necessarily assumes culpable intention for all crimes. The theory of negligence affirms that the law demands the presence of a positive (will) or negative (lack of foresight) mental element. Responsibility thus involves

> ... a minimum of volitional and cognitive involvement. Minimum volitional involvement means that conduct is an action (that is, an intentional corporeal movement, not one that was merely endured; the effect of some physiological mechanism or of an external cause, such as physical force exerted by another person). Minimal cognitive involvement means that the agent is aware of what he does. [...This involvement] is minimum in the sense that it is not necessary that one acted willingly, that one subscribed to one's act or that one had desired or intended the consequences of one's act, in order to be responsible for it. One is therefore responsible for acts carried out under threat because, although it is true that in such cases one acts unwillingly, one acts despite everything intentionally and with a precise aim, which is to avoid that the other carries out the harm that threatens us. (Neuberg, 1996: 1308-1309)

In the definition of a crime and its punishment, most systems of law distinguish according to whether it is the product of a particular mental state disposing the perpetrator to the crime. In other words, intention is introduced as the determining principle of criminal responsibility and of the severity of the punishment. In fact, criminal responsibility is first linked to the fact that the person has committed a crime and, second, that the person carried it out in a certain frame of mind or of will. The question of this mental state is generally raised at two levels, that of culpability and that of the evaluation of the sanction. At the level of culpability, the establishment of intention is generally sufficient, above all for important crimes (although there are some exceptions). At the level of sanction, the character of intention that is established influences the degree of punishment.

'The concept which legal theorists speak of and define as intention diverges from its counterpart in ordinary use at certain points which are of immediate interest to the philosophy of punishment.' (Hart, 1968: 116-117) It is first appropriate to note the existence of a rich vocabulary, which, while always accounting for the concept, nevertheless provides it with nuances: intentionally, maliciously, wilfully and recklessly are so many words used in legal English to express slightly different definitions of intention. Nevertheless, for Hart it is possible to distinguish what, in law, corresponds to intention: three interdependent parts that can be presented as "intentionally doing something", "doing something with a further intention" and "bare intention". In the latter case, what is important is the sole intention of doing something without anything being done to realize the intention in question. This hypothesis is not taken up as such in criminal law, contrary to civil law. In the second case – to do something with a further intention – one can take the example of a man who enters the house of another at night. Here, the question does not bear so much on the intention of entering the house, as on the further intention of stealing something. If the further intention is established, the man would be found guilty of burglary, even though he may not have stolen anything. Numerous crimes are defined in terms of further intention, such as "wounding with intent to kill". Finally, in the first case – intentionally doing something – one can take the example of a man who shot at another with a firearm and wounded or killed him. To the question of whether he wounded him intentionally, the response will be that the physical movement of the body which led the finger to press the trigger expresses, until proven otherwise, a murderous intention, proof to the contrary eventually making it possible to show he thought the weapon was not loaded, or he had not seen his victim at the moment when he fired. Apart from the element of volition, the intervention of three other factors will be noted: a physical element (the movement of the body), the result, and the circumstances.

The combination of all these elements makes it possible to observe one of the points upon which legal theory and common sense are opposed. Legally, a man will be considered guilty if he could foresee the prejudicial consequences, or if he thought that they could result from his wilful act, even if the consequences as such were not desired. In other words, 'The law therefore does not require in such cases that the outcome should have been something intended in the sense that the accused set out to achieve it, either as a means or an end, and here the law diverges from what is ordinarily meant by expressions like "he intentionally killed those men".' (Hart, 1968: 120) Outside the law, a result that was simply foreseen, but not intended, is generally not considered as intentional. Generally, there are also situations where action and result are so connected that it would appear absurd to say that an individual acted in a certain manner without intending that the action should lead to the result (for example, if someone strikes a crystal vase with a hammer, even should he do so with the aim of hearing the sound of metal against the crystal, common sense will consider that he broke the vase intentionally).

Following Bentham and Austin, legal philosophy has classically distinguished oblique intention, which corresponds to the sole foresight of the consequences, and direct intention, in which the consequences are an end that was conceived to be realized. The law condemns the author of an act if the intention was oblique, whereas common sense will consider that he has not acted intentionally. Hart gives the example of a man who, considering himself to be an execrable shot, shoots to kill and, contrary to his expectations, hits the target. In law, the man is guilty of murder. This is no doubt explained by the fact that in the two cases (direct and oblique intention), the author of the act is considered to have control over the alternatives open to him (to shoot or not to shoot). However, it will be noted that English courts distinguish between direct intention and oblique intention in cases of ulterior intent. In this case, it is pertinent to demonstrate that the accused considered the result of his action as an end or as the means to achieve that end. In other words, even when the bare intention is not punishable as such, jurisprudence punishes as an attempt the fact of doing something that is not itself a tort, if it is carried out with the further intention of committing a crime.

In short 'it is [the] principle of individual autonomy that appears to be the point of convergence of our judgments as to responsibility. The fact of linking responsibility either to the wilful and cognitive involvement of the agent, or to his ability in principle to attain a certain level of prudence and of reflection in his social interactions, is explained by a fundamental decision in our system of responsibility in favour of the individual who is master of his choices, and able to orient his conduct in conformity or disagreement with a system of norms.' (Neuberg, 1996: 1309)

That, briefly presented, is where the philosophical and analytical study of the notion of intention arrives. I find it says much and little: much in the sense that the various parameters of representation of intentionality are broken up and analysed in detail to reveal most of the possible scenarios; and little insofar as the common sense of intention is only constructed on the basis of hypotheses founded on the presumed ordinary use of words, whereas its legal concept is conceived only on the basis of a reading of the case-law independent of any examination of the practical construction of meaning in the different stages of the legal procedure.

Intentionality: A Praxeological Approach

I will now attempt to show that concepts of intentionality do not correspond to an *a priori* definable semantic field outside the context of their interactional implementation. In this connection, while Hart raises a number of perfectly relevant questions, he cannot give them an entirely satisfactory response. We must recognize the contingent, contextual and normative nature of intention, which people construct, utilize, reproduce and transform thoroughly in their daily interactions.

Let us take a concrete example from the Egyptian legal context. The following excerpt is familiar to us (cf. excerpt 50).

Excerpt 101 (Prosecution, Case 5471, 1977, Muharram Bey, Alexandria)
Prosecutor's question: What happened
Victim's answer: I was in the street that day … when I met those two … and they told me come with us and they forced me to get in a taxi … and they went behind the Shipyard.
Q: What was their intention when they acted this way
A: They told me don't worry let's have a cup of tea together
Q: Why didn't you call for help when they took you …
A: I tried to shout and I rolled on the ground but the street was empty
Q: What is the number of the taxi they took you in
A: I don't know it happened in the street
Q: Why didn't you ask the taxi driver for help
A: The taxi driver was afraid of them and did what they told him to do
Q: What was their intention when they took you with them
A: I think they wanted to violate my honor otherwise they would not have taken me to that place

This excerpt illustrates several interesting points as regards the question of intentionality. It will be noted that the act is always presented as having a motivation. Here, fear and trust are combined to motivate the woman's decision to go with the two men (Q: 'What was their intention…?' A: 'They told me don't worry, let's have a cup of tea together') and not refuse to get into the taxi ('…and they told me to get into the taxi'). On the other hand, the substitute is always seeking an individual act ('Why didn't you call for help when they took you…?') that was motivated ('Why didn't you ask the taxi driver for help?') and had a purpose ('What was their intention in taking you with them?'). This should be underscored as it shows how the substitute constructs the interrogation with practical ends – that is, in anticipation of the different stages he will have to go through – centred around legally relevant questions of the type "who did what and to what end".

Cases involving minors and the mentally deficient are particularly interesting in the praxeological study of the notion of intention, on at least two levels. The first is the level of the victim's intention or consent. Criminal law presumes absence of consent in sexual relations on the part of a minor. Consequently, the surrogate directs his action towards establishing legal minority. The first example below is taken from a case of abduction and rape of a minor, and the second from a case of attempted rape of a mentally deficient minor (Chapter 8, excerpts 54 to 56).

Excerpt 102 (Prosecution, Case 5719, 1996, Rawd al-Farag, Cairo)
Prosecutor's question: What are the distinctive features of the missing girl and how old is she

Witness's answer: Her name is Sana' Husayn Qasim, she is eight years old, she is fair-skinned and has blond hair, she is wearing jeans and a yellow t-shirt

Excerpt 103 (Prosecution, Case 7158, 1993, Sahil, Cairo)
Prosecutor's question: What is his approximate age
Witness's answer: He is seventeen or eighteen years old and has been mentally retarded since birth

In both cases, however, the substitute attempts to go beyond these presumptions to discover the victim's intention – we shall return later to the intentions of the aggressor and the witness. In the first case, he directs several questions to the parents of the girl so as to determine a background upon which to construct a plausible and legally definable scenario. The explanations given by the victim's parent clearly reveal that the latter is aware of the inferential significance of his responses.

Excerpt 104 (Prosecution, Case No 5719, 1996, Rawd al-Farag, Cairo)
Prosecutor's question: Does the missing girl suffer from a psychological or nervous illness
Witness's answer: No she is well [...]
Q: Has she disappeared before
A: No [...]
Q: Which places does the missing girl frequent
A: None she played in the street [...]

In the second case, even though the mental retardation of the victim does not constitute an aggravating circumstance in the case of indecent assault, the point is to demonstrate that the victim could not have consented because he was mentally deficient.

Excerpt 105 (Prosecution, Case 7158, 1993, Sahil, Cairo)
Prosecutor's question: Based on the facts you witnessed did your son cooperate with this assault or did he resist
Witness's answer: My son is mentally retarded and he knows nothing and remained silent [...]

The intention of the aggressor is also sought in such a manner as to be able to define the act in accordance with the categories of law. The aggressor, whose responses are clearly oriented according to the inferential significance which he knows can be attributed to them, can adopt different attitudes. In the first case, he seems to shift the intention towards an external agency.

Excerpt 106 (Prosecution, Case 5719, 1996, Rawd al-Farag, Cairo)
Prosecutor's question: What is the context of the discussion that took place between yourself and the victim
Witness's answer: The devil sometimes rises in me and I said to myself I should amuse myself with her in whatever way so that she comes to my place with me so that I sleep with her and I said to her...

In the second case, the aggressor has recourse to a strategy to avoid detrimental inferences.

Excerpt 107 (Prosecution, Case 7158, 1993, Sahil, Cairo)
Prosecutor's question: At first glance is he a sentient person (*shakhs mudrik*)
Answer of the accused: He speaks in a jerky way
Q: Is he mentally retarded
A: I don't know
Q: You've seen the victim since 1978 and you don't know whether he's mentally backward or not despite the fact that it is obvious that he's mentally backward
A: I don't know

The intentionality of the witness can also be questioned, as the following excerpt shows.

Excerpt 108 (Prosecution, Case 5719, 1996, Rawd al-Farag, Cairo)
Prosecutor's question: Do you suspect that her disappearance is criminal
Witness's answer: No
Q: What is your purpose in making this deposition
A: To take the steps necessary to find her

This question may appear quite absurd. However, it reveals that the substitute does not want to neglect any hypothesis, including the possibility of the involvement of the parent making the deposition. Raising this question, he is expecting a response, the possible incongruity of which would direct him to explore an alternative track. This explanation is confirmed during a later interrogation, at which time the substitute raises the question of the delay made in informing the police.

Excerpt 109 (Prosecution, Case 5719, 1996, Rawd al-Farag, Cairo)
Prosecutor's question: What do you know about her disappearance from the house on 11 October 1996 until she was found
Witness's answer: I don't know where she was but I heard a child from the corner say that a strange man had called her while she was playing with them and said bring me soap from the grocer's and gave her money and when she returned he gave her twenty-five piasters and he took her into the house where we found her
[…]
Q: When precisely were you given this information
R: I know all that from the little boy since the day my daughter disappeared from the house
Q: How do you explain not having made a deposition about all that until now
R: I told myself those are the words of a child and we were not certain

As seen previously, the substitute is seeking, in the criminal process, a legally relevant characterization (cf. Chapter 6), which he obtains by producing a narration of events centred around the accounts of the persons interrogated and reconstructed for future use in the legal process. The accounts are thus sifted for possible incongruities with an alternative schema in which normality would appear between the lines, as implicitly suggested by the substitute.[2]

The fact that the parties are oriented towards the institutional framework and its procedural implications (the trial) means that they are aware of questions concerning personal involvement and intentions. Here, I seek to show that the definition of intention is inferred from concrete interactional circumstances and information and is not necessarily deduced from theoretical treatises. In the case of intention, as in other instances, what is at work are not representations concerning the profound nature of conscience, but the very practical and concrete orientation of persons towards a very practical and concrete result in an interactional situation inscribed in a legal frame and on the basis of discourse and accounts from which every protagonist seeks to draw a certain number of inferences. The latter operate as the basis of interplay of congruence and incongruity between "normal" typification and factual accounts. Every protagonist is involved in producing a sense of normality and an account, the facts of which are in line with or depart from this normality. This obtains in the case of the accused as well of other protagonists – victim, witness, substitute – all of whom tend to produce an account articulating the intentional or non-intentional character of the act and the inferences that follow. Without entering into details, I give a number of typical excerpts below recapitulating variations of intention in action.

With regard the victim, the following is an excerpt from a case of alleged rape of a schizophrenic victim:

Excerpt 110 (Prosecution, Case 468, 1997, Rawd al-Farag, Cairo)

Prosecutor's question: What is the cause of your presence at that moment and in the aforementioned place

Answer of the victim: I suffer from a psychological disease and depression and during the night I heard a voice while sleeping and it told me go out go on the Corniche and I left my family asleep and I dressed and I went out [...]

Q: In what state was the first accused Hasan Faruq when you met him and what did you talk about

A: He was walking on the Corniche and he stopped me and said come here you where are you going and what are you doing and I asked him what about you and he said I'm with the police and I told him about the voice I heard and he told me come I'll take you home because you shouldn't be walking alone now and I walked with him [...]

Q: Why did the accused menace you with the sharp weapon he brought

2 Cf. ch.ix. Regarding this incongruity procedure, cf. also Matoesian, 1997, and Moerman, 1987: 61: 'The defendant is accused of having killed for hire, a form of murder rather common in northern Thailand at the time of fieldwork. A usual defence in such case is that the accused is not the kind of person who would do such a thing, that he comes from a good family, that he does not need money'.

A: To force me to sleep with them because I stopped and I refused to go with them and then I got scared and again he pushed me with his hands […]
Q: Did you have former conflicts or did you know each other you and one or the other of the two accused Hasan Faruq Husayn and Muhammad `Abd Allah Muhammad
A: No I I didn't know them before that
Q: What are your comments given that both of them state and it's been established by Adjutant Sami Ghunaym in a report dated 9/10/1996 that when the first accused met you he realized you had run away from home and were looking for a shelter and he asked to accompany you and you walked together until you met the third accused whereupon he asked to have sexual relations with you and they were able to achieve what they wanted with your consent
A: What they said never happened and the two of them took me by force (*bi-l-'afiya*) after threatening me with force and they slept with me and I was afraid they'd kill me

This excerpt clearly shows how the victim organizes her words around a certain idea of normality. First, she has to account for the abnormality of walking alone on the Nile Corniche at such a late hour. This breach of the normal scheme (a young Egyptian woman does not walk alone on the Corniche at dawn) is repaired by invoking the psychological problems from which the victim suffers. This restoration of normality (it is not abnormal that an abnormal woman has an abnormal behaviour) in turn furnishes the elements of normalized intention: the goal of achieving something (obeying an order) for explicit reasons (hearing voices). Second, the victim must account for the abnormality of her accepting that the first accused accompanied her. Here again, the abnormality of the situation is repaired by her recourse to normal intentionality: following a policeman who accompanies you back home ('He was walking on the Corniche and he stopped me and said come here you where are you going and what are you doing and I asked him what about you and he said I'm with the police and I told him about the voice I heard and he told me come I'll take you home because you shouldn't be walking alone now and I walked with him […]'). Third, we can note that the victim has to negotiate the credibility of her testimony, from which the status given to her intentions proceeds. Therefore, she has to answer to the suspicion concerning her having consented to sexual intercourse ('Q: […] until your meeting with the third accused where he asked you to have sexual intercourse and they achieved what they wanted with your consent'), which can be considered normal since she had fled her domicile. The negotiation of her credibility proceeds, beside the invocation of her mental illness, from the denial of the accusation ('A: None of what they said happened') and from the reiteration of a constraint effect nullifying any idea of consent ('A: the two of them took me by force after threatening me with force and they slept with me and I was afraid they'd kill me'). Finally, the prosecutor participates in the production of normality and incongruity effects by asking questions about the causes of the victim's behaviour (cf. Chapter 9) and the possible explanations for that behaviour, either by confronting her with testimony from the accused ('they could achieve what they wanted with your consent') or by directly asking her whether she knew her aggressors from before.

Turning now to the accused, the following is an excerpt of the investigation in a case of abduction and rape of an underage girl.

Excerpt 111 (Prosecution, Case 5719, 1996, Rawd al-Farag, Cairo)

Prosecutor's question: When and where did you meet the victim Sana' Husayn Qasim for the first time and in what state were you

Answer of the accused: I saw her when I was washing my father's microbus, which was parked in front of our house

Q: In which state was she and was there someone with her

A: She was playing on the swings with a couple of kids at the corner of our street and she was with the girl with I tried with first and I told her sit down here (?) and she didn't want to answer me and then she went away and I left her

Q: How far were you from where the victim was standing

A: I was in front of the house near the car and she was playing on the swings about two or three meters away and I called her and she came over and nearby there were some boys who were playing on the swings

Q: What did you and the victim talk about

A: Sometimes the devil takes my mind and I thought I have to have fun with her I don't care how and I told her you come to my house so I could sleep with her and I told her [sweet] heart bring me washing powder from the grocer's so I can wash the car and bring it to me in the flat above at the second floor and I'll give you 25 piasters and something wonderful and she went to buy the powder and I stood in front of the door to check that she had brought the powder and she came back and I went ahead of her and I quickly went up the stairs and I opened the flat and I stood at the door until she came and I pushed her inside and I told her wait till I give you the 25 piasters and I closed the door and I gave her the 25 piasters

Q: Were there any ties between you and the victim

A: No I didn't know her before that

Q: How did you recognize her at the door to the building

A: Because I opened the flat and I stood at the door till she went up and I pushed her with my hands and I made her go inside and I told her come so that I give you the 25 piasters

Q: Was it with her consent

A: No but I pushed her and I made her go inside and I told her come so that I give you the 25 piasters

Q: Was there anybody else but you and the victim in the flat

A: No because my father was working the day shift and he's a train driver and my brother `Imâd he had gone down early for work [...]

Q: What was your goal in acting this way toward the victim

A: At that moment I realized that she'd made me do something shameful (*tifdahni*) and I said I have to kidnap her and kill her [...]

Q: The officer who conducted the investigation [says] it's known that you're attracted to underage girls and have even tried to sexually assault one of your [female] relatives
A: Yes the devil sometimes gets into my mind so when I see a little girl I want to undress her and sleep with her and once my family were sleeping and I went into my little girl's [room] and the devil played with my head and I tried to catch her [in my arms] and to kiss her but she cried and my family woke up and beat me and threw me out of the house [...]
Q: What did you seek to achieve through the actions you've reported
R: I want to sleep with every little girl I see and the devil keeps getting into my mind and I don't know what I'm doing

This long excerpt informs us about many tiny things concerning intention. On motivation and initiative, first, we note that the accused, by referring to a third party's intervention (the devil) hides his personal responsibility beyond mental circumstances (A: 'Sometimes the devil takes my mind'; 'Yes the devil sometimes gets into my mind so when I see a little girl I want to undress her and sleep with her'). At no point does he try to contest the facts themselves, acknowledging by so doing the morally reprehensible character of his action. The accused, when confronted with different dilemmas, chooses credibility (he details the facts) and cooperation (he never contests the prosecutor), even though this leads him inexorably to admit to the charges brought against him. The prosecutor testifies to this ('Q: What did you seek to achieve through the actions you've reported?'). The defence of the accused lies elsewhere, i.e. in his invocation of a justifying factor: disease. In this context, intention takes a peculiar shape. It is explicit, public, active, but it is disrupted by an abnormality external to the will of the accused. In some circumstances, indeed, the accused becomes alien to himself, he does not know what he does, he is alienated (A: 'I want to sleep with every little girl I see and the devil keeps getting into my mind and I don't know what I'm doing'). As in the possession case formerly evoked (Chapter 8, excerpts 56-63), the accused seeks to disappear from the scene by invoking an external constraint that erases his personal and intentional agency. Contrary to the previous case, however, he does not push the logic of possession further, and therefore opens the door to the claim that he is legally and morally irresponsible.

The witness is also involved in the contingent production of a notion of intentionality. The latter, of course, bears on the victim and the accused, but also on the witness. By way of illustration, we shall again consider the same case of abduction and rape of a minor and examine the testimony of the victim's father.

Excerpt 112 (Prosecution, Case 5719, 1996, Rawd al-Farag, Cairo)
Prosecutor's question: Why did she leave the house the last time and was someone with her
Witness's answer: She left to play in the building because it was a holiday and she played with the children in the building
Q: Did the child suffer from any psychological or nervous illness
A: No she was very sane and very lively
Q: Was she wearing anything of value

A: No we're poor
Q: Did she show signs of womanhood
A: No she was a little girl but fair-skinned and with beautiful blond hair
Q: Had she already disappeared from home previously
A: No she was always a good girl
Q: What was the nature of her relationship with the family did she have differences with anyone
A: No she was a good girl as far as everyone was concerned and no one ever complained about her
Q: Do you have differences with anyone
A: No I'm a peaceful man and I don't have problems with anyone
[...]
Q: Who was this person exactly and what was your daughter's relationship to him
A: I don't know who he was and the girl also didn't know him because the boy said he was a stranger to the neighbourhood
[...]
Q: Do you suspect that her death was criminal
A: Yes of course
Q: Do you suspect someone of having perpetrated this act
A: God will triumph over whoever did it

The witness gives versions of intention that are closely dependent on his relation to the facts and to main actors involved in them. This relationship is above all marked by exteriority. The witness is not a main protagonist and, as such, his personal agency is not, at least not directly, in question. As noted by Renaud Dulong, the witness plays an auxiliary role and his person and affects are not of interest (Dulong, 1998: 41). When he attests to traits, characteristics, acts and gestures of a person, the witness produces a report of his conduct, his credibility and, consequently, of his intentions. This is directly oriented towards a practical goal of accentuating figures and situations, the typifications to which they are subject, and consequently possible qualifications of the established acts. Thus, in the example given above, the witness gives a description accentuating the normality and qualities of the child: a child who goes out to play during holidays (A: 'She left to play in the building because it was a holiday and she played with the children in the building'); a child without psychological problems ('A: No, she was very sane and very lively'); a child without problems ('A: No, she was always a good girl'); a child without any particular conflict ('A: No, she was a good girl as far as everyone was concerned and no one ever complained about her'). It is even said that she wore nothing of value. The only element contrasting with this apparent banality concerns the girl's physical features ('Q: Did she show signs of womanhood?'; 'A: No, she was a little girl but fair-skinned and with beautiful blond hair'), but it does not refer to the child's responsibility (it is not her behaviour that is at stake). By insisting on this normality, the witness establishes a marked contrast with what took place, upon which background his daughter's death necessarily enters the category of odious crimes and, by the same token, morally qualifies the presumed author. This becomes even more explicit during the mother's testimony.

Excerpt 113 (Prosecution, Case 5719, 1996, Rawd al-Farag, Cairo)

Prosecutor's question: Do you have anything else to say

Witness's answer: Yes I want to say that you should have that fellow hanged

It will also be noted that an ethical quality at the basis of his testimony's veracity is also demanded of the witness (Dulong, 1998: 42). In other words, the witness's relationship to the subject of his testimony is examined so as to judge the quality of his testimony. The witness must, therefore, also orient his testimony so as to avoid detrimental moral implications it could entail. Here, the witness must account for his own intentionality. That could consist in underscoring the typical and normal nature of his situation with respect to the victim through recourse to membership categorization devices (for example, that of father or mother, cf. the father's testimony, excerpt 109), rendering any intention that would be detrimental to oneself incongruous (Watson, 1983). Conversely, any breach of this normal schema (for example, not informing the police of new information reported by the neighbours; cf. excerpt 109) must be redressed, this redress also being upheld by categorization devices with which rights and duties are typically connected (for example, do not trust what is said by a small child; cf. excerpt 109).

The last category to be considered is that of the magistrate. By way of illustration we shall return to the questions asked of the first accused in a case of collective rape, and the text of the inventory of the elements of proof, a document written by the substitute for the judges of the criminal court in the Ma`adi case already studied in detail (excerpts 11-12, 25-30, 47-48).

Excerpt 114 (Prosecution, Case 276, 1985, Ma'adi)

Record of the interrogation

Taking advantage of the presence of the accused, who were being held outside the room where the investigation was taking place, we called them in and asked them to address the charges against them, after having informed them that the prosecutor was opening an investigation against them. They all admitted [that they had understood this information] and we asked them if they had a representative who would appear with them for the investigation. They replied in the negative. We made all the accused leave the room, apart from the first. In appearance, he is a young man in his 30s, around 1.70 meters tall, of average weight, with a dark complexion. He wore a blue suit with checks at the bottom and a blue pullover. We questioned him in detail and he replied as follows:

Q: What are the details of what you admit [...] [the complete investigation follows]

Q: You are accused of participating with others in a kidnapping and violent rape what do you have to say

Q: You are also accused of participating with others in the kidnapping and illegal confinement what do you have to say
Q: Do you have a record
Q: Do you have anything else to say

Inventory of the elements of proof
Miss [...], aged 17 years [...] testifies to the fact that she [...] was in the company of her fiancé [...] and that, while they were stopped in the car [...] the accused ... threatened them by exhibiting a knife (and ordered her fiancé to get out of the car. [...] They forced them to get in the taxi driven by the fifth accused and they left for another place [where the first accused undertook to rape her] [...] when gunshots were heard. [They] hastened to get into the car [...]; they then proceeded to an inhabited area and stopped in front of a building at the foot of which was a garage in which there was no car. The first accused got out and met the sixth accused; he then returned to the car and told the female victim to enter the garage. She obeyed the order while the sixth accused looked on. The first accused then took out a blanket and a cushion and put them in a room adjoining the garage into which the accused, with the exception of the sixth, entered. Each then undertook to remove his clothes and lie on her [...] But she made every effort to resist them and was injured on her left hand as a result of her resistance. She added that the first accused, when he led her into the room adjoining the garage, took possession of two rings she was wearing.

[...]

Observations
1. The first accused said [...] that he had agreed with the second, third, fourth and fifth accused to abduct just any woman whom they met and to rape her. [...] He admitted in the investigation report at the renewal of his detention ... the same thing he had said in the report at his arrest.
2. The second accused said the same thing in the report at arrest. [...] He admitted [...] that the first, third, fourth and fifth accused had stolen from the two victims by force, that he had stolen the watch of the male victim on the public thoroughfare by threatening to use the knife he carried and that he had kissed and seized the female victim.
3. The third accused admitted [...] the same thing [...] and he added that he had seized the female victim by force, had lain on her and had kissed her.
4. The fourth accused admitted the same as what was stated by the first accused and he added that he had grasped the female victim, had seized and kissed her, and he also admitted [...] having participated in the rape of the female victim. [...]
5. The fifth accused admitted [...] the same thing [...] and he added that he had grasped the female victim, had seized and kissed her, and also admitted that he had agreed with the four first accused to abduct the female victim, to rape her and to steal what she possessed by force.

> 6. The sixth accused admitted [...] that he knew the female victim had been abducted and that he had received the two rings and gold chain in return for providing the place where the accused raped the female victim. [...]

Contrary to the victim, the accused or even the witnesses, the substitute for the public prosecutor – the figure of the magistrate in all our examples – saw no dilemma as regards morality, agency or credibility. In the accomplishment of his work, it is essential for him to produce an account fulfilling the formal conditions of the legal category (participation in the abduction and rape by force, theft by force, abduction and illegal confinement). He must construct legally relevant and definable facts (agreement of the accused = premeditation, nature of sexual acts = rape, absence of willingness on the part of the victim = force). In so doing, it is also indispensable for him to bring to light the individual (the terms "admit" and "commit", but also the observations formulated by each of the accused) and intentional (the terms "agree", "admit", "know"). Moreover, because this takes place in the framework of his routine work, which consists of daily repeated procedures, within familiar precincts, at a time in the legal process in which the professional participants are known, as well as their different functions, briefly, in a controlled sequence of the production of legality, the action of the substitute is above all extremely routinized. The document evidently reproduces a stereotyped formula composed of standardized questions which assumes in its broad lines the *General instructions addressed to public prosecutors in criminal cases* as established by circular notice of the Public Prosecutor's office.

Conclusions

We have attempted, from a radically non-mentalistic perspective, to reintegrate the question of intention in a contextual framework. Phenomena such as motivation, purpose, intention, thought, affect, etc., can be neither reified nor disconnected from the fabric of action, interaction and context, through which these phenomena are publicly manifested and hence become observable and relevant (Watson, 1998). Motives, purposes, reasons, intentions can, in effect, only be understood through systems of discursive exchange. In other words, the mental states and their imputation can only be understood in their linguistic publication. In this sense, we have developed a 'praxeological understanding of the "mental".' (Coulter, 1992)

Although the examples given in this text are "small-scale objectives", it should nevertheless be noted, as underscored by Michael Moerman, that they are 'sufficiently actual and unimputed to merit painstaking attention from students of the strategic use of speech and of the relations between intentions and actions.' (Moerman, 1987: 53) They make it possible to see, case by case, how these strategies are deployed and are adapted to greater ends.

To speak of intention in law assumes that it is understood in act and in context. In so doing, we have observed the action of three factors circumscribing this configuration: the interactional nature of the verbal act, the institutional context in which it is inscribed, and the distribution of positions in this context. The intention, its content, the form which it takes, that upon which it has a bearing, vary from one individual to the next according to these factors. We have attempted to show that intention, in law, was not a transcendental property of volition, but a practical orientation. It is thus only in its punctual, contingent and local configurations, in the constraining framework of its context at each different occasion, that it can be analysed. The legal meaning of intention emerges, not from pure legal logic, but from the legal environment and interactions. If the philosophy of law delineates, in the manner of Hart, the possible scenarios, it on the other hand conceals the practical modes of the configuration. These are, however, precisely what constitute the subject of the sociology of legal action.

PART IV
Praxeological Study of Judgments on Morality

Chapter 11
Morality on Trial: Structure and Intelligibility of the Court Sentence

This chapter analyses the structural organization of sentencing in the summary Court of Misdemeanors (State of Emergency) in case 182/2001, Qasr al-Nil, registered as 655/2001, High State Security. Incidentally, we can mention that this trial, known as the "Queen Boat case", made headlines across the world.

The court ruling follows a classical organization: (1) introduction; (2) enunciation of the accusation as formulated by the Public Prosecution; (3) facts and Public Prosecution's investigation; (4) hearing of the pleas; (5) grounds of defence of the accused; (6) examination of the grounds; (7) examination of the constitutive elements of the crime; (8) motivation; (9) enunciation of the ruling. Through the close observation of each of the constitutive elements of this ruling, we can show how a text bears a limited number of possible logical options. To paraphrase Paul Jalbert (1999) having the text and only the text as data, we aim at making explicit the reading possibilities open to potential readers of the ruling. Our analysis of the ruling's structural organization seeks to elucidate the range of possibilities that result from the interaction of the text, the background commitments of the text's producers and addressees, and the positions that result from them.

> The analyst [...] who restricts himself to that form of analysis which begins and ends with the *text*, which locates the *text* at the center of his analytical attention, is *never* interested in criticizing producers or recipients, their background commitments or organizational affiliations. He is interested only in portraying as faithfully as possible the intelligibility structures and devices inhering in the text as well as the background commitments which interact with any such structures or devices so as to generate a given possible understanding and assessment of it" (Jalbert, 1999: 37).

Jalbert makes it clear that there is no reason to consider that the analyst must be the accomplice of a particular account of the text. To the contrary, it seems perfectly reasonable to consider that

> ... given a text *T*, its analysis and a description of background commitment(s) *B*, position *P* can be found as generatable by *T* in its interaction with *B*, where *B* may very well be defensible, conventional knowledge (or indefensible, conventional ignorance) of a particular sort, or where *P* may well be indefensible (or defensible) from other points of view. (Jalbert, 1999: 37)

Introduction

The ruling introduction has a totally standardized form:

Excerpt 115 (Summary Court of Misdemeanors (State of Emergency), Case 182, 2001, Qasr al-Nil)

In the name of God the Compassionate the Merciful

Court of misdemeanors, State Security – emergency
Qasr al-Nil, summary

Ruling

In the name of the people

During the public session held at the court on Thursday 14/11/2001
Under the presidency of His Excellency Mr [...], president of the court
In the presence of His Excellency Mr [...], deputy of the State High security Prosecution
And of Mr [...], clerk of the court

Issued its ruling on

Misdemeanour 182/2001, misdemeanors, State Security – emergency, Qasr al-Nil, registered as 655/2001, High State Security

Against

1 [...] 2 [...]
51 [...] 52 [...]

The court

After the examination of the documents and the hearing of the pleas:
Considering that the Public Prosecution has introduced the criminal petition against the aforementioned accused for the reason that the latter, since 1996 and until 11/5/2001, in the district of the Qasr al-Nil police station, Cairo governorate
1: The first and second accused [...]
2: All the accused [...]

First, we must notice that this document begins with the statement that the ruling is issued in the name of God, a mention that is not legally required, before stating that it is issued in the name of the people, a mention that is required. It must not be concluded, however, that there is anything exceptional in the first of these two mentions, quite to the contrary: it is rare nowadays in Egypt that rulings do not start with these words. It would consequently be wrong to ascribe to the judge, on this basis alone, the explicit will to situate his decision within any particular religious register.

The writing of this document manifests an obvious formalism. Under this standardized form, several elements are made available to the addressee of the text: the concerned institution's identity, respect of different formal requirements, the current number of the case, the identity of the accused. Moreover, the attention given to form expresses the professional qualifications of the person engaged in writing and, therefore, contributes to the production of his neutrality: a document that respects the rules of the genre proceeds from someone qualified in this respect and benefits by extension from the qualities generally attributed to this person. This neutrality effect is strengthened by the fact that the judge who produced the document places himself in the situation of a third party, between the accused and the Public Prosecution. Also, the precise usage of honorific terms shows that the judge in charge of the case does not have the rank of counsellor, which is normal for a Court of Misdemeanors, even in the case of exceptional justice (State Security – State of Emergency). This indication produces, however, a discrepancy between the jurisdiction type (one-judge court) and the volume of the ruling (56 pages written on a PC).

Furthermore, the introduction positions the protagonists in categorial terms from the beginning. The identities listed with reference to the capacity of court president, representative of the Public Prosecution, court clerk, and accused allows for the projection of a particular categorization device: "parties to a criminal ruling". This device includes, on the one hand, the victim (i.e. society as represented by the Public Prosecution) and the offenders (the 52 accused) – who together with the witnesses form the categorial sub-system "parties to the offense" – and, on the other hand, the judge, the Prosecution and the clerk – who form the categorial sub-system "professionals in charge of the procedures resulting in the ruling". The analysis of this categorization device stresses the double affiliation of the Prosecution, which acts as both the victim's proxy and the judicial apparatus's agent. Listing the different parties involved in the criminal procedure in the form of categories also makes it possible to introduce, from the beginning, the bundle of rights, duties, and typical activities that generally attach to membership in these categories: the judge must judge, the Prosecution must accuse, the accused must defend himself, etc. As trivial as this may seem, it is because of the rights, duties and activities typically bound to this or that category that a discrepancy (e.g., the judge accusing, or the accused accusing, or the victim defending) can emerge and is as such subject to sanction and redress.

Finally, the introduction has the effect of an announcement: it projects the character of the text it introduces by specifying and soliciting the activities (accusing, defending, proving, etc.) that constitute it intertextually. In that sense, it is fundamental in allowing the text it introduces to be recognizable as a ruling by all those who might read it. The topic itself with which it is concerned, i.e. the alleged misdemeanour, is introduced in such a way that all the following textual steps appear as concurring relevantly to its judicial assessment.

Accusation

The judge presents the accusation as initiated by a third party, the Public Prosecution.

Excerpt 116 (Summary Court of Misdemeanors (State of Emergency), Case 182/2001, Qasr al-Nil)

Considering that the Public Prosecution filed the criminal petition against the abovementioned accused because, from 1996 until 11/5/2001, in the district of the police office of Qasr al-Nil, governorate of Cairo

1: The first and the second accused:

both abused Islamic religion by propagating (*tarwij*) and encouraging (*tahbidh*) extremist thoughts (*afkar mutatarrifa*) through speech, writing and other means, insofar as they kept interpreting Koranic verses in a wicked (*fasid*) way, they calumniated revealed religions and one of the prophets, they came to [commit] actions contrary to moral behaviour (*adab*) while attributing these [actions] to religion, they had imposed a prayer that was contrary to established prayer, they had founded a place for prayer to perform it, they had ranked perverse (*shadhdha*) sexual practices among its rites and the practices [bound] to these ideas and had encouraged them among the other accused and yet other people, and this in order to denigrate revealed religions, to disdain them and to provoke sedition (*fitna*).

2: All the accused:

practiced debauchery (*fujur*) with men in the way indicated in the investigation.

It [viz. the Prosecution] required that they be condemned to [the penalty stipulated in] Article 98/7 of the Penal Code and Articles 9/3 and 15 of Law-Decree 10/1961 on the repression of prostitution (*da'ara*).

In a thoroughly explicit and intentional manner, the text of the ruling incorporates a series of different voices, which are contextualized so as to adjust to the ongoing performances and to what is relevant within this framework (Matoesian, 2001: 108). The text is, following Bakhtin's expression, polyphonic; it organizes a kind of dialogue between the reporting text and the reported text. In the accusation, the judge repeats what the Public Prosecution petitioned (this petition appearing as a specific text incorporated within the file).

Showing the intertextual dimension of the ruling allows us to see how the judge can formulate an accusation while disengaging himself from it, stipulate a lexical repertoire without making himself its author, announce the membership categorization device that will be ascribed to the accused (beyond their characterization as accused) while claiming not to have categorized them already, and present a question in a formally accusatory manner while actually prefacing his ulterior alignment on one of the existing positions.

The accusation formulated by the Prosecution also extends the introductory announcement by fixing the document's object and thereby restricting the scope of relevant interventions within the sentence. Together, introduction and accusation constitute a formalized solicitation of reactions and positions vis-à-vis the specified object. However, since it is a written exercise, intertextual but not interactional, this announcement cannot be taken as the expression of emerging relevance, but as the reflexive, justificatory, and ex post facto formulation of the constitutive elements of the ruling as purposefully selected and organized by the judge.

Enunciation of the Facts and of the Investigation Conducted by the Prosecution

The judge continues his description of the case by enunciating the different steps followed by the police and the Public Prosecution to constitute and investigate it. He thereby presents the facts of the case and the modalities of their establishment.

> **Excerpt 117 (Summary Court of Misdemeanors (State of Emergency), Case 182/2001, Qasr al-Nil)**
> [The Prosecution] transferred the case to the State Security (Emergency) Summary Court [...], according to the law [...] on the State of Emergency [...]
> The court based its conviction on the facts of the petition and has no doubt with regard to their veracity. Regarding what the court deduced from the examination of the documents and the investigations [...] as well as from the evidence submitted and what was related during the trial, [these facts] amount to what was consigned in the record [...]. This information reached [the Prosecution] from secret and reliable sources, confirmed by its careful investigations, which suffice [to show that the first accused] adopted deviant (*munharifa*) ideas inciting others to hold revealed religions in contempt (*izdira'*) and to call to abject (*radhila*) practices and sexual acts contrary to revealed laws. [...] He undertook to propagate these ideas among his acquaintances and those who are bound to him and to call them to adopt [those ideas]; he is affected by sexual perversion (*musab bi'l-shudhudh al-jinsi*) and practices it with people who are bound to him by considering [these practices] one of their rituals; he and his companions set about organizing decadent parties (*hafalat majina*) every Thursday in their homes or on boats, among them the tourist boat "Queen Nariman" [...] which many of his sexually perverse acquaintances attended [...] He photographed these sexual encounters, then developed and printed the pictures [...], having reached an agreement with the employees at the photography lab, that is [...]
> He set about diffusing pictures of these meetings as well as his confused (*mushawwasha*) ideas through the Internet [...] A warrant was sought to arrest these accused and the other regulars of the tourist boat "Queen Nariman".
> On the basis of the Public Prosecution's warrant [...], the first accused was arrested in the manner established in the record [...] and the following items were seized: (1) 10 books entitled "God's Lieutenancy on Earth"; (2) numerous photographs and negatives showing sexually perverse practices of the accused with many people; (3) numerous Muslim, Christian, and Jewish books; (4) numerous photographs of areas around Cairo, churches, mosques and tourist sites and one Jewish synagogue; (5) commentary papers from Military Unit 1057c; (6) one Star of David; (7) a number of hand-annotated documents; (8) a photograph of the President of the Republic and his wife, (9) photographs of the accused in Jerusalem and the Occupied Territories; (11) numerous photographs of the country's Jewish community and Jewish tombs in Basatin; (12) the Israeli national anthem, a copy of the book [...]; (13) two maps [...]; (14) two maps of Cairo churches; (15) many maps of Cairo mosques.
> When the accused was confronted [...] with what the investigation and information revealed, he admitted that he had embraced certain religious thoughts [...], had

founded God's Lieutenancy […], had used certain religious symbols according to his convictions […], had undertaken to publish these ideas of which he was convinced among the people who were bound to him, among whom the second accused […], so that the latter undertook to found a cell […], had practiced sexual perversion for a long time and during his education at the German School in Duqqi, and had kept on practicing homosexuality (*liwat*) with numerous people; had frequented certain hotels, public places and boats that sexually perverse people frequent; had collected numerous photographs of these perverse practices with certain people, had printed and circulated them, had circulated certain messages through the Internet containing his religious thoughts, besides the exchange of sexually perverse messages.

On the date of […], the second accused was arrested […] On the date of […], the accused from the photo lab were arrested […]

The rest of the accused were also arrested as follows: […]

The General Prosecution conducted the investigation. The major's […] replies to questioning are consigned in the report of […] and he added that the first accused […] has long practiced sexual perversion with men and is a passive participant (*salban*) […] He added that he was convinced that the first accused holds the three revealed religions in contempt […] and that his goal was to provoke sedition and to give rise to gossip among citizens until they are convinced to consider sexual perversion normal. […]

[…] The officer of the State Security inspectors declared that he undertook to implement the General Prosecution's warrant to arrest 31 accused on Queen Nariman when most of them were dancing in a strange and perverse way, and to arrest the employees of the lab […]

[…] [The officer responsible for arresting the second accused]

[…] [The owner of the boat, the manager of the boat, the owner of the lab]

The responses of the first accused in the interrogation […] are in substance what is consigned in the report dated […], previously cited in detail. He added (1) that he had accompanied the officer to his domicile in 'Ayn al-Sira and given him the keys of his apartment willingly, just as he gave him his photos, the personal notes, the books and all the things on the list […]

(2) He had during his sleep a vision of the "Kurdish pageboy" […]

(3) He practiced sexual perversion passively and actively (*ijaban*) with people, the majority [met] on the street and in public places like Tahrir Square, Ma'mura Casino and cinemas. His most important practice dates back to the year 1996 and his last full (*kamila*) practice took place in 1998. Then, he limited himself to incomplete "soft" practices, the last one […] being a mere frivolity (*'abath*) […] He was treating the perversion. His parents knew about that. The practice of perversion began when he was a student at the German School and intensified when he was studying engineering at Cairo University. He took pictures of anything that gave him feelings of danger. He began to take pictures of naked boys or sexual positions and he began to take pictures of himself with those he practiced sexual perversion with. He obtained sexual satisfaction when looking at these pictures. He took the decision to repent since his

> arrest in this case. The goal of his charity project was to cleanse himself of his sins (*takfir 'an dhunubihi*) in matters of sexual perversion.
> (4) He practiced sexual perversion with three of the people arrested, that is [...]
> (5) Faced with the accused, he recognized the three aforementioned accused.
> (6) Faced with the pictures, he declared that three pictures with [...] belonged to him. He was seen by the forensic physician to establish whether he practiced debauchery or not. On the basis of the forensic investigation, the report concluded that there were no signs indicating that he had engaged in homosexuality previously or recently. It is well known that an adult man can engage in homosexuality without it leaving any trace, by using lubricants, by being very careful and with the two parties' consent [...] Interrogated, [...] [the second accused and all the other accused]

This section, devoted to enunciating the facts, has an intertextually imbricated nature. Police and Prosecution records, which report the speech of witnesses (police officers, owner and director of the boat, owner of the photo shop), are organized so as to produce the organized description of the charges against the 52 accused. The narrative scheme is the following: information collected by the police – authorization to proceed to arrest and search – arrest and search (list of the compromising items that were seized) – police interrogation – other interrogations and searches – General Prosecution's investigation (interrogation of witnesses) – General Prosecution's investigation (interrogation of each accused + forensic report). Through someone else's voice, the judge gives a linear and non-contradictory presentation of the facts and the procedure constituting the facts, after announcing he is convinced of their veracity. Two properties of this intertextual organization must be highlighted. First is the ability to import the authority proper to the original document into the text of the sentence. This authority comes from the fact that this is allegedly the first-hand account of a reality presented as objective (secret though reliable information, seizing of evidence, direct testimonies, confessions, forensic expertise) and partly reported by public officials, who by virtue of their position cannot be challenged, or barely so. The second property of intertextuality is its capacity to produce coherence from multiple sources. The actions of many agents, mobilized on various legal bases, interrogated on several accounts and producers of different accounts are aligned to produce a single master document enunciating the authorized version of the facts.

This master document is itself organized around a master narrative, that of the first accused, with the other narratives following under the effect of an explicit inclusion (someone that the first testimony implicates by name) or an implicit inclusion (someone's presence on the boat at the time of the roundup, for instance, justifies his arrest and his appearance before the forensic physician, whose report retrospectively establishes if his inclusion was justified or not). The production of the master document thus gives *ex post facto* coherence to a series of events sharing a very loose unity (if any). By analysing the constitution of this master document we can see how, on the one hand, technically speaking, two cases that were different at the beginning – contempt of religion and debauchery – were merged and integrated so as to mutually reinforce each other. This analysis also shows how, on the other hand, unity can be attributed retrospectively to facts that are bound only by coincidence in time and space. Under the effect of "impregnation by contiguity", several people sit on the dock, and this effect is itself produced in the ruling by the presentation of one single structure of causality: (1) a person is accused, and in turn designates some person or place; (2) said person is arrested or said place is searched; (3) any person found in this place is susceptible as such to be arrested for the same reasons that justified the first search or the arrest. Since this does not hold true for all the people who were on the boat at the time of the police roundup, it is legitimate to think that the mechanism of impregnation by contiguity functions on the basis of background expectations and spontaneous categorizations made by police officers (for instance: considering his physical appearance and clothing, this person presents all the characteristics proper to those whose arrest was ordered; he must consequently be included within the roundup). The ruling gives retrospective coherence to all this, and its cogency is not questioned. It thereby turns impregnation by contiguity into a legitimate basis for presumption of guilt, and it turns the forensic examination conducted on that basis alone into the means to confirm or to reverse the presumption.

One of the clearest consequences of this intertextual, linear, homogenous matrix (I call it thus because it is organized around a master narrative) of factual enunciation is the judge's alignment on a factuality established at the plaintiff's initiative. This holds true in the choice of categories used to describe the facts (cf. below). It equally holds true at the level of narrative organization. In other words, the ruling is structured in such a way that only the judge can ratify different presentations of the facts, which, although they originate from other authorities, are conceived for his benefit and are integrated in a master narrative precisely for this ratifying purpose. The study of the ruling structure shows that the sentence, although officially meant to adjudicate on a legal issue, actually constitutes the formalized justification of a decision taken previously.

At different levels, we noted that the ruling leant on an authoritative argument external to the courtroom. This is the case of evidence whose authority comes from its categorial organization, as we shall show in Chapter 13. For now, let us simply insist that the list of evidence seized by the police at the home of the first accused clearly shows the selective character of its constitution – why mention the picture of the president and his spouse and not the contents of the wardrobe, for instance? – and this reflects the circularity of proof: this or that item is seized because it is considered conclusive and it is considered conclusive because it was seized. Ultimately, proof is conclusive because it was seized in circumstances giving it such authority. This authority also comes from the fact that whoever seized the item was a person endowed with the necessary power to act under these circumstances or even to generate these circumstances (the police officer is entitled to conduct the search and therefore to create the circumstances making it possible to endow an item with the status of proof). This is the second type of authoritative argument external to the courtroom on which the ruling leans. The official character of a function not only allows a person to do what he did, but also gives his action a weight that leads us to assume its rightness and correctness. Whoever wants to contest that version of the facts must bear the heavy burden of proof. Naturally, functional authority does not proceed from enchantment, but from a multiplicity of intertwined references, which systematically recall the official nature of an agent's status, the formal conditions of his various actions, his institutional engagement and his individual disengagement, etc. This holds true – and this is a third authoritative argument external to the courtroom – for the expert report produced by the forensic physician. The production of technical formulae, devoid of any emotional dimension and presenting a clinical and descriptive gloss, foregrounds an impression of objectivity and relegates human agency to the background, whether in the decision to criminalize homosexuality or in the choice to condemn only passive homosexuality (because it is the only form that is supposedly identifiable). In other words, by relying on the authority of expert reports claiming the objective existence of something, the judge spares himself the problem of determining whether this "thing" is criminal in the first place.

Procedure and Hearing of Pleas

The court then undertakes a formal description of the sessions held to hear pleas. This refers directly to my earlier discussion (Chapter 5) of procedure and its constraining effects on judicial activity, as well as the different parties' prospective-retrospective orientation to this procedural constraint. One must note here the specificity of procedure before State Security jurisdictions, viz. that it is impossible to appeal sentences and the Military Governor (i.e. the President of the Republic) must ratify judgments.[1]

Grounds of Defence and Court Argumentation

After having enumerated the different steps of the trial, the ruling returns to the grounds presented by the counsels in defence of their clients.

---

1 Anecdotally, the Military Governor (i.e. the President of the Republic) eventually nullified the ruling concerning the persons only accused of practicing debauchery, and not contempt of religion, on May 2002, and transferred the whole case to an ordinary court. This court, in its ruling of 15 March 2003, condemned the accused to more severe sentences than those issued by the State Security Court. However, in its ruling of 4 June 2003, the Appellate Criminal court reduced the sentence of the accused who appeared to a term equal to the time they had already spent in prison, theoretically enabling their release.

Excerpt 118 (Summary Court of Misdemeanors (State of Emergency), Case 182/2001, Qasr al-Nil)

During the sessions and the pleas, representatives of the accused presented several defences and formulated several requests. They claimed:

1- The unconstitutional character of Law 162/1958 concerning the State of Emergency [...] and the President of the Republic's Order 1/1981 concerning the transfer of certain crimes to State Security Courts – Emergency; as well as the unconstitutional character of the creation of the State Security Prosecution Office.

2- The unconstitutional character of the text of Article 98/7 of the Penal Code and of Decree-Law 10/1961 on the repression of prostitution.

3- The court's incompetence to examine the petition.

4- The nullity of the Prosecution's warrant for arresting and searching because it was delivered on the basis of non-substantial investigations.

5- The nullity of confession because it was obtained under duress (*ikrah*).

6- The nullity of forensic reports because of their non-observance of the rules of the profession (*al-usul al-fanniyya*).

7- The prescription of criminal petitions against the crime of habitual debauchery.

8- The nullity of proof established on the basis of hearsay.

9- The nullity of proof established on the basis of the declarations made by State Security officers.

10- The nullity of proof established on the basis of the additional investigation record on the validity of the names of some of the accused.

11- The nullity of proof established on the basis of the seized booklet because of the absence of any link showing it belongs to the first accused.

In the same way, the defence asked:

1- That press reports concerning the case cease.

2- That the forensic physician be cross-examined.

3- That the accused be transferred before a tripartite commission.

The judge then undertakes to discuss each of these grounds "with perspicacity and discernment". The answers he gives contribute to the textual production of his professionalism: what Jackson calls in semiotic terms the "narrativization of pragmatics" (cf. Chapter 1). Each time, he constructs his rejection of the grounds invoked by the incriminated parties on a legal argumentation foregrounding law, case-law and medical expertise, taken as objective criteria, and relegating to the background the judge as a subjective instance of evaluation. By so doing, on the issue of confession obtained under duress, the judge can invoke the Court of Cassation and the forensic report as exterior instances objectively justifying his subjective feeling:

> **Excerpt 119 (Summary Court of Misdemeanors (State of Emergency), Case 182/2001, Qasr al-Nil)**
> It is established in case-law that it is the right of the court [competent in] substantial issues to divide proof and, if it is a confession, to take what it believes in and leave aside what it excludes [...] (Petition 12712 of Judicial Year 64, session of 23/5/1996). [...] The court is strengthened [in its conviction] that the defence's claim, according to which the accused made their deposition under constraint, is an unfounded statement, which no proof in the documents supports. On the contrary, when the accused appeared before the forensic physician, nothing indicated the existence of constraint. [The court] is convinced that the depositions correspond to the truth, are reliable, and proceed from the freedom and free will of the accused.

The same mechanism works with regard to the validity of forensic reports. The Court of Cassation's objective authority is invoked to justify the judge's right to adjudicate according to his subjective conviction, with no need proceed further with the examination of the defence's arguments. The defence's argument, according to which the penal action instigated against the accused for practice of debauchery was prescribed, is dismissed in an identical way, as is the argument concerning the nullity of proof based on declarations made by the accused about each other, or based on the declarations of State Security officers. Every time, the external authoritative argument grounds the court's subjective interpretation, without further requirement for any form of argumentation.

> **Excerpt 120 (Summary Court of Misdemeanors (State of Emergency), Case 182/2001, Qasr al-Nil)**
> This is not contradicted by the depositions of some of the accused, who claimed they had abstained from practicing perversion for a certain a time or for five years or since 1995. The court does not believe the accused, who claimed they had ceased the aforementioned perversion. Therefore, it dismisses their statements, and the grounds [...], which are not based on facts or a right, must be rejected.

The way the judge deals with the argument that additional information concerning the names of some of the accused is null and void deserves special attention. The defence invoked an error regarding the identity of the four accused. This was not a marginal argument: the two first accused were arrested for contempt of religion, which implied homosexual practices with partners who attended parties on the boat, and these accusations motivated the police roundup on the Queen Nariman and the arrest of several other accused. Logic and law would therefore require that the arrests be carried out on the basis of a list of people designated by the two first accused as their homosexual partners. If the accused were arrested on the boat on the basis of a list established through a prior investigation, and if the identity of the accused persons did not correspond to their actual identity, it is legitimate to doubt the existence of a list and to think that, on the contrary, the list was established after the police roundup. The ruling does not explicitly mention a prior list, but it does not give the reasons for these arrests either (contrary to those that took place outside the boat) and merely mentions 'the arrest of 31 accused who were present on the Queen Nariman'. The sequential analysis of the narrative shows that the roundup on the boat is presented as following the discovery of a sect practicing debauchery among other things, so the Prosecution's narrative, taken up by the judge, can only justify arresting the accused by presenting them as members of this sect. In other words, the close examination of this issue of identity makes it possible to show that the whole case is the product of the police's merger of two different files: one regarding the constitution of a religious sect, and the other concerning the repression of prostitution. The effect of this merger is that each file takes importance and credibility by referring to the other. However, the ruling, when dealing with the issue of the "false names", simply notes the existence of a discrepancy between actual names and 'inaccurate names, which they took during their practice of sexual perversion for fear of being discovered (*khashyatan iftidah amrihim*).' The judge simply makes the rectification and dismisses the defence's argument, which, by indicating this type of error, aimed at invalidating the whole procedure.

Finally, the judge dismisses the three petitions formulated by the defence requiring the interdiction of any press coverage of the case, the forensic physician's cross-examination, and the forensic re-examination of the accused by a tripartite commission, following the same pattern, i.e. the reiteration of general legal principles and their application to the case without any motivation other than the court's conviction. Generally, then, the judge's argument is organized so as to give his subjectivity (i.e. what he is convinced of) a very broad scope, allowing him to dismiss all the defence's grounds and requests by emphasizing the objective authority of the law and the Court of Cassation's case-law and playing down the question of whether these laws are actually relevant to the facts of the case before him.

Crimes and their Constitutive Elements

As we know, the ruling concerns two crimes: contempt of religion and habitual debauchery. At this stage, the judge undertakes the study of the elements constituting each of these crimes. Jurisprudence and Court of Cassation's case-law have formally designated the legal element (a legal text), the material element (the facts of the case) and the moral element (criminal intention) as constitutive elements (cf. Chapter 7). For the present purposes, I shall limit the analysis to debauchery.

In classical jurisprudence, the judge applies the law to facts. This implies that, after he has established the facts of the case, he enunciates the relevant law and, in a third stage, applies it to the facts. In our case, through the emphasis it places on its claim to respect these three steps, the ruling produces a self-ratifying effect. In other words, the writing appears here as the ultimate means of ratifying not only the reasoning followed in the case under scrutiny, but also the authority that conducted the procedure. Moreover, the ruling's legalistic formalism is remarkable if one bears in mind the level of jurisdiction mentioned in the introduction (single-judge misdemeanour court). It clearly reflects the importance of this case, due to the number of accused, the gravity of the charges (contempt of religion and homosexuality), and the publicity the case received outside its judicial setting. In that sense, legalistic formalism is the judge's public expression of the attention he knows is turned upon him.

The legal element of the crime of habitual debauchery (*jarimat al-i'tiyad 'ala mumarasat al-fujur*) is constituted by Article 9 of Law 10/1961 on the repression of prostitution (*da'ara*),[2] which stipulates that '(a) any person who hires or offers in any possible way a place that serves debauchery or prostitution [...]; (b) any person who owns or manages a furnished flat or room or other place open to the public that facilitates the practice of debauchery or prostitution [...]; (c) any person who usually practices debauchery or prostitution is condemned to imprisonment for a period of no less than three months and no more than three years, and to a fine of no less than five pounds and no more than 10 pounds, or to one of these two penalties. When the person is arrested in this last situation, he or she may be subjected to a medical examination and, if it appears that he or she suffers from an ordinary venereal disease, to confine him or her in a medical institution until he or she has recovered [...].' The material element of the crime is constituted, in the terms of the ruling, of the fact that 'a man undertakes to practice debauchery with a man.' Concerning the moral element of the crime, the judge considers that it is constituted by the fact that 'the guilty person committed debauchery [while knowing of the illegal character of the action], without distinction (*duna tamyiz*) and without consideration for financial compensation (*ajr*).' The judge adds that habitual practice is constituted as soon as debauchery is committed more than once.

One can logically wonder how the moral element can be established through knowledge of the condemned act's illegality. Without anticipating later developments concerning the categorization processes, we must already stress that such an establishment of criminal intention is possible only on condition of situating legality in the realm of normality and common sense. Indeed, it is hardly possible to assume that the accused knew the interpretation given by the Court of Cassation, in an unpublished ruling, to legislative provisions with no explicit formulation (there are no texts in Egyptian law formally condemning homosexuality). This is actually why the judge attempts to demonstrate that the 1961 law is applicable to homosexuality. To this end, he refers to a report of the Senate (*majlis al-shuyukh*) presented in 1951 to document a draft law on the repression of prostitution.

---

2 In Arabic, the word *da'ara* also refers to the notion of debauchery. However, it seems that in the case of this law, it directly targeted prostitution, even though the law gives no definition of the terms.

Excerpt 121 (Summary Court of Misdemeanors (State of Emergency), Case 182/2001, Qasr al-Nil)

The crime designated in [this text] is only committed when a man or a woman fornicates (*mubasharat al-fahsha'*) with people without distinction, habitually. When a woman fornicates and sells her virtue to whomever asks for it without distinction, she commits prostitution (*da'ara*) [...]; *fujur* occurs when a man sells his virtue to other men without distinction.

Then the judge cites a 1988 ruling of the Court of Cassation that confirms this conception: 'jurisprudence customarily used the word *da'ara* to [designate] female prostitution (*bagha' al-untha*) and the word *fujur* to [designate] male prostitution (*bagha' al-rajul*).'

The ruling therefore legally demonstrates that prostitution in general and male prostitution in particular is condemned in Egyptian law. Moreover, it shows that repeated sexual relationships are assimilated to prostitution (which is explicitly not defined by the existence of a financial counterpart), insofar as both occur indiscriminately. It does not show on which criteria the notions of repetition and indiscrimination are based. This is important for the purpose of our analysis. Indeed, if we attribute the absence of any criterion to the fact that many of the accused were condemned simply on the basis of the forensic report, the text of the ruling then shows that it constitutes an exceptional, ad hoc argument with a legal shape but devoid, at least in part, of any legal basis.

Applying Law to Facts

After having enunciated the facts and stipulated the law, the judge has only to draw the formal conclusion of his syllogism.

Excerpt 122 (Summary Court of Misdemeanors (State of Emergency), Case 182/2001, Qasr al-Nil)

The General Prosecution has accused all the suspects of habitually practicing debauchery/prostitution (*fujur*). After having scrutinized the documents, the forensic reports, the photographs and what occurred during the sessions, the court is convinced that the accused [...] have committed the crime of habitual debauchery/prostitution, on the grounds of: [...]

The use of this logical form allows the ruling to present itself as the necessary conclusion to an objective situation that did not need to be interpreted but simply to be exposed. In this formally ineluctable way, the judge proceeds to the detailed application of criminal law to the accused, who are organized in different categories.

Excerpt 123 (Summary Court of Misdemeanors (State of Emergency), Case 182/2001, Qasr al-Nil)

(1) As for the first accused, as well as the 34th, the 35th, the 36th and the 37th, their explicit statements during the aforementioned investigation by the Prosecution revealed that they perpetrated the crime of which they are accused. In addition, the first accused stated that he practiced sexual perversion with the 36th accused and both stated that they have compromising (*fadiha*) photographs in their possession.

(2) As for the third, 4th, and 40th accused, beside their explicit statements during the aforementioned investigation of the General Prosecution, the forensic report concludes incontrovertibly that they engaged repeatedly in passive homosexual intercourse.

The aforementioned accused, during the trial sessions, denied the charges, but this does not change anything, since the court is convinced by the statements they made during the General Prosecution's investigation [...]

(3) As for the 47th accused, the first accused testified against him during the investigation [by claiming] that he works as a masseur at the gym [...] (Initially, he gave him a normal massage, and afterwards said that he engaged in sexual activity with many men and women at the gym and that those who had experienced [it] wanted to continue. He asked the first accused whether he wanted sex and the first accused responded see what is good and do it. He masturbated the first accused on a regular basis during a period of approximately one month.) The 47th accused stated that the first accused came to the gym but had only one session, and he denied the charges.

(4) As for the 49th accused, the first accused testified against him [by claiming] that he practiced sexual perversion with him, that he had three photographs of the two of them together, and that he had penetrated him anally. In addition, the accused stated that he had 12 compromising photographs among the photos seized, of which eight [show] him naked and four [show him] practicing sexual perversion with someone else.

The fact that the aforementioned accused, during the trial, denied the charges does not change anything, since the court is convinced of what appears from [...]

(5) As for the 4th, 6th, 7th, 8th, 10th, 11th, 12th, 13th, 38th, 39th, 41st, and 42nd accused, the forensic reports concluded incontrovertibly that they had been subjected to repeated anal penetration. This is what [the court] is convinced of and it carries the authority of perfect evidence, sustaining what appears from the investigation and consolidating imperfect evidences.

The court is convinced of the fact that the accused [...] committed the crime of habitual debauchery/prostitution. It is therefore necessary to condemn them to the [penalties stipulated by] articles 9c and 15 of Law 10/1961 on the practice of prostitution since they practiced habitual debauchery/prostitution in the aforementioned manner.

This enunciation of the reasons for condemning some of the accused corroborates what our analysis of the document showed previously, i.e. that the ruling, although it organizes the sanction of debauchery/prostitution in a formally legal way, actually results in the (legally baseless) sanction of homosexuality as such. Thereafter, the accused are dealt with in an ad hoc manner, according to any element tending to prove homosexual inclination and not through the systematic collection of elements constitutive of what Egyptian law condemns under the title of debauchery/prostitution, that is, repeated and indiscriminate sexual practices. In other words, the characterization of the facts for which the accused are blamed represents the conclusion of a syllogism whose invoked major (the law repressing debauchery) does not correspond to its underlying major (the condemnation of homosexuality) and whose minor (the facts for which the accused are blamed) refers to the underlying major while resulting in a conclusion referring to the invoked major. This is confirmed by the fact that the court clears all those for whom there is no evidence of homosexual practice (and not those for whom there is no evidence of debauchery/prostitution).

> **Excerpt 124 (Summary Court of Misdemeanors (State of Emergency), Case 182/2001, Qasr al-Nil)**
>
> As for the rest of the accused [...], the court examined the documents with discernment and proper judgment and looked into the circumstances with the evidence [available]; it appeared that there was insufficient evidence to justify condemning these accused. The accused protected themselves by denying the charges at all the steps of the procedure. Nobody testified to the fact that they had committed the crimes of which they were accused, and none of them was caught red-handed. It was therefore necessary to [issue] a ruling clearing them of the charges [...] What appears in detail from the aforementioned investigation does not change anything since the investigation, the [accuracy] of which the court is convinced, would not hold water if it were based on simple presumption and not on evidence. Criminal rulings that condemn must be grounded on evidence and not only on presumption, as established by the Court of Cassation [...]
>
> The court indicates that, for the accused it condemned, it stipulated the penalty it considered to correspond to each of them according to the circumstances and the conditions of the request it examined, in the limits established by the law when it exists and according to what appears from the Court of Cassation's case-law [...]

In sum, the ruling discloses that the judge, in order to condemn homosexuality without saying so, made use of the law repressing debauchery/prostitution and that, in order to establish the latter, he took into consideration all the tokens tending to establish the former. He emphasized his legalistic concern for identifying the penal law text on which to ground the characterization of facts and conditioned criminal condemnation upon the production of material evidence.

Sentence

At the end of this highly structured journey, the formulation of the sentence appears as the anticipated, unsurprising outcome of a reasoning process whose conclusion was clear from the beginning. In this regard, one must remember the retrospective nature of such a written document, meaning that, although it presents itself as a demonstration progressively enfolding before the reader's eyes, this text is actually the justificatory formalization of a prior decision. This part of the ruling is concise and precise, in the sense that the reader in a hurry (or the audience attending to the verdict before the publication of its conclusions) can find quickly what he/she is mainly interested in: the formulation of an acquittal or a condemnation and, possibly, its term and/or amount. Contrary to what the ruling's written organization can allow the reader to assume, the sentence constitutes generally the starting point of the reading. What comes before it has little chance of ever being read by laypeople, whereas this is where professionals will find the data on which to ground their work (and especially the basis for an appeal). Thus, whereas the analytical reading of the ruling spoils the suspense of the sentence, the usual practice of this reading makes it the impatiently awaited element.

Excerpt 125 (Summary Court of Misdemeanors (State of Emergency), Case 182/2001, Qasr al-Nil)

For these reasons

The Court of Misdemeanors State Security (Emergency) decides:

1°) Five years' prison with hard labuor for the first accused [...], effective immediately, for the two charges simultaneously, and placement under police probation for a term of three years starting at the end of the prison sentence, in addition to expenses.

2°) Three years' prison with hard labour for the second accused [...], effective immediately, along with expenses, for the crime sanctioned by Article 98/7 of the Penal Code; acquittal from the second crime sanctioned by Articles 9c and 15 of Law 10/1961 on the repression of prostitution.

3°) Two years' prison with hard labour for the [3rd, 4th, 5th, 6th, 7th, 8th, 10th, 11th, 12th, 13th, 34th, 35th, 36th, 37th, 38th, 39th, 40th, 41st, 42nd, 49th accused], effective immediately, and placement under police control for a term equivalent to the stipulated penalty starting at the end of the prison sentence, along with expenses.

4°) One year's prison with hard labour for the 47th accused [...], effective immediately, placement under police control for a term equivalent to the stipulated penalty starting at the end of the prison sentence, and expenses.

5°) Confiscation of the items seized.

6°) Acquittal of the [9th, 14th, 15th, 16th, 17th, 18th, 19th, 20th, 21st, 22nd, 23rd, 24th, 25th, 26th, 27th, 28th, 29th, 30th, 31st, 32nd, 33rd, 43rd, 44th, 45th, 46th, 48th, 50th, 51st, 52nd accused] from the charges.

The clerk The court's president

Chapter 12
Questions of Morality: Sequential, Structured Organization of the Interrogation

Returning to the interrogations led by deputy public prosecutors, I will now focus on the structure of requests for information, their sequential organization, and the linguistic characteristics of the interaction. The material used here is mainly the transcript of the interrogation of the first accused in the Queen Boat trial, the sentence of which was examined in the previous chapter. In the present chapter, I will seek first to observe the interrogation's general structure. Then I will study some of its linguistic characteristics, leaving the analysis of the category systems at work in judicial activity to the following chapter. Finally, I will focus on the deputies' activity as a practice of the rule of law, which we take to mean a "declaration of law".

Structural and Sequential Organization of the Interrogation

The deputy public prosecutor's work, as we saw previously (Chapter 6), consists of leading the investigation, and, in particular, the interrogations on the basis of which a report of the "facts of the case" is established to all practical judicial ends. The interrogation, which, in theory, transcribes verbatim the words of the person being interrogated, is organized in a systematic manner that can be described step by step.

First, the interrogation is situated in a wider procedural sequence and, as such, is the object of a preface that sums up the police's initial conclusions, establishes a few procedural elements, establishes the identity of the person being interrogated, and lays out the charges. Then, the interrogation proper begins with a request for a global narrative from the accused, in which s/he is asked to present his or her version of the facts in a linear, detailed manner. Third, the deputy goes over the various elements of this narrative point by point, so as not to leave out a single element of procedural correctness and legal relevance. Finally, in conclusion, the deputy reiterates the charges against the suspect and offers him or her the opportunity to have the last word.

Preface

The interrogation of a suspect is situated inside a file, which is the compilation of all the procedures put in place by the Prosecution in the framework of an investigation into a case for which it is responsible. The Prosecution's representative, the deputy, is responsible for taking note systematically of the concrete modes whereby the file is opened and closed, the observations suggested to him procedurally, and, of course, the actions carried out in the framework of the investigation, whether it consists of a search warrant, a reconstitution of the facts, or, more generally, an interrogation. The interrogation is therefore preceded by a series of references that situate it within the file's general architecture and the procedural sequence.

Excerpt 126 (High State Security Prosecution, Case 655, 2001)

General Prosecution
Office of the Prosecutor-general
High State Security Prosecution

Investigation report

Report opened on Saturday 12/5/2001 at 10:00 p.m., Prosecution headquarters
We, Samih Sayf, head of the Prosecution
And Nabil Mus'ad Muhammad Salim, secretary,
Have been requested by the Counselor, general prosecutor of High State Security, to interrogate the accused, Sharif Hasan Mursi Farahat, in case 655 of 2001, High State Security.

The Prosecution's representative then cites the police report, as the document around which his own investigation is articulated.

Excerpt 127 (High State Security Prosecution, Case 655, 2001)

We have perused the original report on the office's specific role, dated 24/4/2001, 9:00 p.m., written by Commander Muhammad 'Abd al-Mun'im, officer of State Security inspectors. In it, he establishes that, on the basis of a warrant to arrest and search the person and domicile of the abovementioned suspect, who resides at 67, 'Abd al-Aziz Al Sa'ud Street, Manyal, and has another residence in Masakin 'Ayn al-Sira, Block 27, Entrance 1, he undertook the close surveillance of the latter residence until he arrested the suspect. At that time, he took him in for searching, and on that occasion found [...; cf. Excerpt 117].

The writer of the report established that, after confronting the accused with the information and the revelations concerning his belief in certain religious ideas, through his reading of several books and his vision [...], he had founded God's Lieutenancy [...] and had chosen a plot of land owned by his father [...].

He also established that [the suspect] had undertaken to spread his ideas among people who were linked to him, among them the suspect Mahmud Ahmad 'Allam [...], and that he has long practiced sexual perversion, since the time when he was a student in the German School, Duqqi. He continued his homosexual practices (*liwat*) with many people and was accustomed to frequent certain hotels, public places, and boats frequented by sexual perverts. He photographed these practices, and printed and distributed the photographs. Furthermore, he undertook to send e-mails containing religious ideas, besides the fact that he participated in message exchanges involving sexual perversion. The writer of the report also established at the end of the report that he had placed the seized items in a cardboard box sealed with red wax, with four seals [...].

In procedural terms, the police report is not an authoritative reference, in the sense that the Prosecution's investigation seeks to establish the facts independently of what may have been said and written previously. The fact remains, however, that inserting the summary of that report as a preface to the interrogation tightly conditions its organization and explicitly places the suspect's narrative in a reversal of presumption. The presence of this summary testifies to the fact that the Prosecutor's representative has before him the first report on the facts of the case. The prior availability of this police report thus allows the deputy to conduct his interrogation in an informed (and prejudiced) manner, rather than learning the facts gradually, as the person being interrogated reveals them. This gives the interrogation a "driving" tone (Komter, 2001: 390): the deputy's reading of the police report drives the interrogation and leads him to orient it toward the elements underlined by the police as relevant.

To this general preface, in which the reasons that led the Prosecution to take charge of the case are presented, is added a preface specific to the interrogation itself, in which the deputy – in this instance, the head of the Prosecution – takes note of the fact that the person under interrogation is present at Prosecution headquarters, lays out the modalities of the suspect's presence, and undertakes to describe his or her physical aspect.

Excerpt 128 (High State Security Prosecution, Case 655, 2001)

The accused was present outside the interrogation room, and we called him in. We found him to be a man in his early thirties, tall, of medium built, with white skin and light hair. He is wearing gray pants and a western-type blue blazer. We cannot see the slightest trace of beating on the visible parts of his body. We inform him that the General Prosecution is in charge of leading investigation procedures related to him.

Note that this stage provides the deputy with the opportunity to carry out three tasks: to ensure the procedural accuracy of his actions, to ascertain the identity of the person being interrogated, and to anticipate objections that might be made later with regard to the validity of a confession made under duress.

Once the validity of the interrogation he is about to undertake has been demonstrated, the deputy stipulates in writing that he has informed the accused of the charges against him, and begins the interrogation proper.[1]

1 In a research paper, Hélène Sallon provides a full translation of the interrogation of the first suspect in the Queen Boat trial (Sallon, 2002). We refer readers interested in the case to her excellent analysis of the 'judicialization of a question of public morality in Egypt'.

Excerpt 129 (High State Security Prosecution, Case 655, 2001)
Next, we interrogate him with regard to the charges brought against him, after having informed him of their nature and of the penalty they carry: attacks on religion through the spread and encouragement of extremist ideas, with the aim of degrading and denigrating religion and of fomenting sedition, in speech and in writing. He denies the charges. Next, we ask him whether he has witnesses we should question and someone to help him in the investigation procedures. He replies that he does not. We then undertake to interrogate him in detail in the following manner and he replies as follows:
A: My name is Sharif Hasan Mursi Farahat I'm 32 and I work as a training engineer in IBM the computer company I live at 67 'Abd al-'Aziz Al Sa'ud Street in Manyal Ruda Cairo and right now I don't have ID papers on me

The Suspect's Master Narrative

After providing a preface to the interrogation in the form of the charges brought against the person he is interrogating, the Prosecution deputy poses an open question along the lines of "what happened?" He is thereby asking the accused to give his global narrative of the facts as an alternative to that formulated by the police. In the Queen Boat case, the first suspect's narrative is especially long. For reasons of economy, we will only cite the passages related to the charges of homosexuality.

Excerpt 130 (High State Security Prosecution, Case 655, 2001)
Question of the deputy: What do you have to say with regard to the charges against you
Answer of the suspect: This accusation is untrue
Q: Then what happened
A: What happened is that on Thursday 12/4/2001 my father told me there were people from State Security who had met him through a go-between and had sent him to meet my father in the elevator and he told him that they were calling me in and my father told them that I wasn't there at that time and there was a phone call with the State Security agents and they set a time for me to meet them on Sunday 15/4/2001 at 11:00 a.m. and I went to work that day as usual and I asked permission [to go] to State Security headquarters in Lazughli and I met a colonel named Muhammad 'Abd Allah and he talked to me and told me he had found out that I had taken pictures of the Israeli embassy and that I took lots of photos of people and that I had been seen in the Fustat area taking pictures and he wanted me to explain to him privately why I was interested in [practicing] photography in that way and because I respected that man I told him my story from the beginning and I told him why I was interested in photography in general […] and I also told him that I engaged in perverse sexual practices […] then on Tuesday 24/4/2001 I contacted them and asked for the officer I had talked to and I didn't find him and another officer spoke to me and told me come get your things tonight at 9:00 p.m. and he lied and starting from then I was kept at State Security and I was surprised to hear them say I've been calling people to a new religion […] and they asked me where did you develop the pictures you had at your

> house [...] and they asked me the names of the people I have sex with and I told them most of them come from the street and places where it's well known that there are people like them [...] and the truth and what actually happened is that the people who were arrested and appeared today before the Prosecution are not those I mentioned they have no relation with me and I didn't bring them to a new religion nor have I had sex with them and the first time I saw them was when they were arrested here and came here today of course that's not the case with Yahya and Ahmad Ahlam and Muhammad the masseur whose full names I don't know and those from the photo lab and Mahmud 'Allam with whom I've had only respectable relations ever since he was training at the Mercedes center where I was working until 1999 and he has never had sex with me and my relations with him are very respectable and in general I don't have extremist ideas in religion and all I hope is that I can do something to get myself out of my sinful perversion and this is what encouraged me to set up the God's Agency project which they misunderstood

Although this narrative is supposed to transcribe verbatim the story told by the accused, ethnographic experience suggests that this is not the case and that, in fact, this is a version dictated by the deputy to his secretary. In it, what the deputy sees as essential in the suspect's narrative is cited in terms that are close or identical to those used by the suspect. Furthermore, the exhaustive nature of the master narrative, which formulates all the elements that will be dealt with in detail in the interrogation, suggests that the suspect's narrative has already been structured by the deputy's questions, although these questions are erased when the narrative is dictated to the secretary. A series of elements nevertheless seems to indicate clearly that the deputy's intervention operates in such a way that the suspect's story, the words he uses, and the Prosecution's transcription are closely intertwined. We may thus note the relatively unorganized structure of the narrative, the frequent shifts from one theme to another, the grammatical and narrative weakness of the whole, the proliferation of explanatory clauses, the mixture of direct and indirect styles, and the weak technical character of the lexicon. We will return to some of these linguistic properties in the following section. For now, it is important to note that, contrary to the police interrogation described by Komter (2002), it is plausible that the suspect's master narrative is not the result of a summary written up by the deputy after it was uttered, but rather, as mentioned earlier, the result of information requested through a series of questions that were removed during the transcription process. The Prosecution's representative is thereby merely following the rules of how to conduct an interrogation as they may be found in the *Instructions of the General Prosecution* (cf. below).

I have called the first linear narration of the facts by the suspect a "master narrative" because it appears clearly as a means of structuring the order and content of the detailed questions that follow in the interrogation proper. In that sense, the master narrative replaces the police report as a document on which the deputy can base the interrogation. From this initial narrative, the legally relevant elements that the deputy must document, one after another, in the ensuing sequence of questions emerge.

The Interrogation

The interrogation strictly defined therefore consists of a series of questions through which the deputy systematically takes up the legally relevant elements from the master narrative provided by the accused. The questions asked here take a specific closed form similar to what follows.

Excerpt 131 (High State Security Prosecution, Case 655, 2001)
Q: Who is the person you met in 1996 in this case [...]
Q: How did you meet him [...]
Q: And how did the abovementioned person find you boys as you stated [...]
Q: When did your relationship with him end [...]

The questions are initially ordered according to the sequence in which the various elements of the master narrative are uttered. Then this order evolves as the elements contained in the replies determine the nature of the following question, as in the following excerpt.

Excerpt 132 (High State Security Prosecution, Case 655, 2001)
Q: You mentioned earlier that you had alluded to your sexual perversion in your speech when you had the conversation with State Security when did you start these practices

Schematically, the master narrative and the interrogation may be juxtaposed thus:

Table 12.1 The production of a master narrative

Master narrative	Interrogation
first contact with State Security	summoning to State Security
interest in photography	photography
dream of the Kurdish boy	sexual perversion
interest in religion	partners
perverse sexual practices	God's Agency
search of the apartment	sexual relations
God's Agency	deviant religious beliefs
developing the photographs	confrontation with the police report
partners	

As far as its content is concerned, the interrogation is simply a repetition of what was already said in the master narrative. The only difference is that control over speech turns and their orientation has been transferred entirely to the Prosecution's representative. While the master narrative allowed for the suspect to take the discursive initiative, the interrogation allows the deputy to serialize and systematize the information to the practical legal ends of qualification. To demonstrate this point, we need only compare the enunciation of an element in the master narrative (excerpt 133) with the reference to it in the interrogation (excerpt 134).

Excerpt 133 (High State Security Prosecution, Case 655, 2001)
- master narrative:
[…] and I mentioned their names and it's Yahya and Ahmad also known as Ahlam and another one called Muhammad who works as a masseur at a gym called Top Gym but the last one didn't have sex with me and when I say sex I just mean he touched me during the massage […]

Excerpt 134 (High State Security Prosecution, Case 655, 2001)
- interrogation
Q: Does this mean that you completely stopped having that kind of relation from that time on
A: The feelings didn't stop completely because I can't help that and I had relations in 1998 but then I stopped full relations apart from [?] and would only engage in light sexual touching but not the whole way and the last time was a hand job when I went to a masseur at Top Gym in Duqqi and that happened once with him about a month ago but I engaged in masturbation while looking at photos I had taken of the boy and kept
Q: What is the name of the masseur you just mentioned
A: His name is Muhammad and he's one of the people who were arrested an he's a weight-lifting trainer
Q: So what are the acts you committed together
A: He started massaging my body normally and after he told me that he did sexual things with lots of people boys and girls at the gym and those who came to him kept wanting the same thing and he asked me if I wanted that or not and I said show me and he used his hands outside [i.e. over the suspect's clothes] although I was hesitating because I was trying to stay away from that as much as possible but my physical feelings take over and I hope I'll repent (*tawba*) someday
Q: Didn't the abovementioned individual have full intercourse with you
A: No just with his hand
Q: And did you fully consent
A: Yes I accepted and I let him go ahead

From the above, we may conclude that the interrogation amplifies and systematizes the master narrative. It amplifies that narrative in the sense that the investigation of the element in question takes up much more space in the interrogation, which corresponds to a more intense search for the legally relevant detail, without fear of the redundancy that such a search might occasionally induce. It systematizes that narrative to the extent that one observes the search for all elements endowed with legal relevance: time frame, identity, precise nature of the acts undertaken, consent.

Confrontation with the Accusation and Enunciation of the Accusation

At the end of the interrogation, the deputy presents the suspect with the version of the facts established in the police report and asks him or her to take a standpoint on that report.

Excerpt 135 (High State Security Prosecution, Case 655, 2001)
Q: Investigations indicate that you are afflicted with sexual perversion you engage in sexually perverse practices with those who are convinced of your beliefs and you rank these practices among the rituals of your faith
A: God preserve me may He be pleased with His lieutenant whoever said these things about me put the ten yellow books that people attribute to me [i.e. they are responsible for the booklets they attribute to me]
Q: What is your response to what the investigations established that you and those who follow your beliefs used to hold wild parties in your homes and on certain boats like the tourist boat Queen Nariman anchored in front of the Marriott hotel in Cairo every Thursday night
A: These statements these things didn't occur and I don't know the boat
Q: Do you know the suspects whose names appear on the investigation report and who were arrested
A: I don't know anyone apart from Mahmud 'Allam and I have good relations with him and I know Ahmad also known as Ahlam and Yahya also known as 'Adil I think and Muhammad the weight-lifting trainer and masseur and I don't even know their full names and I know the people from the photo lab

This confrontation corresponds to the requirement that the deputy take up the investigation from the beginning, taking none of the police's statements for granted. The suspect's replies translate his perception that this stage is an opportunity for justification, excuses, or mitigation. At this level of the interrogation, the refutation of the police's version of the facts can take place. Faced with the police's accusation, which he perceives as far more incriminating, the suspect demonstrates the legal knowledge he has acquired – the Prosecution's interrogation is the opportunity for him to retract earlier statements, denounce a confession obtained under duress, and try to obtain the least severe qualification of the facts possible – as well as his mistrust of the police, whose statements he denies. The fact that the accusation emanates from the police allows the suspect to defend himself without having to face the dilemma that often threatens him, in which he has to protect his interests while appearing to cooperate with the interrogator (Komter, 1998).

Immediately after reading the police report to the suspect, the prosecutor presents (or repeats, in the present case) the charges brought against the person being interrogated. This accusation appears indifferent to the denials and mitigations that preceded it. The formulation of the accusation nevertheless gives the suspect a second opportunity to contest the version of the facts it implies.

Excerpt 136 (High State Security Prosecution, Case 655, 2001)

Q: You are accused of having defamed religion by propagating and encouraging extremist beliefs with the aim of denigrating and despising it and of provoking sedition

A: That never happened

Q: You are also accused of having practiced debauchery in the manner indicated in the investigation

A: But the last time that happened with me was in 1996 I mean going all the way

The suspect's defense at this point consists of denying the accusations made against him, either by refuting them straightforwardly or by underlining their anachronistic character.

Conclusion

The last stage of the interrogation consists of an open question that gives the accused the possibility of adding whatever he wants to his previous testimony.

Excerpt 137 (High State Security Prosecution, Case 655, 2001)

Q: Do you have anything else to say

The suspect hastens to seize the opportunity offered to him and invokes the clemency of justice.

Excerpt 138 (High State Security Prosecution, Case 655, 2001)

A: First I would like whoever reads this investigation to know that I've repented and decided not to return to perversion and I think God sent this trial because of that and during the time I spent in prison I thought about my life and I think humans shouldn't think about everything they want and shouldn't puff themselves up to excess and I also thought that intentionally or unintentionally I've caused my family a lot of worry and I fear they will affect their physical and psychological health from the perspective of reputation and I ask God Almighty first to forgive me and for you to forgive me and I trust in His forgiveness and I beg Him to soften your hearts and cause you to help me repent so that I can be cured and not punished and If you punish me my life will be over and so will my family's life as well as all those who care about me and I hope you know that all human beings make mistakes and the best of those who err are those who repent and on Judgment Day and in the afterlife God will protect whoever protected a Muslim in this world and finally I would like to confess before God and then before you that I sinned by practicing sexual perversion but I haven't gone all the way since 1996 and I swear to God I'll never do it again and I also strongly affirm and testify by God first and last that I'm really Muslim and I never adopted a religion other than Islam and there is no Prophet but Muhammad may God bless him and bring him peace and God is our only lord and there is no other god but Him and I read about different religions and the mystery is evident to me and with regard to all strange things they influenced my personality in a way I didn't anticipate and it's attracted people to me

> and it's led me to think about my situation among them and they're interested in me and give me value and respect me and I think this is a mistake on my part but it's what happened and I beg you to help me lead a respectable life far from original sin and to follow the good I've received from God in a moderate not an extremist manner and as I said cure me and don't punish me and with all my strength I say I've never had an extremist idea and I never propagated such ideas among people and I ask God for forgiveness for He is the Merciful Forgiver

Thus, the accused immediately understands the open nature of the deputy prosecutor's question as providing him with an opening to assert his cooperation (confessing to perversion), produce his excuses (repentance), and ask for understanding (help in finding a cure). Recognizing the accusations made against him and unable to see how he can defend himself against them (his homosexuality, proven in photographs), while denying the accusations against which he believes he has a defence (his attack on religion), the accused endeavours to show his good intentions, his good faith, his moral character, and his desire to do the right thing. He expresses the hope that, in return for all this, justice – which he always places immediately after God ('I ask God Almighty first to forgive me and for you to forgive me'; 'I would like to confess before God and then before you') – will adopt a therapeutic rather than a punitive attitude.

The interrogation ends with the repetition of the same open question, but this time the accused does not follow up. A note that the interrogation is closed and the procedural requirements have been fulfilled confirms the material conclusion of this chapter in the legal dossier. Among these requirements is the suspect's signature testifying that these are indeed his words.

> **Excerpt 139 (High State Security Prosecution, Case 655, 2001)**
> Q: Do you have anything to add
> A: No
> End of statement and signature

The Language of the Interrogation

A number of characteristics specific to the interrogation deserve our attention, particularly the constrained sequential distribution of speech turns, the recourse to certain resources affirming or erasing personal agency in the action, and the lexical choices of the deputy and the accused.

Interrogation and Speech Turns

For the protagonists, the insertion of the interrogation in a judicial-type procedural framework is translated through the production, distribution, and formatting of speech turns in an asymmetrical, pre-allocated way: asymmetrical in the sense that the possibility of initiating a speech turn and formatting it is not the same for the different parties to the interrogation; and pre-allocated because the purpose of the interrogation specifies in advance the tasks each party must carry out in order to accomplish it. The parties must produce an interactional situation on site, in a way that can be perceived and described, and in such a way that the initiative of questioning is the deputy's prerogative, while the duty of answering falls upon the accused.

Excerpt 140 (High State Security Prosecution, Case 655, 2001)
Q: Who is the person you met in 1996 in this case
A: This person is called Nasir I don't know the rest of his name and he was a bellhop at a hotel called Happy House at the Pyramids but he left the hotel a long time ago and I don't know where he is now and I cut off ties between me and him
Q: How did you meet him
A: I met a boy called 'Id whom I met by chance in Tahrir Square to have sex and I asked him if he knew a place so he took me to Nasir's
Q: And how did the abovementioned find you boys as you have stated
A: I don't know how but he said if you like come anytime and he would make an appointment and bring one boy or two depending and he always took money
Q: When did your relationship with him end
A: The same year that is 1996 because the owner of the hotel fired him and I don't know where he went and in general the issue of perversion lessened during the time from 1997 till today because I went on *'umra*[2] three times and I swore as much as possible that I would stop that thing especially after I had a car accident in 1998 and I felt it was because God was displeased

The pre-allocation of speech turns does not mean, however, that each party is confined to a single mode of intervention. The preceding section showed us how the accused understood the open (excerpt 141) or closed (excerpt 142) nature of the questions asked by the deputy as defining the format of the response he was being invited to formulate. Inversely, this shows how the deputy concretely achieves mastery of the interrogation and control over speech turns by adopting a particular form of questioning.

Excerpt 141 (High State Security Prosecution, Case 655, 2001)
Q: Do you have anything else to say
A: First I would like [...]
Excerpt 142 (High State Security Prosecution, Case 655, 2001)
Q: Among the arrested suspects is there anyone who practiced perversion with you
A: Yes

We also pointed out that the master narrative, although it is transcribed in the form of a single, continuous narrative, was the fruit of an interaction one of the

2 A reduced form of pilgrimage.

parties to which was hidden in the dictation. From this perspective, it seems that the only free and spontaneous intervention is that made in the conclusion. The very fact that it is not the opportunity for questions from the deputy aiming to detail and specify it suggests that, although it is procedurally necessary, this speech turn does not require from the turn that follows it any intervention with legal relevance deserving to be dealt with specifically by the deputy. One can even think legitimately that the deputy was not expecting a detailed answer to his question, which, more than a question, was actually an announcement that the end of the interrogation was approaching (the preface of the conclusion, as it were), but was still obliged to let the suspect freely use the opportunity offered him. If so, this had no effect beyond leading the deputy to repeat his prefatory question in the conclusion – a question that was understood for what it was the second time around, and obtained from the suspect the sought-for closing response.

Excerpt 143 (High State Security Prosecution, Case 655, 2001)

Q: Do you have anything else to say

A: First I would like […]

Q: Do you have anything to add

A: No

End of statement and signature

Engagement and Neutrality in the Formatting of Speech Turns

The deputy and the suspect mobilize a series of specific linguistic resources to make their respective positions manifest and open to analysis and evaluation. The deputy's neutrality is not a given, but the interactional product of systematic position-taking. In the same way, the suspect's engagement or disengagement are practical achievements realized through cooperation. This emerges particularly clearly from an analysis of the use of personal pronouns as well as the formatting of the questions and, in consequence, the answers they bring about.[3]

The deputy's use of personal pronouns translates as a constant: the absence of the first person. Various factors thus operate to downplay the deputy's personal agency, emphasizing instead that of the suspect, the other accused, or the police.

Excerpt 144 (High State Security Prosecution, Case 655, 2001)

Q: When were you summoned to State Security for the first time

A: On Thursday 12/4/2001

Q: What was the reason

A: In the beginning my father told me I had been summoned by State Security […]

3 These techniques of engagement and neutrality are involved in the work that consists of imputing responsibility, causality, and intentionality, as described in Chapters 8, 9, and 10.

Excerpt 145 (High State Security Prosecution, Case 655, 2001)

Q: You mentioned earlier that you had alluded to your sexual perversion in your speech when you had the conversation with State Security. When did you start these practices

A: The beginning was […]

In this excerpt, we note that the deputy addresses the accused directly, using the second person singular, and puts him in relation with a third party, State Security services. It is also interesting to note, in the same excerpt, that several times the deputy is led to ask the accused questions to which he already knows the answer. These are what we call "leading questions". By asking such questions, it seems that the deputy is positioning himself as the external receptacle for information while showing that it has been produced and collected without his participation. He is displaying his externality to the investigation process and, in so doing, participating in the affirmation of his neutrality. One might argue that the deputy is actually attempting to obtain the suspect's version of the facts, as opposed to the version provided by the police. In that case, his questions are not leading but rather investigative. The fact remains that, even then, the deputy presents himself as a neutral, impartial element. The suspect confirms this position by refraining from engaging the deputy directly through the use of the second person, except when he is corroborating the Prosecution's image of impartiality and equity, and presenting it as the human version of divine justice.

Excerpt 146 (High State Security Prosecution, Case 655, 2001)

A: […] and I ask God Almighty first to forgive me and for you to forgive me and I trust in His forgiveness and I beg Him to soften your hearts and cause you to help me repent so that I can be cured and not punished and If you punish me my life will be over and so will my family's life as well as all those who care about me and I hope you know that all human beings make mistakes and the best of those who err are those who repent and on Judgment Day and in the afterlife God will protect whoever protected a Muslim in this world and finally I would like to confess before God and then before you that I sinned by practicing sexual perversion but I haven't gone all the way since 1996 and I swear to God I'll never do it again and I also strongly affirm and testify by God first and last that I'm really Muslim and I never adopted a religion other than Islam and there is no Prophet but Muhammad may God bless him and bring him peace and God is our only lord and there is no other god but Him and I read about different religions and the mystery is evident to me and with regard to all strange things they influenced my personality in a way I didn't anticipate and it's attracted people to me and it's led me to think about my situation among them and they're interested in me and give me value and respect me and I think this is a mistake on my part but it's what happened and I beg you to help me lead a respectable life far from original sin and to follow the good I've received from God in a moderate not an extremist manner and as I said cure me and don't punish me and with all my strength I say I've never had an extremist idea and I never propagated such ideas among people and I ask God for forgiveness for He is the Merciful Forgiver

The deputy's recourse to the second person singular takes multiple forms; their coercive and even incriminating character varies. Thus, in excerpt 147 (Q1), one can detect a broad request for a narrative: the subject is presupposed, but the information can be administered freely; (Q2) a restricted request for a narrative: information can come to bear only on the restricted topic of the question; (Q3-5) the formulation of questions of the "who-what-where-when" type (wh-questions): the nature of the information requested is specified; (Q6) the formulation of questions of the "how-why" type: substantive information is expected but a degree of freedom is allowed in the administration of this information; (Q7) the formulation of polarized questions (that request a yes or no answer): the information is provided in the question, but open to contestation; (Q8) the formulation of questions containing prior information: the request for information is specifically limited; (Q9) the formulation of "either-or" type questions: the answer can only be either of the two alternatives, but it is sometimes possible to insert additional information; (Q10) the formulation of questions that call for an expression of agreement or disagreement: the answer appears free, but disagreement is always more difficult to express than agreement; (Q11) the formulation of questions related to knowledge and memory: an answer invoking forgetfulness has a number of consequences on the person's credibility (Gibbons, 2003: 100-8; cf. also Drew, 1992, and Komter, 1998).

Excerpt 147 (High State Security Prosecution, Case 655, 2001)
Q1: Then what happened
Q2: Do you have anything else to say
Q3: Who is the person you met in 1996 in this case
Q4: You mentioned earlier that you had alluded to your sexual perversion in your speech when you had the conversation with State Security and when did you start these practices
Q5: Where did you engage in these practices when you got into the habit
Q6: How did you meet him
Q7: And did you fully consent
Q8: How did the two abovementioned individuals practice perversion with you
Q9: Does this mean you completely stopped such relations thereafter
Q10: What is your response to what the investigations established that you and those who follow your beliefs used to hold wild parties in your homes and on certain boats like the tourist boat Queen Nariman anchored in front of the Marriott hotel in Cairo every Thursday night
Q11: What is the name of the masseur you just mentioned

As for the accused, he also plays with pronouns to highlight or dismiss his personal agency in the facts he is narrating. Thus, as we have already pointed out, he never addresses the deputy directly, unless it is to appeal to his clemency and justice; in that case, he uses the second person plural. By calling on the judiciary in general terms, the accused is demonstrating his desire to avoid personalizing the interaction.

Excerpt 148 (High State Security Prosecution, Case 655, 2001)
A: [...] and I ask God Almighty first to forgive me and for you to forgive me and I trust in His forgiveness and I beg Him to soften your hearts and cause you to help me repent so that I can be cured and not punished [...] I hope you know that all human beings make mistakes [...] Finally I would like to confess before God and then before you that I sinned by practicing sexual perversion [...] I beg you to help me lead a respectable life far from original sin and to follow the good I've received from God in a moderate not an extremist manner and as I said cure me and don't punish me [...]

In this interrogation, we may note in passing that the accused resorts to the direct style several times. In these occurrences, however, it is impossible to observe the foregrounding or backgrounding of personal agency that is usually characteristic of plays on direct or indirect style. At most, this is a dynamic and less complex mode of expression than the grammatically correct form.

Excerpt 149 (High State Security Prosecution, Case 655, 2001)
A: Yes he asked me what does God's Soldiers mean it means I belong to the fighters who want to liberate Jerusalem [...]

Excerpt 150 (High State Security Prosecution, Case 655, 2001)
A: [...] and they asked me where did you develop the photos you had at home and I told them the S.S. photo lab on Sudan Street in Giza and I gave them the names of the people who worked with me there

Excerpt 151 (High State Security Prosecution, Case 655, 2001)
A: He started massaging my body normally and after he told me that he did sexual things with lots of people boys and girls at the gym and those who came to him kept wanting the same thing and he asked me if I wanted that or not and I said show me and he used his hands outside [i.e. over the suspect's clothes] although I was hesitating because I was trying to stay away from that as much as possible but my physical feelings take over and I hope I'll repent (*tawba*) someday

In contrast, the formatting of the suspect's speech turns manifestly responds to the possibilities offered by the different kinds of the questions the deputy is asking. Almost every opening is systematically exploited to mitigate incrimination, nuance the suspect's involvement, or produce excuses and justifications. Thus, to questions of a more technical nature, the suspect may provide a response that establishes technical distinctions; these are liable to induce distinctions in the incriminated acts at a later stage, and therefore relativize all or part of the charges.

Excerpt 152 (High State Security Prosecution, Case 655, 2001)

Q: What does active and passive mean in this case

A: It means either I penetrate the person from behind or he penetrates me in the same way and that happens sometimes and often it's manual meaning only touching and kissing, and that's called soft [...]

Q: Does this mean that you completely stopped having that kind of relation from that time on

A: The feelings didn't stop completely because I can't help that and I had relations in 1998 but then I stopped full relations apart from [?] and would only engage in light sexual touching but not the whole way and the last time was a hand job when I went to a masseur at Top Gym in Duqqi and that happened once with him about a month ago but despite this I engaged in the secret habit [i.e. masturbation: *al-'ada al-sirriyya*] while looking at photos I had taken of the boy and kept

The wh-questions leave the accused with less room to maneuver, and often all he can do is formulate counter-suggestions along the lines of "if it's this, then it can't be that".

Excerpt 153 (High State Security Prosecution, Case 655, 2001)

Q: Where did you engage in these practices when you got into the habit

A: When soft was possible we did it in the street or in cars or in a third-rate cinema or the toilets but when it was full penetration it was in a hotel or someone's house but nothing happened in my house though and most of these practices took place in 1996 because at that time I met someone by chance who could bring boys and he had a kind of hotel at the Pyramids and meetings took place there repeatedly and I took pictures of those boys there

Excerpt 154 (High State Security Prosecution, Case 655, 2001)

Q: Who is the person you met in 1996 in this case

A: This person is called Nasir but I don't know the rest of his name and he was a bellhop at a hotel called Happy House at the Pyramids but he left the hotel a long time ago+ and I don't know where he is now and I cut off ties between me and him

Questions of time also provide the opportunity for a sequential reframing of perspective that aims to present the charge as if it belonged to the past and had no current relevance.

Excerpt 155 (High State Security Prosecution, Case 655, 2001)

Q: Just as you are accused of practicing debauchery in the manner indicated in the investigation

A: The last time it happened for me was in 1996 I mean going all the way

The temporal presentation of events also makes it possible to introduce the idea of a break in the incriminated practice, which not only mitigates the accusation but also, through the use of a religious vocabulary referring to conversion and repentance, shifts the story from the register of blame to that of virtue.

Excerpt 156 (High State Security Prosecution, Case 655, 2001)
Q: When did your relationship with him end
A: The same year that is 1996 because the owner of the hotel fired him and I don't know where he went and in general the issue of perversion lessened during the time from 1997 till today because I went on *'umra* three times and I swore as much as possible that I would stop that thing especially after I had a car accident in 1998 and I felt it was because God was displeased

The same vocabulary of repentance intervenes on different occasions, but always after a question regarding practices to which the accused confesses, while seeking to attenuate their scope.

Excerpt 157 (High State Security Prosecution, Case 655, 2001)
Q: How did these perverse practices occur
A: First I would like to say that I've repented and I will never commit this sin again because I realized that it was the reason for this problem and as for the way it was practiced sometimes I was active and sometimes passive

Excerpt 158 (High State Security Prosecution, Case 655, 2001)
Q: So what are the acts you committed together
A: He started massaging my body [...] although I was hesitating because I was trying to stay away from that as much as possible but my physical feelings take over and I hope I'll repent someday

Finally, note that the accused formulates categorical denials only when the charges against him are issued not by the deputy but by State Security. In other words, it is because the denial does not place him in direct conflict with the deputy that the accused can allow himself to make it.

Excerpt 159 (High State Security Prosecution, Case 655, 2001)
Q: What is your response to what the investigations established that you and those who follow your beliefs used to hold wild parties in your homes and on certain boats like the tourist boat Queen Nariman anchored in front of the Marriott hotel in Cairo every Thursday night
A: These statements these things didn't occur and I don't know the boat

The Interrogation and its Lexicon

We may formulate a few brief remarks on the choice of words used by the deputy and the accused in their respective speech turns. For the deputy, these remarks concern first and foremost what we might call a phenomenon of hyper-correctness. Given the type of material on which this study is based, it is difficult to know to what extent this hyper-correctness intervenes at the very moment of the deputy's speech turn or

Table 12.2 The lexicon of the interrogation

Formal expressions	Technical expressions	Stereotypes	Vocabulary of precision
"to undertake" (*qama bi*)	"convoked" (*istid'a*)	"what do you have to say" (*ma qawlak*)	"precisely" (*tahdidan*)
"to mention" (*dhakara*)	"the abovementioned" (*salif al-dhikr*)	"what is the reason for" (*ma al-sabab fi*)	"what is meant by" (*ma al-maqsud fi*)
"from your personal point of view" (*min manzurak al-khass*)	"to engage in intercourse" (*'ashara jinsiyyan*)	"the preceding" (*ma taqaddama*)	"does this mean that" (*hal ya'ni an*)
"locations characterized by" (*mawaqi' dhata sifa*)	"with absolute consent" (*bi irada khalisa*)	"how did this occur" (*kayfa kana dhalik*)	
"in this matter" (*fi hadha al-sha'n*)	"search" (*taftish*)	"in which manner" (*'ala ay nahw*)	
"was accomplished" (*tamma*)	"photographs" (*suwar futughrafiyya*)	"does this mean that" (*hal ya'ni an*)	
"in the manner indicated" (*'ala al-nahw al-mubayyan*)			

in a deferred way, when the narrative is dictated to the secretary.[4] The fact remains that a series of syntactical turns of phrase and lexical choices explicitly manifest the register to which the deputy's discourse belongs. We have already pointed out the preference for closed questions and the limits imposed on open questions at certain precise places, in response to the instructions to the Prosecution to request a global narrative at the beginning of the interrogation and to ask whether there are further remarks before the interrogation is closed. We have also mentioned the different kinds of questions, the search for precision, and therefore the preference for wh-questions, at the risk of redundancy. We may now add to this the choice of a formal vocabulary, manifesting the fact that the deputy's discourse belongs to the lexical register of the legal professional, which combines very formal expressions, technical formulas, stereotypes, and a vocabulary oriented toward precision.

It is difficult, however, to use these lexical specificities to argue, as O'Barr does (1982), that the interrogation is totally structured by the power relations uniting the deputy and the substitute. These characteristics are not found in the suspect's language, which, on the contrary, immediately appears as less technical and formal.

4 Cf. excerpt 23 and related comments for a situation where hyper-correctness is so manifest, heavy, and redundant that it only seems possible that it was introduced at the time of dictation, after the speech turn.

With regard to syntax and lexicon, Egyptian dialect is much more present here,[5] even when the suspect's speech turn cites the formula used by the deputy in his question.

Excerpt 160 (High State Security Prosecution, Case 655, 2001)
Q: You mentioned that places that are dangerous to you attract you what do you mean by danger and what is its extent
A: What I mean is strangeness in other words [...]

There is, however, no reason to discard the hypothesis that the transcription of some expressions with a dialectal ring to them is itself the result of an editing process that affects the suspect's statements in a realist perspective; in other words, perhaps the aim was to produce the effect of a literal transcription using the exact words of the person being interrogated. The recurrent use of certain expressions[6] supports this interpretation.

The Practice of Interrogation: The Rule of Law on Trial

In its treatment of law as a resource and not an object of study in its own right, formal socio-legal research all but forgot that, before being a resource in any explanatory framework, the legal rule is an action, a practice, and an achievement. This assertion takes us down to the level of the "law factory" (Latour, 2002), where it is manufactured, or of what Garfinkel (2002) calls the shop floor problem.

In many professions, practitioners must read descriptive reports as if they were guides to an action they must undertake.

> They do so occupationally, as a skilled matter of course, as vulgarly competent specifically ordinary and unremarkable work-site-specific practices. (Garfinkel, 2002: 105)

Eric Livingston (1986; 1987) was thus able to demonstrate the social nature and praxeological character of mathematical proof. Without seeking to assimilate the rule of law to a mathematical theorem, it is interesting to note that the activity that consists of referring to a legal text, using it, and applying it is one of the phenomena Livingston calls "Lebenswelt pairs" or "L pairs". This means, in the

5 As in the following phrases, for example: 'or that are difficult to photograph' (*aw elli fi su'ubat fi taswirha*); 'frankly I had two chains one with the Star of David I don't know where the other one went I bought them in front of the two synagogues' (*bi saraha kana 'andi silsiltein minhum negmet Dawud ma'rafsh el-tanya rahit fein ishtarithum min amam el-ma'badein*); 'where Nasir the bellhop worked' (*elli kan shaghghal fih Nasir el-bawwab*).

6 For example: 'what happened is that' (*elli hasal huwa an*); 'that never happened' (*mahasalsh*).

case of the phenomenon (legal rule), that it is composed of the two segments of a pair made of (a) the [instruction manual] and (b) the work that consists, in any real situation, of <following these instructions>.

An anecdote will clarify this point. In the Prosecution offices at Shubra al-Khayma, a Cairo neighbourhood, one day when I was sitting at the back of the room in the ethnographic position of the fly on the wall,[7] a woman came in to make a deposition about her son, who had died after drinking rubbing alcohol (*sbirtu* in Egyptian dialect). In such cases, the Prosecution is legally obliged to open an inquest. It has to provide answers to a series of questions, among them whether death was accidental or not, intentional or not, and whether it is necessary to order an autopsy of the victim. The mother expresses her pain and grief, accompanying the deputy's interruptions with prayers and various gestures. The deputy seems uneasy, however. He crosses the room to talk to his colleague, questions the credibility of the testimony, and feels that these manifestations of pain are weak coming from someone who has lost a son. The mother does not seem sufficiently grief-stricken, according to him. He borrows a book titled *General Instructions for the Prosecution* (*al-Ta'limat al-'Amma lil-Niyaba*) from his colleague, and looks for the sections instructing him how to behave with witnesses and how to lead investigations – in other words, the rules telling him how to carry out his work in this case. He is looking for the first segment of the pair we mentioned earlier – to wit, the objective instructions that clearly indicate what he must do. Of course, he does not find exactly what he is looking for. All he finds is a "docile instruction manual", a disengaged text, and he must still give it time-bound, effective, situated meaning. He must still produce the second segment of the pair, i.e. the work of following these instructions. In other words, the phenomenon that consists of enunciating the law, applying it, and referring to it is identical with the inextricable pair (codified instructions/application of the instructions). The law is a practical achievement that consists of stipulations in a legal text and the application of these stipulations. The first part provides a disengaged set of rules while the second is the practice that aims to discover the clear meaning, coherence, truth, and precision of the legal text.

On the basis of what has just been said, it is possible to present the interrogation of the first suspect in the Queen Boat case in the form of a synopsis, setting up a parallel between the two segments of the pair that constitute the (legal rule), i.e. [legal stipulations] on one hand and the <application of legal stipulations> on the other. This will make it possible to see how, even in this simple case, the phenomenon of the legal rule is that of an instructed action.

Here are some [legal stipulations] taken from the General Instructions for the Prosecution (GIP), the Penal Code (CP), decree 10/1961 on the repression of prostitution (DRP), and general principles of criminal law (GP).

---

7 To cite the expression used by Bruno Latour (2002).

Excerpt 161 (GIP)

Article 204 – The first and last name of the accused must be noted in the report and, if available, the day, month, and year of his birth […]

Article 205 – The questions asked of suspects and witnesses, as well as the answers to these questions, must be noted in the interrogation report in their entirety, without summary, suppression, or correction, under the supervision of the responsible [representative of the Prosecution]

Article 216 – The representative of the Prosecution […], after having examined the accused and established the points he considers useful, interrogates the accused orally with regard to the charges against him; if [the accused] admits to these charges, then [the representative] undertakes to question him in detail, making sure to emphasize what confirms his confession. If [the accused] denies the charges, [the representative] asks him if he has evidence and witnesses to corroborate his denial […]

Article 218 – If the accused admits to the charges during the interrogation, [the Prosecution's representative] must not simply accept this confession, but rather must seek evidence to consolidate it […]

Excerpt 162 (DRP)

Article 9 – Condemned to detention for a period of no less than three months and no more than three years and to a fine of no less than five pounds and no more than ten pounds, or to one of these two penalties: (a) any person renting or providing in any way a lodging or place for debauchery or prostitution […]; (b) any person who owns or manages a furnished lodging or room or a place open to the public that facilitates the practice of debauchery or prostitution […]; (c) any person who habitually practices debauchery or prostitution. A person arrested in the last situation may be subjected to a medical examination and, if found to be suffering from a common venereal disease, may be kept in a medical institution until cured […]

Excerpt 163 (CP)

Article 40: Considered as an accomplice:

- whoever instigates an action constitutive of a crime if the action took place as a consequence of this instigation;
- whoever agrees with another person to commit a crime, if the crime accord as a consequence of this agreement;
- […]

Article 48: Criminal complicity occurs when two or several people agree to commit a crime or a misdemeanor or to do something that facilitates same […]

Excerpt 164 (PG, following Husni, 1989)

The constitutive elements of a crime (see Chapter 7)

- the material element (*rukn maddi*): active or passive; the consequence of this action and the offense that harmed an interest or a right that legislators had considered worthy of protection [mat. elt.]

- the moral element (*rukn ma'nawi*): the infliction of a penalty is linked to the intentional or imprudent commission of an offense by a human being [mor. elt.]
- the legal element (*rukn shar'i*): there must be a text criminalizing the act and stipulating the penalty that must be inflicted on its author [leg. elt.]

At the same time, we have the following excerpt from the interrogation of the first suspect in the Queen Boat case. It may be read as the <application of legal stipulations> provided by legal texts.

The (legal rule), as a practice endowed with phenomenological properties, must be read, in this case and thus in each particular case, as a pair of which the

Excerpt 165 (High State Security Prosecution, Case 655, 2001)

<application of legal stipulations>

1. A: My name is Sharif Hasan Mursi Farahat I'm 32 and I work as a
training engineer in IBM the computer company I live at 67
'Abd al-'Aziz Al Sa'ud Street in Manyal Ruda Cairo and right now I
don't have ID papers on me
5. Q: You mentioned earlier that you had alluded
in your speech when you had the conversation with State Security to your
sexual perversion and when did you start these practices
8. A: The beginning was at the time when I was studying at the German
School in Duzzi and it only happened once with three of my
friends and I didn't do it at school after that but at university
so when I was studying in the Faculty of Engineering at Cairo
University [I had] relations with people from the street
so the first time it happened around 1983
14. Q: How did these perverse practices occur
15. A: First I would like to say that I've repented and I will never
commit this sin again because I realized that it was the
reason for this problem and as for the way it was
practiced sometimes I was active and sometimes
passive […]
20. Q: Does this mean that you completely stopped having that kind of relation
from that time on
22. A: The feelings didn't stop completely because it isn't
I practiced it actively and I had relations in 1998 but then I totally stopped
full relations apart from [?] and it became
light sexual touching but not the whole way and the last time
it was relations with the hands when I went to a
masseur at the gymnasium Top Gym in Duqqi and that happened once
with him about a month ago but despite this I was satisfied with
the secret practice [i.e. masturbation] while looking at photos
I had taken of the boy and kept
31. Q: What is the name of the masseur you just mentioned
32. A: His name is Muhammad and he's one of the people who were arrested and
he's a weight-lifting trainer […]
34. Q: Didn't the abovementioned individual have full
intercourse with you
36. A: No just with his hand
37. Q: And did it take place with your full consent
38. A: Yes and I accepted and I let him go ahead […]

two parts, the [legal stipulations] and the <implementation of legal stipulations>, are inextricably linked.

Excerpt 166 (High State Security Prosecution, Case 655, 2001)

[legal stipulations]		<application of legal stipulations>
GIP	1. A:	My name is Sharif Hasan Mursi Farahat I'm 32 and I work as a
204		training engineer in IBM the computer company I live at 67
205		'Abd al-'Aziz Al Sa'ud Street in Manyal Ruda Cairo and right now I
216		don't have ID papers on me
DRP 9	5. Q:	You mentioned earlier that you had alluded
PG mat;		in your speech when you had the conversation with State Security to your
Elt;		sexual perversion and when did you start these practices
	8. A:	The beginning was at the time when I was studying at the German
		School in Duzzi and it only happened once with three of my
		friends and I didn't do it at school after that but at university
		so when I was studying in the Faculty of Engineering at Cairo
		University [I had] relations with people from the street
		so the first time it happened around 1983
GIP 218	14. Q:	How did these perverse practices occur
	15. A:	First I would like to say that I've repented and I will never
DRP 9		commit this sin again because I realized that it was the
PG mat.		reason for this problem and as for the way it was
elt.		practiced sometimes I was active and sometimes
		passive […]
PG mat.	20. Q:	Does this mean that you completely stopped having that kind of relation
elt.		from that time on
	22. A:	The feelings didn't stop completely because it isn't
		I practiced it actively and I had relations in 1998 but then I totally stopped
CP		full relations apart from [?] and it became
40		light sexual touching but not the whole way and the last time
48		it was relations with the hands when I went to a
		masseur at the gymnasium Top Gym in Duqqi and that happened once
		with him about a month ago but despite this I was satisfied with
		the secret practice [i.e. masturbation] while looking at photos
		I had taken of the boy and kept
	31. Q:	What is the name of the masseur you just mentioned
	32. A:	His name is Muhammad and he's one of the people who were arrested and
DRP 9		he's a weight-lifting trainer […]
PG mat.	34. Q:	Didn't the abovementioned individual have full
elt.		intercourse with you
PG mor.	36. A:	No just with his hand
elt.	37. Q:	And did it take place with your full consent
	38. A:	Yes and I accepted and I let him go ahead […]

This synopsis shows us how a set of instructions, in this instance legal rules, 'can be read alternatively so that the reading provides for a phenomenon in two constituent segments of a pair: (a) the-first-segment-of-a-pair that consists of a collection of instructions; and (b) the work, just in any actual case of following which somehow turns the first segment into a description *of the pair*.' (Garfinkel, 2002: 105-6) This pair may be designated as an "instructed action".

When formal/classical analysis examines the second part of the pair, it is only insofar as it is situated in a more or less adjusted correspondence between the [instructions] and the <implementation of instructions>. This type of analysis looks at the case as an example of a general pattern of rule implementation, corresponding to legal stipulations in a deterministic way. This is why such analyses, when they look at a particular case, transform its phenomenological nature and place it in a situation of conformity to or deviance from the abstract and general corresponding version of the legal stipulation. Here, I suggest that we consider [instructions] and <implementation of the instructions> (or the <instructions in use>) as linked: two inseparable segments of a pair. Together, these two segments also allow us to establish the praxeological validity of instructed actions. Questions such as the factual appropriateness of the instructions, their complete nature, the clear or ambiguous meaning of the terms used, their capacity to be implemented, or the effective nature of the procedure used to this end then appear to the analyst as they are asked "live". Only in this framework does it become possible to deal with everything this signifies.

Let us now return in detail to the interrogation transcribed in 38 lines in the synoptic table, above. Lines 1-4 consist of the suspect providing details about his identity, in response to a question from the deputy, which is not the transcription of oral statements but rather follows a stereotype ('We then undertook to interrogate him in detail in the following manner and he replied'). The answer is explicitly about identity, even though the formula that initiates it does not require this. We may easily deduce that, despite its written formulation, the interaction related to the suspect's identity, and therefore conformed to a pattern that is not only obligatory according to the GIP, but also routinely practiced in an interrogation sequence where concern for procedural correctness competes with the search for substantive factuality. In lines 5-7, the deputy begins the interrogation with a question relating to "perverse practices" and how longstanding they are. First, however, he mentions the fact that the suspect has already admitted to these practices. His question therefore aims to give this confession substance and to establish the material nature of the charges. This question should therefore be read in the context of the Prosecution's instructions not to take a confession at face value without seeking to confirm its terms, and of the general principles of criminal law that make materiality one of the constitutive elements of a crime. From this perspective, the deputy's question is the pure expression of the rule of law in action, and cannot be dissociated from a theoretical formulation, although such a formulation would run dry immediately without its practical instantiation. There is no criminal stipulation saying what the material nature of "perversion" might consist of, and it is therefore impossible to claim that the deputy is following the rule. To the contrary, the question of when "perverse relations" began has no meaning outside the principle according to which a crime must be composed of legal, material, and moral elements. This search for the crime's materiality may be found at lines 14, 20-21, 31, 34-35, and 37. Although no definition of perversion exists (such a definition allowing for a circumstantial qualification of the facts), the deputy undertakes an investigation into the substantive character of an action, taking its existence as well as its criminal dimension as given and evident. The deputy therefore endeavours to bring together the constitutive elements of a crime, of which the existence is supposed but not proven, by asking questions about the manner ("how"), the timing ("since when"), and intentionality ("absolute consent"). Regarding the question of timing, we should also note that the Prosecution representative orients to the legal question of prescription, i.e. the time span beyond which a misdemeanour (like that of perversion, regardless of its putative nature) can no longer be tried as such. This is found explicitly in lines 20-21, when the deputy asks about when the incriminated practices came to an end. As for the accused, he cooperates in his answers, adding many details, but also endeavouring to make them the least damaging possible. Thus, at lines 8-13, he resorts to vague deictics of time ("around 1983"), space ("at university"), and relation ("people from the street"), which allow him to show his good faith toward the magistrate while referring the details of the charges against him to a distant past – rendering their memory hazy and their criminalization problematic. At lines 15-19, the accused also attempts to put forth a temporal and moral excuse to avoid answering the deputy's question or, at least, to try to attenuate its scope preventatively. The motive of repentance is produced in such a way as to refer the "crime" to an irrevocably vanished time; it is understood that the punishment should be erased since the perpetrator has recognized the criminal character of the act and has affirmed that he has abandoned it. Once repentance has been asserted, the accused can engage in cooperation with the deputy in a way he deems less damaging. Finally, at lines 22-30, the accused seeks to establish a sort of typology of perversion, between practices that might be punishable ("full intercourse") and others that are shameful but should not be sanctioned ("touching" and "masturbation"). At line 31, we note that the deputy pays no attention to the nuances highlighted by the accused, but instead focuses only on the partner's identity ("the name of the masseur"), which seems to refer directly to the stipulations of the Penal Code relative to participation in a crime. At line 37, the third constitutive element of a crime (the moral element) underlies the deputy's question, as he seeks to verify criminal intent and the lack of victimization of the participants in the massage session.

As a whole, lines 5-30 show the existence of a complete disjunction, within the interrogation, between the deputy's investigative practices and the suspect's defensive practices. Contrary to what Conley and O'Barr argue (1990), this is not really due to the different representations of justice held by legal professionals, who are attached to the rules, and laypeople, who are keen to express their complaints and maintain their membership in the social thread. Rather, this is due to the parties' orientation to positions and goals that are specific to their contextual engagement in the judicial action. Out of professional concern for the routine accomplishment of his work, the deputy seeks to give factual substance to the rule of law, even if that rule is putative; in contrast, the accused, desiring to cooperate with the law, seeks to resolve a dilemma by recognizing the rule's materiality (even if it is just as putative) while emptying it of its damaging content in a bid to protect himself. At the same time, the protagonists share the fact that they are referring to an identical rule (even if it is putative). The (rule of law), as an instructed action made up of the pair [legal stipulations]–<implementation of the legal stipulations>, is therefore not the rule for professionals alone, but rather for all the participants in the judicial action. In that sense, the (rule of law) is a collaborative product of all those who take it as a reference.

In conclusion, let us rapidly review our argument. The legal rule and its uses make up a pair endowed with phenomenological properties. By focusing exclusively on the first segment of the pair, to wit [legal stipulations], formal/classical analysis loses sight of the work that makes up legal reasoning and is concerned only with bringing the finished product to light. In this way, it neglects the elements that constitute the workplace. It paraphrases legal rules, but ignores the effective reasoning carried out by real people in real places and circumstances. There are nevertheless two components that make up the work problem at its true performance level, which the study of practices faces. The first component is made up of rules that practitioners are supposed to follow, while the second is made up of the work that consists of following these rules in any concrete case. While the first component, which is largely recognized by the formal/classical literature, is a property "extracted" from legal activity, the properties of the second component are specifically absent from the literature. And yet we are still irremediably faced with "this particular case" in "this particular context" with "this particular team of people associated in this particular job". By failing to take the second segment of the pair seriously, the analyst runs the risk of missing the entire phenomenon, and of developing only a general gloss that extrapolates present and future from the past and the general from the particular. The question remains, however, of how to keep sight of the phenomenon of workplace practices in each real case.

Chapter 13
The Categories of Morality: Homosexuality between Perversion and Debauchery

In this last chapter, I want to identify the categories that judicial members mobilized in the context of the Queen Boat trial. Insofar as there is no explicit characterization of homosexuality in Egyptian law, its sanction could only operate through assimilation to penal categories that were judged as analogous. We thus witnessed the activation of a whole categorial device through which homosexuality was designated, labelled and provided with penal consequences. I seek now to observe the production of these categories, their organization, their praxeological grammar, the functioning of their inferential power, and their legal fixation and formalization.

The various legal documents concerning the accused in the Queen Boat trial refer to perversion and debauchery. It is exceptional for homosexuality to be assimilated explicitly to these categories. No definition or criterion for establishing a categorial membership is ever given. This is why, in the examination of this practical grammar of categories and their intelligibility, the analysis must also concentrate on the place of the implicit. The implicit results from a conception of normality that is never given once and for all, but rather is constantly produced and reproduced; invoking this conception fixes categories temporarily, allows for responsibility to be ascribed, and leads to the imputation of bound consequences. In the practical production of legal meaning, the place occupied by implicit categories deserves special attention, because of their fluidity and the strength of the support they provide for interactions.

In order to treat these different categorial devices, I will follow the broad lines of the approach taken by membership categorization analysis as developed by Sacks and extended by many scholars, among them Jayyusi, Hester, Eglin, Watson, Jalbert, Nekvapil, and Leudar. After sketching out the idea of a practical grammar of categories and identifying various types of operating categorizations in different documents related to the Queen Boat case, I focus on inferential mechanisms acting in the production and transformation of categories. Next, I concentrate on the open texture of law, which is made of the intertwining of multiple categorial devices and of close relationships between rational and moral dimensions. Then I analyse the paired functioning of many categories. In particular, I study the categorial organization of relational pairs (depraved/society), disjunctive pairs (depraved/sick) and antithetic pairs (normal/aberrant), that all operate in an important way in this case. Fourth, I elaborate on the sequential organization of categorizations, not only at the internal level of documents, but especially at the dialogical level constituted by all the pieces of a judicial file. The last section gives us the opportunity to reflect on the implicit, the ambiguous and the unsaid in the enfolding of categories in the context of a legal case.

Law, Categories and Inferences

The Practical Grammar of Categories

As Coulter puts it (1989: 33-4), the epistemic behaviour of the members of a given social group deserves to be studied in itself and in its own right, not as the basis for general explanations of a quasi-transcendental nature. To this effect, 'we need to reveal, not the putative "causes" or conditions unknown to agents, but the *logic* of agents' actual conceptual, communicative, relational and instrumental conduct as they constitute their object-universes.' (*id.*: 36)

The study of categorizations begins with a relatively simple statement: there is no homothetical relationship between an object and the predicate that is ascribed to it. To say that an ideology is bourgeois does not mean that it is exclusively the ideology of the bourgeois class or that any member of the bourgeois class shares this ideology. Sociology classically treats the knowledge of any community and its members' activities in terms of this community's body of knowledge. Assuming the connection between this community's body of knowledge and its members' activities nevertheless implies the existence of such a relationship between this body and the social group as it permits the ascription of the body to one or another community (Sharrock, 1974: 45). In fact, the ascription of a collective predicate to a body of knowledge is not necessarily literally descriptive of the community in which this body is supposed to exist, but constitutes a "device-for-describing" (*id.*: 49; cf. also Ireton, 2000; Hester and Housley, 2002). So, for instance, the predicate "Roman" in the expression "Roman law" means neither that it is the law of all the Romans, without exception, nor that it is the law of Romans to the exclusion of any other. England has inherited the institution of Roman law, but this does not imply that all English people are Roman or that Roman law immediately became English, nor that the English became Romans because they apply their law. The same holds true for someone who is said to be "stupid as a Sa'idi". This alleged stupidity is not the prerogative of Upper Egypt's inhabitants; nor can it be ascribed to them as a group. However, in certain circumstances, subscription to a body of knowledge or beliefs is effectively constitutive of the community itself. The community of Muslims grows each time an individual professes his or her faith in Islam. In any case, while the relationship between the body of knowledge and the predicate attached to it is analogous to relationship of ownership, there is nevertheless 'a consequential difference that is displayed in the way these different sorts of category-concepts may be said to behave.' (Jayyusi, 1984: 53)

All this allows us to see 'how *categories of social membership* and their "grammars" of application are significantly bound up with our everyday, practical appreciation of the distribution of knowledge and belief.' (Coulter, 1989: 38) The use of these categories permits members of a social group to produce accountable inferences, judgments and ascriptions with regard to "who knows what", "who does what", "who is who", "what is what", "who owns what", "who is what", etc. Among all the categories available for designating a social identity, some function in a paired manner, like for instance the pairs "friend-friend", "parent-child", "husband-wife". Although these categories are elementary, the knowledge that their use allows is complex. Ordinary knowledge is largely bound to this category organization. Many types of activities can be considered as bound to some membership categorizations, so that, 'for an observer of a category-bound activity the category to which the activity is bound has a special relevance for formulation an identification of its doer.' (Sacks, 1974: 225) Descriptions of persons and their activities are, in a very characteristic way, co-selected so that they can exhibit an orientation to issues of category boundedness. For instance, coming across someone who is crying, of whom it can be said that she is not an adult, might incite us to speak not in terms of "boy" or "girl" but in terms of "baby" or "child", because the activity that consists of "crying" is a "baby's" or a "child's" predicate, whatever her gender. In the same way, arresting somebody in the context of a party might lead a prosecutor to suspect him of having abnormal or illicit sexual practices and thus to designate him as debauched or adulterous. There are certainly other ways to designate these persons (young people, revellers, patrons at a club, friends, etc.), and all are factually as true as the category chosen. The selection that is made of an activity (partying), a place (the boat), and a gender (male), however, is linked here to a retrospective gaze that gives the facts coherence oriented toward a practical goal (a morality trial) and incites prejudicial ascription to the category of "perverse" and its corollary legal characterization, "debauched". The choice of descriptors is heavily consequential in the reading of facts and their legal implications. In that sense, we can speak of a practical grammar of notions and concepts, and this grammar determines the intelligibility the world has for us in a way that is both evolutionary and constant (Coulter, 1989: 49; cf. Introduction).

To speak in terms of a practical grammar of meaning and categories means to give special attention to the contextual insertion of discourse and words that make it up. Categorizing devices, categories, and predicates attached to them have a reflexive and indexical relationship with the context of their production. The meaning of a categorizing device is not a static given, but the object of some practical reasoning that is collaboratively elaborated. Categorizing is thus an activity accomplished in particular local circumstances, in a way that is irremediably bound to the practical activity and reasoning of those who collaborate in its production. Categories and categorizing devices do not pre-exist the various contexts of their mobilization; they are an integral part of these contexts, and indeed are constitutive of them. In that sense, excerpts of the Queen Boat case reproduced in this and the two former chapters constitute a corpus of categorizations created by the different steps of the case. Zimmerman and Pollner (1971: 94) use this idea of an "occasioned corpus" to stress the idea that 'the features of socially organized activities are particular contingent accomplishments of the production and recognition work of parties to the activity.'

The Categories of Law

According to Hester and Eglin (1992: 17), ethnomethodological legal research operates at three levels. First, it aims at describing the methods through which actions of a legal and judicial nature are produced and recognized. Second, it concerns the methods through which legal and judicial contexts and situations are socially organized. Third, it seeks to analyse the methods through which legal and judicial identities are accomplished within social interaction. At each level, the point is to observe how the social world is a moral and cognitive phenomenon producing order and constituted by its members' practical methods of reasoning. When it comes to law, it is then necessary to discover through which mechanisms, categorial among others, some factuality is submitted to a formally constituted and organized jurisdiction. In this sense, categorization is at the heart of legal and judicial action.

The whole file of the Queen Boat case is full of categorizations. These are of different types, as it appears from the reading of the examination of the main accused. We find categorizations of a bodily nature:

Excerpt 167 (High State Security Prosecution, Case 655, 2001)
Q: Describe the two abovementioned suspects for us
A: When I met him Yahya had a very athletic body of medium build and at the time he was around 19 Ahmad is on the small side and dark-skinned they're the ones in the pictures

We also find categories of a temporal nature:

Excerpt 168 (High State Security Prosecution, Case 655, 2001)
Q: When did your relationship with him end
A: The same year that is 1996 because the owner of the hotel fired him and I don't know where he went and in general the issue of perversion lessened during the time from 1997 till today because I went on *'umra* three times and I swore as much as possible that I would stop that thing especially after I had a car accident in 1998 and I felt it was because God was displeased

Categorizations can even assume a professional dimension:

Excerpt 169 (High State Security Prosecution, Case 655, 2001)
Q: What was the reason [for the suspect being summoned to State Security]
A: In the beginning my father told me I had been summoned by State Security because there was a question about Natco company and the officer wanted to have a chat with me and the question about Natco was that when I was working there some of the workers who were training there were forced to sign checks to guarantee that they would stay on after the end of the training and some of these workers complained but when I went to

State Security I was astonished that the officer talked to me about another topic that is the reason why I was interested in taking pictures of the Israeli embassy and the Jewish synagogue and some other places

These categorizations also take on a geographical dimension:

Excerpt 170 (High State Security Prosecution, Case 655, 2001)
Q: Where did you engage in these practices when you got into the habit?
A: When soft was possible we did it in the street or in cars or in a third-rate cinema or the toilets but when it was full penetration it was in a hotel or someone's house but nothing happened in my house though and most of these practices took place in 1996 because at that time I met someone by chance who could bring boys and he had a kind of hotel at the Pyramids and meetings took place there repeatedly and I took pictures of those boys there

Geographical categorizations sometimes acquire overtones of identity, ethnicity, or even nationality:

Excerpt 171 (High State Security Prosecution, Case 655, 2001)
Q: You mentioned earlier that you had alluded to your sexual perversion in your speech when you had the conversation with State Security and when did you start these practices
A: The beginning was at the time when I was studying at the German School in Duqqi and it only happened once with three of my friends and I didn't do it at school after that but at university so when I was studying in the Faculty of Engineering at Cairo University [I had] relations with people from the street so the first time it happened around 1983

Some categorizations are more of a legal nature:

Excerpt 172 (High State Security Prosecution, Case 655, 2001)
Q: And did you fully consent
A: Yes I accepted and I let him go ahead

Other categorizations appear as more straightforwardly moral:

Excerpt 173 (High State Security Prosecution, Case 655, 2001)
Q: How did these perverse practices take place
A: First I would like to say that I've repented and I will never commit this sin again because I realized that it was the reason for this problem and as for the way it was practiced sometimes I was active and sometimes passive

Last, in this non-exhaustive list, there are categorizations of a relational nature:

Excerpt 174 (High State Security Prosecution, Case 655, 2001)
Q: How did you meet him

A: I met a boy called ‘Id who I met by chance in Tahrir Square to have sex and I asked him if he knew a place so he took me to Nasir’s

People routinely use descriptions, categorizations and typifications in order to perform certain tasks like legally characterizing a set of facts. To say of someone that he indulges in sexual perversion means providing an anticipatory justification of his condemnation as debauched or licentious. From this point of view, the typification of perversity serves as an underlying scheme for the performance of an interpretation of facts purporting to give them a legal value.

Excerpt 175 (Summary Court of Misdemeanours (State of Emergency), Case 182/2001, Qasr al-Nil)

The responses of the first accused in the interrogation [...] are in substance what is consigned in the report dated [...], previously cited in detail. He added (1) that he had accompanied the officer to his domicile in ‘Ayn al-Sira and given him the keys of his apartment willingly, just as he gave him his photos, the personal notes, the books and all the things on the list [...]

(2) He had during his sleep a vision of the “Kurdish pageboy” [...]

(3) He practiced sexual perversion passively and actively (*ijaban*) with people, the majority [met] on the street and in public places like Tahrir Square, Ma‘mura Casino and cinemas. His most important practice dates back to the year 1996 and his last full (*kamila*) practice took place in 1998. Then, he limited himself to incomplete “soft” practices, the last one [...] being a mere frivolity (*‘abath*) [...] He was treating the perversion. His parents knew about that. The practice of perversion began when he was a student at the German School and intensified when he was studying engineering at Cairo University. He took pictures of anything that gave him feelings of danger. He began to take pictures of naked boys or sexual positions and he began to take pictures of himself with those he practiced sexual perversion with. He obtained sexual satisfaction when looking at these pictures. He took the decision to repent since his arrest in this case. The goal of his charity project was to cleanse himself of his sins (*takfir ‘an dhunubihi*) in matters of sexual perversion.

(4) He practiced sexual perversion with three of the people arrested, that is [...]

(5) Faced with the accused, he recognized the three aforementioned accused.

(6) Faced with the pictures, he declared that three pictures with [...] belonged to him.

Conversely, the suspect’s legal characterization as debauched makes it possible to fix the meaning of the underlying scheme of perversity.[1]

---

1 ‘The descriptions form part of a “gestalt contexture” built up around each case and not separable from it, in which background and foreground, context and particulars, mutually constitute one another.’ (Hester and Eglin, 1992: 221)

Excerpt 176 (Summary Court of Misdemeanours (State of Emergency), Case 182/2001, Qasr al-Nil)

The crime designated in [this text] is only committed when a man or a woman fornicates (*mubasharat al-fahsha'*) with people without distinction, habitually. When a woman fornicates and sells her virtue to whomever asks for it without distinction, she commits prostitution (*da'ara*) [...]; *fujur* occurs when a man sells his virtue to other men without distinction.

The General Prosecution has accused all the suspects of habitually practicing debauchery/prostitution (*fujur*). After having scrutinized the documents, the forensic reports, the photographs and what occurred during the sessions, the court is convinced that the accused [...] have committed the crime of habitual debauchery/prostitution, on the grounds of: [...]

The importance of categorization practices comes from the fact that the mobilization of a category orients participants to the interaction to the category's attributes and vice versa. Indeed, there is an inferential relation between membership categories and their predicates: one can deduce a membership category from the use of a predicate, as one can infer a certain number of rights, duties and consequences from the tying of someone or something to a category. In the Queen Boat case, for instance, it clearly appears that the activity of the masseur referred – at least in the way of a presumption that the accused was responsible for negating – to the categories "perverse"/"homosexual" and to the legal category circumstantially constituted as an equivalent, i.e., that of "debauched".

Excerpt 177 (Summary Court of Misdemeanours (State of Emergency), Case 182/2001, Qasr al-Nil)

(3) As for the 47th accused, the first accused testified against him during the investigation [by claiming] that he works as a masseur at the gym [...] (Initially, he gave him a normal massage, and afterwards said that he engaged in sexual activity with many men and women at the gym and that those who had experienced [it] wanted to continue. He asked the first accused whether he wanted sex and the first accused responded see what is good and do it. He masturbated the first accused on a regular basis during a period of approximately one month.) The 47th accused stated that the first accused came to the gym but had only one session, and he denied the charges.

As mentioned, the receiver of a categorial ascription, after having been categorized, is susceptible of being described in the moral terms bound to the category, without need for any additional evidence. Categorization processes can therefore be analysed as resources allowing people to situate, construct or foreground certain events, persons, groups or actions as being of a non-problematic nature (Stetson, 1999: 94) and, starting from the identification of a "problem", to give it a "solution". This naturally pertains to the activity of ruling itself, which aims at sanctioning the behaviour that is identified with a penal category.

Excerpt 178 (Summary Court of Misdemeanours (State of Emergency), Case 182/2001, Qasr al-Nil)

The court is convinced of the fact that the accused [...] committed the crime of habitual debauchery/prostitution. It is therefore necessary to condemn them to the [penalties stipulated by] articles 9c and 15 of Law 10/1961 on the practice of prostitution since they practiced habitual debauchery/prostitution in the aforementioned manner.

The same remark holds true for activities that took place prior to the court's decision, therefore anticipating this decision and giving it a prejudicial character. In the excerpt reproduced below, the suspects are accused of activities selected on the basis of a police report, which is also oriented toward the description of behaviours already defined as perverse. This pre-definition and the description of what is supposed to substantiate it make the "criminal" character of the activity obvious. Almost automatically, what was initially defined as perverse is transformed into a punishable action.

Excerpt 179 (High State Security Prosecution, Case 655, 2001)

Q: Just as the investigations indicated insofar as you are afflicted with sexual perversion you engage in these perverse sexual practices with those who are convinced of your thoughts and you rank them among the rituals of your faith

A: God preserve me and my He be satisfied with His delegate the person who said this about me put the ten yellow books attributed to me

Q: What is your response to what the investigations established that you and those who follow your beliefs used to hold wild parties in your homes and on certain boats like the tourist boat Queen Nariman anchored in front of the Marriott hotel in Cairo every Thursday night

A: These statements these things didn't occur and I don't know the boat

[...]

Q: You are accused of having defamed religion by propagating and encouraging extremist beliefs with the aim of denigrating and despising it and of provoking sedition

A: That never happened

Q: You are also accused of having practiced debauchery in the manner indicated in the investigation

One of the major properties of legal categories is to make explicit the inferential character of categorial linkages. Once the charges in the Queen Boat case are characterized as "debauchery", the penalty stipulated by Egyptian law is the necessary result. In this sense, the question, in legal terms, is not that of linking a characterization with its consequences, but that of the former categorial definition: that is, the assimilation of an action, a behaviour or even a situation to a legal definition endowed with precise consequences. As a result, if the 1961 law repressing prostitution and debauchery reduces the uncertainty that might hang over the penalty inflicted for acts of prostitution and debauchery, it leaves untouched the problem of what these two terms refer to. I mentioned Sudnow's work on "normal crimes" (cf. Chapter 6; Sudnow, 1987), i.e. the class of crimes and misdemeanours that are not defined legally but correspond to ways of characterizing and typifying behaviours encountered in the performance of routine activities or in everyday life. This class includes typifications of the modalities of incriminated behaviour, the people who practice it, the context of their performance, and their possible victims. If the crime is said to be "normal", it is because it is endowed with certain general features: it concerns types of behaviour rather than specific persons, its attributes are not legally codified, and its features are proper to a particular social group, socially shared, and ecologically specified.

Sudnow links the identification and repression of crimes of a "normal" type to the performance of routine professional practice. In the Queen Boat case, this probably holds true of the police in its ordinary activity of vice control, even though in Egypt until that point repressing homosexuality was not common practice. At least in this case, it seems that the normality of the crime is not limited to routine police activities but is linked upstream to the ordinary disqualification of exposed homosexual intercourse and the police decision to organize its repression. In that sense, the Queen Boat case constitutes the creation of a normal crime. It must be noted, however, that this creation does not proceed unilaterally, by criminalizing an activity (homosexuality) that was totally legal until then, but collaboratively: the parties do not clash with regard to whether homosexuality should be condemned,[2] but try to negotiate the degree of responsibility and possible excuses (at least as far as the accused is concerned).[3]

Excerpt 180 (High State Security Prosecution, Case 655, 2001)

Q: How did these perverse practices take place

A: First I would like to say that I've repented and I will never commit this sin again because I realized that it was the reason for this problem and as for the way it was practiced sometimes I was active and sometimes passive

Excerpt 181 (High State Security Prosecution, Case 655, 2001)

Q: Do you have anything else to say?

A: First I would like whoever reads this investigation to know that I've repented and decided not to return to perversion and I think God sent this trial because of that [...] and I ask God Almighty first to forgive me and for you to forgive me and I trust in His forgiveness and I beg Him to soften your hearts and cause you to help me repent so that I can be cured and not punished [...] and I hope you know that all human beings make

2 To the contrary, they collaborate to produce its categorization in terms of "perversion", law professionals asserting the criminal character of the behavior and the accused expressing their assent to this characterization while seeking to escape its detrimental consequences. This constitutes a concrete example of what J.N. Ferrié (2004) calls "negative solidarity".

3 This is not a trial about whether homosexuality can be criminalized or not, but a trial about whether X or Y practices homosexuality, having assumed that homosexuality is a criminalized practice.

mistakes and the best of those who err are those who repent and on Judgment Day and in the afterlife God will protect whoever protected a Muslim in this world and finally I would like to confess before God and then before you that I sinned by practicing sexual perversion but I haven't gone all the way since 1996 and I swear to God I'll never do it again

Lexical Choices and Categorial Co-selection, Connection and Transformation: An Inferential Grammar

In this collaborative production of homosexuality as debauchery, and in the negative solidarity around homosexuality as an activity deserving condemnation, a mechanism is operating to enable the co-selection of terms. This means that the understanding of a word does not operate in an isolated way, but with a choice of the words preceding or following it. For instance, the word "perversion" is understood conjunctively with the word "practice", which is the operator of an intentional action, or with the word "afflicted", which is the operator of a pathological ailment explaining aberrant practices. This co-selection determines the register in which an action is collaboratively situated – e.g. penal law – and therefore, consequently, the register in which it is possible for the parties to operate without any risk of discrepancy or disqualification. In this way, the defence can play credibly on the absence of participation in the incriminated facts or on the lack of responsibility.

In the Queen Boat case, the various parties, professional and profane, use a category with no legal standing: "perversion" (*shudhudh*), the contextual meaning and implication of which they collaboratively produce and negotiate. "Perversion" is a commonsense category endowed with features (place, time, culture, morality, role allocation, technique), which, far from functioning autonomously, are closely intertwined and morally and normatively loaded. The strength of the argument criminalizing perversion comes from its capacity to call tacitly upon "what-everybody-knows-about-homosexuality-and-need-not-be-detailed-here". The argument is simple: homosexuality is a perversion assimilated with debauchery.

Excerpt 182 (Summary court of Misdemeanors (State of Emergency), Case 182/2001, Qasr al-Nil)

The court based its conviction on the facts of the petition and has no doubt with regard to their veracity. Regarding what the court deduced from the examination of the documents and the investigations [...] as well as from the evidence submitted and what was related during the trial, [these facts] amount to what was consigned in the record [...]. This information reached [the Prosecution] from secret and reliable sources, confirmed by its careful investigations, which suffice [to show that the first accused] adopted deviant (*munharifa*) ideas inciting others to hold revealed religions in contempt (*izdira'*) and to call to abject (*radhila*) practices and sexual acts contrary to revealed laws. [...] He undertook to propagate these ideas among his acquaintances and those who are bound to him and to call them to adopt [those ideas]; he is affected by sexual perversion (*musab bi'l-shudhudh al-jinsi*) and practices it with people who are bound to him by considering

> [these practices] one of their rituals; he and his companions set about organizing decadent parties (*hafalat majina*) every Thursday in their homes or on boats, among them the tourist boat "Queen Nariman" [...] which many of his sexually perverse acquaintances attended [...] He photographed these sexual encounters, then developed and printed the pictures [...], having reached an agreement with the employees at the photography lab, that is [...]
> The court is convinced of the fact that the accused [...] committed the crime of habitual debauchery/prostitution. It is therefore necessary to condemn them to the [penalties stipulated by] articles 9c and 15 of Law 10/1961 on the practice of prostitution since they practiced habitual debauchery/prostitution in the aforementioned manner.
> The court indicates that, for the accused it condemned, it stipulated the penalty it considered to correspond to each of them according to the circumstances and the conditions of the request it examined, in the limits established by the law when it exists and according to what appears from the Court of Cassation's case-law [...]
> For these reasons
> The Court of Misdemeanors State Security (Emergency) decides:
> 1°) Five years' prison with hard labor for the first accused [...], effective immediately, for the two charges simultaneously, and police probation for a term of three years starting at the end of the prison sentence, in addition to expenses.

In our study of categorization mechanisms, it must be stressed that the game of inferences that opens linkages to some category functions through anticipation, allows the reflexive transformation of categorization if these functions do not materialize. We can take the example of a child. When he is taken to the dentist and does not cry, it might be said that "he's a big boy!" because his behaviour is associated with that of a "man", conventionally implying the exclusion of the activity of "crying". Since the child has ceased to perform a category-bound activity (e.g., crying) his categorization is opened to transformation (he has become a "man") (Jalbert, 1989: 238). Here again, law appears as the institutionalized form of this type of reasoning. Someone can be characterized as "debauched" because he practices activities characterized as sexual perversion, and these practices are proven by confession (duress in the extraction of confession must itself be eventually proved) or through medical expertise. In consequence, this person is condemned as a criminal to the penalty stipulated by the law for the type of misdemeanour to which his behaviour is assimilated. Evidence works here as a categorial connector. Indeed, it confirms the membership category or transforms it into another category, translating from the status of "presumed pervert" to the status of "pervert" or "innocent".

> **Excerpt 183 (Summary court of Misdemeanors (State of Emergency), Case 182/2001, Qasr al-Nil)**
> As for the rest of the accused [...], the court examined the documents with discernment and proper judgment and looked into the circumstances with the evidence [available]; it appeared that there was insufficient evidence to justify condemning these accused. The accused protected themselves by denying the charges at all the steps of the procedure.

> Nobody testified to the fact that they had committed the crimes of which they were accused, and none of them was caught red-handed. It was therefore necessary to [issue] a ruling clearing them of the charges [...] What appears in detail from the aforementioned investigation does not change anything since the investigation, the [accuracy] of which the court is convinced, would not hold water if it were based on simple presumption and not on evidence. Criminal rulings that condemn must be grounded on evidence and not only on presumption, as established by the Court of Cassation [...]

An important part of the activity of parties to a judicial case consists of acting on categorial connections and transformations, not only at the formal level of the bill of indictment or the ruling, but also at all the levels leading from the police investigation to the implementation of the judicial sentence. The description of facts, the choice of the applicable rule and the production of evidence are so many levels at which parties intervene collaboratively (although at the same time conflictually). As far as the professionals are concerned, the practical purpose of such collaboration is to produce a procedurally correct, legally relevant and adequate decision vis-à-vis the "normalcy" of the crime. For the laypeople, the practical purpose is to obtain the least harmful solution legally (a reduced penalty) as well as morally (attenuation of blame without contesting dominant categories). It generally operates, in the former case, through the production of some legal category that the ruling will tend to confirm and, in the latter case, through the search for the transformation of the category selected by the accusing party.

Within descriptive practices, a connection is sometimes created that is neither constitutive nor associative of categorized persons with the activity that was performed. Instead, it relates various categories through the creation of an affiliation between two activities perceived as similar enough to guarantee their linking (Jayyusi, 1984: 44sq.) This form of categorial transitivity occurs when activities ascribed to one category's members are transferred to another category whose members can be said to have activities that appear similar at first glance. For instance, when an observer perceives a man as having an "effeminate walk", this activity can cause the same observer to select the category "homosexual". The observer's stereotypical prejudice operates to link the man's activity with those perceived by the observer as bound to the category "homosexual", therefore assimilating the man in question to that category (Jalbert, 1989: 238). This is obviously the situation of the aforementioned accused in the Queen Boat case who practices the profession of masseur. The charges against him proceed from the sole testimony of the main accused, to the exclusion of any forensic report. Nevertheless, it is clear that the professional category to which he is attached binds him directly, by transitivity, to the category of sexual pervert and thus debauched (cf. above, excerpt 171).

Finally, I stress the existence of categorial reasoning grounding the recourse to forensic expertise and the use of its conclusions. In the background, there is the presumption that homosexual practice leaves physical marks. Suspects are thus referred to the forensic physician to confirm a presumption that is based (cf.

above, Chapter 11), for the majority of the accused, on suspicion (their frequenting of suspicious places or a police indicator's report) or on a mere contiguity effect (their presence at the place of the police roundup). In theory, the report confirms or invalidates the presumption, but in practice it works to confirm the presumption or to leave open the possibility of confirmation if the medical report is not conclusive. Categorial transitivity, which allows the forensic physician to associate physical symptoms with the passive practice of sodomy, does not function in both directions, since the absence of symptoms does not automatically transform the categorization of the accused.

Excerpt 184 (Forensic Medicine, Case 655, 2001)
Drawing on what precedes in our examination of the Prosecution's report and the former forensic report and from our re-examination of the accused Sharif Hasan Mursi Farahat, we state:
- that the aforementioned is an adult male of approximately 32 years, of ordinary build and muscular strength, and in ordinary health, devoid of the suspected wounds.
Following our local examination of his anal area, [it is clear that] he does not present the forensic marks of repeated homosexual penetration of the rear.
- that it is known that touching and external sexual contact do not leave marks that can be testified to upon examination.
- that it is also known that adult homosexual penetration, whether exceptionally or repeatedly, with the use of lubricants and appropriate positioning of the active (*al-fa'il*) and passive (*al-maf'ul bihi*) parties, leaves no marks that can be testified to on examination.

The Open Texture of Legal Categories

The Intertwined Nature of Legal Categorization Devices

The simultaneous and intertwined mobilization of two categorization devices can often be observed in the course of judicial activity and its specific categorizations. Drawing from another case than the Queen Boat, we can observe how the Egyptian press was concerned with the legitimacy of hymen reconstruction for a rape victim (cf. Chapter 2). Two categorization devices coexisted in the debate. One was organized around the notion of sexual honour, which implies the possibility for someone (generally a man, the protector of the family name) to be seriously affected in his dignity or even stained by the sexual situation of another person (generally a woman)[4] (Ferrié, 1998a: 133; Douglas, 1981). The other was organized around the notion of sexual morality, in which someone bears an individual responsibility for his/her own deliberate sexual behaviour due to external obligations (Ferrié, 1998:

4 In other words, sexual honour is the process whereby what A does to the body of B has an incidence on C because of his kinship with B.

135). In the former device, categorizations are independent from any voluntary act by the person whose honour has to be defended, whereas in the latter device, categorizations proceed from the linking of an individual's deliberate behaviour with the rules s/he must obey. A communiqué from the Mufti of the Republic makes it religiously legitimate for a woman's virginity to be restored if she lost it due to rape. The same surgery is deemed illegitimate when it aims at erasing the marks of the woman's deliberate behaviour. This introduces a clear distinction of status between women according to the use they make of their deliberate intention. Stain, however, is totally impervious to people's intentions.[5] Those who opposed hymenoplasty for a rape victim argued that the woman has to bear the stigma of the sexual relationships she has had so that her future husband cannot be cheated "on quality". A physician commented thus: 'If one gives a woman the right to recover her virginity, how shall we know if this membrane is artificial or not?'[6] These two categorization devices are closely intertwined: on one side, facts are considered independent of any human agency; on the other side, human agency is allowed to act to modify facts. While, in the device centered on honor, the loss of virginity outside legitimate wedlock affects the woman and depreciates her status, independent of any act of will on her part, in the moral device people are still allowed to act on their own body so as to change, erase or modify their condition, providing they are not taken as individually responsible for this situation.

Various categorization devices coexist and intermingle in the production of categorizations in the Queen Boat case, as we shall see below, especially when

5 Stain is the effect of something, like a homicide. Its occurrence is independent of any intention, like the intention to kill, and it demands reparation (Williams, 1993: 84).

6 The coexistence of two categorization devices is particularly obvious in the law. In Syria, for instance, the Criminal Code makes crimes of honour a distinct category with a lesser penalty. Moreover, legal practice indicates the judiciary is very tolerant of this kind of behaviour (Ghazzal, 1996). However, one must also consider the fact that Syrian law, though lenient, punishes honour killings as crimes that have their own justifications, while customary law can consider it a duty for people to kill those relatives who stain their kinship, though they may not bear any responsibility in what happened to them. Safia Mohsen gives the example of a young girl who was raped by her uncle and then killed by her brother. The latter maintained before the court that he was defending the honour of the family and of his sister (Mohsen, 1990: 22). These two devices, one centred on stain and the other centred on the intentional individual, influence each other. In Egypt, as in Syria, the law explicitly or implicitly recognizes the category of "crimes of honour" and gives it a different treatment according to whether a man or a woman is the offender. Article 237 of the Egyptian Penal Code states that a man who surprises his wife in the act of adultery and kills her and/or her partner is punishable by a maximum sentence of six months in prison instead of being sentenced to the legal punishment for wilful homicide. However, if it is the wife who surprises her husband in the act of adultery and kills him and/or his partner, there are no grounds for reduction of the sentence. It must be added that the provision of Article 237 does not apply if the husband himself has been convicted of adultery or if he has not acted in the heat of the moment (Mohsen, 1990).

the first accused refers to the pathological argument in the conclusion of his questioning by the Prosecution. For the time being, I want to stress, in the same excerpt, the association of the categories of human and divine justice.

> **Excerpt 185 (High State Security Prosecution, Case 655, 2001)**
> Q: Do you have anything else to say
> A: First I would like whoever reads this investigation to know that I've repented and decided not to return to perversion and I think God sent this trial because of that and during the time I spent in prison I thought about my life and I think humans shouldn't think about everything they want and shouldn't puff themselves up to excess [...] and I ask God Almighty first to forgive me and for you to forgive me and I trust in His forgiveness and I beg Him to soften your hearts and cause you to help me repent so that I can be cured and not punished [...] I hope you know that all human beings make mistakes and the best of those who err are those who repent and on Judgment Day and in the afterlife God will protect whoever protected a Muslim in this world and finally I would like to confess before God and then before you that I sinned by practicing sexual perversion but I haven't gone all the way since 1996 and I swear to God I'll never do it again [...] I beg you to help me lead a respectable life far from original sin and to follow the good I've received from God in a moderate, not an extremist manner [...] I ask God for forgiveness for He is the Merciful Forgiver

The repentance argument shifts the suspect's conclusion to the theme of religious morality, which is confirmed when he presents the trial as a test coming from God. Religious morality works here as the ultimate criterion for the evaluation of human action. Human justice, which is another categorization device the relevance of which imposes itself inexorably on the accused, proceeds from this superior authority: forgiveness belongs firstly to God, and secondly to the judges; pity belongs to God, so as to soften the judges' heart afterwards; mistakes must be confessed to God, and only after to the judges. The categorization device of human justice, on which many activities like investigating, imprisoning, caring, or punishing depend, is therefore embedded, in the suspect's discourse, as the continuation of the divine categorization system, if justice is dispensed in conformity with his expectations of clemency ('on Judgment Day and in the afterlife God will protect whoever protected a Muslim in this world'). The opposite situation is tantamount to negation of the same divine categorization device: to devastate the culprit means failing to protect the good Muslim and thus incurring God's anger. When the suspect says that 'all human beings make mistakes', we are meant to understand that the judge can also make mistakes, in his ruling among other things, and that his failure to repent would exclude him from the category of 'the best of those who err'. In this epilogue (but also formerly; cf. excerpt 174), the accused makes use of categorization devices that are different, though intertwined. The use of these devices corresponds not only to a semantic behaviour allowing him to express his worldview, but also and mainly to the practical finalities of action in which he is engaged, that is, his defence against the accusations formulated against him and thus the formulation of justifications, excuses, and mitigating circumstances.

The Moral, the Rational, and the Legal

The intrinsically categorial nature of law proceeds from the articulation of its moral and rational dimensions. Criminal law is grounded on two fundamental assumptions. On one hand, crimes are evil deeds. In that sense, criminal law is based on a value judgment and on the individual's capacity to exert this judgment. On the other hand, there is the assumption that those who are subject to the law are rational, that is, they have the capacity to understand the concept of crime, to know the law, to evaluate circumstances, to define their objectives, to identify the means that are at their disposal and, therefore, to adopt a behavior that avoids the sanctioned deed. In other words, the assumption is that a morally evil deed can only be ascribed to a reasonable being. Here we find two of the constitutive elements of crime, as defined by criminal jurisprudence (cf. Chapter 11).

As shown by Jayyusi, however, morality and rationality do not evolve in parallel, but are closely interdependent. In order to acknowledge the benefit of belonging to the human community, 'we are drawing the boundaries of rational membership through the use of a standard of moral membership.' (Jayyusi, 1984: 183) Causality and motivation constitute the centre of gravity of this intertwining of morality and rationality (cf. above, Chapters 9 and 10). This is why a deed characterized as deviant will be considered as pathological if it does not proceed from some rationally explicable motivation (e.g., the attraction of profit), then inducing the possibility of justification, whereas the identification of a rational cause will lead to its criminalization as a consequence. This flexibility of categories, in general, and of the pathological, in particular, can be observed in the Queen Boat case. In the conclusion of the questioning, the first accused constantly invokes his fault as a disease requiring a cure. This would spare him and his family the stain attached to criminal condemnation.

Excerpt 186 (High State Security Prosecution, Case 655, 2001)

Q: Do you have anything else to say

A: First I would like whoever reads this investigation to know that I've repented [...] and I ask God Almighty first to forgive me and for you to forgive me and I trust in His forgiveness and I beg Him to soften your hearts and cause you to help me repent so that I can be cured and not punished [...] and if you punish me my life will be over and so will my family's life as well as all those who care about me [...] and I beg you to help me lead a respectable life far from original sin and to follow the good I've received from God in a moderate not an extremist manner [...] as I said cure me and don't punish me

In his verdict, the judge considers that the first accused – as well many other suspects – performed specific sexual deeds with full knowledge of the facts. It remains to be seen how the accused was supposed to know the interpretation given by the Court of Cassation, in a non-published ruling, to legal provisions whose formulation is not explicit (there is no text explicitly condemning homosexuality in Egyptian law). Establishing criminal intention is possible only if legality is situated in the field of normality and common sense, that is, if the criminalization of homosexuality refers to something evident whose explicit legal formulation is not a necessity, because its assimilation to debauchery imposes itself in an apodictic manner, morally as well as factually and legally. This is why the judge draws on a report presented by the Senate in 1951 in support of a draft law on the repression of prostitution and a 1988 ruling of the Court of Cassation, according to which 'jurisprudence customarily used the word *da'ara* to [designate] female prostitution (*bagha' al-untha*) and the word *fujur* to [designate] male prostitution (*bagha' al-rajul*).' On this basis, the judge seeks to demonstrate that the law of 1961 is applicable to homosexuality.

Excerpt 187 (Summary court of Misdemeanors (State of Emergency), Case 182/2001, Qasr al-Nil)

The crime designated in [this text] is only committed when a man or a woman fornicates (*mubasharat al-fahsha'*) with people without distinction, habitually. When a woman fornicates and sells her virtue to whomever asks for it without distinction, she commits prostitution (*da'ara*) [...]; *fujur* occurs when a man sells his virtue to other men without distinction.

The General Prosecution has accused all the suspects of habitually practicing debauchery/prostitution (*fujur*). After having scrutinized the documents, the forensic reports, the photographs and what occurred during the sessions, the court is convinced that the accused [...] have committed the crime of habitual debauchery/prostitution, on the grounds of: [...]

(1) As for the first accused, as well as the 34th, the 35th, the 36th and the 37th, their explicit statements during the aforementioned investigation by the Prosecution revealed that they perpetrated the crime of which they are accused. In addition, the first accused stated that he practiced sexual perversion with the 36th accused and both stated that they have compromising (*fadiha*) photographs in their possession.

All this underscores the open texture of legal rules, in the sense that the concrete circumstances of concrete cases give rules their local and punctual meaning. In the background of this circumstantial setting down of the rule's significance, one must stress all the ordinary mores and usages toward which people orient in order to ground their conception of the normal and the natural. This reliance on commonsense procedures, shared practices and ordinary knowledge is organized around categorization processes. 'In describing persons, their actions, their motives, reasons, obligations, knowledge and the like, we build our accounts in accordance with substantive and formal features of a cultural grammar of possibilities.' (Hester and Eglin, 1993: 84) These assumptions of criminal law about mores and usages make it available as a device to draw borders of social membership for any particular person in cases that are always particular.

Categorization Pairs

The "Pervert" and "Society": A Relational Categorization Pair

In any criminal trial, a whole series of standardized relational pairs are present: offender-victim, accused-judge, prosecutor-witness. Criminal law, in the civil-law family, has an important specificity, however: the person who is physically the victim is not a party to the trial, because the harm is deemed to be done to society, which is represented by the General Prosecution. In the Queen Boat case, indeed, there is no "victim" other than society, in the conception of public order and good manners that is put forward. The relational pair that comes first in the categorization device of this case links "perverts" and "society", although the latter only appears by default and is embodied by "law and order officials". The various parties select words in a process articulated around this categorization pairing. Terms are coherent for each other. 'Certain categories are routinely recognized as paired categories, and [this] pairing is recognized to incorporate standardized relationships of rights, obligations and expectations.' (Payne, 1976: 36) Each member of the pair implies the other so that the mention of one makes the other relevant. In a criminal trial, to speak of the "offender" invites us to look for the "society" to which some evil was done.

Moreover, the attributes specific to each element of the pair are also paired: "to harm" is predicated to the "offender", while "being a victim" of this offence is predicated to "society". "To be arrested" is predicated to the "offender", while "being protected" is predicated to "society". To say that someone "he was arrested" implies that "representatives of the social order" did so, and this in turn implies that the person belongs to the category of "offender". To say that someone is "sexually depraved" implies that he breached "the social order", which in turn implies that he belongs to the legal category of "perverts".

The many activities linked to the different categorization pairs are also linked to each other: "arresting", "interrogating", "accusing", "judging", which are activities linked to the category "law and order officials", are paired with, respectively, "committing a crime", "breaching public order", and "acting against morality" – activities linked to the category of "perverts". The invocation of one of these activities confirms the identity of the other element of the pair and the sense of its activity. To speak of "practicing debauchery" immediately suggests that the practitioner is an "offender", because it goes without saying that debauchery constitutes a "breach of the social order" which must be protected by "representatives", i.e., the "law and order officials". The "representatives of social order" will protect it by suing "offenders". The "offence" therefore becomes the cause of the action taken by "law and order representatives". Hester and Eglin (1993: 127) speak of a "motivational attribute". In the Queen Boat case, the law professionals can identify the "breach of social order" constituted by homosexuality as the motivational attribute of the accusation formulated by the police and the Prosecution or of the condemnation issued by the judge.

"Debauchery" and "Insanity:" A Disjunctive Categorization Pair

In his praxeological exploration of cognition, Coulter (1979) shows that it is possible to speak of the categories "belief" and "knowledge" as a disjunctive categorization pair. Other pairs of the same type would be vision/hallucination, ghost/optical illusion or ideology/science, moderate/extremist, and resistant/terrorist. When one of the two constitutive parts of such a pair is called upon to characterize a phenomenon seriously, 'the speaker's belief-commitment may be inferred, and the structure of subsequent discourse may be managed in terms provided for by the programmatic relevance of the disjunctive category-pair relationship.' (Coulter, 1979: 181) So, for the non-believer, Joan of Arc suffered from hallucinations, whereas these are divine visions for the believer; on the Palestinian street, a Hamas activist is a resistance fighter, but a terrorist according to the Israeli government spokesman. Disjunctive categorization pairs often operate by selecting the categorization in which the categorized person does not recognize him or herself (for instance, calling the Hamas candidate for a suicide attack a "terrorist"). The praxeological upshot of the use of this type of non-self-avowable category is the depreciation of these persons, collectivities or activities through the presentation to the receiving third party of a first preferential and non-critical reading (Jalbert, 1989: 240).

The categorization device of criminal liability is largely organized around disjunctive pairs. This is the case, for instance, of the pair "capable of distinction/ lacking the capacity of distinction". The selection of one part of the pair over the other has such implications that subsequent discourse can be inferred and managed accordingly. Each of the parts of this categorization pair conveys a sum of conventional assumptions like "capable of distinction – legally capable – intentional – criminal intention" or "lacking the capacity of distinction – legally incapable – unconscious – legally irresponsible". Thus, category selection is not only descriptive, but presupposes opposite belief affiliations, with clear epistemic consequences.

As a pair, "debauchery/insanity" belongs to these disjunctive categories. In a case of sex change, the identification of some pathological cause in the request for a sex change organized the whole debate about whether or not the surgery was legitimate.

In 1982, Sayyid 'Abd Allah, a medical student at al-Azhar University who claimed to be suffering from severe depression, consulted a psychologist. After examining him, the psychologist concluded that the young man's sexual identity was disturbed. After three years of treatment, she referred him to a surgeon so that he might undergo a sex change operation. The operation, performed on 29 January 1988, had many administrative and legal consequences for the patient. First, the dean of al-Azhar University's Faculty of Medicine refused to allow Sayyid (who in the meantime had changed her name to Sally) to sit her examinations and also refused to transfer her to the Faculty of Medicine for Women. In her effort to obtain such a transfer, Sayyid/Sally submitted a request for a name change to the Civil Status Administration Office. Al-Azhar University maintained that Sayyid/Sally had committed a crime. According to the university, the surgeon who performed the operation had not changed his sex but had mutilated him for the purpose of allowing Sally to engage in legitimate homosexual relations. Meanwhile, the representative of the Giza Doctors Syndicate summoned the two doctors who had performed the operation before a medical board. The board ruled that the doctors had made a serious professional error by failing to establish the existence of a pathological condition prior to the surgery. On 14 May 1988, the Doctors' Syndicate sent a letter to the Mufti of the Republic, Sayyid Tantawi, asking him to issue a fatwa on the matter. In a fatwa issued on 8 June, Tantawi concluded that if the doctor demonstrated that surgery was the only cure for the pathological condition, the treatment should be authorized. However, a sex change operation cannot be performed solely because of an individual's desire to change his/her sex. Tantawi was not clear as to whether or not the "psychological hermaphroditism" from which Sayyid/Sally suffered constituted an acceptable medical cause. Thus, each side claimed that the fatwa supported its position. On 12 June, al-Azhar brought the matter before the courts, claiming that the surgeon had to be punished for inflicting permanent injury upon his patient, in compliance with Article 240 of the Penal code. At this point, the Attorney General and his deputy public prosecutor decided to examine the case. They referred it to a medical expert, who concluded that, from a physical point of view, Sayyid had been born a male, but that, from a psychological point of view, he was not a male. Thus the diagnosis of psychological hermaphroditism was relevant and surgery was the proper treatment. According to the report, the surgeon had followed the rules of his profession, since he had consulted the competent specialists, had performed the operation correctly, and had not inflicted a permanent physical disability on the patient (Niyaba 1991). The patient could thus be considered a woman. The Doctors' Syndicate rejected the expert's conclusions and organized a press conference in which it made the issue a question of public concern that required a moral and social choice. On this basis, the Syndicate decided to remove the surgeon from its membership list and to impose a fine on the anesthesiologist for his participation in the surgery. On 29 December, the Attorney General decided not to pursue the charge. The final report confirms that the operation was carried out according to the appropriate regulations. One year later, the file was closed and, in November 1989, Sally received a certificate establishing her status as a female. In view of the continuing refusal of al-Azhar to admit her into the Faculty of Medicine for Women, she submitted another claim to the Council of State, which, one year later, nullified al-Azhar's decision and authorized Sally to register at whatever university she wished in order to complete her final exams. The case did not end with this ruling. In September 1999, the Cairo Administrative Court issued another ruling, which recognized that Sally had taken all the necessary legal measures to register at al-Azhar University. The court therefore ordered the university to admit her to the Faculty of Medicine for Women (al-Hayat, 30 September 1999; Court of Administrative Justice, Case 4019/50, 1st circuit, 28 September 1999). On November 14, 1999, al-Azhar filed an appeal against the administrative court decision, charging that Sally did not meet its moral and ethical standards (according to the court, al-Azhar held that belly dancing 'is contrary to the provisions of Islamic shari'a' and 'contradicts the conduct which must be adopted by someone who belongs to one of the faculties for women depending on al-Azhar University, which is singular in that it strictly imposes a specific conduct which may not be trespassed'; Court of Administrative Justice, Case 1487/54, 20 June 2000) in view of the fact that 'she performs as a belly dancer in night clubs and has been arrested several times on vice charges.' (Middle East Times, 18-24 November 1999) The same Administrative Court issued a ruling, on 20 June 2000, suspending the implementation of the September 1999 ruling, on the grounds that new evidence had been produced (interviews with newspapers, including photographs of Sally dressed as a belly dancer), which was not in keeping with the conduct required of a woman belonging to this Faculty. Accordingly, the Court transferred the case to the State Litigation Office for further inquiry (Court of Administrative Justice, Case 1487/54, 20 June 2000).

In this case, those who sued the transsexual and her doctors argued that Sayyid/ Sally had made an unjustified request for mutilation, which the doctors had fulfilled. The Public Prosecution summarized their position as follows:

Excerpt 188 (Report of the General Prosecution, Case 21, 1988)

[The student registered at the University] was male and only male. He had no internal or external female reproductive organ, but underwent surgery that led to the suppression of his male reproductive organs and to the creation of an artificial orifice slightly behind (*khalf*) the external urinary orifice. As a consequence of this surgery, the student in question became a male lacking his external reproductive organs, so that the diagnosis of the physician [...] establishing his psychological hermaphroditism totally contradicted the committee's report and the examination of the student. The surgery performed on the student was not related to any organic medical requirement; to the contrary, instead of this surgery, psychological therapy should have been implemented and the course of female hormones terminated. Al-Azhar's report concludes by claiming that this constitutes a serious professional mistake on the part of the physician [...] and that, because of his defective intention, what he dared to undertake constitutes battery leading to permanent incapacity.

On the other side of the debate, the Public Prosecution and its representative could accept the sex-change surgery, not on the basis of the concerned person's free will and consent, but through the identification of some pathology, namely psychological hermaphroditism. As soon as this pathology was identified, the surgeons' therapeutic intention was presumed and the surgery could be considered licit.

Excerpt 189 (Report of the General Prosecution, Case 21, 1988)

We recommend concluding to the legality of these change-sex surgeries, since they correspond to bodily or psychological medical necessities, provided the transformation is performed with the patient's consent; [provided] the latter is an adult, not previously married, not having (in the future) the capacity of giving birth; and [provided] he presented his request to the competent government authority, which will examine its validity. If convinced of the validity of these justifications,

> the competent authority will refer the request to one of the competent governmental psychological institutions, for a term of at least two years, under the supervision of a team of psychiatrists, psychotherapists, specialists in social problems, plastic surgeons, urologists, and gynecologists. If, at the end of this term, they conclude that the patient effectively suffers from psychological hermaphroditism, that he presents the symptoms of dementia and that he will not make any profit from this surgical intervention, these surgeries are legal.

Condemning certain people to criminal penalties or on the contrary excusing them and allowing them therapeutic treatment depends on the former categorization of their “deviance” in terms of amorality or biological abnormality, that is, in other words, in terms of morality or nature. This categorization is nothing if not contradictory. Thus, al-Azhar University or the Doctors’ Syndicate might consider Sally alternatively as “a-man-seeking-to-illegitimately-frequent-women”, “a-man-seeking-to-engage-in-deviant-behaviour-with-other-men”, or “a-man-sexually-mutilated-for-non-therapeutic-purposes”. In the Queen Boat case, as we saw, the first accused failed to invoke the pathologic character of his homosexuality, instead presenting it as a given that escaped his control and caused him suffering. He wished for a cure, but argued that he could not be held responsible for being homosexual (cf. above, excerpts 175, 179, 180). All the legal institutions (police, Public Prosecution, and judge), in contrast, were keen to describe the suspect’s behaviour in terms of “satisfying perverse desires”.

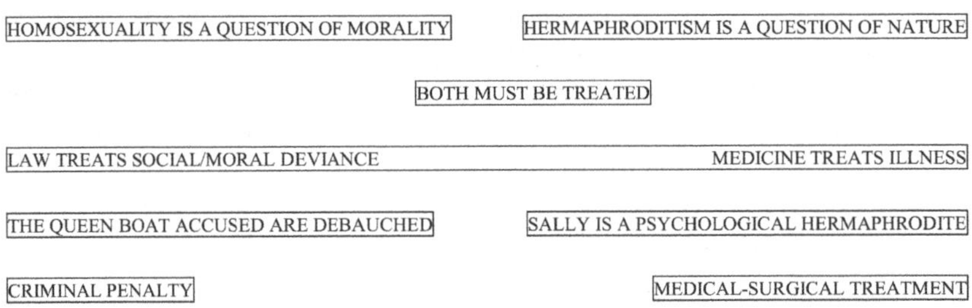

Figure 13.1 Disjunctive pairs

When comparing the treatment of transsexualism in the Sally case and of homosexuality in the Queen Boat case, it is easy to show that the management of sexuality is judicially organized, in Egypt, around the disjunctive categorization pair opposing “morality” and “nature”.[7]

---

7 On the topic of granting political asylum to Cuban refugees, contrasted with the deportation of Haitian refugees in the US in the 1980s, Jalbert (1989: 242) shows the existence and the functioning of a disjunctive categorization pair opposing “economic” and “political” refugees.

'Normal' and 'Aberrant': An Antithetic Categorization Pair

Beside relational pairs and particular cases like disjunctive (cf. above) and asymmetrical pairs (cf. Chapter 2; Jayyusi, 1984), there are antithetic relational pairs that unify a thesis and its antithesis in a single categorization device.

In the Queen Boat case, such a standardized antithetic pair exists in the categorization device "sexual relationships", which brings together "heterosexual" and "homosexual" relationships. The first part of the pair, i.e. "heterosexual relationships", can itself host another antithetic pair, that is, "legitimate" and "illegitimate" heterosexual relationships. However, the second part of the pair, i.e. "homosexual relationships", cannot host any other antithetic pair (e.g. "legitimate" and "illegitimate" homosexual relationships) since there is no recognition of homosexual marriage in Egypt.

Through the identification of these antithetic pairs one can locate the articulation point and flaw in the reasoning followed by the Office of International Co-operation of the Office of the Prosecutor General in a document seeking to justify the Egyptian judicial authorities' attitude against criticism addressed to them from all over the world.

> **Excerpt 190 (General Prosecution, Memorandum Concerning the Apprehension and Trial of 52 Men on Charges of Contempt of Religion and Male Promiscuity)**
>
> [Article 9 (c) of Law 10/1961] criminalizes the material conduct of habitual promiscuity with consent whether perpetrated by a male or a female and without any bearing whatsoever on sexual orientation. Whoever intentionally engages the material conduct described above therefore falls within the ambit of this crime.

Indeed, the argumentation of Ahmed Zohny, the prosecutor who signed the document, is the following: (1) the law of 1961 condemns consenting sexual practice outside wedlock; (2) this law concerns women as well as men; (3) there is therefore no discrimination on the basis of gender or sexual orientation. Using the tool constituted by the categorization analysis of antithetic pairs, we can observe the existence of such a pair "consenting sexual practice within wedlock"/"consenting sexual practice outside wedlock," or in other words – because of the 1961 law prohibiting extramarital sexual relations – the antithetic pair "legitimate sexuality"/"illegitimate sexuality". The prosecutor's argument consists in saying that sexuality is illegitimate because it takes place outside the legal framework of marriage, not because it is homosexual. However, these categorizations operate only at a subsequent level. Formerly, the antithetic pair "heterosexual relationships"/"homosexual relationships" operates, and it is only the first part of this pair, i.e. "heterosexual relationships", that legally authorizes the activity that is bound to it and reflexively legitimates it, that is, "marriage". In other words, it is indeed because they are homosexual that certain sexual relationships are prohibited, because they do not open the right to marriage that solely legitimates sexual relationships. Consequently, the prohibition depends first on the partners' sexual orientation. The category "homosexual relationships" does not open the possibility of a subsequent antithetic pair "legitimate relationships"/"illegitimate relationships", because it constitutes, in the categorization device of sexual relationships, the antithesis "aberrant relationships" of the thesis "normal/natural relationships".[8]

Antithetic pairs are endowed with a number of particular properties. Among them, we notice first that the distribution of rights and duties specific to each of the two parts operates in a way that is neither asymmetrical nor disjunctive, but inverted. If the first part of the antithetic pair "heterosexual relationships"/"homosexual relationships" permits marriage, the second part excludes it. If the first part of the antithetic pair "legitimate sexual relationships"/"illegitimate sexual relationships" permits the procreation of "legitimate children", the second part implies the procreation of "bastards". It is moreover a standardized relational pair that constitutes the border between the two parts of an antithetic pair. Thus, the relational pair "man/woman" constitutes the border of the antithetic pair "heterosexual relationships/homosexual relationships". In the same manner, the relational pair "spouse/spouse" constitutes the border of the antithetic pair "legitimate sexual relationships/illegitimate sexual relationships". In that sense, it is the standardized relational pair "man/woman" that draws the border of the antithetic pair "heterosexual relationships/homosexual relationships", which in turn draws the border of the disjunctive pairs "natural/pathological" and "normal/deviant".

Categorizations and Sequentiality

The mobilization of categorization devices operates on a contextual, circumstantial, local, and time-bound basis. Therefore, the institutional and sequential positioning of the parties concerned exerts a direct influence on the categorizations they will produce. We already saw how the parties in charge of investigation, prosecution, and adjudication manifest a tendency to construct legally the moral condemnation of sexual behaviour. The incriminated parties, on their side, produce what J.N. Ferrié calls negative solidarity: they first acknowledge the norm and its constraining character and then seek to justify the discrepancy between that norm and the misdemeanour committed.[9]

8 The counter-argument to the Prosecutor's reasoning is therefore the following: (1) since sexual relationships outside wedlock are prohibited; (2) and since the law does not recognize homosexual marriage; (3) there is indeed a discrimination on the basis of sexual orientation when condemning sexual relationships that are excluded from any legal framework.

9 In rape cases, it generally consists for the accused in the acknowledgement of having had sexual intercourse while claiming that the woman was willing or even that the

The sequential structure of categorization performances deserves attention. In various articles, Watson shows how, in an often discrete or even surreptitious way, the study of the sequential dimension of conversational interactions has resorted to membership categorizations as an analytical resource (Watson, 1994; 1997). Such is the case with my own analysis, which systematically reproduced the Prosecution's investigations preceding each turn by the mention Q (for question) and A (for answer), following in this the original Arabic texts using the letters *sin* (for *su'al*) and *gim* (for *gawab*). Through the use of these letters, we rendered the categorization work of the Prosecution's clerk – for it was he, and not the parties to the interview, who provided all the participants with their membership category (the letter Q referring to the deputy prosecutor, who is the only one entitled to ask questions, and the letter A referring to the person interviewed, who is required to answer the questions without asking any him/herself). These letters, which provide a sense of the sequentiality specific to the interview, can be studied as categorization terms and, in particular, as adjacent relational pairs (and not only as the evidence of the pre-allocated character of turns in institutional context). In fact, this technique of transcription of categorial incumbencies belongs to the textual practices that seek to make institutional discourse visible and readable as such (Watson, 1997: 52). What emerges most clearly from this technique are the intertwined nature of categorizing operations (like being the deputy prosecutor or the witness) and the sequential organization of interactions (like the linking of questions and answers). Categorizing a speaker as "deputy prosecutor" and an addressee as "witness" can help give meaning to their speech as constitutive of a "judicial investigation". In the same way, the features of a sequence (how it is constituted and placed, what it performs) make it possible to identify that sequence as category-bound, i.e. conventionally identifiable as an investigation sequence pairing a deputy prosecutor with a witness. Independently of the letters assigned to each turn, the interview continuously provides the means of categorial and sequential identification necessary to its "normal" accomplishment, i.e. its accomplishment according to what any competent member of society expects from an interaction within the law courts between a magistrate and a witness. Categorization and sequentiality together point towards the underlying scheme of the interview, which simultaneously serves as a documentary means of considering the various turns as questions and answers situated in the framework of a judicial investigation.

Watson's work on membership categories and their sequentiality is situated mainly at an intra-conversational level, that is a level circumscribed by a sequence the parameters (participants, place, moment) of which are available within one single set of turns. It is however possible to give sequentiality a broader meaning that resituates a succession of turns within the course of a larger process like a judicial procedure in its entirety. This second way of considering the judicial

rape took place at the woman's initiative (cf. Matoesian, 1993, 1995, 1997, 2001; Drew, 1992; cf. also Mozère, 2002, and Ans, 2003).

sequence has direct implications on the categorization work of the many parties to the procedure. In the Queen Boat case, the categorizations operating in the documents are distributed differently according to the time and the document in which they appear. By way of illustration, one can list in the form of short excerpts the different steps of the chronological and procedural sequence of their production:

– Police record:

Excerpt 191 (Police, Record, 25 May 2001)

Information from our secret and reliable sources was given and our careful secret investigations confirmed it. […], living in […], adopted some deviant ideas inciting to the contempt of revealed religions and to the call to abject (*radhila*) practices and to sexual acts contrary to revealed laws […]

Information and investigations also showed that […] is affected by sexual perversion (*shudhudh jinsi*) and practices some sexual acts with people who are bound to him and adopted the same thoughts, considering these acts as one of the rituals [aiming] at infringing revealed laws. [These rituals], according to their erroneous convictions, led him and his associates to organize wild parties in their homes or on boats, among them the tourist boat "Queen Nariman", anchored in front of the Marriott Hotel. Many acquaintances of the abovementioned sexually perverse people attended, every Thursday evening […]

– Prosecution record:

Excerpt 192 (High State Security Prosecution, Case 655, 2001)

Q: What happened then

A: […] I also told him that I engaged in perverse sexual practices that had happened suddenly when I was at the German School and had increased when I was at the Faculty of Engineering at Cairo University and I explained to him that I tried to repent especially after going on *'umra* three times and I took pictures of naked boys in sexual positions and I took pictures of myself with the ones I had these sexual practices with and I enjoy looking at these pictures like just about any young man of my age who has this type of conversation […]

Q: Just as the investigations indicated insofar as you are afflicted with sexual perversion you engage in these perverse sexual practices with those who are convinced of your thoughts and you rank them among the rituals of your faith

A: God preserve me and my He be satisfied with His delegate the person who said this about me put the ten yellow books attributed to me

Q: What is your response to what the investigations established that you and those who follow your beliefs used to hold wild parties in your homes and on certain boats like the tourist boat Queen Nariman anchored in front of the Marriott hotel in Cairo every Thursday night

A: These statements these things didn't occur and I don't know the boat

– Ruling

Excerpt 193 (Summary court of Misdemeanors (State of Emergency), Case 182/2001, Qasr al-Nil)

The court based its conviction on the facts of the petition and has no doubt with regard to their veracity. Regarding what the court deduced from the examination of the documents and the investigations [...] as well as from the evidence submitted and what was related during the trial, [these facts] amount to what was consigned in the record [...]. This information reached [the Prosecution] from secret and reliable sources, confirmed by its careful investigations, which suffice [to show that the first accused] adopted deviant (*munharifa*) ideas inciting others to hold revealed religions in contempt (*izdira'*) and to call to abject (*radhila*) practices and sexual acts contrary to revealed laws. [...] He undertook to propagate these ideas among his acquaintances and those who are bound to him and to call them to adopt [those ideas]; he is affected by sexual perversion (*musab bi'l-shudhudh al-jinsi*) and practices it with people who are bound to him by considering [these practices] one of their rituals; he and his companions set about organizing decadent parties (*hafalat majina*) every Thursday in their homes or on boats, among them the tourist boat "Queen Nariman" [...] which many of his sexually perverse acquaintances attended [...] He photographed these sexual encounters, then developed and printed the pictures [...], having reached an agreement with the employees at the photography lab, that is [...] The crime designated in [the 1961 law] is only committed when a man or a woman fornicates (*mubasharat al-fahsha'*) with people without distinction, habitually. When a woman fornicates and sells her virtue to whomever asks for it without distinction, she commits prostitution (*da'ara*) [...]; *fujur* occurs when a man sells his virtue to other men without distinction.

The General Prosecution has accused all the suspects of habitually practicing debauchery/ prostitution (*fujur*). After having scrutinized the documents, the forensic reports, the photographs and what occurred during the sessions, the court is convinced that the accused [...] have committed the crime of habitual debauchery/prostitution, on the grounds of: [...]

(1) As for the first accused, as well as the 34th, the 35th, the 36th and the 37th, their explicit statements during the aforementioned investigation by the Prosecution revealed that they perpetrated the crime of which they are accused. In addition, the first accused stated that he practiced sexual perversion with the 36th accused and both stated that they have compromising (*fadiha*) photographs in their possession.

For these reasons

The Court of Misdemeanors State Security (Emergency) decides:

1°) Five years' prison with hard labor for the first accused [...], effective immediately, for the two charges simultaneously, and placement under police control for a term of three years starting at the end of the prison sentence, in addition to expenses.

These various speeches and documents, which all belong to the same material entity, i.e. the file of the Queen Boat case, can be read in the perspective suggested by Ivan Leudar and Jiří Nekvapil, 'as collaborative "turns" in a developing dialogical network.' (Nekvapil and Leudar, 2003: 62) This notion of dialogical network (Leudar, 1995, 1998; Leudar and Nekvapil, 1998; Nekvapil and Leudar, 1998, 2002; Leudar, Marsland, Nekvapil, 2004) seeks to show that media events like TV and radio programs, press conferences and newspaper articles function in a network, meaning that they are interactively, thematically and argumentatively connected, even though this dialogical interconnection is distributed in time and space.

This idea of a dialogical network allows us to observe the particular configuration of the judicial sequence in its entirety. In the judicial context, the composition and organization of the dialogical network are constrained by the institutional framework in which it is embedded. Therefore, the importance of the dialogical network constituted by the whole judicial file depends on legal and procedural complexity, the number of parties concerned, and the solicitation of expertise (medical or otherwise). However, it does not depend on the spontaneous involvement of people in an ongoing social debate, unless we extend it to media coverage of the case – which might be justified in particular cases. It must be stressed that the dialogical network constituted by the judicial file does not constitute any notion imposed from outside, through the analyst's sociological imagination, on social phenomena that do not proceed from it in any way; rather, it is a phenomenological, social, legal and judicial unit toward which the various protagonists explicitly orient at every step of their activity in relation to that file.

We can first observe the thematic cohesion of the many documents constituting the file of the Queen Boat case. This cohesion is made of shared statements, re-use of arguments, and sequential structures. We find the features of the face-to-face conversation, but with time deferred from one turn to another, which allows different documents (possibly originating from different people and partly contradictory) to play the role of the second part in an adjacent pair. Thus, for instance, to the question asked by the magistrate, at a time v, with regard to the suspect's passive practice of sodomy, an answer is formulated, at a time w, by the forensic report, which concludes to the inexistence of any mark testifying to that practice (while adding that the lack of evidence does not equate to the lack of practice) and, at a time x, by the suspect's testimony admitting to that practice several years ago. All this leads the judge, at a time z, to consider the facts constitutive of debauchery as established, grounding his decision on his inner conviction and despite the retraction of the confession, at a time y.

The legal file also functions in an intertextual way (cf. Chapter 7). At several points, the participants to a judicial interaction orient toward two different audiences, one present and the other virtual (Livet, 1994). In the conclusion of the interview, when he asks God and the judge for their pity and forgiveness, the first accused addresses the deputy prosecutor as well as the judicial authorities that will judge him afterwards. The intertextuality of the many documents in a dialogical network shows how the authors of these documents formulate them in a constantly evolutionary manner, as the case unfolds and the file is constituted. For instance, the Prosecution's interview bases itself on the police record, but aims at establishing a foundation on which the judge will later on ground his decision, which includes, as we saw (cf. Chapter 11), direct or indirect references to the former stages of the trial. If the trial exerts any impact on its protagonists and more broadly on society, it is through the production of documents providing argumentative resources that will be used at further procedural and media stages and times. The notion of a dialogical network shows how this use can be considered prospectively, in the projection on later stages at each moment of the procedure's course, and retrospectively, in the support given by former documents to every ongoing activity.

The relevance of the idea of a dialogical network to the constitution and unfolding of the judicial file as a material unit comprising the many activities that lead from the police investigation to the successive rulings and their implementation can be observed in the permanence and evolution of the terms used to characterize the incriminated behaviours. Categorizations, far from being understood in a frozen manner (a purely semantic approach), function in sequential dynamics that must be accounted for. This is how the expression "sexual perversion" (*shudhudh jinsi*) passes through the whole judicial sequence, from the police record (cf. excerpt 191) to the ruling of the State Security Court (cf. excerpt 193), via the Prosecution's interview (cf. excerpt 192). However, the characterization of the incriminated action changes along the way: whereas the reprehensible character of homosexuality, presented as sexual perversion, was absolutely obvious in the police and Prosecution documents, its legally problematic character (Egyptian law does not explicitly prohibit homosexual behaviour), pointed out by the defence and by human rights organizations, brought about the transformation of its wording, which became the "habitual practice of debauchery" (*mumarasat al-fujur*), an expression that first appeared at the end of the Prosecution's interview, when the deputy prosecutor spelled out the accusation (cf. excerpt 179). Consequently, categorizations, far from proceeding from formal semantics, are sensitive to the context of their formulation, which is necessarily situated in space and time. However, this time is not instantaneous but sequential, made of a before and providing the basis for an after, an actualization in the present and a projection in the future. This is strengthened by the fact that the categorization observed belongs explicitly to a dialogical unit, i.e. a legal case and its file.

Implicitness, Ambiguity, and Implication

In the study of common beliefs, we must analytically develop the notion of presupposition. As Coulter (1979: 167) points out, 'members display and assign beliefs to each other in virtue of the occasioned production and understanding of utterances analysable for what they presuppose.' Categorization devices largely lean on these tacit meanings, which take form and substance only when mobilized. As I said before, predicates ascribed to people, situations, activities and collectivities are not simply denotative and descriptive; they are also connotative in the sense that they associate the categorized person, situation, activity or collectivity with a set of features made available by the mere fact of their categorization. The selection of the relevant category, the identification of the categorization device on which they depend and the tying-up of the features, rights and duties that can be associated to it is mainly performed in a tacitly understood manner.

Let us return to the issue of sexuality that focused our attention throughout this study. Legal professionals involved in the Queen Boat case sought to define neither sex nor gender, but rather the concept of sexual relationships for all legal practical purposes in the specific context of a homosexuality trial. This definition operates on the basis of the underlying scheme of sexual-relationships-as-an-activity-binding-a-man-and-a-woman-within-wedlock. Sex and gender here take on the dimension of a legal-organizational concept (Hester and Eglin, 1993: 77). Beyond this concept, however, stands a set of commonsense assumptions about the world's sexual organization, sexual normalcy, natural sexuality, deviant sexuality, the pathological character of sexuality, the sharing of active and passive roles in sexual relationships, places where relationships are established, the role of medicine in the establishment of scientific truth in cases exceeding the normal framework, and so forth. As Garfinkel (1967: 122) showed, sexuality is an organized accomplishment that answers to 'a preliminary list of properties of "natural, normally sexed persons" as cultural objects.' Normalcy here is assimilated to the orderliness of things, i.e. uses and mores as well as nature, with criminality being what contravenes it.

The definition that the Egyptian judges and magistrates spontaneously provided in response to questions about "sexual relationships" underscores the efficiency of categorizations, the intertwining of their technical and commonsense dimensions, and the importance of what is tacitly taken for true by the members of a given social group. For the male lawyers with whom I spoke during a series of lectures given at the National Center for Judicial Studies between 1995 and 1996, the category "licit sexual relations" that binds an adult man and an adult woman within the frame of a legal marriage constitutes the basic reference for evaluating any sexual action (cf. also Chapter 4). The creation of such a legal tie involves the right to sexual relationships, independent of the issue of consent or the use of constraint, so that the concept of rape can never characterize relationships within a legally married couple. More precisely, "sexual relationships" implicate the relationship of a man and a woman through the insertion in the woman's genitals of any of the man's organs or any object he holds, and these relationships become "licit" as soon as they take place within the framework of marriage. It is against this underlying notion that the conception of rape becomes the performance by way of constraint of sexual relationships between a man and a woman outside the legal framework of marriage. In turn, this categorization of rape excludes any inversion of the protagonists' roles (a woman cannot rape a man), any relationship that does not correspond strictly to the one described above (like sodomy), and any homosexual situation (a man cannot rape another man).

At first glance, it seems that there is a discrepancy in the way the many texts constitutive of the judicial file account for the Queen Boat case. On the one hand, there is the account of the case as a telling-in-so-many-words and, on the other hand, the account as a telling-of-despite-itself (Jayyusi, 1991). The properties and organization of these different texts make an equivocal reading possible, although this was obviously not their authors' intent. At one level, these documents, whose authors seek procedural correctness and legal relevance in their capacity as legal professionals, systematically produce the marks of their logic and validity (cf. above, Chapter 7). Nevertheless, these documents present a second level that cannot be totally concealed by the force of legal formalism, a level at which a common sense of morality and normalcy can be constantly observed. Without having to be analytically opposed to legal sense, this common sense of morality and normalcy offers another intelligibility structure for the case. To know which one of these two discourses is conclusive and imposes itself as the authoritative reading depends on the institutional position of its addressee,[10] his knowledge of the case, his propensity to believe what police and judicial sources tell him, the extent to which he shares the background of morality and normalcy, his legal knowledge, his own experience of the police and judicial institutions, and his willingness to tie principles, values, or even national sovereignty to respect for the judiciary and its decisions. However, all the activities bound to the criminalization of homosexuality – police, Public Prosecution, judges, attorneys, forensic physician, accused – are intelligible only in the context and the practice of "what everybody knows" about "sexual perversion". Understanding these activities depends on knowing what can be analysed as the articulation of the membership categorization methods used by the people concerned. The ease with which the protagonists of the Queen Boat case refer to this category can only be explained through the seen but unnoticed production of meaning and of interpretive procedures, among them categorization devices.

10 Whether for instance the document is addressed to an absent audience (i.e. the judge, for the Prosecution's interview; or the appellate judge, for the first instance decision) or a human rights militant.

Conclusion

The Morality of Judgment and the Judgment of Morality: A Praxeological Approach[1]

This book directly addressed the study of mechanisms producing court rulings. It is this part of law, located in the wake of statutory provisions, that was examined afresh, in its work of enunciation, interpretation, implementation, invention, perpetuation, and transformation of the law. This book also represents, on the specific issue of the relationship between law and morality, an endeavor to "repatriate" morality to a totally mundane setting. Morality, far from being able to rise above human action, merely constitutes its daily structure and expression. Its configuration and realization are located only in human action, even though the latter gives itself the task of performing justice.

What kind of articulation is there between the morality of judgment, on one side, and judgments and rulings concerning issues of morality, on the other? Judicial activities must not necessarily deal with moral issues in order to be morally constituted, organized, and practiced. However, judicial activities can sometimes concern issues belonging to the domain of morality. In the conclusion of this book, my aim is to observe and describe how the morality of the action of judging and the action of judging morality reciprocally constitute and redouble each other. In the praxeological spirit that has suffused this work, this does not mean I wish to propose a model abstractly framing the different configurations these relationships can take on in the concrete course of events. On the contrary, I aimed to document two mechanisms: first, how the activity of judging, ruling, and adjudicating transforms moral issues into legal objects, while constantly remaining morally informed; second, how the domain of morality constantly informs the law and serves as a basis to ground judgments in normality, while never being totally able to replace the law and people's orientations to the many practical purposes they ascribe to it.

There are two radically distinct ways of considering the place of morality in action. The first consists of claiming that morality is characterized by a series of dispositions internalized by people and generally governing their actions, consciously or not. A classical version of this position stands at the centre of Durkheim's sociology. It supports the idea that people cooperate because they share the same "representations". In that sense, actors follow stable and efficient rules. Such stability and efficiency comes precisely from the fact that human beings have no direct access to the rules determining their actions. The second way

1 This text is the outcome of a reflection conducted together with Jean-Noël Ferrié.

to consider the place of morality in action consists, on the contrary, of considering that morality is characterized by actors' orientation towards what they identify, through their action and speech, in a necessarily situated and punctual manner, as proceeding from a moral order. These orientations are common and intelligible because they are public. These public orientations are prospectively constitutive of the background understanding of future courses of action, while retrospectively validating the background on which the current course of action is based. This is why the action of somebody who drifts away from a routine procedure remains meaningful to me, in the sense that, if it publicly creates a gap with my expectations of normality that proceed from this background, it nevertheless does not prevent me from giving a meaning to his/her action – not because it is endowed with some kind of nature or intrinsic "truth", but because it is indexed on things that are already accomplished and others that will be accomplished. According to this way of considering action, actors do not really follow rules; however, their actions are neither random nor relative nor idiosyncratic, since they are grounded on a public, not a private language. Such a position is praxeological.

The difference separating the two positions is fundamental and irreducible. In other words, although both agree that the cognitive agency of action is located in the social sphere, they nevertheless give that claim radically different meanings. The followers of the former position state that, since morality is social, it exists as an undifferentiated totality, overhanging individuals; they consider the social sphere as a transcendent position within immanence. The followers of the latter position consider, on the contrary, that, since morality is social, it does not exist outside the course of interactions among people, as so many adjustment positions concerning specific cases. Because they are reflexively grounded on some background understanding, these adjustment positions are deemed intelligible outside the cases to which they apply. According to the followers of this conception, the social is located in the fact that human practices are grounded on human practices, while society does not exist as a separated and undifferentiated reality overhanging individuals.

What is the problem the first position (that is, transcendence within immanence) is supposed to solve? Apparently, it seeks to explain the stability of "human institutions". This question is also that of moral realism, even though philosophers formulate it differently. Stability of "human institutions" means that things instituted by human beings must exist independently of personal preference; otherwise society is chaos. The moral grounds of society obviously belong to human institutions. Beside this sociological concern, there is also a philosophical concern, i.e. moral realism, which seeks to justify our moral beliefs in a way that shelter them from human weakness or evil. It thus claims that there are normative propositions that are not preferences, since they can be true or false, independently of our capacity to prove truth or falsehood. It is the flexibility of so-called "preferences" that lies at the heart of many philosophers' and sociologists' will to support the transcendence of moral values, understood as the permanent yet inaccessible character of the "a person's interior moral positions". Is it possible to rely upon preferences? The rejection of approaches to human action in terms of immanent practices largely proceeds from this doubt. In moral philosophy, it is the starting point for wrong descriptions of ethical life and human action. The idea that there are "true" and "false" values, an order of appearances and an order of truth, as well as the idea that a moral action is an action dictated by a system of obligations is typical of these erroneous descriptions. In sociology, the same doubt is certainly at the origin of the attitude that consists of taking people as cognitive dupes. It seems that – for both philosophers and sociologists seeking the origin of human practices in transcendence – human beings can never act simply in order to act, or for trivial reasons. They must always look for grand and noble reasons, within which they are supposed to accomplish the essence of their humanness.

Of course, it is possible to understand this point of view: it is not absurd to suppose that action is constrained (one cannot do just anything in whatever way) and intelligible (one cannot act in an absurd way or for motives inaccessible to other people). However, this can be taken into account without adopting a transcendent or internal and ineffable (the two going together) conception of morality and practice. Human practices can be grounded on human practices and axiological choices can be considered as preferences that become stable within the course of interactions instead of realities constituted beforehand. Indeed, what stabilizes practices and preferences is not located in their transcendence but in their publicity. It is the publicizing of practices and preferences that stabilize them within a common world whose borders are neither submitted to people's fantasies nor independent of the conscious course of their actions. The specificity of this "publicizing" consists in the fact that issues of practice and preference receive the same treatment: they become stable in the course of a necessarily "public" interaction. To claim that this stabilization process is "public" does not mean that it is independent of people. It is exactly the contrary that is meant. Stabilization depends on people, first, because people are its engine; and second, because the backgrounds of understanding mobilized in the course of interaction are not necessarily identical from one actor to another, since they largely depend on the specific experience of each party to the action. The intelligibility of an action and the possibility of performing it correctly do not depend on the parties consciously sharing the same references. Nor do they depend on these parties sharing it "grossly" or in a thoughtless (not to mention unconscious) manner. They depend, first, on the fact that each of these parties can think that the others share the same assumptions and act according to the same practical procedures of mundane reason. Second, they depend on the parties' capacity to adjust, in sequences of action, to what they think are the other's positions, because of public exhibitions of these positions during the interaction. These adjustments naturally cannot be considered as mechanical; communication is not devoid of stuttering and mumbling; repairs occurring after such failures testify to these contingencies and to the fact that social order, to which communication actively contributes, is not free of uncertainties.

Throughout this book, I have shown how courses of action depend thoroughly on what Heritage (1984) calls "the morality of cognition", that is, the routinely normative and evaluative dimension of interaction. Moral order is not specific to some circumscribed field of activities. Morality percolates, in an empirically observable way, into all courses of action. Nevertheless, some activities explicitly address the issue of morality. There is a specific and circumscribed domain of morality within which the morality of cognition is redoubled by the cognition of morality. My work was primarily concerned with the ways the moral order unfolds in courses of action specifically oriented to the domain of morality. The question here is to determine the capacity of morality, as a specific domain of human action (and judicial action in particular), to retroact on the constitution and revision of backgrounds for understanding the moral order.

First, we must stress that the morality of cognition needs guides and standards to express itself. As Wittgenstein (1970: §124) points out, 'We need judgments as principles of judgment.' In other words, the moral order that structures the functioning of cognition must rely upon external marks or objectivations serving as standards in the moral evaluation of action. These standards, which are objective because they are the object of a common identification for a given group's members, are criteria to which these people can orient, either to conform to them or to seek to transform, deny (publicly or secretly), or even manipulate them. The identification of the existence and strength of these moral standards, not necessarily any consensus on their validity, makes them shared guides. For instance, to say that a lie is a vice can be an objective and shared moral standard in a specific social context. Defining what belongs to this category, however, can be the object of different appreciations, in the same way as deciding whether this or that action refers to the vice defined as such. We see here how the domain of morality, that is, this set of shared guide marks, retroacts on the moral order of action, that is, on the evaluative and normative embedding of ordinary behaviours. As parties to a given social context, people know the conventional implications of any contextual description and of particular disagreements and invalidations, and they shape their actions and speech accordingly. The moral values that parties assume, exhibit, imply, and acknowledge in their different courses of action are shared, although not in a uniform and absolute way. At the same time, these moral values are not abstract questions automatically implemented or proposing instructions for their implementation. They are circumstantial questions; that is, their mobilization and expression are not detachable from the circumstances within which it makes sense for members to use them (Jayyusi, 1984: 198).

Morality is thus both the structuring dimension of action and the topicalization of the value of something, in a constant seesaw motion. Whereas, on one side, something can be instated as a value and therefore become an object of morality, action, interaction, and even more specifically interactional reasoning are, on the other side, thoroughly structured by norms and evaluations – that is, by morality. However, it is not because morality is all of these things (topicalization, practical theorization, procedural frame and evaluation criterion) that these many levels should be analytically confused. An action can be morally structured without concerning a moral issue. It is more difficult to conceive of the opposite – an activity concerning a moral issue that would not be morally structured. It is nevertheless interesting to analytically distinguish these levels for three reasons: (1) it makes it possible to focus on the perspicuous character of morality in the accomplishment of ordinary (and extraordinary) actions; (2) it makes it possible to observe how the topicalization of morality also falls within the moral structuring of action; (3) it makes it possible to analyse how the same topicalization of morality recursively structures the moral criteria and standards of ordinary cognition and action. At the opposite, moral philosophy and sociology consider a truncated object. They ascribe themselves the task to give morality a specific domain and, therefore, to define it restrictively – to such good effect that the normative and evaluative operation at work in cognition, action and interaction, 'while it can be called *a* morality[,] is not morality.' (Warnock, 1971: 149) Moral philosophy and sociology thus dodge the issue of the mechanisms of morality in action, whether at the level of its topicalization or of the structuring it recursively gives to cognition, action and interaction. This is particularly true of the sociology that studies activities related to moral objects: while it is expected that such sociology seeks to describe the practices of people when oriented to these objects, it seems that it produces metaphysics in order to understand people's ethical concerns and 'ironically – that is, overhanging these activities – glosses the nature of ethics and the trajectory of reason within the world.' (Ferrié, 2002: 570)

The topicalization of morality retroacts on the morality of cognition. This, indeed, is how the categories on which actions are grounded are not definitely frozen in a cultural or idiosyncratic solipsism. Among other things, Harvey Sacks (1979) was interested in the issue of social and cultural change. Categories, their transformation, their shrinking or their expansion play an essential role in that respect. People have "stocks of knowledge" on what "women" are, for instance, and on what makes them different from "tarts" or "hos"; on what "men" are, including what makes them different from "faggots"; or on what "foreigners" are, including the difference between them and "niggers" or "ragheads". This knowledge is contextually bound, which means that the use of an ordinary concept summons a whole body of knowledge tacitly bound to it. A series of shifts can occur in this knowledge and its categories, following interventions that seek this change either purposefully or in a fuzzier way. Strategies devised by NGOs defending the rights of women or gays or fighting against racism illustrate the former case. The latter case is illustrated by ordinary personal events and encounters and their impact on my personal life, for at least two reasons: because they have an exemplary value; and because they happened in my close environment. For instance, my mother-in-law was the first female professor at the Faculty of Medicine at the University of Louvain, and her professional life illustrates the latter case; similarly, Michel's or Jean-Michel's cleverness and friendship provided homosexuality with a face that is both sympathetic and familiar to me; and Momo, a real live Moroccan, is like an older brother to me. Moral categories constitute, on one hand, 'intersubjective resources for the characterization (including descriptions, inferences and judgments) of [oneself] and others *and* [since, on the other hand, the question of knowing] who someone is is a function of what one is doing, when, where and with whom.' (Stetson, 1999: 93) In consequence, changing any element of the equation is enough to alter it deeply. These categorial shifts occur constantly, but even more when certain things are morally topicalized and identified as a problem, leading people to produce, activate and transform the categorial structures on which they rely.

This book was concerned with the praxeological study of law as it unfolds on matters of morality. It addressed both the morality of judicial cognition, that is, the whole set of normative and evaluative processes involved in the practice of adjudication, and the judicial cognition of morality, that is, adjudicating practices when dealing with cases concerning morality. This study showed that, though analytically distinct, these levels were empirically tightly intertwined. Action, including that consisting of dealing with moral issues, is morally structured. Judicial action, including that concerning cases of morality, is morally structured. Conversely, judicial discourse concerning moral issues can retroact on the moral structuring of cognition, action and interaction, through the activation and transformation of the categories upon which these issues rely.

Starting from this statement, I would like to respecify the issue of the relations between legality (in the sense of an action oriented to law) and morality (in the sense of the specific domain of human action and its topicalization in terms of good and evil). Legality and morality are obviously not identical. According to Jayyusi (1984: 194), '[t]he law, of course, enters our life and *provides further instances of our use*; in some areas it may eventually not only introduce new language games or new steps into our existing language games but it may change some of these games over the years. But *in the first instance*, the law provides a formalization of some lay uses and procedures and is not simply identical with them. Routinely, what is legally relevant is not taken to be identical with what is morally relevant.' This quotation creates a number of confusions. First, as I said elsewhere (Chapter 1), the idea that law mirrors social reality is very problematic. Second, the law is not the mere formalization of daily life. Third, whereas morality is, among other things, a modality of action, law is not. However, it is important to stress that the same thing can be the object of two topicalizations, one legal and one moral, which can coincide or diverge. For instance, a homicide can be described legally and morally as murder; it can be legally characterized as murder and morally as resistance; it can even find legal justifications and nevertheless be morally blameworthy. There are also many situations where conflicting legal characterizations (e.g., a homicide characterized in international law as terrorism or resistance) or moral descriptions (e.g., the same homicide described as barbaric or heroic) can concern the same object.

Although legality and morality are not identical, the institution responsible for the implementation of legality, i.e. the judiciary, sometimes has to adjudicate on issues relating to moral order. In such cases, this institution is led to fix morality legally. Even though law is not equivalent to morality, which means that the judicial treatment of a moral issue is a non-moral mode of reduction of moral indeterminacy, the judicial ruling nevertheless relies upon a whole set of categorizations, which are partly legal and partly moral. It thereby participates in the activation of legal and moral categories as well as in their evolution and transformation. In all cases – the morality of judicial cognition and the judicial cognition of moral issues – normality functions as the reference point of practical reasoning. The argument of incongruity originates in the "abnormality" of the object it deals with, while in moral affairs justice is called upon because of the breach caused by an action to what is perceived as moral normality. In every situation, the force of normality proceeds from the fact that, once it is invoked, it becomes extremely hard to retract. It activates a mechanism of solidarity without consensus and, even more, a mechanism of negative solidarity. By solidarity without consensus, I mean that a community's members acknowledge the same references and symbols, but interpret them differently (Kertzer, 1988: 57-76). By negative solidarity, I mean the additional fact that members use shared references and symbols because they think other members expect them to do so and will not consider them as respectable members if they do not (Ferrié, 2004a). At the same time – and this is fundamental – law and justice, when dealing with a moral issue, transform this issue into a legal object, which brings morality into the distinct (but not autopoietic) language game of the law.

I shall resort once again to empirical data to examine how, at one and the same time, law, while morally structured, "legalizes" morality. The events took place in the district of Heliopolis, where a police operation led to the arrest of a several men and women. The police record describes the motives of the inquiry (procuring and prostitution), its procedural enfolding (surveillance, warrants issued by the Prosecution) and characterizations of the protagonists ("wicked women", "men looking for sexual pleasure"). An excerpt from the interrogation of one of the women accused of prostitution follows:

Excerpt 194 (Vice Squad, Case 2677, 1983, Heliopolis)

We interrogated Inas 'Isa 'Abd al-Ghani as follows

Q: How long have you been a prostitute

A: Three years

Q: Do you habitually practice prostitution with men without compensation[2]

A: Yes

Q: How many times have you practiced prostitution

A: More than once but I don't do it a lot and I do it once or twice a month because I don't like it

Q: When was it the last time you had extramarital sex

A: Approximately two weeks ago or a little bit less

Q: Did you have extramarital sex today

2 The question is contradictory and could be due to an error in the transcript.

A: Yes
Q: What induced you to do these things
A: The one I was telling you about a moment ago who is called Fatna her name is well known and she kept on calling me at the doctor where I work and asking me to come and sleep with a guy who was at her place and these people are Egyptian and she settles the bill with me and then I leave
Q: Did the abovementioned undertake to facilitate and exploit your prostitution
A: Yes
Q: When was the last time the abovementioned undertook to exploit your prostitution
A: Approximately one month ago
Q: What financial compensation did the abovementioned get in exchange
A: She sat with the client and she paid me the money and I don't know how much she took from the client
Q: How did you learn about the presence of Ja'far in Cairo in the home for which a search warrant was obtained
A: Fawqiyya came home yesterday and told me that Ja'far was at her flat and had asked for me and she told me to stay with her because he wanted me very much and she told me this time and I understood that she didn't want to let me speak with Ja'far about marriage because she was in no mood for that
Q: Did Fawqiyya get some financial advantage from you in exchange for that
A: I'm like her I take from the one who sleeps with me and naturally she takes a part of this
Q: Are there other women who used to frequent this apartment for which a search warrant was obtained at the [home] of Fatna and Amal to commit adultery there
A: There are other girls than me who go there and I know it but they don't let more than one man in the flat because Fawqiyya is scared and she prefers to go out and leave the flat because she's scared
Q: Have you been arrested before
A: No
Q: You're accused of having exposed yourself to the practice of prostitution with men without distinction in exchange for compensation
A: I do and our Lord will punish the person who's the cause of it
Q: Do you have something to add
A: No

Once again, I want to stress how much the judicial process seeks to reduce indeterminacy. This translates, at the formal level, into a sorting out of all possible characterizations. The scope of legal interpretation is necessarily constrained by the choice of definition and the order of the words used. In Egypt, Law 10/1961 criminalizes "prostitution" (*da'ara*). However, it does not define it, which at least opens a possibility of interpretation. The Court of Cassation, in its ruling of 2 March, 1988, explains that "prostitution" means committing an indecent action (*fahsha'*) without distinction (*tamyiz*); repetition is not a relevant factor. Such a definition leaves open many, but not all, possibilities. Legal activities are characterized by their embeddedness within a procedural sequence: the public prosecutor to whom a case of prostitution is referred must deal with the case according to the law of 1961. Moreover, he must rely upon former procedures (police reports) and anticipate forthcoming procedures (the reading made by the judge in order to build his ruling). Finally, judicial activities are constrained by their institutional embeddedness. The parties to a trial do not have the same status or the same rights and duties. In a nutshell, they are engaged in asymmetrical relationships. Although there is a turn-taking system among the different parties, this system is partly determined by the pre-allocation of turns, by initiative in and control over the content of exchanges, and by the unequal distribution of knowledge and the capacity of one party to orient to a specific goal the other can guess and whose harmful content he or she can anticipate or even avert, but which he or she cannot decide.

More precisely, we see through the reading of this excerpt how the accusing party orients the exchanges toward the legal specification of facts (place, circumstances, people concerned) and toward the interrogated person's acceptance of the accusation addressed to her. There is no "normative overload" in the sense that the police officer seeks only to get a legally clear, coherent and fact-centered narrative and abstains from evaluating this narrative from the point of view of morality. So, the accused is not interrogated on what she might have felt when doing what she did. It is up to her to use answers to precise questions and add a couple of words formulating her moral position. To the question: 'How many times did you practice prostitution', she answers: 'More than once', but adds: 'I don't do it a lot!' This interjection does not seek to clarify frequency, but to indicate the limited character of a punishable practice. Then, she adds something specific concerning frequency: '... once or twice a month', which actually works as a preface to her expressing a moral position that was not solicited by her interlocutor: '... because I don't like it'. The same method is used after the enunciation of the accusation by the police officer: she uses the enunciation as if it had introduced a speech turn, notwithstanding the fact that it does not entail any invitation to speak, in order to introduce a formulation that exempts her from at least part of the responsibility: 'Our Lord will punish the person who's the cause of it.' Such a formulation designates an anonymous or even virtual responsible person and a divine agent, who do not constitute relevant figures in the legal process of responsibility ascription. Nor does it abide by the institutional and procedural order, since the accused is taking her turn before, not after a question, while the interrogator does not assent to it and directly asks a question that should have taken its place after the accusation was formulated. Such bracketing of a statement, which is precisely not treated as a statement (even though it is mentioned in the record), suggests the incongruity and uselessness of this exit from legal relevance (it does not deal with facts that could be legally characterized) and from the institutional and procedural order (there is no possible intervention outside the accusing party's invitation and no possible orientation to anything but the judicial sequence).

Facing a legal accusation that gives her responsibility for a misdemeanour she obviously perceives as a moral reprimand, even though this cannot be observed directly in the accusing party's formulations, the accused woman produces a moral response. The moral order has no place in the characterizing enterprise conducted by the police officer. At best, it takes its place in an interstitial way, in a totally asymmetrical relationship, without having been solicited and with no direct consequence on the ongoing procedure. The accused woman, without being ever asked to do so, is keen to exhibit her moral identity vis-à-vis her accuser, who, in the performance of his job, does not care at all. It can therefore be argued that legal normativity can function independently of moral normativity, even though both go together from the commonsense perspective (here expressed by the accused).[3] At the same time, it is equally obvious that the criminalizing of prostitution corresponds to the fixation of a moral proscription. In that sense, the law was asked to intervene in the sphere of morality and morality became law. However, such transubstantiation of morality into law was only achieved, by the police officer in this case, with the help of standards and categories, partly formal and partly implicit, with a more or less open texture, through work of a moral nature (that is, normative and evaluative) describing facts, and identifying and characterizing the law.

It should be clear by now that the morality of cognition is continuously fed by the cognition of morality; that the cognition of morality is bound by the structuring specific to the morality of cognition; that, nevertheless, law and morality keep on being specific and non-mistaken activities, because they are embedded in their particular contexts, naturally, but also because they unfold for practical purposes that intersect only occasionally and circumstantially. At the same time, action has only one world; it is not embedded in a plurality of "cities" (Boltanski and Thévenot, 1991). Like baron von Munchhausen, it cannot rise above its mundane condition. To the contrary, it depends thoroughly on such a condition and is integrally situated within mundane reason. Its relative plurality proceeds from the fact that contexts in which it is embedded have specific practical purposes and singular configurations, which people recognize as such and to which they orient, something that necessarily exerts a degree of constraint on its accomplishment.

This last case study having served as a conclusion, I shall close by insisting on the point that, throughout this book, I dealt with the ontology of law and its part of morality. As Bruno Latour (2002: 295-6) puts it, 'To say that law is symbolic, that it is something mental, the product of human brains, an arbitrary social construct, means to capitulate from the start by renouncing the discovery of the specific ontology that fits it.' On the contrary, I faced the question directly. According to what I said in the introduction, I engaged in respecifying the study of law and its relation with morality by observing, in context, how different real persons strive, when accomplishing their many jobs and activities, to concretely

3 It does not mean that the accusing party does not subscribe to such commonsense point of view outside the frame of his professional activity.

establish the facts, to implement the rules, and to refer facts to rules in the routine course of their work or in their less ordinary encounters with justice. My task was not to gloss on this or that quasi-metaphysical truth with the law as a resource, but only to describe law in its most precise phenomenological reality. According to some scholars, such a perspective is poor: 'It convinces us easily, but also gives the impression it has taught nothing, beyond simply making explicit, albeit occasionally in more refined form, what we always knew.' (Bouvier, 1999: 14) In a word, the praxeological approach is accused of not having contributed to progress, 'either in knowledge or in comprehension or in a real call to reflection.' (*ibid.*: 14, fn.2) This book is grounded on the opposite conviction: that returning to law as an object of analysis "in its own right", caring for the empirical as the only object of sociology, and paying attention to practice as the only place where the social is achieved, not only saves us from the 'debilitation of the soul' (Latour, 2002: 296) constituted by sociologies without phenomenology, but also represents a step toward understanding our mundane world.

Bibliography

Ans (d'), André-Marcel (2003) "La Cour d'assises en examen. Réflexion-témoignage d'un juré sociologue" *Droit et Société* 54: 403-431.

Arabi, Oussama (2004) "The Regimentation of the Subject: Madness in Islamic and Modern Arab Civil Laws" in Baudouin Dupret (ed.) *Standing Trial: Law and People in the Modern Middle East*. London: Tauris.

Arabi, Oussama (1997) "Intention and Method in Sanhûrî's Fiqh: Cause as Ulterior Motive" *Islamic Law and Society* 4(2): 200-223.

Arnaud, André-Jean (1993) "liberté" in André-Jean Arnaud *et al.* (eds.) *Dictionnaire encyclopédique de théorie et de sociologie du droit* (deuxième édition corrigée et augmentée) Paris: LGDJ.

Assier-Andrieu, Louis (1996) *Le droit dans les sociétés humaines*. Paris: Nathan.

Atkinson, J. Maxwell (1982) "Understanding Formality: The Categorization and Production of 'Formal' Interaction" *The British Journal of Sociology* 33(1): 86-117.

Atkinson, J. Maxwell and Paul Drew (1979) *Order in Court: The Organization of Verbal Interaction in Courtroom Settings*. Basingstoke: Macmillan.

Austin, John (1954) *The Province of Law Determined*. London: Weidenfeld and Nicolson (1st edition 1832).

Austin, John L. (1970) "A Plea for Excuses" in John L. Austin *Philosophical Papers* (edited by J.O. Urmson and G.J. Warnock). New York: Galaxy Books.

Austin, John L. (1973) *How to do Things with Words*. New York: Oxford University Press.

Bakhtin, Michail (1981) *The Dialogic Imagination*. Austin: University of Texas Press.

Bakhtin, Michail (1986) *Speech Genres and Other Late Essays*. Austin: University of Texas Press.

Batrân, Hamdî al- (1998) *Yawmiyyât zâbit fî-l-aryâf* (Journal d'un officier de campagne) Le Caire: Dâr al-Hilâl.

Becker, Howard (1963) *Outsiders*. Glencoe: The Free Press.

Bennett, W. Lance and Martha S. Feldman (1981) *Reconstructing Reality in the Courtroom*. New Brunswick: Rutgers University Press.

Benson, Douglas and John Hughes (1991) "Method: evidence and inference – evidence and inference for ethnométhodology" in Graham Button (ed.) *Ethnomethodology and the Human Sciences*. Cambridge: Cambridge University Press.

Berger, Maurits (2001) "Public Policy and Islamic Law: The Modern *Dhimmî* in Contemporary Egyptian Family Law" *Islamic Law and Society* 8(1): 88-136.

Bernard-Maugiron, Nathalie (1999) "La Haute Cour constitutionnelle égyptienne et la *shari'a* islamique" *Awrâq* 19: 103-141.
Bogen, David (1999) *Order Without Rules: Critical Theory and the Logic of Conversation*. New York: SUNY Press.
Boltanski, Luc, and Laurent Thévenot (1991) *De la justification. Les économies de la grandeur*. Paris: Gallimard.
Botiveau, Bernard (1989) "L'adaptation d'un modèle français d'enseignement du droit au Proche-Orient" in M. Flory and J.R. Henry (eds) *L'enseignement du droit musulman*. Marseille: Ed. du CNRS 229-252.
Bouvier, Alban (1999) *Philosophie des sciences sociales*. Paris: PUF.
Brown, Nathan (1997) *The Rule of Law in the Arab World*. Cambridge and New York: Cambridge University Press.
Brunet, Pierre (2002) "Alf Ross et la conception référentielle de la signification en droit" in Eric Millard *Droit et Société* ("Une théorie empiriste du droit est-elle possible? Lectures d'Alf Ross") 50: 19-28.
Burns, Stacy (1997) "Practicing Law: A Study of Pedagogic Interchange in a Law School Classroom" in Max Travers and John F. Manzo (eds.) *Law in Action: Ethnomethodological and Conversation Analytic Approaches to Law*. Aldershot: Dartmouth/Ashgate.
Button, Graham (1991) "Introduction: Ethnomethodology and the Foundational Respecification of the Human Sciences" in Graham Button (ed.) *Ethnomethodology and the Human Sciences*. Cambridge: Cambridge University Press.
Button, Graham (2001) "L'ethnométhodologie est-elle constructiviste?" in Michel de Fornel, Albert Ogien, Louis Quéré (eds) *L'ethnométhodologie: Une sociologie radicale*. Paris: La Découverte (colloque de Cerisy).
Button, Graham, and Wes Sharrock (1993) "A disagreement of agreement and consensus in constructionist sociology" *Journal for the Theory of Social Behaviour* 23(1): 1-25.
Canto-Sperber, Monique (ed.) (1996) *Dictionnaire d'éthique et de philosophie morale*. Paris: PUF.
Cayla, Oliver (1996) "Droit" in Monique Canto-Sperber (ed.) *Dictionnaire d'éthique et de philosophie morale*. Paris: PUF.
Cefaï, Daniel (1994) "Type, typicalité, typification. La perspective phénoménologique" in Bernard Fradin, Louis Quéré and Jean Widmer (eds) *L'enquête sur les categories*. Paris: Ed. de l'EHESS (Raisons pratiques, no. 5).
Cefaï, Daniel (1998) *Phénoménologie et sciences sociales. Alfred Schütz. Naissance d'une anthropologie philosophique*. Geneva: Droz.
Chazel, François (1991) "Emile Durkheim et l'élaboration d'un 'programme de recherche' en sociologie du droit" in François Chazel and Jacques Commaille (eds) *Normes juridiques et régulation sociale*. Paris: LGDJ.
Cicourel, Aaron (1968) *The Social Organization of Juvenile Justice*. New York: John Wiley & Sons, Inc.

Clémence, Alain, and Willem Doise (1995) "La représentation sociale de la justice: une approche des droits dans la pensée ordinaire" *L'Année sociologique* 45(2): 371-400.

Conley, John M., and William M. O'Barr (1998) *Just Words: Law, Language and Power*. Chicago: University of Chicago Press.

Conley, John M., and William M. O'Barr (1990) *Rules Versus Relationships: The Ethnography of Legal Discourse*. Chicago: University of Chicago Press.

Corten, Olivier (1998) "La référence à la nature des choses dans l'herméneutique de l''Ecole de Bruxelles': une critique sociologique" *Revue interdisciplinaire d'études juridiques* 40: 79-113.

Coulon, Alain (1987) *L'ethnométhodologie*. Paris: PUF (Que sais-je?).

Coulon, Alain (1994a) "Alfred Schütz (1899-1959) – Le Chercheur et le quotidien (1962-1966)" in Karl van Meter (ed.) *La sociologie*. Paris: Larousse.

Coulon, Alain (1994b) "Harold Garfinkel (né en 1917) – Studies in Ethnomethodology (1967)" in Karl van Meter (ed.) *La sociologie*. Paris: Larousse.

Coulter, Jeff (1979) "Beliefs and Practical Understanding" in G. Psathas (ed.) *Everyday Language*. New York: Irvington Publishers, Inc.

Coulter, Jeff (1989) *Mind In Action*. Atlantic Highlands, NJ: Humanities Press International.

Coulter, Jeff (1991) "Logic: ethnomethodology and the logic of language" in Graham Button (ed.) *Ethnomethodology and the Human Sciences*. Cambridge: Cambridge University Press.

Danet, Brenda (1980) "Language in the Legal Process" *Law and Society Review* 14(3): 445-564.

Dingwall, Robert (1976) "Accomplishing Profession" *The Sociological Review* 24: 331-49.

Dingwall, Robert (2000) "Language, Law, and Power: Ethnomethodology, Conversation Analysis, and the Politics of Law and Society Studies" *Law and Social Inquiry* 25(3): 885-911.

Douglas, Mary (1981) *De la souillure, essai sur les notions de pollution et de tabous*. Paris: Maspéro.

Drew, Paul (1992) "Contested Evidence in Courtroom Cross-Examination: The Case of a Trial for Rape" in Paul Drew and John Heritage (eds.) *Talk at Work. Interaction in Institutional Settings*. Cambridge: Cambridge University Press (reprinted in Travers et Manzo, 1997).

Drew, Paul and Heritage, John (eds.) (1992) *Talk at Work: Interaction in Institutional Settings*. Cambridge: Cambridge University Press.

Drew, Paul, and John Heritage (1992) "Analyzing Talk at Work: An Introduction" in Paul Drew and John Heritage (eds.) *Talk at Work. Interaction in Institutional Settings*. Cambridge: Cambridge University Press.

Drieskens, Barbara (2003) "The Misbehavior of the Possessed: On Spirits, Morality and the Person" in Baudouin Dupret (ed.) *Standing Trial: Law and People in the Modern Middle East*. London: Tauris.

Dupret, Baudouin (1997) "A propos de la constitutionnalité de la sharî`a: Présentation et traduction de l'arrêt du 26 mars 1994 (14 Shawwâl 1414) de la Haute Cour Constitutionnelle (*al-mahkama al-dustûriyya al-`ulyâ*) égyptienne" *Islamic Law and Society* 4(1): 91-113.

Dupret, Baudouin (2000) *Au nom de quel droit. Répertoires juridiques et référence religieuse dans la société égyptienne musulmane contemporaine.* Paris: LGDJ/ Maison des sciences de l'homme.

Dupret, Baudouin, and Nathalie Bernard-Maugiron (2002) "Introduction: A general Presentation of Law and Judicial Bodies" in Nathalie Bernard-Maugiron and Baudouin Dupret (eds) *Egypt and Its Laws*. London, The Hague and New York: Kluwer Law International.

Durkheim, Emile (1924) *Sociologie et philosophie*. Paris: Alcan.

Durkheim, Emile (1960) *La division du travail social.* (1st edition 1893). Paris: PUF.

Dworkin, Ronald (1977) *Taking Rights Seriously*. London: Duckworth.

Dworkin, Ronald (1986) *Law's Empire* Cambridge: Harvard University Press.

El Hakim, Tewfik (1974) *Un substitut de campagne en Egypte. Journal d'un substitut du procureur égyptien.* Paris: Plon (trans. by G. Wiet and Z.M. Hassan, originally published as *Yawmiyyât nâ'ib fî al-aryâf*, 1942).

Emerson, Robert M. (1983) "Holistic Effects In Social Control Decision-Making" *Law and Society Review* 17(3): 425-455.

Emerson, Robert M., and Melvin Pollner (1976) "Dirty Work Designations: Their Features and Consequences in a Psychiatric Setting" *Social Problems* 23: 243-254.

Engel, Laurence (1993) "Vers une nouvelle approche de la responsabilité. Le droit français face à la dérive américaine" *Esprit* 6: 5-31.

Evans-Pritchard, E.E. (1937) *Witchcraft, Oracles and Magic Among the Azande.* Oxford: Oxford University Press.

Ferrié, Jean-Noël (1995) "Lieux intérieurs et culture publique au Maroc" *Politix* 31: 187-202.

Ferrié, Jean-Noël (1997) "Solidarité sans consensus en Egypte: un cadre d'analyse" *Les Annales de l'autre islam* 4: 73-83.

Ferrié, Jean-Noël (1998a) "Figures de la moralité en Egypte: typifications, conventions et publicité" in J. Dakhlia (ed.) *Urbanité arabe. Hommage à Bernard Lepetit.* Arles: Actes Sud/Sindbad.

Ferrié, Jean-Noël (1998) "La Petite robe, ou le dépassement des limites en régime de civilité" *Hermès* 22: 111-20.

Ferrié, Jean-Noël (2002) "Ladrière Paul, *Pour une sociologie de l'éthique*" (notice bibliographique) *Droit et Société* 51-52: 567-570.

Ferrié, Jean-Noël (2004a) *Le régime de la civilité. Public et réislamisation en Egypte.* Paris: Presses du CNRS.

Ferrié, Jean-Noël (2004b) *La Religion de la vie quotidienne chez les Marocains musulmans. Rites, règles et routine*. Paris: Karthala.

Fish, Stanley (1989) *Doing What Comes Naturally*. Durham: Duke University Press.

Fletcher, G. (1978) *Rethinking Criminal Law*. Boston: Little, Brown.

Foriers, Paul (1982) *La pensée juridique de Paul Foriers*. 2 vol. Bruxelles: Bruylant.

Fornel, Michel de, Albert Ogien, Louis Quéré (2001) "Introduction" in Michel de Fornel, Albert Ogien, Louis Quéré (eds) *L'ethnométhodologie: Une sociologie radicale.* Paris: La Découverte (colloque de Cerisy).

Fradin, Bernard, Louis Quéré and Jean Widmer (eds) (1994) *L'enquête sur les catégories.* Paris: Ed. de l'EHESS (Raisons pratiques, no. 5).

Frank, Jerome (1949) *Courts on Trial*. Princeton: Princeton University Press.

Freeman, Michael D.A. (1979) "Milgram's Obedience to Authorité – Some Lessons for Legal Theory" *Liverpool Law Review* 1: 45-61.

Freeman, Michael D.A. (2001) *Lloyd's Introduction to Jurisprudence* (7e édition). London: Sweet & Maxwell.

Fuller, Lon L. (1964) *The Morality of Law.* New Haven: Yale University Press.

Fuller, Lon L. (1969) *The Morality of Law.* New Haven: Yale University Press.

Garfinkel, Harold (1948) "A Research Note on Inter- and Intra-Racial Homicides" *Journal of Social Forces* 4: 369-81.

Garfinkel, Harold (1963) "A conception of, and experiments with, 'trust' as a condition of stable concerted actions" in O.J. Harvey (ed.) *Motivation and Social Interaction.* New York: Ronald Press.

Garfinkel, Harold (1967) "Practical Sociological Reasoning: Some Features in the Work of the Los Angeles Suicide Prevention Center" in E.S. Schneidman (ed.) *Essays in Self-Destruction.* New York: International Science Press.

Garfinkel, Harold (1967) *Studies in Ethnomethodology*. Cambridge: Polity Press.

Garfinkel, Harold (1974) "'Good' Organizational Reasons for 'Bad' Clinic Records" in Roy Turner (ed.) *Ethnomethodology*. Harmondsworth: Penguin Books Ltd.

Garfinkel, Harold (1974) "The Origins of the Term 'Ethnomethodology'" in Roy Turner (ed.) *Ethnomethodology*. Harmondsworth: Penguin Books Ltd.

Garfinkel, Harold (1997) "Practical Sociological Reasoning: Some Features in the Work of the Los Angeles Suicide Prevention Center" in Max Travers and John F. Manzo (eds.) *Law in Action: Ethnomethodological and Conversation Analytic Approaches to Law*. Aldershot: Dartmouth/Ashgate.

Garfinkel, Harold (2001) "Postface – L'ethnométhodologie et le legs oublié de Durkheim" in Michel de Fornel, Albert Ogien, Louis Quéré (eds) *L'ethnométhodologie. Une sociologie radicale.* Paris: La Découverte (colloque de Cerisy).

Garfinkel, Harold (2002) *Ethnomethodology's Program: Working Out Durkheim's Aphorism* (edited and introduced by Anne Warfield Rawls). Lanham: Rowman & Littlefield Publishers.

Garfinkel, Harold, and Harvey Sacks (1986) "On formal structures of practical actions" in Harold Garfinkel (ed.) *Ethnomethodological Studies of Work*. London: Routledge and Kegan Paul [version réimprimée du même article paru in John C. McKinney and Edward Tiryakian (eds.) *Theoretical Sociology.* New York: Appleton Century Crofts, 1970].

Geertz, Clifford (1983) *Local Knowledge: Further Essays in Interpretive Anthropology.* New York: Basic Books.

Gemei, Hassan (1997) *Introduction to Law: Theory of Law, Theory of Right*. Cairo: Cairo University.

Génard, Jean-Louis (1997) "Responsabilité et normativité dans l'école et la pensée de Durkheim" in Philippe Robert, Francine Soubiran-Paillet, Michel van de Kerchove (eds) *Normes, normes juridiques, normes pénales: Pour une sociologie des frontiers*. Paris: L'Harmattan.

Ghazzal, Zouheir (1996) "Honor Crimes in Syrian Courts: The Art of Finding Good Reasons to Kill Your Wife" *Paper presented at the Middle East Studies Association*, 30th Annual Meeting, November 21-24, Providence, Rhode Island.

Ghurâb, Muhammad `Abd al-Hamîd (1986) *Jugements islamiques contredisant les lois positives* (en arabe). Le Caire: Dâr al-i`tisâm.

Gibbons, John (2003) *Forensic Linguistics: An Introduction to Language in the Justice System*. Oxford: Blackwell.

Goffman, Erving (1959) *Presentation of Self in Everyday Life*. Garden City: Doubleday.

Goffman, Erving (1981) *Forms of Talk*. Philadelphia: University of Pennsylvania Press.

Goldman, Alvin I. (1971) "The Individuation of Action" *Journal of Philosophy* 62: 761-774.

Greimas, Algirdas J. and Joseph Courtès (1979) *Sémiotique. Dictionnaire raisonné de la théorie du langage, vol. 1*. Paris: Hachette.

Greimas, Algirdas J. and Joseph Courtès (1986) *Sémiotique. Dictionnaire raisonné de la théorie du langage, vol. 2*. Paris: Hachette.

Griffiths, John (1984) "What Is Legal Pluralism?" *Journal of Legal Pluralism* 24: 1-55.

Gumperz, John (1982) *Discourse Strategies*. Cambridge: Cambridge University Press.

Habermas, Jürgen (1988) *The Tanner Lectures on Human Values, VIII*. Salt Lake City: University of Utah Press.

Hâkim, Tawfîq al- (1942) *Journal d'un substitut de campagne* (en arabe).

Hart, Herbert L.A. (1961) *The Concept of Law*. Oxford: Oxford University Press (translation by M. van de Kerchove, *Le concept de droit*. Bruxelles: Publications des Facultés universitaires Saint-Louis, 1976).

Hart, Herbert L.A. (1968) *Punishment and Responsibility: Essays in the Philosophy of Law*. Oxford: Clarendon Press.

Hart, Herbert L.A. and Tony Honoré (1985) *Causation in the Law*. Oxford: Clarendon Press (2nd edition).

Hasan, Najîb (s.d.) "Droit de la protection de la pudeur" (in Arabic) *Majallat al-qânûn wa l-iqtisâd – huqûq al-insân*.

Have, Paul ten and George Psathas (1995) "Introduction" in Paul ten Have and George Psathas *Situated Order: Studies in the Social Organization of Talk and Embodied Activities*. Washington, D.C.: University Press of America.

Heritage, John (1984) *Garfinkel and Ethnomethodology*. Cambridge: Polity Press.

Hester, Stephen and Peter Eglin (1992) *A Sociology of Crime.* London and New York: Routledge.

Hester, Stephen and Peter Eglin (1997a) "Membership Categorization Analysis: An Introduction" in Stephen Hester and Peter Eglin (eds.) *Culture in Action: Studies in Membership Categorization Analysis.* Washington, D.C.: University Press of America.

Hester, Stephen and Peter Eglin (1997b) "The Reflexive Constitution of Category, Predicate and Context in Two Settings" in Stephen Hester and Peter Eglin (eds.) *Culture in Action: Studies in Membership Categorization Analysis.* Washington, D.C.: University Press of America.

Hester, Stephen, and Peter Eglin (1997c) "Conclusion: Membership Categorization Analysis and Sociology" in Stephen Hester and Peter Eglin (eds.) *Culture in Action: Studies in Membership Categorization Analysis.* Washington, D.C.: University Press of America.

Hester, Stephen, and William Housley (2002) "Introduction: Ethnomethodology and National Identity" in Stephen Hester and William Housley (eds.) *Language, Interaction and National Identity: Studies in the Social Organisation of National Identity in Talk-in-Interaction.* Aldershot: Ashgate.

Hill, Enid (1987) *Al-Sanhuri and Islamic Law.* Cairo: Amercian University in Cairo Press (Cairo Papers in Social Science 10/1).

Holstein, James A. (1993) *Court-Ordered Insanity: Interpretive Practice and Involuntary Commitment.* New York: Aldine De Gruyter.

Hume, David (1969) *A Treatise on Human Nature.* London: Penguin (1st edition 1739-40) [French translation *Traité de la nature humaine*. Paris: Aubier].

Husni, Muhammad N. (1989) *Sharh qânûn al-`uqûbât, 1. al-qânûn al-`âmm* (Précis de droit pénal, 1. Droit général). Le Caire: Dâr al-Nahda al-`arabiyya.

Hüsserl, Edmund (1970) *Expérience et jugement* (translation of *Erfahrung und Urteil: Untersuchungen zur Genealogie der Logik* par D. Souche-Dagues). Paris: PUF.

Ireton, François (2000) "A propos de la (re)production d'une identité 'sa'idi'" in Chr. Décobert (ed.) *Valeur et distance: Identités et sociétés en Egypte.* Paris: Maisonneuve and Larose.

Isambert, François-André (1989) "Alfred Schütz entre Weber et Hüsserl" *Revue française de sociologie* 30(2): 299-319.

Isambert, François-André (1991) "Durkheim et la sociologie des normes" in François Chazel and Jacques Commaille (eds) *Normes juridiques et régulation sociale.* Paris: LGDJ.

Jackson, Bernard S. (1985) *Semiotics and Legal Theory.* Liverpool: Deborah Charles Publications.

Jackson, Bernard S. (1988) *Law, Fact and Narrative Coherence.* Liverpool: Deborah Charles Publications.

Jackson, Bernard S. (1994) "Towards a semiotic model of professional practice, with some narrative reflections on the criminal process" *International Journal of the Legal Profession* 1(1): 55-79.

Jackson, Bernard S. (1995) *Making Sense in Law: Linguistic, Psychological and Semiotic Perspectives.* Liverpool: Deborah Charles Publications.

Jackson, Bernard S. (1996) *Making Sense in Jurisprudence.* Liverpool: Deborah Charles Publications.

Jacquemet, Marco (1996) *Credibility in Court: Communicative Practices in the Camora Trials.* Cambridge: Cambridge University Press.

Jalbert, Paul L. (1989) "Categorization and Beliefs: News Accounts of Haitian and Cuban Refugees" in D.T. Helm, W.T. Anderson, A.J. Meehan, A.W. Rawls (eds.) *The Interactional Order: New Directions in the Study of Social Order.* New York: Irvington Publishers, Inc.

Jalbert, Paul L. (1999) "Critique and Analysis in Media Studies: Media Criticism as Practical Action" in Paul L. Jalbert (ed.) *Media Studies: Ethnomethodological Approaches.* Lanham: University Press of America.

Jamî`î, Hasan (1996) *Mabâdi' al-qânûn* (Les principes du droit). Le Caire: Faculté de commerce.

Jayyusi, Lena (1984) *Categorization and the Moral Order.* Boston: Routledge & Kegan Paul.

Jayyusi, Lena (1991) "Values and Moral Judgement: Communicative Praxis as a Moral Order" in Graham Button (ed.) *Ethnomethodology and the Human Sciences.* Cambridge: Cambridge University Press.

Jayyusi, Lena (1991b) "The Equivocal Text and the Objective World: An Ethnomethodological Analysis of a News Report" *Continuum: The Australian Journal of Media and Culture* 5(1): 166-190.

Jayyusi, Lena (1993) "Premeditation and Happenstance: The Social Construction of Intention, Action and Knowledge" *Human Studies* 16: 435-454.

Jefferson, Gail (1979) "The Transcript Symbols" in George Psathas (ed.) *Everyday Language: Studies in Ethnomethodology.* New York: Irvington Publishers.

Kelsen, Hans (1996) *Théorie générale des normes* (translation by O. Beaud and F. Malkani of *Allgemeine Theorie der Normen*, Manz Verlag, 1979). Paris: PUF.

Kertzer, David (1988) *Rituals, Politics and Power.* New Haven: Yale University Press.

Komter, Martha (1994) "Accusations and Defences in Courtroom Interactions" *Discourse and Society* 5(2): 165-87.

Komter, Martha (1995) "The Distribution of Knowledge in Courtroom Interaction" in Paul ten Have and George Psathas *Situated Order: Studies in the Social Organization of Talk and Embodied Activities.* Washington, D.C.: University Press of America.

Komter, Martha (1997) "Remorse, Redress, and Reform: Blame-Taking in the Courtroom" in Max Travers and John F. Manzo (eds.) *Law in Action: Ethnomethodological and Conversation Analytic Approaches to Law.* Aldershot: Dartmouth/Ashgate (reprint of an article original published in 1995).

Komter, Martha (1998) *Dilemmas in the Courtroom: A Study of Trials of Violent Crime in the Netherlands.* Mahwah: Lawrence Erlbaum Associates.

Komter, Martha (2001) "La construction de la preuve dans un interrogatoire de police" in Baudouin Dupret (dossier coordonné par) *Droit et Société* ("Le droit en action et en contexte. Ethnométhodologie et analyse de conversation dans la recherche juridique") 48: 367-93.

Kripke, Saul (1982) *Wittgenstein on Rules and Private Language.* Cambridge: Harvard University Press.

Landowski, Eric (1989) *La société réfléchie. Essais de socio-sémiotique.* Paris: Seuil.

Latour, Bruno (2002) *La Fabrique du droit. Une ethnographie du Conseil d'Etat.* Paris: La Découverte.

Latour, Bruno and Steve Woolgar (1986) *Laboratory Life: The Social Construction of Scientific Facts.* Princeton: Princeton University Press (2nd edition).

Lenoble, Jacques and François Ost (1980) *Droit, mythe et raison. Essai sur la dérive mytho-logique de la rationalité juridique.* Brussels: Publications des Facultés universitaires Saint-Louis.

Leudar, Ivan (1995) "Reporting Political Arguments" in F.H. van Eemeren, R. Grootendorst, J.A. Blair and C.A. Willard (eds.) *Reconstruction and Application: Proceedings of the Third Conference on Argumentation* Vol. III. Amsterdam: Sic Sat.

Leudar, Ivan (1998) "Who Is Martin McGuiness 1: On Contextualizing Reported Political Talk" in S. Čmejrková, J. Hoffmannová, O. Müllerová and J. Světlá (eds.) *Dialogue Analysis 6* Vol. 2. Tübingen: Niemeyer.

Leudar, Ivan and Jiří Nekvapil (1998) "On the Emergence of Political Identity in the Czech Mass Media: The Case of the Democratic Party of Sudetenland" *Czech Sociological Review* 6: 43-58.

Leudar, Ivan, and Philip Thomas (2000) *Voices of Reason, Voices of Insanity: Studies of Verbal Hallucinations.* London and Philadelphia: Routledge.

Leudar, Ivan, Victoria Marsland, Jiří Nekvapil (2004) "On Membership Categorization: 'Us', 'Them' and 'Doing Violence' in Political Discourse" *Discourse and Society* 15(2-3): 243-266.

Levinson, Stephen C. (1992) "Activity types and language" in Paul Drew and John Heritage (eds.) *Talk at Work. Interaction in Institutional Settings.* Cambridge: Cambridge University Press (reprinted in Travers and Manzo, 1997).

Livet, Pierre (1994) *La communauté virtuelle. Action et communication.* Combas: Editions de l'éclat.

Livet, Pierre (2001) "Dynamiques ethnométhodologiques. De la perception des mouvements à la révision des interprétations" in Michel de Fornel, Albert Ogien and Louis Quéré (eds) *L'ethnométhodologie: Une sociologie radicale.* Paris: La Découverte (colloque de Cerisy).

Livingston, Eric (1986) *The Ethnomethodological Foundations of Mathematics.* London: Routledge & Kegan Paul.

Livingston, Eric (1987) *Making Sense of Ethnomethodology.* London: Routledge & Kegan Paul.

Llewellyn, Karl (1960) *The Common Law Tradition, Deciding Appeals.* Boston: Little, Brown & Co.

Lukes, Steven (1985) "Conclusion" in Michael Carrithers, Steven Collins, Steven Lukes (eds.) *The Category of the Person: Anthropology, Philosophy, History.* Cambridge: Cambridge University Press.

Lynch, Michael (1991) "Method: Measurement – Ordinary and Scientific Measurement as Ethnomethodological Phenomena" in Graham Button (ed.) *Ethnomethodology and the Human Sciences.* Cambridge: Cambridge University Press.

Lynch, Michael (1993) *Scientific Practice and Ordinary Action: Ethnomethodology and Social Studies of Science.* Cambridge: Cambridge University Press.

Lynch, Michael (1997) "Preliminary Notes on Judges' Work: The Judge as a Constituent of Courtroom 'Hearings'" in Max Travers and John F. Manzo (eds.) *Law in Action: Ethnomethodological and Conversation Analytic Approaches to Law.* Aldershot: Dartmouth/Ashgate.

Lynch, Michael (2001) "Après Wittgenstein. Le tournant de l'épistémologie à la sociologie des sciences" in Michel de Fornel, Albert Ogien, Louis Quéré (eds) *L'ethnométhodologie: Une sociologie radicale.* Paris: La Découverte (colloque de Cerisy).

Lynch, Michael (2001) "Les fondements ethnométhodologiques de l'analyse de conversation" in Michel de Fornel, Albert Ogien, Louis Quéré (eds) *L'ethnométhodologie: Une sociologie radicale.* Paris: La Découverte (colloque de Cerisy).

Lynch, Michael and David Bogen (1996) *The Spectacle of History: Speech, Text, and Memory at the Iran-contra Hearings.* Durham: Duke University Press.

Lynch, Michael and Ruth McNally (2003) "'Science,' 'common sense,' and DNA evidence: a legal controversy about the public understanding of science" *Public Understanding of Science* 12: 83-103.

MacCormick, D. Neil (1984) "Coherence in Legal Justification" in W. Krawietz *et al.* (eds.) *Theorie der Normen, Festgabe für Ota Weinberger zum 65. Geburtstag.* Berlin: Duncker & Humblot.

Marmor, Andrei (1992) *Interpretation and Legal Theory.* Oxford: Clarendon Press.

Matoesian, Gregory (1993) *Reproducing Rape: Domination Through Talk in the Courtroom.* Chicago: University of Chicago Press.

Matoesian, Gregory (1995) "Language, Law, and Society: Policy Implications of the Kennedy Smith Rape Trial" *Law and Society Review* 29: 669-701.

Matoesian, Gregory (1997) "'I'm sorry we had to meet under these circumstances': Verbal Artistry (and Wizardry) in the Kennedy Smith Rape Trial" in Max Travers and John F. Manzo (eds.) *Law in Action: Ethnomethodological and Conversation Analytic Approaches to Law.* Aldershot: Dartmouth/Ashgate.

Matoesian, Gregory (2001) *Law and the Language of Identity: Discourse in the William Kennedy Smith Rape Trial.* New York: Oxford University Press.

Matoesian, Gregory and James R. Coldren (2001) "Evaluer la police de proximité. Style indirect, ambiguïté et paroles rapportées dans un contexte juridique bureaucratique" in Baudouin Dupret (dossier coordonné par) *Droit et Société*

("Le droit en action et en contexte. Ethnométhodologie et analyse de conversation dans la recherche juridique") 48: 395-415.

Mauss, Marcel (1938) "Une catégorie de l'esprit humain: la notion de personne, celle de 'moi'" *Journal of the Royal Anthropological Institute* Vol. LXVIII.

Maynard, Douglas W. (1984) *Inside Plea Bargaining: The Language of Negotiation.* New York: Plenum Press.

Maynard, Douglas and John F. Manzo (1993) "On the Sociology of Justice: Theoretical Notes From an Actual Jury Deliberation" *Sociological Theory* 11(2): 171-193.

Maynard, Douglas and John F. Manzo (1997) "Justice as a Phenomenon of Order: Notes on the Organization of a Jury Deliberation" in Max Travers and John F. Manzo (eds.) *Law in Action: Ethnomethodological and Conversation Analytic Approaches to Law.* Aldershot: Dartmouth/Ashgate.

McBarnet, Doreen J. (1981) *Conviction: Law, the State and the Construction of Justice.* London: Macmillan Press.

Meehan, Albert J. (1988) "Record-Keeping Practices in the Policing of Juveniles" *Urban Life* 15: 70-102.

Meehan, Albert J. (1997) "Record-Keeping Practices in the Policing of Juveniles" in Max Travers and John F. Manzo (eds.) *Law in Action: Ethnomethodological and Conversation Analytic Approaches to Law.* Aldershot: Dartmouth/Ashgate.

Mellinger, Wayne Martin (1992) "Accomplishing Fact in Police 'Dispatch Packages': The Situated Construction of an Organizational Record" *Perspectives on Social Problems* 4: 47-72.

Merry, Sally E. (1988) "Legal Pluralism" *Law and Society Review* 22(5): 869-901.

Mill, John S. (1886) *A System of Logic Ratiocinative and Inductive* (8th ed.) London.

Millard, Eric (2002) "Présentation" in Eric Millard *Droit et Société* ("Une théorie empiriste du droit est-elle possible? Lectures d'Alf Ross") 50: 13-8.

Mir-Hosseini, Ziba (1993) *Marriage on Trial: A Study of Islamic Family Law.* London: I.B. Tauris.

Moerman, Michael (1974) "Accomplishing Ethnicity" in Roy Turner (ed.) *Ethnomethodology.* Harmondsworth: Penguin Books Ltd [reprint of "Being Lue: Uses and Abuses of Ethnic Identification", in June Helm (ed.), *Essays on the Problem of Tribe.* Washington: University of Washington Press, 1968].

Moerman, Michael (1987) *Talking Culture.* Cambridge: Cambridge University Press.

Mohsen, Safia (1990) "Women and Criminal Justice in Egypt" in D.H. Dwyer (ed.) *Law and Islam in the Middle East.* New York, Westport, London: Bergin & Garvey Publishers.

Moore, Sally F. (1993) "Introduction" in Sally F. Moore (ed.) *Moralizing States and the Ethnography of the Present.* American Ethnological Society Monograph Series No 5.

Mozère, Liane (2002) "Jurée sous influence ou la résistible jouissance du jugement?" *Droit et Société* 51/52: 399-414.

Mungham, G. and Philip Thomas (1979) "Advocacy and the Solicitor-Advocate in Magistrates' Courts in England and Wales" *International Journal of the Sociology of Law* 7: 169-196.

Nadel, Siegfried F. (1954) *Nupe Religion*. London: Routledge and Kegan Paul.

Naveh, Immanuel (2002) "The Tort of Injury and Dissolution of Marriage at the Wife's Inititiative in Egyptian *Mahkamat al-Naqd* Rulings" *Islamic Law and Society* 9(1): 16-41.

Nekvapil, Jiří, and Ivan Leudar (1998) "Of Police Interrogations and Interviews" *Victimology* 8: 31-52.

Nekvapil, Jiří, and Ivan Leudar (2002) "On Dialogical Networks: Arguments about the Migration Law in Czech Mass Media in 1993" in S. Hester and W. Housley *Language, Interaction and National Identity*. Aldershot: Ashgate.

Niyaba (1991) "Taqrîr al-niyâba al-'âmma fî-l-qadiyya raqam 21 li-l-sana 1988" *Majalla hay'a qadâyâ al-dawla* 35(4): 159-169.

Neuberg, Marc (1996) "responsabilité" in Monique Canto-Sperber (ed.) *Dictionnaire d'éthique et de philosophie morale*. Paris: PUF.

O'Barr, William M. (1982) *Linguistic Evidence: Language Power and Strategy in the Courtroom*. New York: Academic Press.

Olivecrona, Karl (1939) *Law as Fact*. Copenhagen: Munksgaard.

Olivecrona, Karl (1953) "Preface" in Axel Hägerström *Inquiries into the Nature of Law and Morals*. Uppsala: Almquist and Wiesbaden: Harrassowitz.

Olivecrona, Karl (1971) *Law as Fact*. London: Stevens (2nd edition).

Payne, G.C.F. (1976) "Making a Lesson Happen: An Ethnomethodological Analysis" in M. Hammersley and P. Woods (eds.) *The Process of Schooling*. London: Routledge & Kegan Paul.

Perelman, Chaïm, and Lucie Olbrechts-Tyteca (1992) *Traité de l'argumentation. La nouvelle rhétorique* (5th édition). Brussels: Ed. de l'ULB.

Peters, Rudolph (1995) "Sharia and the State: Criminal Law in Nineteenth-Century Egypt" in C. van Dijk and A.H. de Groot (eds.) *State and Islam*. Leiden: CNWS.

Peters, Rudolph (1999) "Administrators and Magistrates: The Development of a Secular Justice in Egypt, 1842-1871" *Die Welt des Islams* 39: 378-397.

Pollner, Melvin (1974) "Sociological and common-sense models of the labelling process" in Roy Turner (ed.) *Ethnomethodology*. Harmondsworth: Penguin Books Ltd.

Pollner, Melvin (1975) "'The Very Coinage of Your Brain': The Anatomy of Reality Disjunctures" *Philosophy of the Social Sciences* 5: 411-30.

Pollner, Melvin (1979) "Explicative Transactions: Making and Managing Meaning In Traffic Court" in George Psathas (ed.) *Everyday Language: Studies in Ethnomethodology*. New York: Irvington Publishers.

Pollner, Melvin (1987) *Mundane Reason: Reality in Everyday and Sociological Discourse*. Cambridge: Cambridge University Press.

Qabbânî, al-Sâwî Y. al- (1989), *Compendium des règles juridiques décidées par la Cour de cassation en 50 ans, section pénale, 1ère partie, Droit pénal et législations pénales spéciales, vol.2, lettre* alif *à* bâ (in Arabic). Le Caire: Matkabat rijâl al-qadâ'.

Qadrî, Muhammad (1347 H.) *Le livre des statuts légaux en matière de statut personnel selon l'école de l'imâm Abû Hanîfa al-Nu`mân* (in Arabic). Le Caire: al-Matba`a al-`uthmâniyya al-misriyya.

Qâyid, `Umar `A. (1987) *La responsabilité pénale des médecins. Etude comparée* sharî`a *islamique - droit positif* (in Arabic). Le Caire: s.e..

Quéré, Louis (1994) "Présentation" in Bernard Fradin, Louis Quéré and Jean Widmer (eds) *L'enquête sur les categories.* Paris: Ed. de l'EHESS (Raisons pratiques, no. 5).

Rady, Wael (2000) "L'acquisition de la connaissance juridique par les professionnels du droit en Egypte – les substituts du Parquet et les juges en particulier" Texte présenté au First Mediterranean Social and Political Research Meeting (European University Institute, Florence, 22-26 March 2000).

Rady, Wael (2002) "Les degrés de jugement. Raisons d'un différentiel empirique dans le contenu des décisions" Texte présenté au Third Mediterranean Social and Political Research Meeting (European University Institute, Montecatini Terme et Florence, 20-24 March 2002).

Reid, Donald (1981) *Lawyers and Politics in the Arab World.* Minneapolis-Chicago: Bibliotheca Islamica.

Ricœur, Paul (1995) *Le Juste.* Paris: Editions Esprit.

Ross, Alf (1958) *On Law and Justice.* London: Stevens.

Sacks, Harvey (1972) "Notes on Police Assessment of Moral Character" in David Sudnow (ed.) *Studies in Social Interaction.* New York: The Free Press.

Sacks, Harvey (1974) "On the Analyzability of Stories by Children" in Roy Turner (ed.) *Ethnomethodology.* Harmondsworth: Penguin Books Ltd.

Sacks, Harvey (1979) "Hotrodder: A Revolutionary Category" in G. Psathas (ed.) *Everyday Language: Studies in Ethnomethodology.* New York: Irvington.

Sacks, Harvey (1989) "On doing 'being ordinary'" in J. Maxwell Atkinson and John Heritage (eds.) *Structures of Social Action: Studies in Conversation Analysis.* Cambridge: Cambridge University Press.

Sacks, Harvey (1995) *Lectures on Conversation* (vol. I and II). Oxford: Blackwell.

Sacks, Harvey (1997) "The Lawyer's Work" in Max Travers and John F. Manzo (eds.) *Law in Action: Ethnomethodological and Conversation Analytic Approaches to Law.* Aldershot: Dartmouth/Ashgate.

Sallon, Hélène (2002) *La Judiciarisation d'une question de moralité publique en Egypte: l'affaire des homosexuels du Queen Boat.* Aix-en-Provence: Mémoire pour l'obtention du DEA de Science politique comparative.

Sarat, Austin and William L.F. Festiner (1986) "Law and Strategy in the Divorce Lawyer's Office" *Law and Society Review* 20: 94-134.

Sbisà, Marina and Pietro Fabbri (1981) "Models (?) for a Pragmatic Analysis" *Journal of Pragmatics* 4: 301-319.

Schegloff, Emmanuel (1984) "On some questions and ambiguities in conversation" in J. Maxwell Atkinson and John Heritage (eds.) *Structures of Social Action: Studies in Conversation Analysis.* Cambridge: Cambridge University Press.

Schegloff, Emmanuel (1989/90) "From Interview to Confrontation: Observations of the Bush/Rather Encounter" *Research on Language and Social Interaction* 22: 215-40.

Schegloff, Emmanuel (1992) "On talk and its institutional occasions" in Paul Drew and John Heritage (eds.) *Talk at Work. Interaction in Institutional Settings.* Cambridge: Cambridge University Press.

Schegloff, Emmanuel (1995) "Introduction" in Harvey Sacks, *Lectures on Conversation* (vol. I). Oxford: Blackwell.

Schegloff, Emmanuel (1997) "Whose Text? Whose Context?" *Discourse and Society* 8: 165-188.

Schegloff, Emmanuel and Harvey Sacks (1973) "Opening Up Closings" *Semiotica* 7: 289-327.

Schulte, Joachim (1992) *Lire Wittgenstein: Dire et montrer* (translation by M. Charrière and J.P. Cometti). Combas: Editions de l'éclat.

Schütz, Alfred (1987) *Le chercheur et le quotidien. Phénoménologie des sciences sociales* (translation of a selection of texts by A. Noschis-Gilliéron).

Schütz, Alfred (1990) *Collected Papers I – The Problem of Social Reality.* Dordrecht: Kluwer Academic Publishers.

Searle, John R. (1969) *Speech Acts: An Essay in the Philosophy of Language.* Cambridge: Cambridge University Press.

Searle, John R. (1995) *The Construction of Social Reality.* London: Penguin Books.

Serverin, Evelyne (2002) "Quels faits sociaux pour une science empirique du droit ?" in Eric Millard (dossier coordonné par) *Droit et Société* ("Une théorie empiriste du droit est-elle possible ? Lectures d'Alf Ross") 50: 59-68.

Shaham, Ron (1997) *Family and the Courts in Modern Egypt: A Study Based on Decisions by Sharî'a Courts, 1900-1955.* Leiden, New York and Cologne: Brill.

Shanker, Stuart G. (1987) *Wittgenstein and the Turning-Point in the Philosophy of Mathematics.* Albany: State University of New York Press.

Sharaf al-Dîn, Ahmad (1987) *Les dispositions légales régissant les actes médicaux* (en arabe). Le Caire: s.e..

Sharrock, Wes (1974) "On Owning Knowledge" in Roy Turner (ed.) *Ethnomethodology.* Harmondsworth: Penguin Books Ltd.

Sharrock, Wes and Bob Anderson (1991) "Epistemology: Professional Skepticism" in Graham Button (ed.) *Ethnomethodology and the Human Sciences.* Cambridge: Cambridge University Press.

Sharrock, Wes and Graham Button (1991) "The Social Actor: Social Action in Real Time" in Graham Button (ed.) *Ethnomethodology and the Human Sciences.* Cambridge: Cambridge University Press.

Sharrock, Wes,and R.J. Anderson (1982) "On the Demise of the Native: Some Observations on and a Proposal for Ethnography" *Human Studies* 5: 119-135.

Sharrock, Wes and Rodney Watson (1988) "Autonomy among social theories. The incarnation of social structures" in G. Fielding (ed.) *Actions and Structures.* London: Sage Publications.

Sharrock, Wes and Rodney Watson (1990) "L'unité du faire et du dire. L'action et l'organisation sociales comme phénomènes observables et descriptibles" in Patrick Pharo and Louis Quéré (eds) *Les formes de l'action.* Paris: Ed. de l'EHESS (collection Raisons Pratiques, vol. 1).

Sidqî, `Abd al-Rahîm (1986) *Droit pénal: le crime, la peine* (en arabe). Dâr al-ma`ârif.

Stetson, Jeff (1999) "Victim, Offender and Witness in the Emplotment of News Stories" in Paul L. Jalbert (ed.) *Media Studies: Ethnomethodological Approaches.* Lanham: University Press of America.

Stockinger, Peter (1993) "Autonomie" in André-Jean Arnaud *et al.* (eds.) *Dictionnaire encyclopédique de théorie et de sociologie du droit* (2nd edition). Paris: Librairie Générale de Droit et de Jurisprudence.

Sudnow, David (1987) "Normal Crimes" in E. Rubington and M. Weinberg (eds.) *Deviance: The interactionist perspective.* New York: Macmillan (réédition de l'article paru en 1965 dans *Social Problems* 12: 251-276).

Tamanaha, Brian Z. (1993) "The Folly of the 'Social Scientific' Concept of Legal Pluralism" *Journal of Law and Society* 20(2): 192-217.

Tamanaha, Brian Z. (1997) *Realistic Socio-Legal Theory: Prgagmatism and A Social Theory Of Law.* Oxford: Clarendon Press.

Tamanaha, Brian Z. (2000) "A Non-Essentialist Version of Legal Pluralism", *Journal of Law and Society* 27(2): 296-321.

Tamanaha, Brian Z. (2001) *A General Jurisprudence of Law and Society.* Cambridge: Cambridge University Press.

Travers, Max (1997) *The Reality of Law: Work and Talk in a Firm of Criminal Lawyers.* Aldershot: Ashgate/Dartmouth.

Travers, Max (2001) "Ethnométhodologie, analyse de conversation et droit" in Baudouin Dupret (dossier coordonné par) *Droit et Société* ("Le droit en action et en contexte. Ethnométhodologie et analyse de conversation dans la recherche juridique") 48: 349-366.

Travers, Max and John F. Manzo (eds.) (1997) *Law in Action: Ethnomethodological and Conversation Analytic Approaches to Law.* Aldershot: Dartmouth/Ashgate.

Umphrey, Martha M. (1999) "The Dialogics of Legal Meaning: Spectacular Trials, the Unwritten Law, and Narratives of Criminal Responsibility" *Law and Society Review* 33(2): 393-423.

Voloshinov, Valentin N. (1973) *Marxism and the Philosophy of Language.* Cambridge: Harvard University Press.

Warnock, Geoffrey J. (1971) *The Object of Morality.* New York: Methuen.

Watson, Rodney (1976) "Some Conceptual Issues in the Social Identification of Victims and Offenders" in Emilio C. Viano (ed.) *Victims and Society.* Washington: Visage Press.

Watson, Rodney (1983) "The Presentation of Victim and Motive in Discourse: The Case of Police Interrogations and Interviews" *Victimology: An International Journal* 8(1-2): 31-52 (reprinted in Travers and Manzo, 1997).

Watson, Rodney (1994) "Catégories, séquentialité et ordre social" in Bernard Fradin, Louis Quéré and Jean Widmer (eds) *L'enquête sur les categories.* Paris: Ed. de l'EHESS (Raisons pratiques, no. 5).

Watson, Rodney (1995) "Angoisse dans la 42e rue" in Patricia Paperman and Ruwen Ogien (eds) *La couleur des pensées.* Paris: Ed. de l'EHESS (Raisons pratiques, no. 6).

Watson, Rodney (1997) "Some General Reflections on 'Categorization' and 'Sequence' in the Analysis of Conversation" in Stephen Hester and Peter Eglin (eds.) *Culture in Action: Studies in Membership Categorization Analysis.* Washington, D.C.: University Press of America.

Watson, Rodney (1998) "Ethnomethodology, Consciousness and Self" *Journal of Consciousness Studies* 5(2): 202-223.

Watson, Rodney (2001) "Continuité et transformation de l'ethnométhodologie" in Michel de Fornel, Albert Ogien, Louis Quéré (eds) *L'ethnométhodologie. Une sociologie radicale.* Paris: La Découverte (colloque de Cerisy).

Weber, Max (1986) *Sociologie du droit* (translation by J. Grosclaude du vol.II, ch.VII, of *Wirtschaft und Gesellschaft*, 1922). Paris: PUF.

Wieder, D. Lawrence (1974) *Language and Social Reality: The Case of Telling the Convict Code.* The Hague: Mouton.

Williams, Bernard (1993) *Shame and Necessity*. Oxford: University of California Press [French translation, *Honte et nécessité*, 1997, Paris: PUF].

Wittgenstein, Ludwig (1967) *Philosophical Investigations* (Translation by G.E.M. Anscombe de *Philosophische Untersuchungen*, Suhrcamp, 1953). Oxford and Cambridge: Blackwell [French translation: P. Klossowski, Paris, Gallimard, 1961].

Zappulli, Luisa (2001) "Les savoirs en action. La répartition géographique des auditeurs de justice à l'intérieur du dispositif de formation professionnelle" in Baudouin Dupret (dossier coordonné par) *Droit et Société* ("Le droit en action et en contexte. Ethnométhodologie et analyse de conversation dans la recherche juridique") 48: 417-437.

Ziadeh, Farhat (1968) *Lawyers, the Rule of Law and Liberalism in Modern Egypt.* Stanford: Hoover Institution.

Zimmerman, Don H. (1970) "The Practicalities of Rule Use" in J. Douglas (ed.) *Understanding Everyday Life: Toward the Reconstruction of Sociological Knowledge*. Chicago: Aldine.

Zimmerman, Don H. (1974) "Fact as a Practical Accomplishment" in Roy Turner (ed.) *Ethnomethodology*. Harmondsworth: Penguin Books Ltd.

Zimmerman, Don H., and Melvin Pollner (1971) "The Everyday World as a Phenomenon" in J.D. Douglas (ed.), *Understanding Everyday Life: Towards the Reconstruction of Sociological Knowledge*. London: Routledge and Kegan Paul.

Index

For Product Safety Concerns and Information please contact our EU representative GPSR@taylorandfrancis.com Taylor & Francis Verlag GmbH, Kaufingerstraße 24, 80331 München, Germany